The Booklover's Almanac

Country Calendar

Gwenda Morgan

The Booklover's Almanac

Compiled and Edited by
Robert Brittain

HarperPerennial
A Division of HarperCollins*Publishers*

LIBRARY OF CONGRESS CATALOG CARD NUMBER 90-56422

ISBN 0–06–097409–5

91 92 93 94 95 RRD 10 9 8 7 6 5 4 3 2 1

Art thou for something rare and profitable?
Wouldest thou see a Truth within a Fable?
Art thou forgetful? Wouldest thou remember
From New-year's day to the last of December?
Then read my Fancies, they will stick like Burrs,
And may be to the Helpless, Comforters.

John Bunyan, "The Author's Apology for His Book"

ACKNOWLEDGMENTS

Dr. Robert Brittain and the Publishers acknowledge with grateful
thanks permission to quote from copyright works as follows:

Arnold Bennett: Mrs. D. Cheston Bennett, Hodder & Stoughton Ltd.
Christopher Brennan: Angus & Robertson Ltd.
G. K. Chesterton: Miss D. Collins, Methuen & Co.
Sir Arthur Conan Doyle: Trustees of the Estate of Sir Arthur Conan Doyle,
John Murray (Publishers) Ltd.
Joseph Conrad: The Trustees of the Joseph Conrad Estate
Hart Crane: Liveright Publishing Corporation, Oxford University Press
Daphne Du Maurier: Curtis Brown Ltd.
Gabriel Fallon: Routledge & Kegan Paul Ltd.
Ford Madox Ford: The Bodley Head
E. M. Forster: Edward Arnold (Publishers) Ltd.
Robert Frost: The Estate of Robert Frost, Jonathan Cape Ltd.
John Galsworthy: The Society of Authors as the literary representative
of the Estate of John Galsworthy
Robert Graves: Robert Graves
Thomas Hardy: The Trustees of the Thomas Hardy Estate, Macmillan & Co.
James Joyce: The Bodley Head
Rudyard Kipling: Mrs. George Bambridge, Macmillan & Co; Methuen & Co.
D. H. Lawrence: The Estate of the Late Mrs. Frida Lawrence,
Laurence Pollinger Ltd.
T. E. Lawrence: The Executors of the Estate of T. E. Lawrence,
Jonathan Cape Ltd.
Vachel Lindsay: The Macmillan Company, New York
Hugh MacDiarmid: The Macmillan Company, New York
Wilfred Owen: Oxford University Press; Mr. Harold Owen,
Chatto & Windus Ltd.
Eugene O'Neill: The Executors of the Eugene O'Neill Estate,
Jonathan Cape Ltd.
Beatrix Potter: Frederick Warne & Co. Ltd.
Leo Rosten: Victor Gollancz Ltd.
Siegfried Sassoon: Mr. G. T. Sassoon
George Bernard Shaw: The Society of Authors, for the Bernard Shaw Estate
Edith Sitwell: David Higham Associates Ltd., Macmillan & Co.
J. Duncan Spaeth (Tr.): Princeton University Press
Brian Stone (Tr.): Penguin Books Ltd.
Dylan Thomas: The Trustees for the Copyrights of the Late Dylan Thomas
Terence Tiller (Tr.): Penguin Books Ltd.

LIST OF ILLUSTRATIONS

The twelve engravings of the months are taken from the unique copy of the first edition of Edmund Spenser's *The Shepheardes Calendar*, 1579.

PREFACE

'Wouldest thou remember/From New-year's-day to the last of December?' The question permitted, it seemed to me, of only one answer. But I have the kind of memory that needs to be jogged; and being always in quest of the pleasures that only reading can give, and the richer pleasures that come only from re-reading, I began to wish for a guide. What I wanted was a book I could keep on my bedside table or by my favourite chair, that would remind me of delights once tasted but ripe to be savoured again; or better, perhaps, one that would sometimes nudge me into reading something I had heard about but never got round to; or even, on occasions, might suggest a pleasurable stroll along some literary lane of whose very existence I had never been aware.

Once one puts one's mind to it, the memories flood in. But the landscape of literature in English is so vast, and the features so rich and varied, that although one may be as 'certain of the spot as if a chart were given' a chart is nevertheless needed. Since daily reminders were wanted, the calendar seemed the obvious device for plotting them. Dates can be interesting in themselves, and many of them are already firmly embedded in our minds as anniversaries, calling to mind some event we remember with pleasure or pain: Christmas, the Fifth of November, the Fourth of July, or some such occurrence in our personal histories as a really happy birthday or, if we are spiritually akin to anyone like Samuel Pepys, an unexpected encounter with some oddity singled out for a moment from the swirling complexity of experience because it was 'the first that ever I saw!' Just as religiously inclined people have found the Church calendar useful in reminding them of saints they might well remember on specific occasions in their daily devotions, so it seemed to me that booklovers might welcome an almanac that would identify each day in the year as the anniversary of some event in the history of literary activity, and would offer a page of reading matter appropriate to the occasion.

At any rate, that is the plan on which I have made this book. The actual doing of it was much more pleasurable than one might expect. At the first, there was the pleasure of putting in the familiar dates—when the Brownings were married, when Gibbon conceived the idea of writing *The Decline and Fall*, when Keats first saw his name in print, when Hardy wrote the final sombre page of *The Mayor of Caster-bridge*, when Caxton published Malory's *Morte d'Arthur* – and of reading again some of the great passages these dates call to mind. After this initial flurry came the slower business of hunting for dates and passages that might be worth remembering. The easiest dates to find in the history of literature are of course those of the births and deaths of authors. They are also commonly the least interesting occasions in a writer's life, and I soon began to avoid using them except when they had been the occasion of some really fine (or at least characteristic) piece of writing, such as Cuthbert's moving description of Bede's last day, or Aubrey's account of Francis Bacon catching his death of cold as a result of his insatiable curiosity; occasionally

I have used a death date (e.g., the suicide of Hart Crane) simply because it seemed an appropriate time to recall one of an author's best productions. On the whole, however, it seemed better to use dates the writers themselves thought interesting and worth memorializing.

Sometimes I have strayed from fact into fiction because I found, somewhat to my surprise, that many delightful passages I wanted to remember were fictionally dated: Gulliver's awakening in the land of the Lilliputians, Alice's adventures at the mad tea-party, or Tristram Shandy's conception as recounted in the hilarious opening chapter of one of the world's most amusing books.

Other booklovers, hearing of what I was up to, have encouraged and aided me with dates and quotations from their favourite authors, and to all of them I am grateful; two, in particular, deserve my deepest gratitude for many hours of patient searching and copying-up of material: Mrs Barbara Harvey and Mr Gerhardt Beckmann contributed so much to this book that without their help it could never have been finished in time for its present publication. Mr Charles Skilton deserves not only my thanks but those of any reader into whose hands this book may fall for the beauty and clarity of its type and page design, as does Mr Dulan Barber for his patient editing and the removal of many faults; those that remain must be laid at my own door.

All of us who have had a hand in the making of this book have had a thoroughly good time. Compiling an anthology can still be as exciting as it was when the first one in our language was undertaken by the royal booklover of whom it is written:

> Now when the first quotation was copied, he was eager at once to read, and to interpret in Saxon, and then to teach others; ... and he continued to learn the flowers collected by certain masters, and to reduce them into the form of one book, as he was then able, although mixed with one another, until it became almost as large as a psalter. This book he called his *Enchiridion* or *Manual*, because he carefully kept it at hand day and night and found, as he told me, no small consolation therein.

We hope this book may serve its users as well as King Alfred's served him; and if they follow his practice with it, we think it may.

ROBERT BRITTAIN

London, 25 August 1970

Januarye.

1600—The Shoemaker's Holiday, Thomas Dekker's comedy of London life, was first produced

Cold's the wind, and wet's the rain,
 Saint Hugh be our good speed;
Ill is the weather that bringeth no gain,
 Nor helps good hearts in need.

Troll the bowl, the jolly nut-brown bowl,
 And here, kind mate, to thee;
Let's sing a dirge for Saint Hugh's soul,
 And down it merrily.

Down-a-down, hey, down-a-down,
 Hey derry derry down-a-down,
 Close with the tenor, boy;
Ho! well done, to me let come,
 Ring compass, gentle joy.

Troll the bowl, the nut-brown bowl,
 And here, kind, &c. (*As often as there be men to drink.*)

(*At last, when all have drunk, this verse.*)

Cold's the wind, and wet's the rain,
 Saint Hugh be our good speed;
Ill is the weather that bringeth no gain,
 Nor helps good hearts in need.

'*The Second Three-Man's Song*', Shoemaker's
Holiday, *Act V, scene 4*

2 January

1492—Granada fell to the Catholic Kings

While these transactions were passing in the Alhambra, and its vicinity, the sovereigns remained with their retinue and guards near the village of Amilla, their eyes fixed on the towers of the royal fortress. . . . At length they saw the silver cross, the great standard of this crusade, elevated on the Torre de la Vela, or great Watch-Tower, and sparkling in the sunbeams. . . . Beside it was planted the pennon of the glorious apostle St. James, and a great shout of 'Santiago! Santiago!' rose throughout the army. Lastly was reared the royal standard by the king-of-arms, with the shout of 'Castile! Castile! For King Ferdinand and Queen Isabella!' . . .

The King now advanced with a splendid escort of cavalry and the sound of trumpets, until he came to a small mosque near the banks of the Xenil. . . . Here he beheld the unfortunate King of Granada approaching on horseback, at the head of his slender retinue. Boabdil, as he drew near made a movement to dismount, but, as had previously been concerted, Ferdinand prevented him. He then offered to kiss the King's hand, which, according to arrangement, was likewise declined, whereupon he leaned forward and kissed the King's right arm; and at the same time he delivered the keys of the city with an air of mingled melancholy and resignation: 'These keys', said he, 'are the last relics of the Arabian empire in Spain: thine, O King, are our trophies, our kingdom, and our person. Such is the will of God! Receive them with the clemency thou hast promised, and which we look for at thy hands.'

King Ferdinand restrained his exultation into an air of serene magnanimity. 'Doubt not our promises', replied he, 'nor that thou shalt regain from our friendship the prosperity of which the fortune of war has deprived thee.' . . .

Having rejoined his family, Boabdil set forward with a heavy heart for his allotted residence in the valley of Purchena. At two leagues' distance, the cavalcade, winding into the skirts of the Alpuxarras, ascended an eminence commanding the last view of Granada. As they arrived at this spot, the Moors paused involuntarily, to take a farewell gaze at their beloved city, which a few steps more would shut from the sight forever. Never had it appeared so lovely in their eyes. While they yet looked, a light cloud of smoke burst forth from the citadel, and presently a peal of artillery, faintly heard, told that the city was taken possession of, and the throne of the Moslem Kings was lost forever. The heart of Boabdil, softened by misfortunes and overcharged with grief, could no longer contain itself. 'Allah Achbar! God is Great!' said he; but the words of resignation died upon his lips, and he burst into tears.

Washington Irving: from Chronicle of the Conquest of Granada, *vol. ii, chapter liii*

1841—Herman Melville began at Fairhaven his 18-month voyage to the South Seas on the whaling-ship 'Acushnet' (described in Moby Dick)

Call me Ishmael. Some years ago – never mind how long precisely – having little or no money in my purse, and nothing particular to interest me on shore, I thought I would sail about a little and see the watery part of the world. . . .

Why is almost every robust healthy boy with a robust healthy soul in him, at some time or other crazy to go to sea? . . . Why did the old Persians hold the sea holy? Why did the Greeks give it a separate deity, and own brother of Jove? Surely all this is not without meaning. And still deeper the meaning of the story of Narcissus, who because he could not grasp the tormenting, mild image he saw in the fountain, plunged into it and was drowned. But that same image, we ourselves see in all rivers and oceans. It is the image of the ungraspable phantom of life; and this is the key to it all. . . .

Though I cannot tell why it was exactly that those stage managers, the Fates, put me down for this shabby part of a whaling voyage, when others were set down for magnificent parts in high tragedies, and short and easy parts in genteel comedies, and jolly parts in farces – though I cannot tell why this was exactly; yet, now that I recall all the circumstances, I think I can see a little into the springs and motives which being cunningly presented to me under various disguises, induced me to set about performing the part I did, besides cajoling me into the delusion that it was a choice resulting from my own unbiased freewill and discriminating judgment.

Chief among these motives was the overwhelming idea of the great whale himself. Such a portentous and mysterious monster roused all my curiosity. Then the wild and distant seas where he rolled his island bulk; the undeliverable, nameless perils of the whale; these, with all the attending marvels of a thousand Patagonian sights and sounds, helped to sway me to my wish. With other men, perhaps, such things would not have been inducements; but as for me, I am tormented with an everlasting itch for things remote. I love to sail forbidden seas, and land on barbarous coasts. Not ignoring what is good, I am quick to perceive a horror, and could still be social with it – would they let me – since it is but well to be on friendly terms with all the inmates of the place one lodges in.

By reason of these things, then, the whaling voyage was welcome; the great flood-gates of the wonder-world swung open, and in the wild conceits that swayed me to my purpose, two and two there floated into my inmost soul, endless processions of the whale, and, mid most of them all, one grand hooded phantom, like a snow hill in the air.

Herman Melville: from Moby Dick, *chapter I*

Between twelve hours and eleven
I dreamed an angel came from heaven
With sweet voice saying pleasantly,
'Tailors and cobblers, blest be ye.'

'Your place in heaven's ordainéd higher
Than that to which all saints aspire,
Next God Himself in dignity:
Tailors and cobblers, blest be ye.

'The cause to you is not unkenned:
What God mis-makes, ye do amend
By craft and great agility:
Tailors and cobblers, blest be ye.

'Cobblers, with shoes well-made and neat
Ye mend the faults of ill-made feet,
Wherefore to heaven your souls will flee:
Tailors and cobblers, blest be ye. . . .

'And ye tailors with well-made clothes
Can mend the worst-made man that goes
And make him seemly for to see:
Tailors and cobblers, blest be ye.

'In earth ye do such miracles here,
In heaven ye shall be saints full clear;
Though ye be knaves in this countree,
Tailors and cobblers, blest be ye.'

William Dunbar: from 'Tailyouris and Sowtaris'
(*Anglicized by RB*)

1895—H. G. Wells, on his second assignment as a drama critic [his first and only regular newspaper work], saw Henry James for the first time

On the fifth I had to do *Guy Domville*, a play by Henry James at the St. James's Theatre. . . . It was an extremely weak drama. James was a strange unnatural human being, a sensitive man lost in an immensely abundant brain, which had had neither a scientific nor a philosophical training, but which was by education and natural aptitude alike, formal, formally aesthetic, conscientiously fastidious and delicate. Wrapped about in elaborations of gesture and speech, James regarded his fellow creatures with a face of distress and a remote effort at intercourse, like some victim of enchantment placed in the centre of an immense bladder. . . . He had always been well off and devoted to artistic ambitions; he had experienced no tragedy and he shunned the hoarse laughter of comedy; and yet he was consumed by a gnawing hunger for dramatic success. . . .

Guy Domville was one of those rare ripe exquisite Catholic Englishmen of ancient family conceivable only by an American mind, who gave up the woman he loved to an altogether coarser cousin, because his religious vocation was stronger than his passion. I forget the details of the action. . . . Guy was played by George Alexander, at first in a mood of refined solemnity and then as the intimations of gathering disapproval from pit and gallery increased, with stiffening desperation. Alexander at the close had an incredibly awkward exit. He had to stand at a door in the middle of the stage, say slowly 'Be keynd to Her . . . *Be* keynd to Her' and depart. By nature Alexander had a long face, but at that moment with audible defeat before him, he seemed the longest and dismallest face, all face, that I have ever seen. The slowly closing door reduced him to a strip, to a line, of perpendicular gloom. The uproar burst like a thunderstorm as the door closed and the stalls responded with feeble applause. Then the tumult was mysteriously allayed. There were some minutes of uneasy apprehension. 'Author' cried voices. 'Au-thor!' The stalls, not understanding, redoubled their clapping.

Disaster was too much for Alexander that night. A spasm of hate for the writer of those fatal lines must surely have seized him. With incredible cruelty he led the doomed James, still not understanding clearly how things were with him, to the middle of the stage, and there the pit and gallery had him. James bowed; he knew it was the proper thing to do. Perhaps he had selected a few words to say, but if so they went unsaid. I have never heard any sound more devastating than the crescendo of booing that ensued. . . . For a moment or so James faced the storm, his round face white, his mouth opening and shutting, and then Alexander, I hope in a contrite mood, snatched him back into the wings.

H. G. Wells: from Experiment in Autobiography

1560/61—The first performance of Gorboduc, *the 'first English tragedy', by Thomas Norton and Thomas Sackville, Earl of Dorset*

O Love, how are these peoples harts abusde!
What blind fury, thus headlong carries them!
That though so many bookes, so many rolles
Of auncient time recorde, what grevous plagues
Light on these rebelles aye, and though so oft
Their eares have heard their aged fathers tell
What iuste rewarde these traitours still receyve,
Yea, though them selves have sene depe death and bloud,
By strangling corde and slaughter of the sword,
To such assigned, yet can they not beware,
Yet can not stay their lewde rebellious hands,
But suffring loe fowle treason to distaine
Their wretched myndes, forget their loyall hart
Reject all truth and rise against their prince.
O ruthefull case, that those whom duties bond
Whom grafted law by nature, truth and faith,
Bound to preserve their countrey and their king,
Borne to defend their common wealth and prince,
Even they should geve consent thus to subvert
Thee Brittaine land, & from thy wombe should spring
(O native soile) those that will needs destroy
And ruine thee and eke themselves in fine.

From the speech of Eubulus, Act V, scene ii

'Our tragedies and comedies not without cause cried out against, observing rules neither of honest civility nor of skillful poetry, excepting *Gorboduc* (again I say of those that I have seen), which notwithstanding as it is full of stately speeches and well-sounding phrases, climbing to the height of Seneca's style, and as full of notable morality, which it doth most delightfully teach, and so obtain the very end of poesy; yet in truth it is very defectious in the circumstances, which grieveth me, because it might not remain as an exact model of all tragedies.'

Sir Philip Sidney: from The Defence of Poesy,
1595

Friend of the wise! and teacher of the good!
Into my heart I have received thy lay
More than historic, that prophetic lay
Wherein (high theme by thee first sung aright)
Of the foundations and the building up
Of a Human Spirit thou hast dared to tell . . .

Ah! As I listened with a heart forlorn,
The pulses of my being beat anew:
And even as Life returns upon the drowned,
Life's joy rekindling roused a throng of pains –
Keen pangs of Love, awakening as a babe
Turbulent with an outcry in the heart;
And fears self-willed, that shunned the eye of Hope;
And Hope that scarce would know itself from Fear;
Sense of past Youth, and Manhood come in vain,
And Genius given, and Knowledge won in vain,
And all which I had culled in wood-walks wild,
And all which patient toil had reared, and all,
Commune with thee had opened out – but flowers
Strewed on my corse, and borne upon my bier
In the same coffin, for the selfsame grave! . . .

And when – O friend! my comforter and guide!
Strong in thyself, and powerful to give strength! –
Thy long sustained song finally closed,
And thy deep voice had ceased – yet thou thyself
Wert still before my eyes, and round us both
That happy vision of beloved faces –
Scarce conscious, and yet conscious of its close
I sate, my being blended in one thought
(Thought was it? or aspiration? or resolve?)
Absorbed, yet hanging still upon the sound –
And when I rose, I found myself in prayer.

S. T. Coleridge, 7 January 1807

1604—'The Vision of the Twelve Goddesses': A Royal Masque, by Samuel Daniel. Presented in the Greate Hall at Hampton Court, and Personated by the Queenes Most Excellent Majestie, attended by Eleven Ladies of Honour

The Night *represented, in a blacke Vesture, set with Starres, comes and wakens her Sonne Somnus, (sleeping in his Cave) with this Speech.*

> Awake, darke *Sleepe* rouse thee from out this Cave
> Thy Mother *Night* that bred thee in her wombe
> And fed thee first with silence and with ease,
> Doth here thy shadowing operations crave:
> And therefore wake my Sonne, awake, and come
> Strike with thy Horny wand, the spirits of these
> That here expect some pleasing novelties:
> And make their slumber to beget strange sights,
> Strange visions and unusual properties.
> Unseene of later Ages, ancient Rites,
> Of gifts divine, wrapt up in mysteries,
> Make this to seem a Temple in their sight,
> Whose maine support, holy Religion frame:
> And 1 *Wisdome*, 2 *Courage*, 3 *Temperance*, and 4 *Right*,
> Make seeme the Pillars that sustaine the same.
> Shadow some *Sybill* to attend the Rites,
> And to describe the Powers that shall resort,
> With th'interpretation of the benefits
> They bring in clouds, and what they do import.

Somnus

> Deare Mother *Night*, I your commandement
> Obay and Dreames t'interpret Dreames will make,
> As waking curiosity is wont.
> Though better dreame a sleep, the dreame awake.
> And this white horny Wand shall worke the deed;
> Whose power doth *Figures* of the light present:
> When from this sable *radius* doth proceed
> Nought but confused shewes, to no intent.
> Be this a Temple; there *Sybille* stand,
> Preparing reverent Rites with holy hand,
> And so bright visions go, and entertaine
> All round about, while Ile to sleepe again.

1805—Horatio Nelson was buried in the crypt of St Paul's Cathedral

At Viscount Nelson's lavish funeral,
  While the mob milled and yelled about St. Paul's,
A General chatted with an Admiral:

'One of your Colleagues, Sir, remarked today
  That Nelson's *exit*, though to be lamented,
Falls not inopportunely, in its way.'

'He was a thorn in our flesh,' came the reply –
  'The most bird-witted, unaccountable,
Odd little runt that ever I did spy.

'One arm, one peeper, vain as Pretty Poll,
  A meddler, too, in foreign politics
And gave his heart in pawn to a plain moll.

'He would dare lecture us Sea Lords, and then
  Would treat his ratings as though men of honour
And play at leap-frog with his midshipmen!

'We tried to box him down, but up he popped
  And when he'd banged Napoleon at the Nile
Became too much the hero to be dropped.

'Yet,' cried the General, 'six and twenty sail
  Captured or sunk by him off Trafalgar –
That writes a handsome *finis* to the tale.'

'Handsome enough. The seas are England's now.
  That fellow's foibles need no longer plague us.
He died most creditably, I'll allow.'

'And, Sir, the secret of his victories?'
  'By his unServicelike, familiar ways, Sir,
He made the whole Fleet love him, damn his eyes!'

Robert Graves: Collected Poems (*1914–1947*)

10 January 📖

1776—Thomas Paine published Common Sense, *'addressed to the Inhabitants of America'*

Volumes have been written on the subject of the struggle between England and America. Men of all ranks have embarked in the controversy, from different motives, and with various designs: but all have been ineffectual, and the period of debate is closed. Arms, as the last resource, decide the contest. . . .

The sun never shined on a cause of greater worth. It is not the affair of a city, a county, a province, or of a kingdom, but of a continent – of, at least, one eighth-part of the habitable globe. It is not the concern of a day, a year, or an age; posterity are involved in the contest, and will be more or less affected, even to the end of time, by the proceedings now. Now is the seed-time of continental union, faith, and honour. . . .

I have heard it asserted by some, that as America had flourished under her former connection with Great Britain, the same connection is necessary towards her future happiness, and will always have the same effect. Nothing can be more fallacious than this kind of argument. We may as well assert, that because a child has thriven upon milk, it is never to have meat, or that the first twenty years of our lives are to become a precedent for the next twenty. But even this is admitting more than is true, for I answer roundly, that America would have flourished as much, and probably much more, had no European power had any thing to do with her. . . .

Alas! we have been long led away by ancient prejudices, and made large sacrifices to superstitition. We have boasted of the protection of Great Britain, without considering that her motive was *interest* not *attachment*; that she did not protect us from our *enemies* on *our* account, but from *her enemies* on *her own account*, from those who had no quarrel with us on any *other account*. . . .

But Britain is the parent country, say some. Then the more shame upon her conduct. Even brutes do not devour their young, nor savages make war on their families; wherefore the assertion, if true, turns to her reproach; but it happens not to be true, or only partly so, and the phrase *parent* or *mother country* hath been jesuitically adopted by the king and his parasites, with a low papistical design of gaining an unfair bias on the credulous weakness of our minds. Europe, and not England, is the parent country of America. This new world hath been the asylum for the persecuted lovers of civil and religious liberty in *every part* of Europe. Hither have they fled, not from the tender embraces of the mother, but from the cruelty of the monster; and it is so far true of England, that the same tyranny which drove the first emigrants from home, pursues their descendants still.

1804—'William Blake, an engraver at Felpham, was tried [on a charge exhibited against him by two soldiers], for having uttered seditious and treasonable expressions, such as "D—n the king, d—n all his subjects, d—n his soldiers, they are all slaves ; when Bonaparte comes, it will be cut-throat for cut-throat, and the weakest must go to the wall ; I will help him ; &c." ' – Sussex Advertiser

---

I am at Present in a Bustle to defend myself against a very unwarrantable warrant from a Justice of Peace in Chichester, which was taken out against me by a Private in Captn Leathes's troop of Ist or Royal Dragoons, for an assault & seditious words. The wretched man has terribly Perjur'd himself, as has his Comrade; for, as to Sedition, not one Word relating to the King or Government was spoken by either him or me. His Enmity arises from my having turned him out of my Garden, into which he was invited as an assistant by a Gardener at work therein, without my knowledge that he was so invited. I desired him, as politely as was possible, to go out of the Garden; he made me an impertinent answer. I insisted on his leaving the garden; he refused. I still persisted in desiring his departure; he then threaten'd to knock out my Eyes, with many abominable imprecations & with some contempt for my Person; it affronted my foolish Pride. I therefore took him by the Elbows & pushed him before me till I had got him out; there I intended to have left him, but he, turning about, put himself into a Posture of Defiance, threatening & swearing at me. I, perhaps foolishly & perhaps not, stepped out at the Gate, &, putting aside his blows, took him again by the Elbows, &, keeping his back to me, pushed him forward down the road about fifty yards – he all the while endeavouring to turn round & strike me, & raging & cursing, which drew out several neighbours; at length, when I had got him to where he was Quarter'd, which was very quickly done, we were met at the Gate by the Master of the house, The Fox Inn (who is the proprietor of my Cottage), & his wife & Daughter & the Man's Comrade & several other people. My Landlord compell'd the Soldiers to go indoors, after many abusive threats against me & my wife from the two Soldiers; but not one word of threat on account of Sedition was utter'd at that time. This method of Revenge was Plann'd between them after they had got together into the stable. This is the whole outline. I have for witnesses: The Gardener, who is Hostler at the Fox & who Evidences that, to his knowledge, no word of the remotest tendency to Government or Sedition was utter'd; Our next door Neighbour, a Miller's wife, who saw me turn him before me down the road, & saw & heard all that happen'd at the Gate of the Inn, who Evidences that no Expression of threatening on account of Sedition was utter'd in the heat of their fury by either of the Dragoons; . . . The Landlord of the Inn & his Wife & Daughter will Evidence the same, and will evidently prove the Comrade perjur'd, who swore that he heard me, while at the Gate, utter Seditious words & D— the K—, without which perjury I could not have been committed.

William Blake to Thomas Butts, 16 August 1803

12 January 📖

1893—Jack London, on his seventeenth birthday, signed on the sealer, 'Sophie Sutherland' ; in The Sea Wolf (*published 1904*) *he drew on the experience of that voyage, both for descriptions of the sea and for such characters as the brutal book-lover, Wolf Larsen.*

After breakfast I had another unenviable experience. When I had finished washing the dishes, I cleaned the cabin stove and carried the ashes up on deck to empty them. Wolf Larsen and Henderson were standing near the wheel, deep in conversation. The sailor, Johnson, was steering. As I started toward the weather side I saw him make a sudden motion with his head, which I mistook for a token of recognition and good morning. In reality, he was attempting to warn me to throw my ashes over the lee side. Unconscious of my blunder, I passed by Wolf Larsen and the hunter and flung the ashes over the side to windward. The wind drove them back, and not only over me, but over Henderson and Wolf Larsen. The next instant the latter kicked me, violently, as a cur is kicked. I had not realized there could be so much pain in a kick. I reeled away from him and leaned against the cabin in a half-fainting condition. Everything was swimming before my eyes, and I turned sick. The nausea overpowered me, and I managed to crawl to the side of the vessel. But Wolf Larsen did not follow me up. Brushing the ashes from his clothes, he had resumed his conversation with Henderson. Johansen, who had seen the affair from the break of the poop, sent a couple of sailors aft to clean up the mess.

Later in the morning I received a surprise of a totally different sort. Following the cook's instructions, I had gone into Wolf Larsen's state-room to put it to rights and make the bed. Against the wall, near the head of the bunk, was a rack filled with books. I glanced over them, noting with astonishment such names as Shakespeare, Tennyson, Poe, and De Quincey. There were scientific works, too, among which were represented men such as Tyndall, Proctor, and Darwin. Astronomy and physics were represented, and I remarked Bulfinch's 'Age of Fable', Shaw's 'History of English and American Literature', and Johnson's 'Natural History' in two large volumes. Then there were a number of grammars, such as Metcalf's, and Reed and Kellogg's; and I smiled as I saw a copy of 'The Dean's English'. . . .

I could not reconcile these books with the man from what I had seen of him, and I wondered if he could possibly read them. But when I came to make the bed I found, between the blankets, dropped apparently as he had sunk off to sleep, a complete Browning, the Cambridge edition. It was open at 'In a Balcony', and I noticed, here and there, passages underlined in pencil. Further, letting drop the volume during a lurch of the ship, a sheet of paper fell out. It was scrawled over with geometrical diagrams and calculations of some sort.

It was patent that this terrible man was no ignorant clod, such as one would inevitably suppose him to be from his exhibitions of brutality. At once he became an enigma. One side or the other of his nature was perfectly comprehensible; but both sides together were bewildering.

Jack London : from The Sea Wolf, *chapter V*

1669—Samuel Pepys made another of his many visits to the theatre to see again Nell Gwynn's great performances as Florimel in Dryden's Secret Love, or The Maiden Queen

He who writ this, not without pains and thought,
From French and English theatres has brought
The exactest rules, by which a play is wrought.

The unities of action, place, and time;
The scenes unbroken; and a mingled chime
Of Jonson's humour, with Corneille's rhyme.

But while dead colours he with care did lay,
He fears his wit, or plot, he did not weigh,
Which are the living beauties of a play.

Plays are like towns, which, howe'er fortified
by engineers, have still some weaker side,
By the o'erseen defendant unespied.

And with that art you make approaches now;
Such skillful fury in assaults you show,
That every poet without shame may bow.

Ours, therefore, humbly would attend your doom,
If, soldier-like, he may have terms to come,
With flying colours, and with beat of drum.

John Dryden: Prologue to The Maiden Queen

[Despite Dryden's uncertainties about the weakness of his plot, Nell Gwynn had carried the play to triumph and a long life in the repertory. After the opening night (2 March 1667), Pepys, who had entertained a puritanical dislike of the pert actress because of her relations with Charles II, had been obliged to admit: 'I never can hope ever to see the like done again by man or woman . . . as Nell do this, both as a mad girl, then most and best of all when she comes in like a young gallant; and hath the motions and carriage of a spark the most that ever I saw any man have. It makes me, I confess, admire her.']

14 January 📖

1604/5—'I have sent and bene all thys morning huntyng for players Juglers &
Such kinde of Creaturs, but fynde them harde to finde, wherfore Leavinge notes
for them to seeke me, Burbage ys come, & Sayes ther ys no new playe that the
quene hath not seene, but they have Revyved an olde one, Cawled Loves Labore
lost, *which for wytt & mirthe he sayes will please her excedingly. And thys ys*
appointed to be playd to Morowe night . . .'

Sir Water Cope to Robert Cecil

Love's Labour Lost, I once did see a play
Ycleped so, so called to my pain,
Which I to hear to my small joy did stay,
Giving attendance on my froward dame;
 My misgiving mind presaging to me ill,
 Yet was I drawn to see it 'gainst my will.

This play, no play but plague was unto me,
For there I lost the Love I liked most:
And what to others seemed a jest to be,
I, that, in earnest, found unto my cost:
 To every one save me 'twas comical,
 Whilst tragic-like to me it did befall.

Each actor played in cunning-wise his part,
But chiefly those entrapped in Cupid's snare:
Yet all was feigned, 'twas not from the heart,
They seemed to grieve, but yet they felt no care;
 'Twas I that grief indeed did bear in breast,
 The others did but make a show in jest.

Yet neither feigning theirs, nor my mere truth,
Could make her once so much as for to smile:
Whilst she, despite of pity mild and ruth,
Did sit as scorning of my woes the while.
 Thus did she sit to see Love lose his Love,
 Like hardened rock that force nor power can move.

'R. T., Gentleman' (Robert Tofte): from Alba:
The Month's Mind of a Melancholy Lover

Know, that I would accounted be
True brother of a company
That sang, to sweeten Ireland's wrong,
Ballad and story, rann and song;
Nor be I any less of them,
Because the red-rose-bordered hem
Of Her, whose history began
Before God made the angelic clan,
Trails all about the written page.
When Time began to rant and rage
The measure of her flying feet
Made Ireland's heart begin to beat;
And Time bade all his candles flare
To light a measure here and there;
And may the thoughts of Ireland brood
Upon a measured quietude. . . .

While still I may, I write for you
The love I lived, the dream I knew.
From our birthday, until we die,
Is but the winking of an eye;
And we, our singing and our love,
What measure Time has lit above
And all benighted things that go
About my table to and fro,
Are passing on to where may be,
In truth's consuming ecstasy,
No place for love and dream at all;
For God goes by with white footfall.
I cast my heart into my rhymes,
That you, in the dim coming times,
May know how my heart went with them
After the red-rose-bordered hem.

W. B. Yeats: 'To Ireland in the Coming Times'

1604—On the second day of the Hampton Court conference, James I accepted proposals for a new translation of the Bible, which became the Authorized Version of 1611

On Monday, Januarie sisteene, betweene 11. and 12. of the clock, were the 4 plaintiffes called into the privy Chamber, (the two Bishops of London and Winchester being there before) and after them all the Deanes and Doctors present ... the Kings Majesty, entring the Chamber, presently took his Chaire ... where making a short but a pithy and sweet speech ... he said ... he was now ready to heare at large, what they could object or say; and so willed them to begin: whereupon the foure kneeling downe, D. Reinalds the Foreman, after a short Preamble gratulary ... reduced all matters disliked or questioned. ...

After that, he moved his Majesty, that there might be a new translation of the Bible, because, those which were allowed in the reigne of King Henry the Eight, and Edward the sixt, were corrupt, and not answerable to the truth of the Original ... to which motion, there was, at the present, no gainsaying ... Whereupon his Highnesse" "wished, that some especiall paines should bee taken in that behalfe for one uniforme" "translation (professing that he could never, yet, see a Bible well translated in" "English, but the worst of all his Majesty thought the Geneva to bee) and this to" "bee done by the best learned in both the Universities, after them to bee reviewed" "by the Bishops, and the chiefe learned of the Church; from them to be presented" "to the Privy Councel; and lastly, to be ratified by his Royall authority; and so this" "whole Church to be bound unto it, and none other: Mary, withall, he gave this" "caveat (upon a word cast out by my Lord of London) that no Marginall Notes" "should be added, having found in them which are annexed to the Geneva translation" "(which he saw in a Bible given him by an English Lady) some Notes very partiall," "untrue, seditious, and savouring too much of dangerous, and traiterous conceits." "As for example, the first Chapter of *Exodus* and the nineteenth Verse, where the" "marginall Note alloweth Disobedience unto King. And 2. *Chro.* 15. 16. the note" "taxeth Asa for deposing his mother, onely, and not killing her: And so concludeth" "this point as all the rest, with a grave and judicious advice. First, that errors in" "matters of Faith might bee rectified and amended. Secondly, that matters indifferent" "might rather be interrupted [*sic*], & a glosse added; alleaging from *Bartolus de*" "*regno*, that, as better a King with some weaknesse, than still a change; so rather a" "Church with some faults, than an Innovation. And surely, saith his Majesty, if" "these be the greatest matters you be grieved with, I need not have been troubled" "with such importunities & complaints, as have been made unto me; some other" "more private course might have beene taken for your satisfaction, and withall," "looking upon the Lords, hee shooke his head, smiling.

> *William Barlow: from* The Summe and Substance of the Conference ... at Hampton Court

1775—Richard Brinsley Sheridan's comedy, The Rivals, *was first produced (the first appearance of 'Mrs Malaprop' on the English stage)*

LYDIA: Here, my dear Lucy, hide these books. Quick, quick! – Fling *Peregrine Pickle* under the toilet – throw *Roderick Random* into the closet – put *The Innocent Adultery* into *The Whole Duty of Man* – thrust *Lord Aimworth* under the sofa – cram *Ovid* behind the bolster – put *The Man of Feeling* into your pocket – so, so – now lay *Mrs. Chapone* in sight, and leave *Fordyce's Sermons* open on the table.

LUCY: O burn it, ma'am! the hair-dresser has torn away as far as *Proper Pride.*

LYDIA: Never mind – open at *Sobriety.* – Fling me *Lord Chesterfield's Letters.* – Now for 'em.
    [Exit *Lucy.* Enter *Mrs. Malaprop* and *Sir Anthony Absolute*]

MRS. M.: There, Sir Anthony, there sits the deliberate simpleton who wants to disgrace her family, and lavish herself on a fellow not worth a shilling.

LYDIA: Madam, I thought you once –

MRS. M.: You thought, Miss! I don't know any business you have to think at all – thought does not become a young woman. But the point we would request of you is, that you will promise to forget this fellow – to illiterate him, I say, quite from memory.

LYDIA: Ah, madam! our memories are independent of our wills. It is not so easy to forget.

MRS. M.: But I say, it is, miss; there is nothing on earth so easy as to forget, if a person chooses to set about it. I'm sure I have as much forgot your poor dear uncle as if he had never existed – and I thought it my duty to do so; and let me tell you, Lydia, these violent memories don't become a young woman.

SIR A.: Why sure she won't pretend to remember what she's ordered not! – ay, this comes of her reading!

LYDIA: What crime, madam, have I committed to be treated thus?

MRS. M.: Now don't attempt to extirpate yourself from the matter; you know I have proof controvertible of it. . . .

Sheridan: from The Rivals, *Act I, scene* 2

1529—Hugh Latimer preached, 'in the covered place called "The Shrouds" ' outside St Paul's, the hell-fire-and-damnation sermon 'of the Plough'

Nowe what shall we saye of these ryche citizens of London? what shall I saye of them? Shal I call them proud men of London, malicious men of London, mercylesse men of London. No, no, I may not saye so, they will be offended wyth me than. Yet must I speake. . . . But London cannot abyde to be rebuked, suche is the nature of man. If they be prycked, they wyll kycke. If they be rubbed on the gale, they wil wynce. But yet they wyll not amende theyr faultes, they wyl not be yl spoken of. But howe shal I speke wel of them. If you could be contente to receyve and folowe the worde of God and favoure good preachers, if you coude bear to be tolde of youre faultes, if you could amende when you heare of them: if you woulde be gladde to reforme that is amisse: if I mighte se anie suche inclinacion in you, that leave to be mercilesse and begynne to be charytable I would then hope wel of you. But London was never so yll as it is now. In tymes past men were full of pytie and compassion but nowe there is no pitie, for in London their brother shal die in the streetes fro colde, he shall lye sycke at theyr doore betwene stocke and stocke – I can not tel what to call it – and peryshe there for hunger. Was there any more unmercifulness in Nebo? I thynke not. In tymes paste when any ryche man dyed in London, they were wonte to healp the pore scholers of the universitye wyth exhibition. When any man dyed they woulde bequeth great summes of money towarde the releve of the pore. When I was a scholer in Cambrydge my selfe, I harde verye good reporte of London and knewe manie that had releve of the rytche men of London, but nowe I can heare no such good reporte, and yet I inquyre of it, and herken for it, but nowe charitie is waxed colde, none helpeth the scholer nor yet the pore. . . . Oh London, London, repente repente, for I thynke God is more displeased wyth London than ever he was with the citie of Nebo. Repente, therefor, repent London, and remember that the same God liveth nowe yat punyshed Nebo, even the same God and none other, and he wyl punyshe synne as well nowe as he dyd then, and he wyl punishe the iniquitie of London as well as he did then of Nebo. Amende therefore and ye that be prelatis loke well to your office, for right preletynge is busye labourynge and not lordyng. Therefore preache and teache and let your ploughe be doynge, ye lordes I say that live lyke loyterers, loke well to your office, the plough is your office and charge.

1619—Ben Jonson, after his visit to Drummond of Hawthornden, discovered he had left something behind

---

My Picture Left in Scotland

I now think, Love is rather deafe, then blind,
For else it could not be,
That she,
Whom I adore so much, should so slight me,
And cast my love behind;
I'm sure my language to her, was as sweet
And every close did meet
In sentence, as of subtile feet,
As hath the youngest Hee,
That sits in shadow of Apollo's tree.

Oh, but my conscious feares,
That flie my thoughts betweene,
Tell me that she hath seene
My hundred of grey haires,
Told seven and fortie years,
Read so much wast, as she cannot embrace
My mountaine belly, and my rockie face,
And all these through her eyes, have stopt her eares.

*Jonson in his 'thank-you' letter to Drummond,
19 January 1619*

20 January (St Agnes's Eve) 📖

1820—'I was nearly a fortnight at Mr John Snook's and a few days at old Mr Dilke's (Chichester in Hampshire). Nothing worth speaking of happened at either place. I took down some thin paper and wrote on it a little poem called St Agnes's Eve'

John Keats to his brother George

St. Agnes' Eve – Ah, bitter chill it was!
The owl, for all his feathers, was a-cold;
The hare limped trembling through the frozen grass,
And silent was the flock in woolly fold;
Numb were the Beadsman's fingers, while he told
His rosary, and while his frosted breath,
Like pious incense from a censer old,
Seem'd taking flight for heaven, without a death,
Past the sweet Virgin's picture, while his prayer he saith.

His prayer he saith, this patient, holy man;
Then takes his lamp, and riseth from his knees,
And back returneth, meagre, barefoot, wan,
Along the chapel aisle by slow degrees:
The sculptured dead, on each side, seem to freeze,
Emprison'd in black, purgatorial rails:
Knights, ladies, praying in dumb orat'ries,
He passeth by; and his vast spirit fails
To think how they may ache in icy hoods and mails. . . .

That ancient Beadsman heard the prelude soft;
And so it chanced, for many a door was wide,
From hurry to and fro. Soon, up aloft,
The silver, snarling trumpets, 'gan to chide;
The level chambers, ready with their pride,
Were glowing to receive a thousand guests;
The carved angels, ever eager-eyed,
Stared, where upon their heads the cornice rests,
With hair blown back, and wings put cross-wise on their breasts . . .

1769—the first of the collected Letters of Junius *appeared in the* Public Advertiser

---

The situation in this country is alarming enough to rouse the attention of every man, who pretends to a concern for the public welfare. Appearances justify suspicion, and, when the safety of a nation is at stake, suspicion is a just ground of inquiry. Let us enter into it with candour and decency. Respect is due to the station of ministers; and, if a resolution must at last be taken, there is none so likely to be supported with firmness, as that which has been adopted with moderation.

The ruin or prosperity of a state depends so much upon the administration of its government, that to be acquainted with the merit of a ministry, we need only observe the condition of the people. If we see them obedient to the laws, prosperous in their industry, united at home, and respected abroad, we may reasonably presume that their affairs are conducted by men of experience, abilities, and virtue. If, on the contrary, we see an universal spirit of distrust and dissatisfaction, a rapid decay of trade, dissensions in all parts of the empire, and a total loss of respect in the eyes of foreign powers, we may pronounce, without hesitation, that the government of that country is weak, distracted, and corrupt. The multitude, in all countries, are patient to a certain point. Ill-usage may rouse their indignation, and hurry them into excesses, but the original fault is in government. Perhaps there never was an instance of a change in the circumstances and temper of a whole nation so sudden and extraordinary as that which the misconduct of ministers has, within these very few years, produced in Great Britain. . . .

In one view, behold a nation overwhelmed with debt; her revenues wasted; her trade declining; the affections of her colonies alienated; the duty of the magistrate transferred to the soldiery; a gallant army, which never fought unwillingly but against their fellow subjects, mouldering away for want of the direction of a man of common abilities and spirit; and, in the last instance, the administration of justice become odious and suspected to the whole body of the people. This deplorable scene admits of but one addition – that we are governed by councils, from which a reasonable man can expect no remedy but poison, no relief but death. . . .

22 January 🎀

1878—George Thomas Lanigan, Canadian journalist, read in the London Times *the terse notice : 'The Ahkound of Swat is dead'. The odd title aroused his sense of parody, and he produced the now-famous 'Threnody'*

What, what, what,
What's the news from Swat?
    Sad news,
    Bad news,
Comes by the cable led
Through the Indian Ocean's bed,
Through the Persian Gulf, the Red
Sea and the Med-
Iterranean – he's dead;
The Ahkound is dead! ...

Dead, dead, dead;
    Sorrow, Swats!
Swats wha hae wi' Ahkound bled,
Swats whom he had often led
Onward to a gory bed,
    Or to victory,
    As the case might be ...

The azure skies that bend above his loved
    Metropolis of Swat
He sees with larger, other eyes,
Athwart all earthly mysteries
    He knows what's Swat.

Let Swat bury the great Ahkound
    With a voice of mourning and of lamentation!
Let Swat bury the great Ahkound
    With the noise of the mourning of the Swattish nation!
        Fallen is at length
        Its tower of strength,
Its sun had dimmed ere it had nooned:
Dead lies the great Ahkound.
        The great Ahkound of Swat
        Is not.

1589—Edmund Spenser addressed his explanation of the allegory of The Faerie Queene *to 'the Right Noble, and Valorous, Sir Walter Raleigh knight, Ld. Warden of the Stanneryes, and her Maiesties lieftenant of the County of Cornwayll'*

Sir knowing how doubtfully all Allegories may be construed, and this booke of mine, which I have entituled the Faery Queene, being a continued Allegory, or darke conceit, I have thought good as well for avoyding of gealous opinions and misconstructions, as also for your better light in reading thereof, (being so by you commanded,) to discover unto you the general intention and meaning, which in the whole course thereof I have fashioned, without expressing of any particular purposes or by-accidents therein occasioned. The generall end therefore of all the booke is to fashion a gentleman or noble person in vertuous and gentle discipline: which for that I conceived should be most plausible and pleasing, being coloured with an historicall fiction, the which the most part of men delight to read . . . I chose the historye of king Arthure, as most fitte for the excellency of his person, being made famous by many mens former workes, and also furthest from the daunger of envy, and suspition of present times. . . .

I labour to pourtraict in Arthure before he was king, the image of a brave knight, perfected in the twelve private morall vertues, as Aristotle hath devised, the which is the purpose of these first twelve bookes: which if I finde to be well accepted, I may be perhaps encoraged, to frame the other part of polliticke vertues in his person, after that he came to be king. To some I know this Methode will seeme displeasaunt, which had rather have good discipline delivered plainly in way of precepts, or sermoned at large, as they use, then thus cloudily enwrapped in Allegorical devises. But such, me seeme, should be satisfide with the use of these dayes, seeing all things accounted by their showes, and nothing esteemed of, that is not delightfull and pleasing to commune sence. . . .

So in the person of Prince Arthure I sette forth magnificence in particular, which vertue for that (according to Aristotle and the rest) it is the perfection of all the rest, and conteineth in it them all, therefore in the whole course I mention the deedes of Arthure applyable to that vertue, which I write of in that booke. Out of the xii. other vertues, I make xii. other knights the patrones, for the more variety of the history: . . .

1924—first performance of Edith Sitwell's Façade, *with music by Sir William Walton, and with Edith Sitwell and Peter Pears as readers*

En Famille

In the early spring-time, after their tea
Through the young fields of the springing Bohea,
Jemima, Jocasta, Dinah, and Deb
Walked with their father Sir Joshua Jebb –
An admiral red, whose only notion,
(A butterfly poised on a pigtailed ocean)
Is of the peruked sea whose swell
Breaks on the flowerless rocks of Hell.
Under the thin trees, Deb and Dinah,
Jemima, Jocasta, walked, and finer
Their black hair seemed (flat-sleek to see)
Than the young leaves of the springing Bohea;
Their cheeks were like nutmeg-flowers when swells
The rain into foolish silver bells.
They said, 'If the door you would only slam,
Or if, Papa, you would once say "Damn" –
Instead of merely roaring "Avast"
Or boldly invoking the nautical Blast –
We should now stand in the street of Hell
Watching siesta shutters that fell
With a noise like amber softly sliding;
Our moon-like glances through these gliding
Would see at her table preened and set
Myrrhina sitting at her toilette
With eyelids closed as soft as the breeze
That flows from gold flowers on the incense-trees.'

　　　·　　　·　　　·　　　·　　　·

The Admiral said, 'You could never call –
I assure you it would not do at all!
She gets down from table without saying "Please",
Forgets her prayers and to cross her T's,
In short, her scandalous reputation
Has shocked the whole of the Hellish nation;
And every turbaned Chinoiserie,
With whom we should sip our black Bohea,
Would stretch out her simian fingers thin
And scratch you, my dears, like a mandolin;
For Hell is just as properly proper
As Greenwich, or as Bath, or Joppa!'

1759—Robert Burns was born

'For my own affairs, I am in a fair way of becoming as eminent as Thomas a Kempis, or John Bunyan; and you may expect henceforth to see my birthday inscribed among the wonderful events, in the Poor Robin and Aberdeen Almanacks, along with the Black Monday and the Battle of Bothwell Bridge.'

Robert Burns in a letter to Gavin Hamilton, written 1786

SONNET on Hearing a Thrush Sing in January,
written on 25th Jan. 1793,
the birthday of the author

Sing on, sweet thrush, upon the leafless bough,
 Sing on, sweet bird, I listen to thy strain;
 See aged Winter, 'mid his surly reign,
At this blythe carol clears his furrowed brow.

So in lone Poverty's dominion drear,
 Sits meek Content with light unanxious heart;
 Welcomes the rapid moments, bids them part,
Nor asks if they bring ought to hope or fear.

I thank thee, Author of this opening day:
 Thou whose bright sun now gilds yon orient skies!
 Riches denied, thy boon was purer joys,
What wealth could never give nor take away.

Yet come, thou child of povery and care,
The mite high Heaven bestowed, that mite with thee I'll share.

Robert Burns

26 January

1788—The penal colony was founded at Botany Bay – an event still viewed with alarm by Sydney Smith fifteen years later

Upon the foundation of a new colony, and especially one peopled by criminals, there is a disposition in Government . . . to convert capital punishments into transportation; and by these means to hold forth a very dangerous, though certainly a very unintentional, encouragement to offences. And when the history of the colony has been attentively perused in the parish of St. Giles, the ancient avocation of picking pockets will certainly not become more discreditable from the knowledge that it may eventually lead to the possession of a farm of a thousand acres on the river Hawkesbury. Since the benevolent Howard attacked our prisons, incarceration has become not only healthy, but elegant; and a county-jail is precisely the place to which any pauper might wish to retire to gratify his taste for magnificence as well as for comfort. Upon the same principle, there is some risk that transportation will be considered as one of the surest roads to honour and to wealth; and that no felon will hear a verdict of '*not guilty*', without considering himself as cut off in the fairest career of prosperity. It is foolishly believed, that the colony of Botany Bay unites our moral and commercial interests, and that we shall receive hereafter an ample equivalent, in bales of goods, for all the vices we export. Unfortunately, the expence we have incurred in founding the colony, will not retard the natural progress of its emancipation, or prevent the attacks of other nations, who will be as desirous of reaping the fruit, as if they had sown the seed. It is a colony, besides, begun under every possible disadvantage; it is too distant to be long governed, or well defended; it is undertaken, not by the voluntary association of individuals, but by Government, and by means of compulsory labour. A nation must, indeed, be redundant in capital, that will expend it where the hopes of a just return are very small.

It may be a curious consideration, to reflect what we are to do with this colony when it comes to years of discretion. Are we to spend another hundred millions of money in discovering its strength, and to humble ourselves again before a fresh set of Washingtons and Franklins? . . . But we confess ourselves not to be so sanguine as to suppose, that a spirited and commercial people would in spite of the example of America, ever consent to abandon their sovereignty over an important colony, without a struggle. Endless blood and treasure will be exhausted to support a tax on kangaroos' skins; faithful Commons will go on voting fresh supplies to support a *just and necessary war*; and Newgate, then become a quarter of the world, will evince a heroism, not unworthy of the great characters by whom she was originally peopled.

Sydney Smith: in a review of Collins' Account of the English Colony of New South Wales, *in* The Edinburgh Review, *1803*

1621—Francis Bacon was created Viscount St Albans, 'touching the highest point of his greatness'

Men in great places are thrice servants: servants of the sovereign or state; servants of fame; and servants of business. So as they have no freedom, neither in their persons, nor in their actions, nor in their times. It is a strange desire, to seek power and to lose liberty; or to seek power over others and to lose power over a man's self. The rising unto place is laborious, and by pains men come to greater pains; and it is sometimes base, and by indignities men come to dignities. The standing is slippery; and the regress is either a downfall, or at least an eclipse, which is a melancholy thing. *Cum non sis qui fueris, non esse cur velis vivere* [When you are no longer the man you have been, there is no reason why you should wish to live]. Nay, retire men cannot when they would; neither will they when it were reason; but are impatient of privateness, even in age and sickness, which require the shadow: like old townsmen, that will be sitting at their street door, though thereby they offer age to scorn. Certainly, great persons had need to borrow other men's opinions, to think themselves happy; for if they judge by their own feeling, they cannot find it; but if they think with themselves what other men think of them, and that other men would fain be as they are, then they are happy as it were by report, when perhaps they find the contrary within. For they are the first that find their own griefs, though they be the last that find their own faults. Certainly, men in great fortunes are strangers to themselves, and while they are in the puzzle of business they have no time to tend their health, either of body or mind. *Illi mors gravit incubat, qui notus nimis omnibus, ignotus moritur sibi.* [Death falls heavy on him, who, too well known to all others, dies to himself unknown.]

In place there is license to do good and evil; whereof the latter is a curse: for in evil the best condition is not to will, the second not to can. But power to do good is the true and lawful end of aspiring. For good thoughts (though God accept them) yet towards men are little better than good dreams, except they be put in act; and that cannot be without power and place, as the vantage and commanding ground. Merit and good works is the end of man's motion; and conscience of the same is the accomplishment of man's rest. For if man can be partaker of God's theatre, he shall likewise be partaker of God's rest. . . .

It is most true that was anciently spoken, *A place sheweth the man*: it sheweth some to the better, and some to the worse.

Francis Bacon: Of Great Place

28 January 🕮

1846—Charlotte Brontë wrote to the publishers, Aylott & Jones, the information about her sisters' poems which she later published

One day in the autumn of 1845, I accidentally lighted on a MS. volume of verse, in my sister Emily's hand-writing. Of course, I was not surprised, knowing that she could and did write verse: I looked it over, and something more than surprise seized me – a deep conviction that these were not common effusions, nor at all like the poetry women generally write. I thought them condensed and terse, vigorous and genuine. To my ear they had also a peculiar music, wild, melancholy, and elevating. My sister Emily was not a person of demonstrative character, nor one, on the recesses of whose mind and feelings, even those nearest and dearest to her could, with impunity, intrude unlicensed: it took hours to reconcile her to the discovery I had made, and days to persuade her that such poems merited publication. . . . Meantime, my younger sister quietly produced some of her own compositions, intimating that since Emily's had given me pleasure, I might like to look at hers. I could not but be a partial judge, yet I thought that these verses too had a sweet sincere pathos of their own. We had very early cherished the dream of one day being authors. . . . We agreed to arrange a small selection of our poems, and, if possible, get them printed. Averse to personal publicity, we veiled our own names under those of Currer, Ellis, and Acton Bell; the ambiguous choice being dictated by a sort of conscientious scruple at assuming Christian names, positively masculine, while we did not like to declare ourselves women, because – without at the time suspecting that our mode of writing and thinking was not what is called 'feminine', – we had a vague impression that authoresses are liable to be looked on with prejudice; we noticed how critics sometimes use for their chastisement the weapon of personality, and for their reward, a flattery, which is not true praise. The bringing out of our little book was hard work. As was to be expected, neither we nor our poems were at all wanted; but for this we had been prepared at the outset; though inexperienced ourselves, we had read the experience of others. The great puzzle lay in the difficulty of getting answers of any kind from the publishers to whom we applied. Being greatly harrassed by this obstacle, I ventured to apply to the Messrs. Chambers, of Edinburgh, for a word of advice; *they* may have forgotten the circumstance, but *I* have not, for from them I received a brief and business-like, but civil and sensible reply, on which we acted, and at last made way.

Charlotte Brontë, in the preface to the 1850 edition of Wuthering Heights and Agnes Grey *(as quoted in Mrs Gaskell's* Life of Charlotte Brontë*)*

1728—First performance of John Gay's The Beggar's Opera, *which subsequently had the longest run of any play on the English stage before the twentieth century*

PEACHUM: And had you not the common views of a Gentlewoman in your Marriage, Polly?

POLLY: I don't know what you mean, Sir.

PEACHUM: Of a Jointure, and of being a Widow.

POLLY: But I love him, Sir; how then could I have Thoughts of parting with him?

PEACHUM: Parting with him. Why that is the whole Scheme and Intention of all Marriage Articles. The comfortable estate of Widowhood, is the only Hope that keeps up a Wife's Spirits. Where is the Woman who would scruple to be a Wife, if she had it in her Power to be a Widow whenever she pleas'd? If you have any Views of this sort, Polly, I shall think the Match not so very unreasonable.

POLLY: How I dread to hear your Advice! Yet I must beg you to explain yourself.

PEACHUM: Secure what he hath got, have him peach'd the next Sessions, and then at once you are made a rich Widow.

POLLY: What, murder the Man I love! The Blood runs cold at my Heart at the very thought of it.

PEACHUM: Fye, Polly! What hath Murder to do in the Affair? Since the thing sooner or later must happen, I dare say, the Captain himself would like that we should get the Reward for his Death sooner than a Stranger. Why, Polly, the Captain knows, that as 'tis his Employment to rob, so 'tis ours to take Robbers; every man in his Business. So that there is no Malice in the Case.

POLLY: (AIR XII.)   Oh, ponder well! be not severe
So save a wretched Wife!
For on the Rope that hangs my Dear
Depends poor Polly's Life.

30 January

1648—Charles I repeated on the scaffold Pamela's prayer from Sidney's Arcadia

Pamela did walk up and down, full of deep though patient thoughts. For her look and countenance was settled, her pace soft and almost still of one measure, without any passionate gesture or violent motion; till at length, as it were awakening and strengthening herself, 'Well,' said she, 'yet this is the best and of this I am sure, that howsoever they wrong me they cannot over-master God. No darkness blinds His eyes, no jail bars Him out. To whom then else should I fly but to him for succour?'

And therewith kneeling down even in the same place where she stood, she thus said: 'O all-seeing Light and eternal Life of all things, to whom nothing is either so great that it may resist or so small that it is contemned, look upon my misery with Thine eye of mercy and let Thine infinite power vouchsafe to limit out some proportion of deliverance unto me as to Thee shall seem most convenient. Let not injury, O Lord, triumph over me, and let my faults by Thy hand be corrected, and make not mine unjust enemy the minister of Thy justice. But yet, my God, if in Thy wisdom this be the aptest chastisement for my inexcusable folly, if this low bondage be fittest for my over-high desires, if the pride of my not-enough humble heart be thus to be broken, O Lord, I yield unto Thy will, and joyfully embrace what sorrow Thou wilt have me suffer. Only this much let me crave of Thee – let my craving, O Lord, be accepted of Thee, since even that proceeds from Thee – let me crave, even by the noblest title which in my greatest affliction I may give myself, that I am Thy creature, and by Thy goodness, which is Thyself, that Thou wilt suffer some beam of Thy majesty so to shine into my mind that it may still depend confidently upon Thee. Let calamity be the exercise but not the overthrow of my virtue; let their power prevail, but prevail not to destruction; let my greatness be their prey; let my pain be the sweetness of their revenge; let them, if so it seem good unto Thee, vex me with more and more punishment. But, O Lord, let never their wickedness have such a hand but that I may carry a pure mind in a pure body.'

Sir Philip Sidney: from The Countess of Pembroke's Arcadia, *Bk. iii, ch. 3*

1864—John Henry Newman published his correspondence with Charles Kingsley, whose reply led Newman to produce his autobiographical Apologia pro vita sua

Lovers of their country and of their race, religious men, external to the Catholic Church, have attempted various expedients to arrest fierce wilful human nature in its outward course, and to bring it into subjection. The necessity of some form of religion for the interests of humanity has been generally acknowledged: but where was the concrete representative of things invisible, which would have the force and the toughness necessary to be a breakwater against the deluge? Three centuries ago the establishment of religion, material, legal, and social, was generally accepted, adopted as the best expedient for the purpose, in those countries which separated from the Catholic Church; and for a long time it was successful; but now the crevices of those establishments are admitting the enemy. Thirty years ago, education was relied upon: ten years ago, there was a hope that wars would cease forever, under the influence of commercial enterprise and the reign of the useful and fine arts; but will anyone venture to say that there is any thing any where on this earth, which will afford a fulcrum for us, whereby to keep the earth from moving onwards? . . .

Supposing then it to be the Will of the Creator to interfere in human affairs, and to make provisions for retaining in the world a knowledge of Himself, so definite and distinct as to be proof against the energy of human scepticism, in such a case . . . there is nothing to surprise the mind, if He should think fit to introduce a power into the world, invested with the prerogative of infallibility in religious matters. Such a provision would be direct, immediate, active, and prompt means of withstanding the difficulty; it would be an instrument suited to the need; and, when I find that this is the very claim of the Catholic Church, not only do I feel no difficulty in admitting the idea, but there is a fitness in it, which recommends it to my mind. And thus I am brought to speak of the Church's infallibility, as a provision, adapted by the mercy of the Creator, to preserve religion in the world, and to restrain that freedom of thought, which of course in itself is one of the greatest of our natural gifts, and to rescue it from its own suicidal excesses. . . . I say, that a power, possessed of infallibility in religious teaching, is happily adapted to be a working instrument in the course of human affairs, for smiting hard and throwing back the immense energy of the aggressive, capricious, untrustworthy intellect: – and in saying this . . . it must still be recollected that I am all along bearing in mind my main purpose, which is a defence of myself.

John Henry Newman: from Apologia pro vita sua

Februarie.

before 1648—Robert Herrick devised 'ceremonies' proper to Candlemas Eve, which falls on this date ; and in a second version elaborated the theme of seasonal decorations throughout the year

Down with the Rosemary, and so
Down with the Baies, and mistletoe:
Down with the Holly, Ivie, all,
Wherewith ye drest the Christmas Hall:
That so the superstitious find
No one least Branch there left behind:
For look how many leaves there be
Neglected there (maids trust to me)
So many *Goblins* you shall see.

Herrick : 'Ceremony upon Candlemas Eve'

Down with the Rosemary and Bayes,
  Down with the mistletoe;
In stead of Holly, now up-raise
  The greener Box (for show).

The Holly hitherto did sway;
  Let Box now domineere;
Until the dancing Easter-day,
  Or Easters Eve appeare.

Then youthfull Box which now hath grace,
  Your houses to renew;
Grown old, surrender must his place,
  Unto the crisped Yew.

When Yew is out, then Birch comes in,
  And many Flowers beside;
Both of a fresh, and fragrant kinne
  To honour Whitsontide.

Green rushes then, and sweetest Bents,
  With cooler Oken boughs;
Come in for comely ornaments,
  To re-adorn the house.

Thus times do shift; each thing his turne do's hold;
New things succeed, as former things grow old.

Herrick : 'Ceremonies for Candlemas Eve'

2 February (Candlemas Day) 🔖

1601/2—John Donne attempted to mollify his father-in-law, Sir George More, after his elopement with Anne More

SIR,

If a very respective feare of your displeasure . . . did not so much increase my sickness as that I cannot stir, I had taken the boldnes to have donne the office of this letter by wayting upon you myself to have given you the truthe and clearnes of this matter between your daughter and me, and to show you plainly the limits of our fault, by which I know your wisdome will proportion the punishment. So long since as her being at York House this had foundacion, and so much then of promise and contract built upon it withowt violence to conscience might not be shaken. At her lyeing in town this last Parliament, I found meanes to see her twice or thrice. We both knew the obligacions that lay upon us, and we adventured equally, and about three weeks before Christmas we married. And as at the doinge, there were not usd above fyve persons, of which I protest to you by my salvation, there was not one that had any dependence or relation to you, so in all the passage of it did I forbear to use any suche person, who by furtheringe of it might violate any trust or duty towards you. The reasons why I did not foreacquaint you with it (to deale with the same plainnes that I have usd) were these. I knew my present estate lesse than fitt for her, I knew (yet I knew not why) that I stood not right in your opinion. I knew that to have given any intimacion of it had been to impossibilitate the whole matter. . . . Sir, I acknowledge my fault to be so great, as I dare scarse offer any other prayer to you in mine own behalf than this, to beleeve this truthe, that I neyther had dishonest end nor meanes. But for her whom I tender much more than my fortunes or lyfe (els I woould I might neyther joy in this lyfe, nor enjoy the next), I humbly beg of you that she may not to her danger feele the terror of your sodaine anger. I know this letter shall find you full of passion; but I know no passion can alter your reason and wisdome, to which I adventure to commend these particulers; that it is irremediably donne; that if you incense my Lord you destroy her and me; that it is easye to give us happines, and that my endevors and industrie, if it please you to prosper them, may soone make me somewhat worthyer of her. . . . Sir, I have truly told you this matter, and I humbly beseeche you so to deale in it as the persuasions of Nature, Reason, Wisdom, and Christianity shall inform you; and to accept the vowes of one whom you may now rayse or scatter, which are that as my love is directed unchangeably upon her, so all my labors shall concur to her contentment, and to show my humble obedience to your self.

Yours in all duty and humbleness,

J. DONNE

1557—Thomas Tusser published the first of many editions of his Good Points of
Husbandry, *a book which long remained the standard 'farmer's almanac'*

What lookest thou here for to have,
    Trim verses thy fansy to please?
Of Surrey (so famous) that crave,
Looke nothing but rudeness in these.

What other thing lookest thou then?
Grave sentences herein to finde?
Such Chaucer had twenty and ten,
Yea thousands to pleasure thy mynde. . . .

What lookest thou then at the last?
Good lessons for thee and thy wyfe,
Then kepe them in memory fast,
From youth, to the last of thy life. . . .

        As true as thy fayth,
        Thus Husandry saith,

I seme but a drudge, yet I passe any king,
    To such as can use me great wealth I do bring.
Since Adam first lived, I never did die,
When Noe was a sea man there also was I.
The earth is my store house, the sea is my fishponde:
What they have to pleasure with, is in my hande.
What hath any life, but I helpe to preserve!
What thing without me, but is ready to sterve.
In Woodland, or Champion, Citie or Towne,
If I be long absent, what falleth not downe!
Of such as do love me (what neede to recite)
(Yea though of the poorest) who I make not knight
Great kings I do succour, else wrong it would go:
The king of al kings hath appointed it so.

        Thomas Tusser: from the Preface to the 1571
        edition of Good Points of Husbandry

4 February

1890—Beatrix Potter visited the Winter Exhibition at the Royal Academy

Tuesday, February 4th. – Uncle Thomas, who looked apoplectic, explained fluently that his cold had left him no voice so he could not talk to us. As to Mr. and Mrs. Gladstone, they came in directly after we did, and I took a good stare at the old gentleman as the rest of the company seemed to be doing so, without putting them out of countenance.

My dear Esther, he really looks as if he had been put in a clothes-bag and sat upon. I never saw a person so creased. He was dressed entirely in rusty black, like a typical clergyman or a Dissenting Minister or Dominie, and has a wrinkled appearance of not filling his clothes.

His trousers particularly were too long, I did not notice his finger tips but one would expect his gloves to be the same. I forgot to look at his collar either, one accepts it as a matter of course, being Friday it may have toned down. You are probably exclaiming at my not describing himself, but indeed he seemed to be shrunk out of sight inside his clothes, in the same fashion that some gray wisps of hair straggled from under his old hat. But very waken, not to say foxy, the old fellow looked, what there is of him.

As for his features, they have lent themselves with singular accuracy to the caricaturist, one villainous skit in particular recurs to me, which represented him as a callow nestling with enormous goggle eyes.

Mrs. Gladstone had on a round velvet cloak edged with sable, probably an heirloom. She rushed about with voluminous skirts, and, when I first noticed her, was pawing a bishop's wife, who appeared in the seventh heaven. Very few people spoke to them. My uncle said he should have done so, and I have no doubt he would, for though his admirers approach him with fawning adulation he does not appear to inspire awe.

They made straight for his own portrait by Millais, and stood in front of it, a shocking daub it is and does not do him justice at all, for however one may dislike him, undeniably he has a face one would notice unknown in a crowd.

I'm sure there were other characters there if one had only known them. There was one lame, elderly Scotchwoman in a frayed plaid gown and old-fashioned jewellery, who must surely have been a Peeress to wear such tips to her boots. Oh, and I must not omit to mention the little man trying to look like Titian, whose appearance immediately provokes my aunt to describe his hanging pictures on a ladder at Palace Gardens.

From The Journal of Beatrix Potter from 1881 to 1897, *transcribed from her code writing by Leslie Linder, London, 1966*

1885—Leopold II of the Belgians established the Congo as a personal possession, and began the regime under which hands of natives were chopped off for petty thievery

Then along that riverbank
A thousand miles
Tattooed cannibals danced in files;
Then I heard the boom of the blood-lust song
And a thigh-bone beating on a tin-pan gong.
And 'Blood' screamed the whistles and the fifes of the warriors,
'Blood' screamed the skull-faced, lean witch-doctors,
'Whirl ye the deadly voo-doo rattle,
Harry the uplands,
Steal all the cattle,
Rattle-rattle, rattle-rattle,
Bing.
Boomlay, boomlay, boomlay, BOOM',
A roaring, epic, rag-time tune
From the mouth of the Congo
To the Mountains of the Moon.
Death is an elephant,
Torch-eyed and horrible,
Foam-flanked and terrible.
BOOM, steal the pygmies,
BOOM, kill the Arabs,
BOOM, kill the white men,
HOO, HOO, HOO.
Listen to the yell of Leopold's ghost
Burning in Hell for his hand-maimed host.
Hear how the demons chuckle and yell
Cutting *his* hands off, down in Hell.
Listen to the creepy proclamation,
Blown through the lairs of the forest-nation,
Blown past the white-ants' hill of clay,
Blown past the marsh where the butterflies play: –
'Be careful what you do,
Or Mumbo-Jumbo, God of the Congo,
And all of the other
Gods of the Congo,
Mumbo-Jumbo will hoo-doo you,
Mumbo-Jumbo will hoo-doo you,
Mumbo-Jumbo will hoo-doo you.

Vachel Lindsay: from 'The Congo'

6 February 📖

1601—Supporters of Essex, on the eve of his planned revolution, persuaded members of Shakespeare's company to perform Richard II *at the Globe. The deposition scene, which had usually been omitted from performances and printed texts, was to be included, in the hope of preparing the audience to accept the deposition of Elizabeth*

BOLINGBROKE:	Are you contented to resign the crown?
RICHARD:	Ay, no: no, ay; for I must nothing be;
	Therefore no no, for I resign to thee.
	Now mark me how I will undo myself,
	I give this heavy weight from off my head,
	And this unwieldy sceptre from my hand,
	The pride of kingly sway from out my heart.
	With mine own tears I wash away my balm,
	With mine own hands I give away my crown,
	With mine own tongue deny my sacred state,
	With mine own breath release all duteous oaths.
	All pomp and majesty I do forswear;
	My manors, rents, revenues I forgo;
	My acts, decrees, and statutes I deny.
	God pardon all oaths that are broke to me. . . .
	What more remains?
NORTHUMBERLAND:	No more; but that you read (*Offers a paper*)
	These accusations, and these grievous crimes,
	Committed by your person, and your followers,
	Against the state and profit of this land;
	That by confessing them, the souls of men
	May deem that you are worthily deposed. . . .
RICHARD:	Mine eyes are full of tears, I cannot see.
	And yet salt water blinds them not so much,
	But they can see a sort of traitors here.
	Now, if I turn mine eyes upon myself,
	I find myself a traitor with the rest.
	For I have given here my soul's consent
	T' undeck the pompous body of a King;
	Made glory base; and sovereignty, a slave;
	Proud majesty, a subject; state, a peasant.

William Shakespeare: from Richard II, *Act iv, scene 1*

1755—Samuel Johnson addressed his famous letter on patronage to the Right Honourable the Earl of Chesterfield

My lord,

I have been lately informed, by the proprietor of the World, that two papers, in which my Dictionary is recommended to the publick, were written by your Lordship. To be so distinguished, is an honour, which, being very little accustomed to favours from the great, I know not well how to receive, or in what terms to acknowledge.

When, upon some slight encouragement, I first visited your Lordship, I was overpowered, like the rest of mankind, by the enchantment of your address, and could not forbear to wish that I might boast myself *Le vainqueur du vainqueur de la terre*; – that I might obtain that regard for which I saw the world contending; but I found my attendance so little encouraged that neither pride nor modesty would suffer me to continue it. When I had once addressed your Lordship in publick, I had exhausted all the art of pleasing which a retired and uncourtly scholar can possess. I had done all that I could; and no man is well pleased to have his all neglected, be it ever so little.

Seven years, my Lord, have now past, since I waited in your outward rooms, or was repulsed from your door; during which time I have been pushing on my work through difficulties, of which it is useless to complain, and have brought it, at last, to the verge of publication, without one act of assistance, one word of encouragement, or one smile of favour. Such treatment I did not expect, for I never had a Patron before. . . .

Is not a Patron, my Lord, one who looks with unconcern on a man struggling for life in the water, and, when he has reached ground, encumbers him with help? The notice which you have been pleased to take of my labours, had it been early, had been kind; but it has been delayed till I am indifferent, and cannot enjoy it; till I am solitary, and cannot impart it; till I am known, and do not want it. I hope it is no very cynical asperity, not to confess obligations where no benefit has been received, or to be unwilling that the Publick should consider me as owing that to a Patron, which Providence has enabled me to do for myself.

Having carried on my work thus far with so little obligation to any favourer of learning, I shall not be disappointed though I should conclude it, if less be possible, with less; for I have been long wakened from that dream of hope, in which I once boasted myself with so much exultation,

My Lord,

Your Lordship's most humble
Most obedient servant,

Sam. Johnson.

8 February

1750—The last series of earthquakes to occur in England began

– You know we have had an earthquake. Mr. Chute's Francesco says, that a few evenings before it there was a bright cloud, which the mob called the *bloody cloud*; that he had been told there never were earthquakes in England, or else he should have known by that symptom that there would be one within a week. I am told that Sir Isaac Newton foretold a great alteration in our climate in the year '50, and that he wished he could live to see it. Jupiter, I think, has jogged us three degrees nearer to the sun. . . .

. . . We have had a second, much more violent than the first; and you must not be surprised if by next post you hear of a burning mountain sprung up in Smithfield. In the night between Wednesday and Thursday last (exactly a month since the first shock) the earth had a shivering fit between one and two; but so slight that, if no more had followed, I don't believe it would have been noticed. I had been awake, and had scarce dozed again – on a sudden I felt my bolster lift up my head. I thought somebody was getting from under my bed, but soon found it was a strong earthquake, that lasted nearly half a minute, with a violent vibration and great roaring. I rang my bell; my servant came in, frightened out of his senses: in an instant we heard all the windows in the neighbourhood flung up. I got up and found people running into the streets, but saw no mischief done: there had been some; two old houses flung down, several chimneys, and much china-ware. The bells rang in several houses. . . .

You will not wonder so much at our earthquakes as at the effects they have had. All the women in the town have taken them upon the foot of *Judgments*; and the clergy, who have had no windfalls of a long season, have driven horse and foot into this opinion. There has been a shower of sermons and exhortations: Secker, the jesuitical Bishop of Oxford, began the mode. He heard the women were all going out of town to avoid the next shock; and so, for fear of losing his Easter offerings, he set himself to advise them to await God's pleasure in fear and trembling. . . .

. . . This frantic error prevails so much, that within these three days seven hundred and thirty coaches have been counted passing Hyde Park Corner, with whole parties removing into the country. . . . Several women have made earthquake gowns; that is, warm gowns to sit out of doors all to-night. These are of the more courageous. One woman, still more heroic, is come to the town on purpose: she says, all her friends are in London, and she will not survive them. . . .

Horace Walpole, from various letters to Sir Horace Mann

1645/6—John Milton wrote and dated his sonnet to Henry Lawes, who composed the music for Comus, A Masque

---

To Mr. H. Lawes, on his Aires

Harry whose tuneful and well measur'd Song
    First taught our English Musick how to span
    Words with just note and accent, not to scan
    With *Midas* Ears, committing short and long;
Thy worth and skill exempts thee from the throng,
    With praise enough for Envy to look wan;
    To after age thou shalt be writ the man,
    That with smooth aire couldst humor best our tongue.

Thou honour'st Verse, and Verse must send her wing
    To honour thee, the Priest of *Phoebus* Quire
    That tun'st their happiest lines in Hymn, or Story.
Dante shall give Fame leave to set thee higher
    Than his *Casella*, whom he woo'd to sing
    Met in the milder shades of Purgatory.

                    John Milton, Sonnet xiii

1671—John Evelyn saw at Whitehall Theater . . . 'the famous Play, cald the *Siege of* Granada *two days acted successively : there were indeede very glorious* *scenes and perspectives, the worke of Mr* Streeter, *who well understands it'*

Epilogue to *The Conquest of Granada*, II

They who have best succeeded on the stage
Have still conformed their genius to their age.
Thus Jonson did mechanic humor show,
When men were dull, and conversation low.
Then comedy was faultless, but 'twas coarse:
Cob's tankard was a jest, and Otter's horse.
And, as their comedy, their love was mean;
Except, by chance, in some one laboured scene
Which must atone for an ill-written play.
They rose, but at their height could seldom stay.
Fame then was cheap, and the first comer sped;
And they have kept it since, by being dead.
But, were they now to write, when critics weigh
Each line, and every word, throughout a play.
None of 'em, no, not Jonson in his height,
Could pass, without allowing grains for weight.
Think it not envy, that these truths are told;
Our poet's not malicious, though he's bold.
'Tis not to brand 'em, that their faults are shown,
But, by their errors, to excuse his own.
If love and honour now are higher raised,
'Tis not the poet, but the age is praised.
Wit's now arrived to a more high degree;
Our native language more refined and free.
Our ladies and our men now speak more wit
In conversation, than those poets writ.
Then, one of these is, consequently, true;
That what this poet writes comes short of you,
And imitates you ill (which most he fears),
Or else his writing is not worse than theirs.
Yet, though you judge (as sure the critics will)
That some before him writ with greater skill,
In this one praise he has their fame surpassed,
To please an age more gallant than the last.

John Dryden

There was in the [Abbess Hilda's] monastery [at Whitby] a certain brother who . . . having lived a secular life until he was well along in years, had never learned anything about making verses. Whenever it was agreed that each person in a company should entertain the others by singing in turn, Caedmon, when he saw the harp coming towards him, would get up from the table and leave the hall. On one such occasion, having gone out to the stable, where he had to take care of the horses that night, he lay down there to sleep. In his sleep, a person appeared to him, called him by name, and said, 'Caedmon, sing me a song.' He answered, 'I cannot sing; that is why I left the entertainment, and came here, because I cannot sing.' 'Nevertheless', said the other, 'you shall sing.' 'What shall I sing?' Caedmon asked. 'Sing about the Creation.' And he immediately began to sing verses in praise of God, which he had never heard, and this was the general theme of them:

> Let us praise the Creator   of heaven's kingdom
> the power and purpose   of the Father of glory
> how He, the eternal   maker of all marvels
> gave men the sky   as a roof to cover them
> and the earth also   for a dwelling-place.

This is the general sense, but not the words in the exact order as he sang them in his sleep; for verses, however well composed, cannot be translated from one language to another without losing much of their beauty and dignity. When he awoke, he remembered the verses he had made in his sleep, and soon added more, equally good, in praise of God.

The next morning, he told his superior, the steward, of the gift he had received; the steward took him to the Abbess, who ordered Caedmon to tell his dream and repeat his verses in the presence of many learned men. They all agreed that his gift was from God; then they selected a passage from Scripture, either history or doctrine, and when they had explained it to him, they told him to express it in verse if he could. The next morning he returned and gave them the passage in most excellent verse; the Abbess, seeing that God had bestowed such grace upon him, urged him to leave the secular life and become a monk, and when she had received him into the Community as a brother, she ordered him to be taught all the events of sacred history. So Caedmon, remembering all he learned and meditating on it, turned it into such melodious verse and sang it so well that his masters became his eager hearers.

Bede: from Ecclesiastical History

Before I went into Germanie, I came to Brodegate in Leicestershire to take my leave of that noble Ladie Jane Grey, to whom I was exceding moch beholdinge. Hir parents, the Duke and Duches, with all the houshold, Gentlemen and Gentlewomen, were hunting in the Parke: I founde her, in her Chamber, readinge Phaedon Platonis in Greeke, and that with as moche delite, as som gentlemen would read a merie tale in Bocase. After salutation, and deutie done, with som other taulke, I asked hir, whie she would lose such pastime in the Parke? Smiling she answered me: I wisse all their sport in the Parke is but a shadoe to that pleasure that I find in Plato: Alas, good folke, they never felt, what trewe pleasure ment. And howe came you, Madame, quoth I, to this deepe knowledge of pleasure, and what did chieflie allure you unto it: seeing, not many women, but verie fewe men have attained thereunto. I will tell you, quoth she, and tell you a troth, which perchance ye will mervell at. One of the greatest benefites, that ever God gave me, is, that he sent me so sharpe and severe Parentes, and so gentle a scholemaster. For when I am in presence either of father or mother, whether I speake, kepe silence, sit, stand, or go, eate, drinke, be merie, or sad, be sowyng, plaiyng, dauncing, or doing anie thing els, I must do it as it were, in such weight, mesure, and number, even so perfitelie, as God made the world, or else I am so sharplie taunted, so cruellie threatened, yea presentlie some tymes, with pinches, nippes, and bobbes, and other waies, which I will not name, for the honor I bear them, so without measure misordered, that I thinke my selfe in hell, till tyme cum, that I must go to M. Elmer, who teacheth me so gentlie, so pleasantly, with soch faire allurements to learning that I thinke all the tyme nothing, whiles I am with him. And when I am called from him, I fall on weeping, because whatsoever I do else, but learning, is ful of grief, trouble, feare, and whole misliking unto me: and thus my booke, hath bene so moch my pleasure, and bringeth dayly to me more pleasure and more, that in respect of it, all other pleasures, in very deede, be but trifles and troubles unto me. I remember this talk gladly, both because it is so worthy of memorie, and because also, it was the last talke that ever I had, and the last tyme, that ever I saw that noble and worthy Ladie.

Roger Ascham: from The Scholemaster

1926—Excerpts from Hugh MacDiarmid's A Drunk Man Looks at the Thistle *appeared in the* Glasgow Herald, *several months before the publication of the complete poem in book form, foreshadowing the advent of the Scottish Movement under the leadership of a poet to rank with Burns and Dunbar*

O wha's the bride that cairries the bunch
O' thistles blinterin' white?
Her cuckold bridegroom little dreids
What he sall ken this night.

For closer than gudeman can come
And closer to'r than hersel',
Wha didna need her maidenheid
Has wrocht his purpose fell.

O wha's been here afore me, lass,
And hoo did he get in?
– *A man that deed or I was born*
This evil thing has din.

And left, as it were on a corpse,
Your maidenheid to me?
– *Nae lass, gudeman, sin' Time began*
'S hed ony mair to gi'e.

But I can gi'e ye kindness, lad,
And a pair o' willin' hands,
And you sall ha'e my breists like stars,
My limbs like willow wands.

And on my lips ye'll heed nae mair,
And in my hair forget,
The seed o' a' the men that in
My virgin womb ha'e met....

'Hugh MacDiarmid' (Dr Christopher Grieve):
from A Drunk Man Looks at the Thistle

14 February (St Valentine's Day)

1477—Margery Brew's 'Valentine' to her future husband, John Paston

Unto my ryght welbelovyd Voluntyn, John Paston, Squyer, be this bill delyvered, &c.

RYGHT reverent and wurschypfull and my ryght welebeloved Voluntyne, I recommande me unto yowe full hertely, desyring to here of yowr welefare, whech I beseche Almyghty God long for to preserve unto hys plesure and yowr hertys desyre. And yf it please yowe to here of my welefare, I am not in good heele of body ner of herte, nor schall be tyll I here from yowe;

> For ther wottys no creature what peyn that I endure,
> And for to be deede, I dare it not dyscure   [discover; reveal]

And my lady my moder hath labored the mater [of Margery's dowry] to my fadure full delygently, but sche can no more gete then ye knowe of, for the wheche God knowyth I am full sory.

But yf that ye loffe me, as I tryste verely that ye do, ye will not leffe me therfor; for if that ye hade not halfe the lyvelode that ye hafe, for to do the grettyst labure that any woman on lyve myght, I wold not forsake yowe.

> And yf ye commande me to kepe me true whereever I go,
> I wyse I will do all my myght yowe to love and never no mo.
> And yf my freendys say that I do amys, thei schal not me let so for to do,
> Myn herte me byddys ever more to love yowe
> Truly over all erthely thing.
> And yf thei be never so wroth, I tryst it schall be bettur in tyme commyng.

No more to yowe at this tyme, but the Holy Trinite hafe yowe in kepyng. And I besech yowe that this bill be not seyn of non erthely creature safe only your selfe, &c. And thys lettur was indyte at Topcroft wyth full hevy herte, &c

Be your own M. B.

From Paston Letters, *edited by Norman Davis*
(Everyman's Library)

1714/15—Lemuel Gulliver departed from the Land of the Houyhnhnms

When all was ready, and the day came for my departure, I took leave of my master and lady, and the whole family, my eyes flowing with tears, and my heart quite sunk with grief. But his Honour, out of curiosity, and perhaps (if I may speak it without vanity) partly out of kindness, was determined to see me in my canoe, and got several of his neighbouring friends to accompany him. I was forced to wait above an hour for the tide, and then observing the wind very fortunately bearing towards the island, to which I intended to steer my course, I took a second leave of my master: but as I was going to prostrate myself to kiss his hoof, he did me the honour to raise it gently to my mouth. I am not ignorant how much I have been censured for mentioning this last particular. Detractors are pleased to think it improbable, that so illustrious a person should descend to give so great a mark of distinction to a creature so inferior as I. Neither have I forgot how apt some travellers are to boast of extraordinary favours they have received. But if these censurers were better acquainted with the noble and courteous disposition of the Houyhnhnms, they would soon change their opinion.

I paid my respects to the rest of the Houyhnhnms in his Honour's company; then getting into my canoe, I pushed off from shore.

I began this desperate voyage on February 15, 1714–5, at 9 o'clock in the morning. The wind was very favourable; however, I made use at first only of my paddles, but considering I should soon be weary, and that the wind might probably chop about, I ventured to set up my little sail; and thus with the help of the tide I went at the rate of a league and a half an hour, as near as I could guess. My master and his friends continued on the shore till I was almost out of sight; and I often heard the sorrel nag (who always loved me) crying out, *Hnuy illa nyha maiah yahoo*, Take care of yourself, gentle yahoo.

My design was, if possible, to discover some small island uninhabited, yet sufficient by my labour to furnish me with the necessaries of life, which I would have thought a greater happiness than to be first minister in the politest court of Europe; so horrible was the idea I conceived of returning to live in the society and under the government of yahoos. For in such a solitude as I desired, I could at least enjoy my own thoughts, and reflect with delight on the virtues of those inimitable Houyhnhnms, without any opportunity of degenerating into the vices and corruptions of my own species.

Jonathan Swift: from Travels into Several Remote Nations of the World. *In Four Parts. By Lemuel Gulliver, first a Surgeon, and then a Captain of Several Ships* (*London, 1726*)

1728—Henry Fielding's first play, Love in Several Masques *was first performed at Drury Lane*

Epilogue
Spoken by Miss Robinson, Jun.

Our author, full of sorrow and repentance,
Has sent me here – to mitigate his sentence.
To you, tremendous critics in the pit,
Who on his first offence in judgment sit!
He pleads – oh gad! how terrible his case is!
For my part, I'm frightened by your faces.
Think on his youth – it is his first essay;
He may, in time, perhaps, – atonement pay,
If but reprieved this execution day.

Methinks I see some elder critic rise,
And daring furious justice from his eyes,
Cry, 'Zounds! what means the brat? Why all this fuss?
What are his youth and promises to us?
For should we from severity refrain,
We soon should have the coxcomb here again.
And, brother, such examples may invite
A thousand other senseless rogues to write!'

From you, then, – ye toupets – he hopes defence:
You'll not condemn him for his want of sense.
What, now you'll say, I warrant with a sneer,
'He's chose too young an advocate, my dear!'
Yet boast not (for if my own strength I know)
I am a match sufficient – for a beau!

Lastly, to you, ye charmers, he applies,
For in your tender bosoms mercy lies,
As certain as destruction in your eyes.
Let but that lovely circle of the fair
Their approbation, by their smiles, declare,
Then let the critics damn him – if they dare.

Henry Fielding: from Love in Several Masques

1776—The first volume of Edward Gibbon's Decline and Fall of the Roman Empire *was published*

The [first] volume of my history, which had been somewhat delayed by the novelty and tumult of a first session, was now ready for the press. After the perilous adventure had been declined by my timid friend Mr. Elmsley, I agreed, on very easy terms, with Mr. Thomas Cadell, a respectable bookseller, and Mr. William Strahan, an eminent printer; and they undertook the care and risk of the publication, which derived more credit from the name of the shop than from that of the author. The last revival of the proofs was submitted to my vigilance; and many blemishes of style, which had been invisible in the manuscript, were discovered and corrected in the printed sheet. So moderate were our hopes, that the original impression had been stinted to five hundred, till the number was doubled by the prophetic taste of Mr. Strahan. During this awful interval I was neither elated by the ambition of fame, nor depressed by the apprehension of contempt. My diligence and accuracy were attested by my own conscience. History is the most popular species of writing, since it can adapt itself to the highest or the lowest capacity. I had chosen an illustrious subject; Rome is familiar to the schoolboy and the statesman, and my narrative was deduced from the last period of Classical reading. I had likewise flattered myself that an age of light and liberty would receive, without scandal, an enquiry into the *human* causes of the progress and establishment of Christianity.

I am at a loss how to describe the success of the work without betraying the vanity of a writer. The first impression was exhausted in a few days; a second and third edition were scarcely adequate to the demand, and the bookseller's property was twice invaded by the pyrates of Dublin. My book was on every table, and almost on every toilette; the historian was crowned by the taste or fashion of the day; nor was the general voice disturbed by the barking of any profane critic. The favour of mankind is most fully bestowed on a new acquaintance of any original merit, and the mutual surprise of the public and their favourite is productive of those warm sensibilities which, at a second meeting, can no longer be rekindled. If I listened to the music of praise, I was more seriously satisfied with the approbation of my Judges. The candour of Dr. Robertson embraced his disciple; a letter from Mr. Hume overpaid the labour of ten years; but I never presumed to accept a place in the triumvirate of British historians.

The Autobiographies of Edward Gibbon, *ed.*
John Murray, London, 1896, page 311

1678—John Bunyan's Pilgrim's Progress, *next to the Bible the most reprinted book in English, was first published*

When at the first I took my Pen in hand
Thus for to write, I did not understand
That I at all should make a little Book
In such a mode; Nay, I had undertook
To make another, which when almost done,
Before I was aware I this begun.
    And thus it was: I writing of the Way
And Race of Saints, in this our Gospel-day,
Fell suddenly into an Allegory
About their Journey, and the way to Glory,
In more than twenty things which I set down.
This done, I twenty more had in my Crown . . .
Nay then, thought I, if that you breed so fast,
I'll put you by yourselves, lest you at last
Should prove *ad infinitum*, and eat out
The Book that I already am about.
    Well, so I did; but yet I did not think
To shew to all the World my Pen and Ink
In such a mode; I only thought to make
I knew not what: nor did I undertake
Thereby to please my Neighbour; no not I,
I did it mine own self to gratifie. . . .
    Thus I set Pen to Paper with delight,
And quickly had my thoughts in black and white.
For having now my Method by the end,
Still as I pull'd, it came; and so I penn'd
It down, until at last it came to be
For length and breadth the bigness which you see.
    Well, when I had thus put mine ends together,
I shew'd them others, that I might see whether
They would condemn them, or them justify:
And some said, Let them live; some, Let them die;
Some said, John, print it; others said, Not so:
Some said, It might do good; others said, No.
    Now was I in a strait, and did not see
Which was the best thing to be done by me:
At last I thought, Since you are thus divided,
I print it will, and so the case decided.

John Bunyan: from 'The Author's Apology for his Book'

1670/71—'This day dined with me Mr. Surveyor, Dr. Christopher Wren, and Mr. Pepys, Clerk of the Acts, two extraordinary, ingenious, and knowing persons, and other friends. I carried them to see the piece of carving [by Grinling Gibbons] which I had recommended [a month earlier] to the King'

John Evelyn : Diary

18th. Jan. This day, I first acquainted his Majesty with that incomparable young man, Gibbons, whom I had lately met with in an obscure place by mere accident, as I was walking near a poor solitary thatched house, in a field in our parish, near Sayes Court. I found him shut in; but looking in at the window, I perceived him carving that large cartoon, or crucifix, of Tintoretto, a copy of which I had myself brought from Venice, where the original painting remains. I asked if I might enter; he opened the door civilly to me, and I saw him about such a work as for the curiosity of handling, drawing, and studious exactness, I never had before seen in all my travels. I questioned him why he worked in such an obscure and lonesome place; He told me it was that he might apply himself to his profession without interruption, and wondered not a little how I found him out. I asked if he was unwilling to be made known to some great man, for that I believed it might turn to his profit; he answered, he was yet but a beginner, but would not be sorry to sell off that piece; on demanding the price, he said £100. In good earnest, the very frame was worth the money, there being nothing in nature so tender and delicate as the flowers and festoons about it, and yet the work was very strong; in the piece were more than one hundred figures of men, etc. I found he was likewise musical, and very civil, sober, and discreet in his discourse. There was only an old woman in the house. So, desiring leave to visit him sometimes, I went away.

Of this young artist, together with my manner of finding him out, I acquainted the King, and begged that he would give me leave to bring him and his work to Whitehall, for that I would adventure my reputation with his Majesty that he had never seen anything approach it, and that he would be exceedingly pleased, and employ him. The King said he would himself go see him. This was the first notice his Majesty ever had of Mr. Gibbons. . . .

1st. March. I caused Mr. Gibbons to bring to Whitehall his excellent piece of carving. . . . It was carried into [the Queen's] bedchamber, where she and the King looked on and admired it again; the King, being called away, left us with the queen, believing she would have bought it, it being a crucifix; but, when his Majesty was gone, a French peddling woman, one Madame de Boord, who used to bring petticoats and fans, and baubles, out of France to the ladies, began to find fault with several things in the work, which she understood no more than an ass, or a monkey, so as in a kind of indignation, I caused the person who had brought it to carry it back to the chamber . . . and this incomparable artist had his labour only for his pains, which not a little displeased me.

Miss Clarissa Harlowe, To Miss Howe (After her Return from her)

Harlowe-Place, Feb. 20

I beg your excuse for not writing sooner. Alas, my dear, I have sad prospects before me! My Brother and Sister have succeeded in all their views. They have found out another Lover for me; an hideous one! Yet he is encouraged by every-body. No wonder that I was ordered home so suddenly. At an hour's warning! – No other notice, you know, than what was brought with the chariot that was to carry me back. It was for fear, as I have been informed (an unworthy fear!) that I should have entered into any concert with Mr. Lovelace had I known their motive for command-ing me home; apprehending, 'tis evident, that I should dislike the man they had to propose to me.

And well might they apprehend so: – For who do you think he is? – No other than that *Solmes*! – Could you have believed it? – And they are all determined too; my Mother with the rest! – Dear, dear excellence! how could she be thus brought over, when I am assured, that on his first being proposed she was pleased to say, That had Mr. Solmes the *Indies* in possession, and would endow me with them, she should not think him deserving of her Clarissa? . . .

Mr. Solmes came in before we had done Tea. My Uncle Antony presented him to me, as a gentlemen he had a particular friendship for. My Uncle Harlowe in terms equally favourable for him. My Father said, Mr. Solmes is my friend, Clarissa Harlowe. My Mother looked at him, and looked at me, now-and-then, as he sat near me, I thought with concern. – I at *her*, with eyes appealing for pity. At *him*, when I could glance at him, with disgust little short of affrightment. While my Brother and Sister Mr. *Solmes*'d him, and *Sirr*'d him up, at every word. So caressed in short, by all; – yet such a wretch! – But I will at present only add, My humble thanks and duty to your honoured Mother (to whom I will particularly write, to express the grateful Sense I have of her goodness to me); and that I am

Your ever obliged,

Cl. Harlowe

Samuel Richardson: from Clarissa Harlowe, or The History of a Young Lady . . . (*1747–8*)

1892—The day after the opening of Oscar Wilde's play Lady Windermere's Fan *at the St James's Theatre, the reviewer for* The Times *wrote this notice*

Stripped of its meretricious ornament, *Lady Windermere's Fan*, in fact, is a play of that simple and ingenious class of which *The Wife's Secret* is a prominent example. In this old play, it will be remembered, much anguish of mind is caused to a worthy husband by his wife's secret interviews with a stranger who, after much tedious misunderstanding, proves to be her brother. To Mr. Wilde's imagination we are indebted for a variant upon this somewhat primitive theme. Lady Windermere, a young and devoted wife, in society is scandalized by her husband's attentions to a woman of uncertain age, passing in Mayfair as a widow, but conducting herself like an adventuress, to whom he pays large sums of money. This Mrs. Erlynne remains a mystery until the last act, when she is discovered to be no other than Lady Windermere's mother – a *declassée* who is supposed to be dead, but whom Lord Windermere befriends for her daughter's sake, though, with a perversity which it is hard to understand, he allows the tongues of the scandal-mongers to wag unchecked for many months and his wife's affections to be almost fatally estranged rather than reveal the woman's identity. No one has hitherto guessed that in Mr. Wilde's eyes the personality of a mother-in-law could be so sacred.

The absurdity of this theme is not to be overlooked on the stage, however much it might have been disguised under an exquisite vellum or morocco binding. . . .

As a set-off to its drawbacks from the constructive point of view, the play has the benefit of Mr. Wilde's fantastic *préciosité* in its dialogue. This in the first act is very well. It is amusing at first to hear that 'nothing is so unbecoming in a woman as a Nonconformist conscience,' that 'scandal is gossip made tedious by morality,' that 'there is nothing like the devotion of a married woman – a thing no married man knows anything about,' and other adaptations of the maxims of La Rochefoucauld and Talleyrand. But the strain becomes fatiguing when it is discovered, as it very soon is, that all the characters talk alike. . . . In order to obtain his *dramatis personæ*, Mr. Wilde seems to have multiplied himself by a process of fission, such as is seen among the lower organisms. . . .

22 February ⚏

1743—Philip Dormer Stanhope, fourth Earl of Chesterfield, spoke in the House of Lords against the Gin Licensing Act

The law before us, my lords, seems to be the effect of that practice of which it is intended likewise to be the cause, and to be dictated by the liquor of which it so effectually promotes the use; for surely it never before was conceived by any man entrusted with the administration of public affairs, to raise taxes by the destruction of the people. . . .

To pretend, my lords, that the design of this Bill is to prevent or diminish the use of spirits, is to trample upon common sense, and to violate the rules of decency as well as of reason. For when did any man hear, that a commodity was prohibited by licensing its sale? or that to offer and refuse is the same action?

It is indeed pleaded, that it will be made dearer by the tax which is proposed, and that the increase of the price will diminish the number of the purchasers; but it is at the same time expected that this tax shall supply the expence of a war on the continent . . . for the re-establishment of the Austrian family, and the repressing of the attempts of France.

Surely, my lords, these expectations are not very consistent, nor can it be imagined that they are both formed in the same head, though they may be expressed by the same mouth. It is however some recommendation of a statesman, when of his assertions one can be found reasonable or true; and this praise cannot be denied to our present ministers; for though it is undoubtedly false, that this tax will lessen the consumption of spirits, it is certainly true, that it will produce a very large revenue, a revenue that will not fail but with the people from whose debaucheries it arises.

Our ministers will therefore have the same honour with their predecessors, of having given rise to a new fund, not indeed for the payment of our debts, but for much more valuable purposes, for the exaltation of our spirits amidst miscarriages and disappointments, and for the cheerful support of those debts which we have lost hopes of paying. They are resolved, my lords, that the nation, which nothing can make wise, shall, while they are at its head, at least be merry; and since public happiness is the end of government, they seem to imagine that they shall deserve applause by an expedient which will enable every man to lay his cares asleep, to drown sorrow, and lose in the delights of drunkenness both the public miseries and his own.

1669—Samuel Pepys celebrated his thirty-sixth birthday

Up: and to the Office, where all the morning, and then home, and put a mouthful of victuals in my mouth: and by a hackney-coach followed my wife and the girls, who are gone by eleven o'clock, thinking to have seen a new play at the Duke of York's House. But I do find them staying at my tailor's, the play being not today, and therefore to Westminster Abbey, and there did see all the tombs very finely, having one with us alone, there being other company this day to see the tombs, it being Shrove Tuesday; and here we did see, by particular favour, the body of Queen Katherine of Valois; and I had the upper part of her body in my hands, and I did kiss her mouth, reflecting upon it that I did kiss a queene, and that this was my birth-day, thirty-six years old, that I did kiss a Queene. But here this man, who seems to understand well, tells me that the saying is not true that she was never buried, for she was buried; only, when Henry the Seventh built his chapel, she was taken up and laid in this wooden coffin; but I did see that, in it, the body was buried in a leaden one, which remains under the body to this day. Thence to the Duke of York's play-house, and there, finding the play begun, we homeward to the Glass-House, and there shewed my cosins the making of glass, and had several things made with great content, and, among others, I had one or two singing-glasses made, which make an echo to the voice, the first that ever I saw; but so thin, that the very breath broke one or two of them. Thence to Mr. Batelier's where we supped, and had a good supper, and here was Mr. Pembleton; and after supper some fiddles, and so to dance; but my eyes were so out of order, that I had little pleasure this night at all, although I was glad to see the rest merry.

Samuel Pepys, Diary, *23 February 1669*

24 February ⬚

1841—'This thing on Heroes *proves to be a stranger kind of Book than I thought it would. Since men do read without reflection, this too was worth writing'*

Thomas Carlyle to J. S. Mill

The Hero as *Man of Letters* . . . is altogether a product of these new ages; and so long as the wondrous art of *Writing*, or of Ready-writing, which we call *Printing*, subsists, he may be expected to continue, as one of the main forms of Heroism for all future ages. . . .

Certainly the Art of Writing is the most miraculous of all things man has devised. Odin's *Runes* were the first form of the work of a Hero: *Books*, written words, are still miraculous *Runes*, the latest form! In Books lies the *soul* of the whole Past Time; the articulate audible voice of the Past, when the body and material substance of it has altogether vanished like a dream. Mighty fleets and armies, harbors and arsenals, vast cities, high-domed, many-engined, – they are precious, great: but what do they become? Agamemnon, the many Agamemnons, Pericleses, and their Greece; all is gone now to some ruined fragments, dumb mournful wrecks and blocks: but the Books of Greece! There Greece, to every thinker, still very literally lives; can be called up again into life. No magic *Rune* is stranger than a Book. All that Mankind has done, thought, gained or been: it is lying as in magic preservation in the pages of Books. They are the chosen possession of men.

Do not Books still accomplish *miracles*, as *Runes* were fabled to do? They persuade men. Not the wretchedest circulating-library novel, which foolish girls thumb and con in remote villages, but will help to regulate the actual practical weddings and households of those foolish girls. So 'Celia' felt, so 'Clifford' acted: the foolish Theorem of Life, stamped into those young brains, comes out as a solid Practice one day. Consider whether any *Rune* in the wildest imagination of Mythologist ever did such wonders as on the actual firm Earth, some Books have done! What built St. Paul's Cathedral? Look at the heart of the latter, it was the divine Hebrew Book, – the word partly of the man Moses, an outlaw tending his Midianitish herds, four-thousand years ago, in the wilderness of Sinai! It is the strangest of things, yet nothing is truer. With the art of Writing, of which Printing is a simple, an inevitable and comparatively insignificant corollary, the true reign of miracles for mankind commenced. It related, with a wondrous new contiguity and perpetual closeness, the Past and Distant with the Present in time and place; all times and all places with this actual Here and Now. All things were altered for men; all modes of important work of men: teaching, preaching, governing, and all else.

Thomas Carlyle: from On Heroes, Hero-Worship, and the Heroic in History

1904—John Millington Synge's Riders to the Sea *was first produced at the Molesworth Hall, Dublin, with Sara Allgood in the role of Cathleen, and Honor Lavelle in that of Maurya*

CATHLEEN (in a whisper to the women who have come in): Is it Bartley it is?
ONE OF THE WOMEN: It is surely, God rest his soul.

(The younger women come in and pull out the table. Then men carry in the body of Bartley, laid on a plank, with a bit of a sail over it, and lay it on the table.)

CATHLEEN (to the women): What way was he drowned?
ONE OF THE WOMEN: The gray pony knocked him over into the sea, and he was washed out where there is a great surf on the white rocks.

(Maurya has gone over and knelt down at the head of the table. The women are keening softly and swaying themselves with a slow movement. Cathleen and Nora kneel at the other end of the table. The men kneel near the door.)

MAURYA (raising her head and speaking as if she did not see the people around her): They're all gone now, and there isn't anything more the sea can do to me. . . . I'll have no call now to be up crying and praying when the wind breaks from the south, and you can hear the surf is in the east, and the surf is in the west, making a great stir with the two noises, and they hitting one on the other. I'll have no call now to be going down and getting Holy Water in the dark nights after Samhain, and I won't care what way the sea is when the other women will be keening. (To Nora.) Give me the Holy Water, Nora, there's a small sup still on the dresser.

(Nora gives it to her.)

MAURYA (drops Michael's clothes across Bartley's feet, and sprinkles Holy Water over him): It isn't that I haven't prayed for you, Bartley, to the Almighty God. It isn't that I haven't said prayers in the dark night till you wouldn't know what I'd be saying; but it's a great rest I'll have now, and it's time surely. It's a great rest I'll have now, and great sleeping in the long nights after Samhain, if it's only a bit of wet flour we do have to eat, and maybe a fish that would be stinking.

(She kneels down again, crossing herself, and saying prayers under her breath.)

J. M. Synge: from Riders to the Sea

Go thou to Rome – at once the Paradise,
The grave, the city, and the wilderness;
And where its wrecks like shattered mountains rise,
And flowering weeds, and fragrant copses dress
The bones of Desolation's nakedness
Pass, till the spirit of the spot shall lead
Thy footsteps to a slope of green access
Where, like an infant's smile, over the dead
A light of laughing flowers along the grass is spread;

And gray walls moulder round, on which dull Time
Feeds, like slow fire upon a hoary brand;
And one keen pyramid with wedge sublime,
Pavilioning the dust of him who planned
This refuge for his memory, doth stand
Like flame transformed to marble; and beneath,
A field is spread, on which a newer band
Have pitched in Heaven's smile their camp of death,
Welcoming him we lose with scarce extinguished breath.

Here pause: these graves are all too young as yet
To have outgrown the sorrow which consigned
Its charge to each; and if the seal is set,
Here, on one fountain of a mourning mind,
Break it not thou! too surely shalt thou find
Thine own well full, if thou returnest home,
Of tears and gall. From the world's bitter wind
Seek shelter in the shadow of the tomb.
What Adonais is, why fear we to become?

The One remains, the many change and pass;
Heaven's light forever shines, Earth's shadows fly;
Life, like a dome of many-coloured glass,
Stains the white radiance of Eternity,
Until Death tramples it to fragments. – Die,
If thou wouldst be with that which thou dost seek!
Follow where all is fled! – Rome's azure sky,
Flowers, ruins, statues, music, words, are weak
The glory they transfuse with fitting truth to speak.

Percy Bysshe Shelley: from Adonais: An Elegy
on the Death of John Keats, Author of Endymion, Hyperion, etc.

1847—Henry Wadsworth Longfellow completed Evangeline

This is the forest primeval. The murmuring pines and the hemlocks
Bearded with moss, and in garments green, indistinct in the twilight,
Stand like Druids of eld, with voices sad and prophetic;
Stand like harpers hoar, with beards that rest on their bosoms.
Loud from its rocky caverns, the deep-voiced neighbouring ocean
Speaks, and in accents disconsolate answers the wail of the forest.
This is the forest primeval; but where are the hearts that beneath it
Leaped like the roe, when he hears in the woodland the voice of the huntsman?
Where is the thatch-roofed village, the home of Acadian farmers, –
Men whose lives glided on like rivers that water the woodlands;
Darkened by shadows of earth, but reflecting an image of heaven?
Waste are those pleasant farms, and the farmers for ever departed!

. . .

Still stands the forest primeval; but under the shade of its branches
Dwells another race, with other customs and language.
Only along the shore of the mournful and misty Atlantic
Linger a few Acadian peasants, whose fathers from exile
Wandered back to their native land to die in its bosom.
In the fisherman's cot the wheel and the loom are still busy;
Maidens still wear their Norman caps and their kirtles of homespun,
And by the evening fire repeat Evangeline's story,
While from its rocky caverns the deep-voiced, neighbouring ocean
Speaks, and in accents disconsolate answers the wail of the forest.

Henry Wadsworth Longfellow : from Evangeline,
the opening and concluding lines

1749—Henry Fielding's novel The History of Tom Jones *was published*

As we do not disdain to borrow wit or wisdom from any man who is capable of lending us either, we have condescended to take a hint from these honest victuallers, and shall prefix not only a general bill of fare to our whole entertainment, but shall likewise give the reader particular bills to every course which is to be served up in this and the ensuing volumes.

The provision, then, which we have here made is no other than *Human Nature* . . . nor can the learned reader be ignorant, that in human nature, though here collected under one general name, is such prodigious variety, that a cook will have sooner gone through all the several species of animal and vegetable food in the world, than an author will be able to exhaust so extensive a subject. . . . But the who!e, to continue the same metaphor, consists in the cookery of the author; for, as Mr Pope tells us –

> True wit is nature to advantage dressed;
> What oft was thought, but ne'er so well exprest.

The same animal which hath the honour to have some part of his flesh eaten at the table of a duke, may perhaps be degraded in another part, and some of his limbs gibbeted, as it were, in the vilest stall in town. Where, then, lies the difference between the food of the nobleman and the porter, if both are at dinner on the same ox or calf, but in the seasoning, the dressing, the garnishing, and the setting forth? Hence the one provokes and incites the most languid appetite, and the other turns and palls that which is the sharpest and keenest.

In like manner, the excellence of the mental entertainment consists less in the subject than in the author's skill in well dressing it up. How pleased, therefore, will the reader be to find that we have, in the following work, adhered closely to one of the highest principles of the best cook which the present age, or that of Heliogabalus, hath produced. This great man, as is well known to all lovers of polite eating, begins at first by setting plain things before his hungry guests, rising afterwards by degrees as their stomachs may be supposed to decrease, to the very quintessence of sauce and spices. In like manner, we shall represent human nature at first to the keen appetite of our reader, in that more plain and simple manner in which it is found in the country, and shall hereafter hash and ragoo it with all the high French and Italian seasoning of affectation and vice which courts and cities afford. By these means, we doubt not but our reader may be rendered to be desirous to read on forever, as the great person above-mentioned is supposed to have made some persons eat.

Henry Fielding: from The History of Tom Jones, *Book I*

'How quaint the ways of Paradox' one year in four

CHANT

KING: For some ridiculous reason, to which, however, I've no desire to be disloyal,
  Some person in authority, I don't know who, very likely the Astronomer Royal,
  Has decided that, although for such a beastly month as February, twenty-eight days as a general rule are plenty,
  One year in every four his days shall be reckoned as nine-and-twenty.
  Through some singular coincidence – I shouldn't be surprised if it were owing to the agency of an ill-natured fairy
  You are the victim of this clumsy arrangement, having been born in leap-year, on the twenty-ninth February.
  And so, by a simple arithmetical process, you'll easily discover,
  That though you've lived twenty-one years, yet, if we go by birthdays, you're only five and a little bit over!
RUTH: Ha! ha! ha! ha!
KING: Ho! ho! ho! ho!
FRED: Dear me!
  Let's see! (*counting on fingers*)
  Yes, yes; with yours my figures do agree!
ALL: Ha, ha, ha, ha! Ho, ho, ho, ho!
  (FREDERIC *more amused than any.*)
FRED: How quaint the ways of Paradox!
  At common sense she gaily mocks!
  Though counting in the usual way,
    Years twenty-one I've been alive,
  Yet reckoning by my natal day,
    I am a little boy of five!
ALL: He is a little boy of five. Ha, ha!
  At common sense she gaily mocks;
  So quaint a wag is Paradox.
    ALL: Ha, ha, ha, ha!
    KING: Ho, ho, ho, ho!
    RUTH: Ha, ha, ha, ha!
    FRED: Ha, ha, ha, ha!
ALL: Ho, ho, ho, ho! (RUTH *and* KING *throw themselves back on seats*, exhausted with laughter.)

W. S. Gilbert : from The Pirates of Penzance

March.

1468/9—William Caxton began to translate the Recueil des Histoires de Troye, *which later became the first English printed book*

And for so much as this book was new and late made and drawn into French, and never had seen it in our English tongue, I thought in myself it should be a good business to translate it into our English to the end that it might be had as well in the realm of England as in other lands, and also for to pass therewith the time, and thus concluded in myself to begin this said work. And forthwith took pen and ink, and began boldly to run forth as blind Bayard, in this present work which is named the Recueil of the Trojan histories. And afterward when I remembered myself of my simpleness and unperfectness that I had in both languages, that is, to wit, in French and in English, for in France was I never, and was born and learned mine English in Kent in the Weald where, I doubt not, is spoken as broad and rude English as in any place of England, and have continued by the space of thirty years, for the most part in the countries of Brabant, Flanders, Holland, and Zeeland; and thus when all these things came before me after that I had made and written a five or six quires, I fell in despair of this work and purposed no more to have continued therein, and those quires laid apart, and in two years after laboured no more in this work. And was fully in will to have left it, till on a time it fortuned that the right high, excellent, and right-virtuous princess, my right redoubted lady, my lady Margaret, by the grace of God sister unto the king of England and of France, my sovereign Lord . . . sent for me to speak with her good grace of divers matters. Among the which . . . she commanded me to amend, and moreover commanded me straitly to continue and make an end of the residue then not translated; whose dreadful commandment I durst in no wise disobey, because I am a servant unto her said grace, and receive of her yearly fee, and other many good and great benefits, and also hope many more to receive of her highness; but forthwith went and laboured in the said translation after my simple and poor cunning; also, nigh as I can, following mine author, meekly beseeching the bounteous highness of my said lady, that of her benevolence list to accept and take in gree this simple and rude work here following. And if there be anything written or said to her pleasure, I shall think my labour well employed, and whereas there is default that she arette it to the simpleness of my cunning which is full small in this behalf, and require and pray all them that shall read this said work to correct it, and to hold me excused of the rude and simple translation.

William Caxton: from 'The Author's Apology' to his translation of the Recueil des Histoires de Troye

2 March 🎭

1924—The final dress rehearsal of Sean O'Casey's Juno and the Paycock *was held at the Abbey Theatre in Dublin*

We could make nothing of the reading of *Juno and the Paycock* as it was called. It seemed to be a strange baffling mixture of comedy and tragedy; and none of us could say, with any certainty, whether or not it would stand up on the stage. . . .

The dress rehearsal . . . would be held at 5 p.m. on the Sunday. I arrived at the theatre at 4:30 p.m. and found the author there before me looking rather glum and wondering if a rehearsal would take place. . . . Gradually the players filed in and went to their dressing-rooms. Lennox Robinson arrived shortly before 5 o'clock and was followed by Yeats and Lady Gregory. . . . The curtain rose about 5:36 p.m. So far as I could see and hear while waiting for my cue in the wings the rehearsal seemed to be proceeding smoothly. As soon as I had finished my part of Bentham at the end of the second act I went down into the stalls and sat two seats behind the author. Here for the first time I had an opportunity of seeing something of the play from an objective point of view. I was stunned by the tragic quality of the third act which the magnificent playing of Sara Allgood made almost unbearable. But it was the blistering irony of the final scene which convinced me that this man sitting two seats in front of me was a dramatist of genius, one destined to be spoken of far beyond the confines of the Abbey Theatre. . . .

We watched the act move on, the furniture removers come and go, the ominous entry of the I. R. A. men, the dragging of Johnny to summary execution, the stilted scene between Jerry Devine and Mary Boyle, and then as with the ensnaring slow impetus of a ninth great wave Allgood's tragic genius rose to an unforgettable climax and drowned the stage in sorrow. Here surely was the very butt and sea-mark of tragedy! But suddenly the curtain rises again: are Fitzgerald and McCormick fooling, letting off steam after the strain of rehearsal? Nothing of the kind; for we in the stalls are suddenly made to freeze in our seats as a note beyond tragedy, a blistering flannel-mouthed irony sears its maudlin way across the stage and slowly drops an exhausted curtain on a world disintegrating in 'chassis'.

I sat there stunned. So, indeed, so far as I could see, did Robinson, Yeats, and Lady Gregory. Then Yeats ventured an opinion. He said that the play, particularly in its final scene, reminded him of a Dostoievsky novel. Lady Gregory turned to him and said: 'You know, Willie, you never read a novel by Dostoievsky.' And she promised to amend this deficiency by sending him a copy of *The Idiot*. I turned to O'Casey and found I could only say to him: 'Magnificent, Sean, magnificent.' Then we all quietly went home.

Gabriel Fallon: from Sean O'Casey, the Man I Knew, *London (Routledge & Kegan Paul), 1965*

1817—Poems by John Keats, his first volume, was published. On the eve of the great day, Keats excitedly thanked his friend Reynolds for a sonnet of congratulation and good wishes, which is still as just an estimation of that first volume as we possess

Thy thoughts, dear Keats, are like fresh gathered leaves,
Or white flowers pluck'd from some sweet lily bed;
They set the heart a-breathing, and they shed
The glow of meadows, mornings, and spring eves
O'er the excited soul. – Thy genius weaves
Songs that shall make the age be nature-led,
And win that coronal for thy young head
Which time's strange hand of freshness ne'er bereaves.
Go on! and keep thee to thine own green way,
Singing in that same key which Chaucer sung;
Be thou companion of the summer day,
Roaming the fields and older woods among:
So shall thy Muse be ever in her May,
And thy luxuriant spirit ever young.

John Hamilton Reynolds to John Keats on the occasion of his first 'one-man show'

[London] Sunday Evening
[March 2, 1817]

My Dear Reynolds – Your kindness affects me so sensibly that I can merely put down a few mono-sentences. Your Criticism only makes me extremely anxious that I should not deceive you.

It's the finest thing by God as Hazlitt would say. However I hope I may not deceive you. There are some acquaintances of mine who will scratch their Beards and although I have, I hope, some Charity, I wish their Nails may be long. I will be ready at the time you mention in all Happiness.

There is a report that a young Lady of 16 has written the new Tragedy, God bless her – I will know her by Hook or by Crook in less than a week. My Brothers' and my Remembrances to your kind Sister.

Yours most sincerely

John Keats

1645—Milton's Tetrachordon, *his fourth tract on divorce, was first published— and created a storm of protest*

'That opinion of a poor shallow-brained puppy, who upon any cause of dis-affection would have men to have a privilege to change their wives or repudiate them, deserves to be hissed at rather than confuted; for nothing can tend more to usher in all confusion and beggary throughout the world.'

James Howell, in his Familiar Letters

Sonnet VI – On the Detraction Which Followed Upon My Writing Certain Treatises

A book was writ of late call'd *Tetrachordon*,
    And woven close, both matter, form and style;
    The subject new: it walk'd the town a while,
    Numbering good intellects; now seldom por'd on.
Cries the stall-reader, 'Bless us! what a word on
    A title-page is this!'; and some in file
    Stand spelling false, while one might walk to Mile-
End Green. Why, is it harder, sirs, than *Gordon*,
Colitto, or Macdonnel, or Galasp?
    Those rugged names to our like mouths grow sleek
    That would have made Quintilian stare and gasp.
Thy age, like ours, O soul of Sir John Cheek,
    Hated not learning worse than toad or asp,
    When thou taught'st Cambridge and King Edward Greek.

Sonnet VII – On the Same

I did but prompt the age to quit their clogs
    By the known rules of ancient liberty,
    When straight a barbarous noise environs me
    Of owls and cuckoos, asses, apes and dogs;
As when those hinds that were transform'd to frogs
    Rail'd at Latona's twin-born progeny,
    Which after held the Sun and Moon in fee.
    But this is got by casting pearls to hogs,
That bawl for freedom in their senseless mood
    And still revolt when truth would set them free.
    Licence they mean when they cry Liberty;
For who loves that must first be wise and good:
    But from that mark how far they rove we see,
    For all this waste of wealth and loss of blood.

John Milton

[17—]—'I was begot in the night, betwixt the first Sunday and the first Monday, in the month of March . . .'

Tristram Shandy, *I. v. 8*

I wish either my father or my mother, or indeed both of them, as they were in duty both equally bound to it, had minded what they were about when they begot me; had they duly considered how much depended upon what they were then doing; – that not only the production of a rational Being was concerned in it, but that possibly the happy formation and temperature of his body, perhaps his genius and the very cast of his mind; – and, for aught they knew to the contrary, even the fortunes of his whole house might take their turn from the humours and dispositions which were then uppermost; – Had they duly weighed and considered all this, and pro-ceeded accordingly, – I am verily persuaded I should have made quite a different figure in the world, from that in which the reader is likely to see me. – Believe me, good folks, this is not so inconsiderable a thing as many of you may think it; – you have all, I dare say, heard of the animal spirits, as how they are transfused from father to son &c. &c. – and a great deal to that purpose: – Well, you may take my word, that nine parts in ten of a man's sense or his nonsense, his successes and mis-carriages in this world, depend upon their motions and activity, and the different tracts and trains you put them into, so that when they are once set a-going, whether right or wrong, 'tis not a half-penny matter, – away they go cluttering like hey-go mad; and by treading the same steps over and over again, they presently make a road of it, as plain and as smooth as a garden walk, which, when they are once used to, the Devil himself sometimes shall not be able to drive them off it.

Pray, my Dear, quoth my mother, *have you not forgot to wind up the clock? – Good G——!* cried my father, making an exclamation, but taking care to moderate his voice at the same time, – *Did ever woman, since the creation of the world, interrupt a man with such a silly question?* Pray, what was your father saying? – Nothing.

Laurence Sterne, The Life and Opinions of *TRISTRAM SHANDY*, Gentleman, *ch. i*

6 March 🎗

1835—John Stuart Mill informed Thomas Carlyle of the catastrophe that had happened to the manuscript of The French Revolution

John Mill, then his closest and most valuable friend, was ardently interested in the growth of the new book. He borrowed the manuscript as it was thrown off, that he might make notes and suggestions, either for Carlyle's use, or as material for an early review. The completed first volume was in his hands for this purpose, when one evening, the 6th of March, 1835, as Carlyle was sitting with his wife, 'after working all day like a nigger' at the Feast of Pikes, a rap was heard at the door, a hurried step came up the stairs, and Mill entered deadly pale, and at first unable to speak. 'Why, Mill,' said Carlyle, 'what ails ye, man? What is it?' Staggering, and supported by Carlyle's arm, Mill gasped out to Mrs. Carlyle to go down and speak to some one who was in a carriage in the street. Both Carlyle and she thought that a thing which they had long feared must have actually happened, and that Mill had come to announce it and to take leave of them. So genuine was the alarm that the truth when it came out was a relief. Carlyle led his friend to a seat 'the very picture of desperation.' He then learnt in broken sentences that his manuscript, 'left out in too careless a manner after it had been read,' was, 'except four or five bits of leaves, irrevocably annihilated.' That was all, nothing worse; but it was ugly news enough, and the uglier the more the meaning of it was realised. Carlyle always wrote in a highly wrought quasi-automatic condition both of mind and nerves. He read till he was full of the subject. His notes, when they were done with, were thrown aside and destroyed; and of this unfortunate volume, which he had produced as if 'possessed' while he was about it, he could remember nothing. Not only were 'the fruits of five months of steadfast, occasionally excessive, and always sickly and painful toil' gone irretrievably, but the spirit in which he had worked seemed to have fled too, not to be recalled; worse than that, his work had been measured carefully against his resources, and the household purse might now be empty before the loss could be made good. The carriage and its occupant drove off – and it would have been better had Mill gone too after he told his tale, for the forlorn pair wished to be alone together in the face of such a calamity. But Carlyle, whose first thought was of what Mill must be suffering, made light of it, and talked of indifferent things, and Mill stayed and talked too – stayed, I believe, for two hours. Mrs. Carlyle told me that the first words her husband uttered as the door closed were: 'Well, Mill, poor fellow, is terribly cut up; we must endeavour to hide from him how very serious this business is to us.'

James Anthony Froude: from Thomas Carlyle, A History of his life in London 1834–1881

1923—One of Robert Frost's best-known poems was first published in the New Republic

---

Stopping by Woods on a Snowy Evening

Whose woods these are I think I know.
His house is in the village, though;
He will not see me stopping here
To watch his woods fill up with snow.

My little horse must think it queer
To stop without a farmhouse near
Between the woods and frozen lake
The darkest evening of the year.

He gives his harness bells a shake
To ask if there is some mistake.
The only other sound's the sweep
Of easy wind and downy flake.

The woods are lovely, dark, and deep,
But I have promises to keep,
And miles to go before I sleep,
And miles to go before I sleep.

Robert Frost

DORINDA:	. . . My Brother is, first, the most constant Man alive.
MRS. SULLEN:	The most constant Husband, I grant'ye . . .
DORINDA:	He allows you a Maintenance suitable to your Quality.
MRS. SULLEN:	A Maintenance! do you take me, Madam, for an hospital Child, that I must sit down, and bless my Benefactors for Meat, Drink and Clothes? As I take it, Madam, I brought your Brother Ten thousand Pounds, out of which, I might expect some pretty things, call'd Pleasures.
DORINDA:	You share in all the Pleasures that the Country affords.
MRS. SULLEN:	Country Pleasures! Racks and Torments! dost think, Child, that my Limbs were made for leaping of Ditches, and clambring over Stiles. . . .
DORINDA:	I'm sorry, Madam, that it is not more in our power to divert you; I cou'd wish indeed that our Entertainments were a little more polite, or your Taste a little less refin'd: But, pray, Madam, how came the Poets and Philosophers that labour'd so much in hunting after Pleasure, to place it at last in a Country Life?
MRS. SULLEN:	Because they wanted Money, Child, to find out the Pleasures of the Town: Did you ever see a Poet or Philosopher worth Ten thousand Pound; if you can shew me such a Man, I'll lay you Fifty Pound you'll find him somewhere within the weekly Bills – Not that I disapprove rural Pleasures, as the Poets have painted them; in their Landscape every *Phillis* has her *Coridon*, every murmuring Stream, and every flowry Mead gives fresh Alarms to Love – Besides, you'll find, that their Couples were never marry'd: – But yonder I see my *Coridon*, and a sweet Swain it is, Heaven knows. – Come, *Dorinda*, don't be angry, he's my Husband, and your Brother; and between both is he not a sad Brute?
DORINDA:	I have nothing to say to your part of him, you're the best Judge.
MRS. SULLEN:	O Sister, Sister! if ever you marry, beware of a sullen, silent Sot, one that's always musing, but never thinks: – There's some Diversion in a talking Blockhead; and since a Woman must wear Chains, I wou'd have the Pleasure of hearing 'em rattle a little.

1680—John Oldham wrote and dated his popular drinking-song, 'The Careless Good Fellow'

A Pox of this fooling and plotting of late,
What a pother and stir has it kept in the State?
Let the Rabble run mad with Suspicions and Fears,
Let them scuffle and jar, till they go by the ears:
    Their Grievances never shall trouble my pate,
    So I can enjoy my dear Bottle at quiet.

What Coxcombs were those who would barter their ease
And their Necks for a Toy, a thin Wafer and Mass?
At old *Tyburn* they never had needed to swing,
Had they been but true Subjects to Drink, and to King;
    A Friend, and a Bottle is all my design;
    He has no room for Treason, that's top-full of Wine. . . .

I mind not grave Asses, who idly debate
About Right and Succession, the trifles of State;
We've a good King already; and he deserves laughter
That will trouble his head with who shall come after:
    Come, here's to his health, and I wish he may be
    As free from all Care, and all Trouble, as we.

The Bully of *France*, that aspires to Renown
By dull cutting of Throats, and vent'ring his own;
Let him fight and be damn'ed, and make Matches, and Treat,
To afford the News-mongers and Coffee-house Chat:
    He's but a brave wretch, while I am more free,
    More safe, and a thousand times happier than He.

Come He, or the Pope, or the Devil to boot,
Or come Faggot and Stake; I care not a Groat;
Never think that in *Smithfield* I Porters will heat:*
No, I swear, Mr. Fox, pray excuse me for that.
    I'll drink in defiance of Gibbet and Halter,
    This is the Profession that never will alter.

John Oldham

* Several Protestants described in Fox's *Book of Martyrs* were burned in Smithfield.

Happily the sunshine fell more warmly than usual on the lilac tufts the morning that Eppie was married for her dress was a very light one. She had often thought, though with a feeling of renunciation, that the perfection of a wedding-dress would be a white cotton, with the tiniest pink sprig at wide intervals; so that when Mrs. Godfrey Cass begged to provide one, and asked Eppie to choose what it should be, previous meditation had enabled her to give a decided answer at once.

Seen at a little distance as she walked across the churchyard and down the village, she seemed to be attired in pure white, and her hair looked like a dash of gold on a lily. One hand was on her husband's arm, and with the other she clasped the hand of her father Silas.

'You won't be giving me away, father,' she had said before they went to church; 'you'll only be taking Aaron to be a son to you.' . . .

In the open yard before the Rainbow, the party of guests were already assembled, though it was still nearly an hour before the appointed feast-time. But by this means they could not only enjoy the slow advent of their pleasure; they had also leisure to talk of Silas Marner's strange history, and arrive by due degrees at the conclusion that he had brought a blessing on himself by acting like a father to a lone motherless child. Even the farrier did not negative this sentiment: on the contrary, he took it up as peculiarly his own, and invited any hardy person present to contradict him. But he met with no contradiction; and all differences among the company were merged in a general agreement with Mr. Snell's sentiment, that when a man had deserved his good luck, it was the part of his neighbours to wish him joy.

As the bridal group approached, a hearty cheer was raised in the Rainbow yard; and Ben Winthrop, whose jokes had retained their acceptable flavour, found it agreeable to turn in there and receive congratulations; not requiring the proposed interval of quiet at the Stone-pits before joining the company.

Eppie had a larger garden than she had ever expected there now; and in other ways there had been alterations at the expense of Mr. Cass, the landlord, to suit Silas's larger family. For he and Eppie had declared that they would rather stay at the Stone-pits than go to any new home. The garden was fenced with stones on two sides, but in front there was an open fence, through which the flowers shone with answering gladness, as the four united people came within sight of them.

'O father,' said Eppie, 'what a pretty home ours is! I think nobody could be happier than we are.'

George Eliot: from Silas Marner, *final chapter*

1696/7—William Congreve's play The Mourning Bride *was advertised in* The London Gazette. *In the last stage of its publication Congreve received a fan-letter in verse, and replied*

CATHARINE TROTTER TO CONGREVE

. . .
Boundless thy fame does on thy genius flow,
Which spread thus far, can now no limits know:
This only part was wanting to thy name,
That wit's whole empire thou mightst justly claim:
. . .
But to express how thou our souls do'st move,
How at thy will, we rage, we grieve, we love,
Requires a lofty, almost equal flight,
Nor dare I aim at such a dang'rous height,
A task, which well might Dryden's muse engage,
Worthy the first, best poet of the age;
Whose long retreat that we might less bemoan,
He left us thee, his greatest darling son,
Possessor of the stage, once his alone. . . .

CONGREVE TO CATHARINE TROTTER

I can never enough acknowledge the honour you have done me, nor enough regret the negligence of those, to whom you delivered your valuable Letter. It is the first thing, that ever happened to me, upon which I should make it my choice to be vain. And yet such is the mortification, that attends even the most allowable vanity, that at the same instant I am robb'd of the means, when I am possessed with the inclination. It is but this moment, that I received your verses; and had scarce been transported with the reading them, when they brought me the play from the press printed off; I hope you will do me the justice to believe, that I was not so insensible, as not to be heartily vexed; and all the satisfaction, that I can take, and all the sacrifice that I make to you, is only to stifle some verses on the same barren subject, which were printed with it, and now, I assure you, shall never appear, whatever apology I am forced to make to the authors. And since I am deprived of the recommendation you designed me, I will be obliged to no other, till I have some future opportunity of preferring yours to everbody's else.

12 March

1711—Joseph Addison realized that The Spectator *was a success*

It is with much Satisfaction that I hear this great City inquiring Day by Day after these my Papers, and receiving my Morning Lectures with a becoming Seriousness and Attention. My Publisher tells me, that there are already Three thousand of them distributed every Day: So that if I allow Twenty Readers to every Paper, which I look upon as a modest Computation, I may reckon about Threescore thousand Disciples in *London* and *Westminster*, who I hope will take care to distinguish themselves from the thoughtless Herd of their ignorant and unattentive Brethren. Since I have raised to myself so great an Audience, I shall spare no Pains to make their Instruction agreeable, and their Diversion useful. For which Reasons I shall endeavour to enliven Morality with Wit, and to temper Wit with Morality, that my Readers may, if possible, both Ways find their Account in the Speculation of the Day. And to the End that their Virtue and Discretion may not be short transient intermittent Starts of Thought, I have resolved to refresh their Memories from Day to Day, till I have recovered them out of that desperate State of Vice and Folly into which the Age is fallen. The Mind that lies fallow but a single Day, sprouts up in Follies that are only to be killed by a constant and assiduous Culture. It was said of *Socrates*, that he brought Philosophy down from Heaven, to inhabit among Men: and I shall be ambitious to have it said of me, that I have brought Philosophy out of Closets and Libraries, Schools and Colleges, to dwell in Clubs and Assemblies, at Tea-Tables and in Coffee-Houses.

I would therefore in a very particular Manner recommend these my Speculations to all well regulated Families, that set apart an Hour in every Morning for Tea and Bread and Butter; and would earnestly advise them for their Good to order this Paper to be punctually served up, and to be looked upon as a Part of the Tea Equipage.

Joseph Addison: The Spectator, *no. 10*

1592/3—Richard Hooker presented the manuscript copy of his book, Of the Lawes of Ecclesiasticall Politie of the Church of England, *to Lord Burghley*

BOOK I, Ch. i 1, 2.
The cause of writing this general Discourse.

1. He that goeth about to persuade a multitude, that they are not so well governed as they ought to be, shall never want attentive and favourable hearers; because they know the manifold defects whereunto every kind of regimen is subject, but the secret lets and difficulties, which in public proceedings are innumerable and inevitable, they have not ordinarily the judgment to consider. And because such as openly reprove supposed disorders of state are taken for principal friends to the common benefit of all, and for men that carry singular freedom of mind; under this fair and plausible colour whatsoever they utter passeth for good and current. That which wanteth in the weight of their speech, is supplied by the aptness of men's minds to accept and believe it. Whereas on the other side, if we maintain things that are established, we have not only to strive with a number of heavy prejudices deeply rooted in the hearts of men, who think that herein we serve the time, and speak in favour of the present state, because thereby we either hold or seek preferment; but also to bear such exceptions as minds so averted beforehand usually take against that which they are loth should be poured into them.

2. Albeit therefore much of that we are to speak in this present cause may seem to a number perhaps tedious, perhaps obscure, dark, and intricate; (for many talk of the truth, which never sounded the depth from whence it springeth; and therefore when they are led thereunto they are soon weary, as men drawn from those beaten paths wherewith they have been inured;) yet this may not so far prevail as to cut off that which the matter itself requireth, howsoever the nice humour of some be therewith pleased or no. They unto whom we shall seem tedious are in no wise injuried by us, because it is in their own hands to spare that labour which they are not willing to endure. And if any complain of obscurity, they must consider, that in these matters it cometh no otherwise to pass than in sundry the works both of art and also of nature, where that which hath greatest force in the very things we see is notwithstanding itself oftentimes not seen. The stateliness of houses, the goodliness of trees, when we behold them delighteth the eye; but that foundation which beareth up the one, that root which ministereth unto the other nourishment and life, is in the bosom of the earth concealed; and if there be at any time occasion to search into it, such labour is then more necessary than pleasant, both to them which undertake it and for the lookers-on. . . .

Richard Hooker: from Laws of Ecclesiastical Polity, *Book I, chapter I*

14 March 📖

1885—The first performance of Gilbert and Sullivan's The Mikado

Gilbert, who had combined the patience of Job with the discipline of a sergeant-major throughout the rehearsals, behaved like a frightened child on the evening of the first performance. Wrought up to the highest pitch of excitement and dread, he went from dressing-room to dressing-room, wishing the actors good luck, asking them how they felt, reminding them of points he had already stressed a hundred times, wondering whether they were sure of their words, begging them to do their best, and making a general nuisance of himself. Then he had a last look round the stage, fussed over the scenery and properties, and worried the life out of the stage-manager. The moment the curtain went up he left the theatre and wandered about the streets in a condition of indescribable anxiety until eleven o'clock struck, when he returned to the theatre to hear the result and to take his bow before the curtain. 'What I suffered during those hours', he once admitted, 'no man can tell. I have spent them at the club; I once went to a theatre alone to see a play; I have walked up and down the street; but no matter where I was, agony and apprehension possessed me.' Strangely enough, he never saw his productions after the final dress-rehearsal, and with a single exception he never witnessed any of his operas as a member of the audience.

Sullivan's first-night demeanour was quite different from Gilbert's, but then the tumultuous applause with which his appearance in the orchestra was always received must have given him assurance. The moment the audience caught sight of the dapper little figure, moving to his seat with quick step and cocksure carriage, the cheers broke out and sometimes lasted for more than a minute. His manner as a conductor was not spectacular. He kept his eyes on the music and his beat was restrained and cramped, the baton moving across the top or up and down the sides of the score. He wore glasses, and people sitting near him observed that the fingers of his well-manicured right hand were stained with nicotine. In spite of his unimpressive manner, he was in complete command of his orchestra and nothing escaped his attention. Once, to prove that he could be as dramatic as anyone, he altered his style of conducting, using whirlwind beats, stamping his feet, jerking his head and twisting his body. Though many people considered it a great improvement, he did not repeat the experiment.

At the conclusion of the performance the theatre resounded with cheers, applause, the thunder of beating feet, and loud cries of 'author', 'composer', 'Gilbert' and 'Sullivan'. The contrast between the tall martial figure of Gilbert and the short tubby figure of Sullivan, as they came before the curtain, was heightened by their difference in bearing. Sullivan bowed gracefully, smiled affably and walked on and off the stage with ease and self-assurance. Gilbert almost had to be dragged on, scowled at the audience, and seemed to resent the occasion as a personal indignity.

Hesketh Pearson: from Gilbert and Sullivan

44 B.C.—Julius Caesar was assassinated, an event which has fascinated many English writers ever since North's translation of Plutarch's Lives *first made it available to English readers*

There was a certain soothsayer that had given Caesar warning long time afore, to take heed of the day of the Ides of March, (which is the fifteenth of the month), for on that day he should be in great danger. That day being come, Caesar going unto the Senate-house, and speaking merrily unto the soothsayer, told him 'the Ides of March be come'; 'So be they,' softly answered the soothsayer, 'but yet they are not past.' . . .

So, Caesar coming into the house, all the Senate stood up on the feet to do him honour. Then part of Brutus' company and confederates stood round about Caesar's chair, and part of them also came towards him, as though they made suit with Metellus Cimber, to call home his brother again from banishment; and thus prosecuting still their suit, they followed Caesar till he was set in his chair; who denying their petitions, and being offended with them one after another, because the more they were denied the more they pressed upon him and were the earnester with him. Metellus at length, taking his gown with both his hands, pulled it over his neck, which was the sign given the confederates to set upon him. Then Casca, behind him, strake him in the neck with his sword; howbeit the wound was not great nor mortal, because, it seemed, the fear of such a devilish attempt did amaze him and take his strength from him, that he killed him not at the first blow. But Caesar, turning straight unto him, caught hold of his sword and held it hard; and they both cried out, Caesar in Latin: 'O vile traitor Casca, what doest thou?' and Casca, in Greek, to his brother, 'Brother, help me.' At the beginning of this stir they that were present, not knowing of the conspiracy, were so amazed with the horrible sight they saw, they had no power to fly, neither to help him, nor so much as once to make an outcry. They on the other side that had conspired his death compassed him in on every side with their swords drawn in their hands, that Caesar turned him no where but he was stricken at by some, and still had naked swords in his face, and was hackled and mangled among them, as a wild beast taken of hunters. For it was agreed among them that every man should give him a wound, because all their part should be in this murder: and then Brutus himself gave him one wound about his middle. Men report also, that Caesar did still defend himself against the rest, running every way with his body: but when he saw Brutus with his sword drawn in his hand, then he pulled his gown over his head, and made no more resistance, and was driven either casually or purposely, by the counsel of the conspirators, against the base whereupon Pompey's image stood, which ran all of a gore-blood till he was slain. Thus it seemed that the image took just revenge of Pompey's enemy, being thrown down on the ground at his feet, and yielding up the ghost there, for the number of wounds he had upon him. For it is reported, that he had three and twenty wounds upon his body. . . .

> *Sir Thomas North: from Plutarch's* Life of Julius Caesar

16 March 🔲

Dear Ezra,

Do exercise a little imagination and try to understand the situation. I am an *extremely* sick man and your incomprehensible scrawls are a torture to me – to read and to have to answer.

The situation is this: I am offering to give up my job at Olivet because you have been making noises about Universities for a long time and it would give you a chance really to do something. I have already answered your question about the press. They have already a press at Olivet. They print a paper. They would no doubt do any necessary scholastic printing you needed. But they probably would not print Musso-lini–Douglas propaganda for you. They might. But it would be up to you to persuade them. They do not, as I have already told you, use your books as text books because 'They' are I and I do not approve of the use of text books. At the same time I con-stantly recommend my classes to read your books. You understand I do not approve of making any reading compulsory. If a boy tells me he does not like Virgil I tell him to find something he does like & read it with attention. That gives results that satisfy me. If you wanted to revert to text books you could. . . .

The number of students at the moment is 305 – the capacity of the college; the number of faculty is 45. The system is tutorial, each teacher having so many students to boss for study and discipline – that not applying to me & not to apply to you unless you wanted it to. I teach what I want to – i.e. comparative literature from the beginning of time to the moment of speaking. No one interferes with me in the slightest degree. Nor would they with you. I don't know just what they would do if you tried to introduce your politics into your teaching – nothing at all probably unless you were too loudly communist in which case the local farmers would shoot you.

Please understand. I am not a confidence trickster trying to induce you into some disastrous folly. *I am not trying to persuade you to take the job.* You would probably turn that pleasant place into a disastrous place of hell. But it is my duty to say that there the place is for you & the College authorities want you because they admire you as a poet and teacher. Nor is it part of a sinister conspiracy on my part to rob you of your claim to be the greatest discoverer of literary talent the world has ever seen. I don't care a damn: I wish to God I had never 'discovered' anyone. . . . The only conspiracy I am in is to get you the Charles Eliot Norton professorship at Boston to which Olivet would be a stepping stone. The snag is that the Professor ought to be an Englishman – but I have tried to persuade the Boston authorities that you are English enough.

PLATE 1

Title page of the first edition (1611) of the Authorised
Version of the Holy Bible. (cf. 16 January)

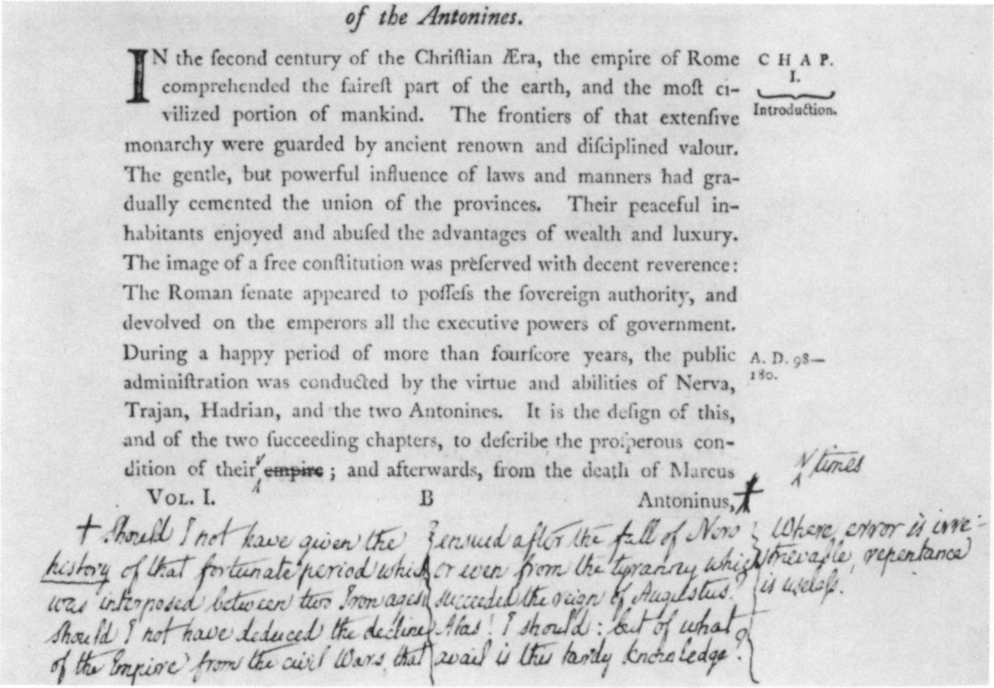

of the Antonines.

IN the fecond century of the Chriftian Æra, the empire of Rome comprehended the faireft part of the earth, and the moft civilized portion of mankind. The frontiers of that extenfive monarchy were guarded by ancient renown and difciplined valour. The gentle, but powerful influence of laws and manners had gradually cemented the union of the provinces. Their peaceful inhabitants enjoyed and abufed the advantages of wealth and luxury. The image of a free conftitution was preferved with decent reverence: The Roman fenate appeared to poffefs the fovereign authority, and devolved on the emperors all the executive powers of government. During a happy period of more than fourfcore years, the public adminiftration was conducted by the virtue and abilities of Nerva, Trajan, Hadrian, and the two Antonines. It is the defign of this, and of the two fucceeding chapters, to defcribe the profperous condition of their ~~empire~~; and afterwards, from the death of Marcus Antoninus, +

CHAP. I. Introduction.

A. D. 98—180.

times

VOL. I. B

+ Should I not have given the history of that fortunate period which was interposed between two Iron ages? Should I not have deduced the decline of the Empire from the civil Wars that ensued after the fall of Nero or even from the tyranny which succeeded the reign of Augustus. Alas! I should: but of what avail is this tardy knowledge? Where error is irretrievable, repentance is useless.

PLATE 2

Part of the first page of Edward Gibbon's own copy of the first edition of his *Decline and Fall of the Roman Empire*, with marginal notes in his handwriting. (cf. 17 February)

Han they of Crete had herd the refolucion of
faturne they were gretly abaffhed. ffor they
knewe well that faturne toke this mater gret
ly to his herte: and that he was a terryble man to of
fende. And fo they knewe that wrongfully he wyl
lyd the deth of his fone Jupiter that had reftored hym
to his lordfhip by his proweffe z vailliance/ Many
ther were that went into an other kyngedom becaufe
they wold not be with the fader ayenft the fone ner
with the fone ayenft the fader/but ther was noman
that durfte be fo hardy to replie agayn faturne ner faie
that he dide euyll/for they dredde more his yre than to
offende Juftyce. what fhall J faye after the comande
ment of faturne/eche man withdrewe hym vnto his
houe full of grete and bitter forowe in herte. And ther
was not oon man but he had his face charged with
grete gref and pefaunt anoyaúce ref ::.

  He day than drewe ouer/And on the morn Sa
turne armed hym felf z fowned Trompettis
vnto armes. They of crete aroos this mornyng
And many ther were of them that knewe thentencon
of faturue. And allfo ther were many that meruailled
of that/that the kyng wold do z coude fynde no refon
wherfore he maad this armee. ffor all Crete was in
pees And all the tyrannoys were difparklid and put
into deftruccion perdurable/ Amonge all other Cybell
wift not what to thynke Seeyng that faturne fent
not after Jupiter Sfhe demanded hym oftentymes whe
ther he wold goo. and for what refon that he toke not
Jupiter with hym in his compaygne. Jupiter was at
that tyme in parthenipe with his wyf Juno/Whan

PLATE 3

Facsimile of a page from William Caxton's *The Receuil of
the Histories of Troye*, 1471, the first book printed in
English. (cf. 1 March)

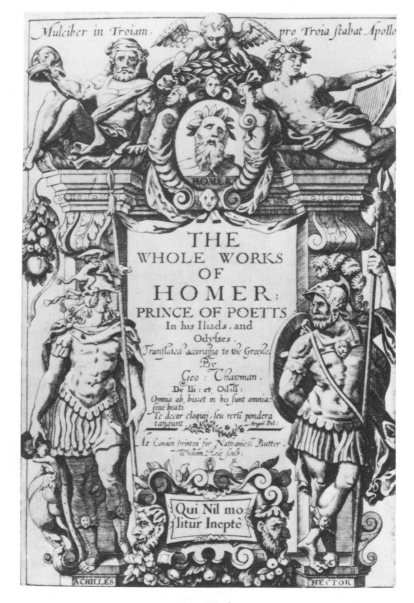

PLATE 4

Title page of the book that inspired John Keats' sonnet 'On
first looking into Chapman's *Homer*'. (cf. 8 April)

are ferrets! Where *can* I have dropped them, I wonder?" Alice guessed in a moment that it was looking for the nosegay and the pair of white kid gloves, and she began hunting for them, but they were now nowhere to be seen — everything seemed to have changed since her swim in the pool, and her walk along the river-bank with its fringe of rushes and forget-me-nots, and the glass table and the little door had vanished.

Soon the rabbit noticed Alice, as she stood looking curiously about her; and at once said in a quick angry tone, "why, Mary Ann! what *are* you doing out here? Go home this moment, and look on my dressing-table for my gloves and nosegay, and fetch them here, as quick as you can run, do you hear?" and Alice was so much frightened that she ran off at once, without

PLATE 5

A page from the original autograph ms. written and illustrated by 'Lewis Carroll', which Charles Dodgson gave to Alice Liddell as a Christmas present, and which he later developed and published in 1865 as *Alice's Adventures in Wonderland*. (cf. 4 May and 25 April)

Page from the Kelmscott edition of Chaucer, designed by
William Morris and Edward Burne-Jones. (cf. 3 June)

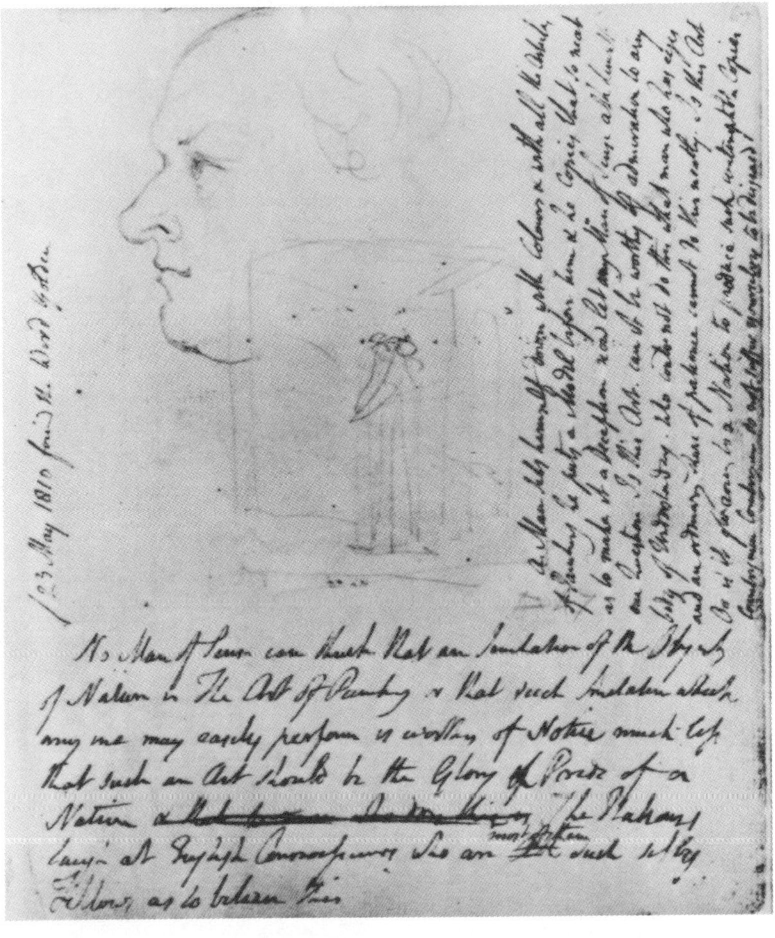

PLATE 7

Page from William Blake's notebook (the 'Rosetti MS')
containing a self-portrait of the artist. (cf. 11 January)

THE MURDERS IN THE

RUE MORGUE

AND OTHER

TALES OF MYSTERY

BY EDGAR ALLAN POE

LONDON

SAMPSON LOW, MARSTON & CO., LTD.,   WILLIAM DAWSON & SONS, LTD.,
St. Dunstan's House, Fetter Lane, E.C.   Cannon House, Bream's Buildings, E.C.

1893

PLATE 8

Title page of an 1893 edition of some of Edgar Allan Poe's
best 'tales of mystery'. (cf. 19 August)

Dickens placing his first literary contribution in the editor's box.

Charles Dickens [signature]

PLATE 9

Contemporary drawing of the young Charles Dickens hopefully placing the manuscript of his first 'Sketches by Boz' in the Magazine Editor's box of *The Morning Chronicle*. (cf. 7 April)

PLATE 10

Title page of Francis Bacon's *Instauratio Magna*.
(cf. 27 January)

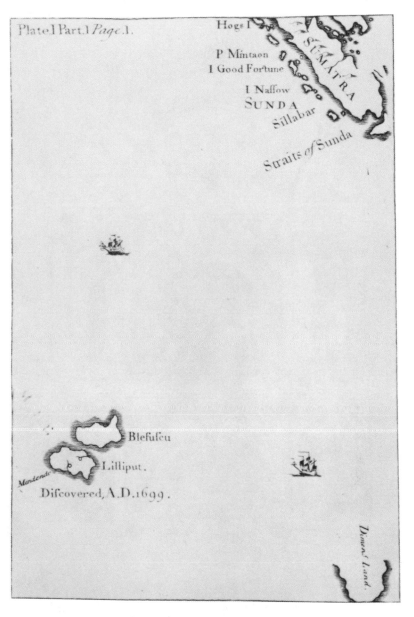

PLATE 11

Map of Lilliput, from an early edition of Jonathan Swift's
Gulliver's Travels. (cf. 6 November)

PLATE 12

Title page designed by John Farleigh for George Bernard
Shaw's *Prefaces*. (cf. 21 April and 24 December)

1889—Gerard Manley Hopkins wrote the sonnet, 'Thou art indeed just', which he sent three days later to Robert Bridges with the caution : 'Observe, it must be read adagio molto *and with great stress'*

---

*Justus quidem tu es, Domine, si disputem tecum : verumtamen justa
loquar ad te : Quare via impiorum prosperatur ? &c.*

Thou art indeed just, Lord, if I contend
With thee; but, sir, so what I plead is just.
Why do sinners' ways prosper? And why must
Disappointment all I endeavour end?
　Wert thou my enemy, O thou my friend,
How wouldst thou worse, I wonder, than thou dost
Defeat, thwart me? Oh, the sots and thralls of lust
Do in spare hours more thrive than I that spend,
Sir, life upon thy cause. See, banks and brakes
Now, leavéd how thick! lacéd they are again
With fretty chervil, look, and fresh wind shakes
Them; birds build – but not I build; no, but strain,
Time's eunuch, and not breed one work that wakes.
Mine, O thou lord of life, send my roots rain.

18 March

1798—The Wordsworths observed a hail-shower

March 18th. The Coleridges left us. A cold, windy morning. Walked with them half way. On our return, sheltered under the hollies, during a hail-shower. The withered leaves danced with the hailstones. William wrote a description of the storm.

Dorothy Wordsworth : The Alfoxden Journal

A whirl-blast from behind the hill
Rush'ed o'er the wood with startling sound;
And showers of hailstones pattered round,
Where leafless Oaks towered high above,
I sat within an undergrove
Of tallest hollies, tall and green;
A fairer bower was never seen.
From year to year the spacious floor
With withered leaves is covered o'er,
You could not lay a hair between;
And all the year the bower is green.
But see! where'er the hailstones drop
The withered leaves all skip and hop,
There's not a breeze – no breath of air –
Yet here, and there, and every where
Along the floor, beneath the shade
By those embowering hollies made,
The leaves in myriads jump and spring,
As if with pipes and music rare
Some Robin Good-fellow were there,
And all those leaves, that jump and spring,
Were each a joyous, living thing.

Oh! grant me Heaven a heart at ease,
That I may never cease to find,
Even in appearances like these,
Enough to nourish and to stir my mind!

William Wordsworth, Lyrical Ballads, *Volume II*
(*published 1805*)

1917—'I am still kept in bed, though I feel fit for a walk. Yesterday I wrote to Mother without knowing it was my birthday! ...'

Wilfred Owen to his brother, from 13th Casualty Clearing Station

Sunday, [18] March [1917]

My dearest Mother,

I am in a hospital bed, (for the first time in life.) [On the 13th of March, while 'going round through pitch darkness to see a man in a dangerous state of exhaustion', Owen had fallen 'into a kind of well, only about 15 ft., but I caught the back of my head on the way down. The doctors (not in consultation!) say I have a slight concussion. Of course I have a slight headache, but I don't feel at all fuddled.']

After falling into that hole (which I believe was a shell-hole in a floor, laying open a deep cellar) I felt nothing more than a headache, for 3 days; and went up to the front in the usual way – or nearly the usual way, for I felt too weak to wrestle with the mud, and sneaked along the top, snapping my fingers at a clumsy sniper. When I got back I developed a high fever, vomited strenuously, and long, and was seized with muscular pains. The night before last I was sent to a shanty a bit farther back, & yesterday motored on to this Field Hospital, called Casualty Clearing Station 13. . . . my head is not broken or even cut in any way. My temperature etc. *may not* have any relation to the knock, and the first doctor said he only hoped it *had*. Anyhow it was normal yesterday, and below today, and the only abnormal thing about me now is that I don't want a cigarette. . . .'

His fingers wake, and flutter up the bed.
His eyes come open with a pull of will,
Helped by the yellow may-flowers by his head.
The blind-cord drawls across the window-sill . . .
What a smooth floor the ward has! What a rug!
Who is that talking somewhere out of sight?
Why are they laughing? What's inside that jug?
'Nurse! Doctor!' – 'Yes, all right, all right.'

But sudden evening muddles all the air –
There seems no time to want a drink of water,
Nurse looks so far away. And here and there
Music and roses burst through crimson slaughter.
He can't remember where he saw blue sky.
More blankets. Cold. He's cold. And yet so hot.
And there's no light to see the voices by;
There is no time to ask – he knows not what.

Wilfred Owen: 'Conscious'

20 March

1727—Sir Isaac Newton died

Shall the great soul of Newton quit this earth,
To mingle with his stars; and every Muse,
Astonished into silence, shun the weight
Of honours due to his illustrious name?
Who, while on this dim spot, where mortals toil
Clouded in dust, from Motion's simple laws,
Could trace the secret hand of Providence,
Wide-working through his universal frame.
 Have ye not listened how he bound the suns
And planets to their spheres? the unequal task
Of humankind till then. Oft had they rolled
O'er erring man the year, and oft disgraced
The pride of schools, before their course was known
Full in its causes and effects to him,
All-piercing sage! Who sat not down and dreamed
Romantic schemes, defended by the din
Of specious words, and tyranny of names;
But, bidding his amazing mind attend,
And with heroic patience years on years
Deep-searching, saw at last the system dawn,
And shine, of all his race, on him alone.
. . .
O Britain's boast! whether with angels thou
Sittest in dread discourse, or fellow-blessed,
Who joy to see the honour of their kind;
Or whether, mounted on cherubic wing,
Thy swift career is with the whirling orbs,
Comparing things with things, in rapture lost,
And grateful adoration, for that light
So plenteous rayed into thy mind below,
From Light himself; oh, look with pity down
On humankind, a frail erroneous race!
Exalt the spirit of a downward world!
O'er thy dejected country chief preside,
And be her Genius called! her studies raise,
Correct her manners, and inspire her youth.
For, though depraved and sunk, she brought thee forth,
And glories in thy name; . . .

*James Thomson: from 'To the Memory of Sir
Isaac Newton'*

1853—Matthew Arnold expressed his opinion of various redoubtable females

I am glad to hear a good account of Emerson's health – I thought his insanity was one of Miss Martineau's terrific lies: sane he certainly is, though somewhat incolere as the French say – very thin and ineffectual, and self-defensive only. Tell me when you can send something about his life and manner of going on – and his standing in the Boston world.

Margaret Fuller – what do you think of her? I have given, after some hesitation, half a guinea for the three volumes concerning her – partly moved by the low price partly by interest about that partly brazen female. I incline to think that the meeting with her would have made me return all the contents of my spiritual stomach but through the screen of a book I willingly look at her and allow her exquisite intelligence and fineness of aperçus. But my G–d what rot did she and the other female dogs of Boston talk about the Greek mythology! The absence of men of any culture in America, where everybody knows that the Earth is an oblate speroid [*sic*] and nobody knows anything worth knowing, must have made her run riot so wildly, and for many years has made her insufferable.

Miss Bronte has written a hideous undelightful constricted novel [Charlotte Bronte's *Villette*] – what does Thackeray say to it. It is one of the most utterly disagreeable books I ever read – and having seen her makes it more so. She is so entirely – what Margaret Fuller was partially – a fire without aliment – one of the most distressing barren sights one can witness. Religion or devotion or whatever it is to be called may be impossible for such people now: but they have at any rate not found a substitute for it and it was better for the world when they comforted themselves with it.

Thackeray's Esmond you know everyone here calls a failure – but I do not think so. It is one of the most readable books I ever met – and Thackeray is certainly a first rate journeyman though not a great artist: – It gives you an insight into the *heaven born* character of Waverley and Indiana and such like when you read the undeniably powerful but most un-heaven-born productions of the present people – Thackeray – the woman Stowe etc. The woman Stowe [this is Harriet Beecher Stowe, the author of *Uncle Tom's Cabin*] by her picture must be a Gorgon – I can quite believe all you tell me of her – a strong Dissenter-religious middle-class person – she will never go far, I think.

Matthew Arnold to Arthur Clough

1812—Charles Lamb contributed 'The Triumph of the Whale' to the issue of The Examiner *which landed Leigh Hunt, its editor, in prison for its attacks on the Prince Regent*

The Triumph of the Whale

Io! Paean! Io! sing
To the finny people's King.
Not a mightier Whale than this
In the vast Atlantic is;
Not a fatter fish than he
Flounders round the polar sea.
See his blubber – at his gills
What a world of drink he swills,
From his trunk, as from a spout,
Which next moment he pours out.
  Such his person – next declare,
Muse, who his companions are, –
Every fish of generous kind
Scuds aside, or slinks behind;
But about his presence keep
All the Monsters of the Deep;
Mermaids, with their tails and singing
His delighted fancy stinging;
Crooked Dolphins, they surround him,
Dog-like Seals, they fawn around him.
Following hard the progress mark,
Of the intolerant sea Shark.
For his solace and relief,
Flat-fish are his courtiers chief. . . .

  Name of title, what has he?
Is he Regent of the Sea?
From this difficulty free us,
Buffon, Banks, or sage Linnaeus.
With his wondrous attributes
Say, what appellation suits?
By his bulk, and by his size,
By his oily qualities,
This (or else my eyesight fails),
This should be the PRINCE OF WHALES.

Charles Lamb

[1798]—March 23rd—'Coleridge dined with us. He brought his ballad finished. We walked with him to the Miner's house. A beautiful evening, very starry, the horned moon'

Dorothy Wordsworth : from The Alfoxden Journal

During the first year that Mr. Wordsworth and I were neighbours, our conversations turned frequently on the two cardinal points of poetry, the power of exciting the sympathy of the reader by a faithful adherence to the truth of nature, and the power of giving the interest of novelty by the modifying colours of imagination. . . . The thought suggested itself (to which of us I do not recollect) that a series of poems might be composed of two sorts. In the one, the incidents and agents were to be, in part at least, supernatural; and the excellence aimed at was to consist in the interesting of the affections by the dramatic truth of such emotions, as would naturally accompany such situations, supposing them real. And real in *this* sense they have been to every human being who, from whatever source of delusion, has at any time believed himself under supernatural agency. For the second class, subjects were to be chosen from ordinary life; the characters and incidents were to be such as will be found in every village and its vicinity, where there is a meditative and feeling mind to seek after them, or to notice them, when they present themselves.

In this idea originated the plan of the 'Lyrical Ballads'; in which it was agreed, that my endeavours should be directed to persons and characters supernatural, or at least romantic; yet so as to transfer from our inward nature a human interest and a semblance of truth sufficient to procure for these shadows of imagination that willing suspension of disbelief for the moment, which constitutes poetic faith. Mr. Wordsworth, on the other hand, was to propose to himself as his object, to give the charm of novelty to things of every day, and to excite a feeling analogous to the supernatural, by awakening the mind's attention from the lethargy of custom, and directing it to the loveliness and the wonders of the world before us. . . .

With this view I wrote the 'Ancient Mariner', and was preparing among other poems, the 'Dark Ladie', and the 'Christabel', in which I should have more nearly realized my ideal, than I had done in my first attempt. But Mr. Wordsworth's industry had proved so much greater, that my compositions, instead of forming a balance, appeared rather an interpolation of heterogeneous matter. Mr. Wordsworth added two or three poems written in his own character, in the impassioned, lofty, and sustained diction, which is characteristic of his genius. In this form the 'Lyrical Ballads' were published; and were presented by him, as an *experiment*, whether subjects, which from their nature rejected the usual ornaments and extra-colloquial style of poems in general, might not be so managed in the language of ordinary life as to produce the pleasureable interest, which it is the peculiar business of poetry to impart.

Samuel Taylor Coleridge : from Biographia Literaria

24 March 🎭

1711—George Frederick Handel's Italian opera, Rinaldo, *was first performed, to the amusement of 'Mr Spectator'*

As I was walking in the Streete about a Fortnight ago, I saw an ordinary Fellow carrying a Cage full of little Birds upon his Shoulder; and, as I was wondering with my self what Use he would put them to, he was met very luckily by an Acquaintance, who had the same Curiosity. Upon his asking him what he had upon his Shoulder, he told him, that he had been buying Sparrows for the Opera. Sparrows for the Opera, says his Friend, licking his lips, what, are they to be roasted? No, no, says the other, they are to enter towards the end of the first Act, and to fly about the Stage.

This strange Dialogue awakened my Curiosity so far, that I immediately bought the Opera, by which means I perceived that the Sparrows were to act the part of Singing Birds in a delightful Grove; though they flew in Sight, the Musick proceeded from a Consort of Flagellets and Birdcalls which was planted behind the Scenes. At the same time I made this Discovery, I found . . . that there was actually a Project of bringing the *New-River* into the House, to be employed in Jetteaus and Water-works. . . . In the meantime, the Opera of *Rinaldo* is filled with Thunder and Lightning, Illuminations and Fireworks; which the Audience may look upon without catching Cold, and indeed without much Danger of being burnt; for there are several Engines filled with Water, and ready to play at a Minute's warning, in case any Accident should happen. . . .

But to return to the Sparrows; there have been so many Flights of them let loose in this Opera, that it is feared the House will never get rid of them; and that in other Plays they may make their Entrance in very wrong and improper Scenes . . . besides the Inconvenience which the Heads of the Audience may suffer from them. I am credibly informed, that there was once a Design of casting into an Opera the Story of *Whittington* and his Cat, and that in order to it there had been got together a great Quantity of Mice; but Mr. Rich, the Proprietor of the House, very prudently . . . would not permit it to be Acted in his House. And indeed I cannot blame him; for, as he said very well upon that Occasion, I do not hear that any of the Performers in our Opera pretend to equal the famous Pied Piper. . . .

Before I dismiss this Paper, I must inform my Reader, that I hear there is a Treaty on foot . . . to furnish the Opera of *Rinaldo and Armida* with an Orange-Grove; and that the next time it is Acted, the Singing Birds will be Personated by Tom-Tits; The Undertakers being resolved to spare neither Pains nor Mony, for the Gratification of the Audience.

Joseph Addison: from The Spectator, *no. 5*

1736—Alexander Pope tried to persuade Jonathan Swift to visit him again

---

If ever I write more epistles in verse, one of them shall be addressed to you. I have long concerted it, and begun it, but I would make what bears your name as finished as my last work ought to be, that is to say, more finished than any of the rest. The subject is large, and will divide into four Epistles, which naturally follow the Essay on Man, *viz.* 1. Of the Extent and Limits of Human Reason and Science. 2. A View of the useful and therefore attainable, Arts. 3. Of the Nature, Ends, Application, and Use of Different Capacities. 4. Of the Use of *Learning*, of the *Science* of the *World*, and of *Wit*. It will conclude with a satire against the mis-application of all these, exemplified by pictures, characters, and examples.

But alas! the task is great, and *non sum qualis eram!* My understanding indeed, such as it is, is extended rather than diminished; I see things more in the whole, more consistent, and more clearly deduced from, and related to, each other. But what I gain on the side of philosophy, I lose on the side of poetry: the flowers are gone, when the fruits begin to ripen, and the fruits perhaps will never ripen perfectly. The climate (under our heaven of a court) is but cold and uncertain; the winds rise, and the winter comes on. I find myself but little disposed to build a new house; I have nothing left but to gether up the reliques of a wreck, and look about me to see how few friends I have left. Pray, whose esteem or admiration should I desire now to procure by my writings? whose friendship or conversation to obtain by them? I am a man of desperate fortunes, that is, a man whose friends are dead: for I never aimed at any other fortune than in friends. . . .

Every man you know or care for here, inquires of you, and pays you the only devoir he can, that of drinking your health. I wish you had any motive to see this kingdom. I could keep you, for I am rich; that is, I have more than I want. I can afford room for yourself and two servants; I have indeed room enough, nothing but myself at home. The kind and hearty housewife is dead! the agreeable and instructive neighbour is gone! yet my house is enlarged, and the gardens extend and flourish, as knowing nothing of the guests they have lost. I have more fruit-trees and kitchen-garden than you have any thought of: nay, I have good melons and pine-apples of my own growth. I am as much a better gardener, as I am a worse poet, than when you saw me; but gardening is near a-kin to philosophy, for Tully says, *Agricultura proxima sapientiae*. For God's sake, why should not you (that are a step higher than a philosopher, a divine, yet have too much grace and wit than to be a bishop) e'en give all you have to the poor of Ireland, (for whom you have already done everything else) to quit the place, and live and die with me? And let *Tales animae concordes* be our motto and our epitaph.

1541—Sir William Howard informed the Privy Council that Sir Thomas Wyatt, who was imprisoned in the Tower on charges of treason, had confessed 'all the things objected to him'; but Wyatt was shortly released

Sighs are my food, my drink are my tears;
Clinking of fetters would such music crave;
Stink and close air, away my life it wears;
Poor innocence is all the hope I have.
Rain, wind, or weather judge I by mine ears;
Malice assaults that righteousness should have.
Sure am I, Brian, this wound shall heal again,
But yet, alas, the scar shall still remain.

'Wyatt being in Prison, to Brian'

The woeful days so full of pain,
The weary night all spent in vain,
The labor lost for no small gain,
To write them all it will not be.
    But ha! ha! ha! full well is me,
    For I am now at liberty.

Everything that fair doth show,
When proof is made it proveth not so,
But turneth mirth to bitter woe;
Which in this case full well I see.
    But ha! ha! ha! full well is me
    For I am now at Liberty. . . .

Was never bird tangled in lime
That brake away in better time
Than I, that rotten boughs did climb,
And had no hurt, but scapèd free.
    Now ha! ha! ha! full well is me,
    For I am now at liberty.

Sir Thomas Wyatt: from 'Tangled I was'

1766—Oliver Goldsmith's The Vicar of Wakefield *was published, after having been held back by the publisher for two years*

'I received one morning a message from poor Goldsmith that he was in great distress, and as it was not in his power to come to me, begging that I would come to him as soon as possible. I sent him a guinea, and promised to come to him directly. I accordingly went as soon as I was drest, and found that his landlady had arrested him for his rent, at which he was in a violent passion. I perceived that he had already changed my guinea, and had got a bottle of Madeira and a glass before him. I put the cork into the bottle, desired he would be calm, and began to talk to him of the means by which he might be extricated. He then told me that he had a novel ready for the press, which he produced to me. I looked into it, and saw its merit; told the landlady I should soon return, and having gone to a bookseller, sold it for sixty pounds. I brought Goldsmith the money, and he discharged his rent, not without rating his landlady in a high tone for having used him so ill. . . . His "Vicar of Wakefield" I myself did not think would have had much success. It was written and sold to a bookseller, before his "Traveller"; but published after; so little expectation had the bookseller from it. Had it been sold after the "Traveller", he might have had twice as much money for it, though sixty guineas was no mean price. The bookseller had the advantage of Goldsmith's reputation from "The Traveller" in the sale, though Goldsmith had it not in selling the copy.'

Samuel Johnson, as quoted by Boswell

*   *   *   *   *

ADVERTISEMENT

There are an hundred faults in this Thing, and an hundred things might be said to prove them beauties. But it is needless. A book may be amusing with numerous errors, or it may be very dull without a single absurdity. The hero of this piece unites in himself the three greatest characters upon earth; he is a priest, an husbandman, and the father of a family. He is drawn as ready to teach, and ready to obey, as simple in affluence, and majestic in adversity. In this age of opulence and refinement, whom can such a character please? Such as are fond of high life, will turn with disdain from the simplicity of his country fireside. Such as mistake ribaldry for humour, will find no wit in his harmless conversation; and such as have been taught to deride religion, will laugh at one, whose chief stores of comfort are drawn from futurity.

Oliver Goldsmith (the 'preface' to The Vicar of Wakefield)

28 March

1735—'I kept this day as the anniversary of my Tetty's death [she had died the previous year, on March 17 Old Style], with prayer and tears in the morning. In the evening I prayed for her conditionally, if it were lawful'

from Samuel Johnson's 'Memorandum', quoted by Boswell

'I have often heard my mother say she perfectly remembered his wife. He has recorded of her that beauty which existed only in his imagination. She had a very red face, and very indifferent features; and her manners in advanced life, for her children were all grown up when Johnson first saw her, had an unbecoming excess of girlish levity, and disgusting affectation. The rustic prettiness, and artless manners of her daughter, the present Mrs. Lucy Porter, had won Johnson's youthful heart, when she was upon a visit at my grandfather's in Johnson's school-days. Disgusted by his unsightly form, she had a personal aversion to him, nor could the beautiful verses he addressed to her, teach her to endure him. The nymph, at length, returned to her parents at Birmingham, and was soon forgotten. Business taking Johnson to Birmingham, on the death of his own father, and calling upon his coy mistress there, he found her father dying. He passed all his leisure hours at Mr. Porter's, attending his sick-bed, and, in a few months after his death, asked Mrs. Johnson's consent to marry the old widow. After expressing her surprise at a request so extraordinary – "no, Sam, my willing consent you will never have to so preposterous a union. You are not twenty-five, and she is turned fifty. If she had any prudence, this request had never been made to me. Where are your means of subsistence? Porter has died poor, in consequence of his wife's expensive habits. You have great talents, but, as yet, have turned them in to no profitable channel." – "Mother, I have not deceived Mrs. Porter; I have told her the worst of me; that I am of mean extraction; that I have no money; and that I have had an uncle hanged. She replied, that she had no more money than myself; and that, though she had not had a relation hanged, she had fifty who deserved hanging." '

Anna Seward, the Swan of Lichfield, to James Boswell, March 25, 1785

To argue from her being much older than Johnson, or any other circumstances, that he could not really love her, is absurd; for love is not a subject of reasoning, but of feeling, and therefore there are no common principles upon which one can persuade another concerning it. Every man feels for himself, and knows how he is affected by particular qualities in the person he admires, the impressions of which are too minute and delicate to be substantiated in language.

James Boswell: from The Life of Johnson

1614—Sir Walter Raleigh's History of the World, *written, it is said, during his final imprisonment in the Tower of London, was first published*

For the rest, if we seek a reason of the succession and continuance of this boundless ambition in mortal men, we may add to that which hath been already said, that the Kings and Princes of the world have always laid before them the actions, but not the ends of those great ones which preceded them. They are always transported with the glory of the one, but they mind the misery of the others, till they find the experience in themselves. They neglect the advice of God, while they enjoy life, or hope it; but they follow the counsel of Death upon his first approach. It is he that puts into man all the wisdom of the world, without speaking a word, which God with all the words of His law, promises, or threats, doth not infuse. Death, which hateth and destroyeth man, is believed; God, which hath made him and loves him, is always deferred: 'I have considered', saith Solomon, 'all the works that are under the sun, and, behold, all is vanity and vexation of spirit'; but who believes it till Death tells it us? It was Death which opening the conscience of Charles the Fifth made him enjoin his son Philip to restore Navarre; and King Francis the First of France, to command that justice should be done upon the murderers of the Protestants in Merindol and Cabrieres, which till then he neglected. It is therefore Death alone that can suddenly make man to know himself. He tells the proud and insolent that they are but abjects, and humbles them at the instant, makes them cry, complain, and repent, yea even to hate their forepast happiness. He takes the account of the rich, and proves him a beggar, a naked beggar, which hath interest in nothing but in the gravel that fills his mouth. He holds a glass before the eyes of the most beautiful, and makes them see therein their deformity and rottenness, and they acknowledge it.

O eloquent, just, and mighty Death! whom none could advise thou hast perswaded; what none have dared thou hast done; and whom all the world hath flattered, thou only hast cast out of the world and despised; thou hast drawn together all the far-stretched greatness, all the pride, cruelty, and ambition of man, and covered it all over with these two narrow words: *Hic jacet.*

Walter Raleigh : from The History of the World
(*conclusion*)

1639—John Milton attempted to repay the scholarly hospitality of the Keeper of the Vatican Library

Although I can, and often do, remember the great courtesy and friendliness which I have received during my passage through Italy, yet there is perhaps no one from whom I could properly say that I have received greater proofs of goodwill than yourself, on so short an acquaintance. For when I went to visit you at the Vatican you received me with the utmost cordiality although I was completely unknown to you, except for anything which Cherubini may have told you previously. You afterwards were so good as to admit me to the Library, where I had the opportunity of seeing the rich collection of volumes and the large number of Greek manuscripts as well, enriched by your annotations. Some of these have never been seen in our time, but lie waiting, like the souls in Virgil 'enclosed within the confines of a green vale, waiting to take their journey to the world above', and seemed to demand the helping hand and obstetric skill of the printer; others have already been published by you, and have been eagerly received by scholars throughout the world. You presented me, moreover, with two copies of one of these as a parting gift. . . .

I do not indeed know, my learned friend Holstenius, whether you have singled me out for such remarkably friendly and hospitable treatment, or whether you make a practice of bestowing similar favours on all Englishmen, on account of your three years' residence at the University of Oxford. If the latter is the case, you have chosen a generous way of repaying your debt to England, and one which reflects honour upon yourself, and you merit equal gratitude from each one of us in particular and from our country in general. But if the former is the case, and you have singled me out above all others and held me worthy to be honoured with your friendship, I congratulate myself on your choice, while attributing the honour to your kindness rather than to my own deserts.

As to the commission which you seemed to entrust to me, of inspecting the Codex Mediceus, I was forward in laying it before my friends, but they give very little hope of its being executed at present. They tell me it is a rule of that library that unless one has previously obtained permission nothing may be copied, and that one is not allowed even to make notes. They say, however, that there is one Giovanni Battista Doni at Rome, who has been appointed public lecturer in Greek at Florence, and is shortly expected. It would be easy to obtain what you desire through him, though I should have been very glad if I could have been of some better service in forwarding an object so desirable, since in so honourable and excellent an undertaking you have the right to command the help of all men everywhere and to expect every possible assistance and facility. . . .

Farewell then, my learned friend Holstenius, and wherever I may be in future, count me, I beg you, among those who are most devotedly attached to you and to your interests, if you hold me worthy of that honour.

1883—Alfred, Lord Tennyson, sent a copy of his early poem, 'Tiresias', to Edward Fitzgerald as a seventy-fifth birthday present, along with these verses

Old Fitz, who from your suburb grange,
    Where once I tarried for a while,
Glance at the wheeling orb of change,
    And greet it with a kindly smile . . .
Who live on milk and meal and grass
    . . . but none can say
That Lenten fare makes Lenten thought
    Who reads your golden Eastern lay,
Than which I know no version done
    In English more divinely well;
A planet equal to the sun
    Which cast it, that large infidel
Your Omar; and your Omar drew
    Full-handed plaudits from our best
In modern letters, and from two,
    Old friends outvaluing all the rest,
Two voices heard on earth no more;
    But we old friends are still alive,
And I am nearing seventy-four
    While you have touched at seventy-five,
And so I send a birthday line
    Of greeting; and my son, who dipped
In some forgotten book of mine
    With sallow scraps of manuscript,
And dating many a year ago,
    Has hit on this [Tiresias], which you will take,
My Fitz, and welcome, as I know,
    Less for its own than for the sake
Of one recalling gracious times,
    When, in our younger London days,
You found some merit in my rhymes,
    And I more pleasure in your praise.

Aprill.

1785—Robert Burns wrote his first verse epistle to John Lapraik

I am nae poet, in a sense,
But just a rhymer, like, by chance,
And hae to learning nae pretence,
 Yet, what the matter!
Whene'er my muse does on me glance,
 I jingle at her.

Your critic folk may cock their nose,
And say, 'How can you e'er propose,
You, wha ken hardly verse frae prose,
 To mak a sang?'
But, by your leaves, my learned foes,
 Ye're maybe wrang.

What's a' your jargon o' your schools,
Your Latin names for horns and stools;
If honest nature made you fools,
 What sairs your grammars?
Ye'd better taen up spades and shools,
 Or knappin'-hammers.

A set o' dull conceited hashes,
Confuse their brains in college classes!
They gang in stirks, and come out asses,
 Plain truth to speak;
And syne they think to climb Parnassus
 By dint o' Greek!

Gie me ae spark o' nature's fire!
That's a' the learning I desire;
Then though I drudge through dub and mire
 At pleugh or cart,
My muse, though hamely in attire,
 May touch the heart.

A LETTER TO DAFNIS

April 2nd. 1685

This to the Crown, and blessing of my life,
The much lov'd husband, of a happy wife.
To him, whose constant passion found the art
To win a stubborn, and ungrateful heart;
And to the World, by tend'rest proof discovers
They err, who say that husbands can't be lovers.
With such return of passion, as is due,
Daphnis I love, Daphnis my thoughts pursue,
Daphnis, my hope, my joys, are bounded all in you:
Ev'n I, for Daphnis, and my promise sake,
What I in women censure, undertake.
But this from love, not vanity, proceeds;
You know who writes; and I who 'tis that reads.
Judge not my passion, by my want of skill,
Many love well, though they express itt ill;
And I your censure cou'd with pleasure bear,
Wou'd you but soon return, and speak itt here.

1843—Sir Robert Peel wrote to William Wordsworth, urging him to accept the Laureateship; to the dismay of liberal young poets, Wordsworth accepted

The Lost Leader

Just for a handful of silver he left us,
    Just for a riband to stick in his coat –
Found the one gift of which fortune bereft us,
    Lost all the others she lets us devote;
They, with the gold to give, doled him out silver,
    So much was theirs who so little allowed:
How all our copper had gone for his service!
    Rags – were they purple, his heart had been proud!
We that had loved him so, followed him, honored him,
    Lived in his mild and magnificent eye,
Learned his great language, caught his clear accents,
    Made him our pattern to live and to die!
Shakespeare was of us, Milton was for us,
    Burns, Shelley, were with us – they watch from their graves!
He alone breaks from the van and the freemen
    – He alone sinks to the rear and the slaves!

We shall march prospering – not through his presence;
    Songs may inspirit us – not from his lyre;
Deeds will be done – while he boasts his quiescence,
    Still bidding crouch whom the rest bade aspire:
Blot out his name, then, record one lost soul more,
    One task more declined, one more footpath untrod,
One more devils'-triumph and sorrow for angels,
    One wrong more to man, one more insult to God!
Life's night begins: let him never come back to us!
    There would be doubt, hesitation and pain,
Forced praise on our part – the glimmer of twilight,
    Never glad confident morning again!
Best fight on well, for we taught him – strike gallantly,
    Menace our heart ere we master his own;
Then let him receive the new knowledge and wait us,
    Pardoned in heaven, the first by the throne!

Robert Browning

4 April 📖

1802—Wordsworth completed, and read to Coleridge, four stanzas which were to become, after two years, the opening section of his 'Ode: Intimations of Immortality'

[The 1802 stanzas ended with the lines: 'Whither is fled the visionary gleam?] Where is it now, the glory and the dream?' After hearing them, Coleridge wrote that night 'A Letter to ——', 340 agonized lines on this theme, addressed to Sara Hutchinson, of which the following are typical:

> I speak not now of those habitual Ills
> That wear out Life, when two unequal Minds
> Meet in one House and two discordant Wills –
>   This leaves me, where it finds,
> Past Cure, and past Complaint, – a fate austere
> Too fix'd and hopeless to partake of Fear! . . .
> Methinks to weep with you
> Were better far than to rejoice alone –
> But that my coarse domestic Life has known
> No Habits of heart-nursing Sympathy,
> No Griefs but such as dull and deaden me,
> No mutual mild Enjoyments of its own,
> No hopes of its own Vintage, None O! none –
> Whence when I mourn'd for you, my Heart might borrow
> Fair forms and living Motions for its Sorrow. . . .

[Coleridge wisely did not publish this long-winded attempt to make his unhappy marriage to Sara Fricker justify his passion for Sara Hutchinson and his failures as a poet. Instead, during the following six months he re-worked his crude and extravagant outburst, ruthlessly pruning most of the personal references and the weak, self-pitying lines, and reducing the whole 'Letter to ——' to the 139 lines we know as *Dejection: An Ode*. This resultant example of the triumph of art and judgment over the 'spontaneous overflow of powerful emotions', he published on October 4, 1802 – the day on which Wordsworth married Sara Hutchinson's sister Mary, and the seventh anniversary of Coleridge's own disastrous marriage.]

1636—Ben Jonson's friends remained troubled by his display of ill manners at a supper party on the previous night, and tried to excuse it

---

I was invited yesternight to a solemn Supper, by *Ben Jonson*, where you were deeply remember'd; there was good company, excellent cheer, choice wines, and jovial welcome. One thing interven'd, which almost spoil'd the relish of the rest, that *Ben* began to engross all the discourse, to vapour extremely of himself, and, by vilifying others, to magnify his own *Muse*. *Thomas Carew* buzz'd me in the ear, that tho' *Ben.* had barrell'd up a great deal of knowledge, yet it seems he had not read the *Ethiques*, which, among other precepts of Morality, forbid self-commendation, declaring it to be an ill-favour'd solecism in good manners. . . . be a Man's breath ever so sweet, yet it makes one's praise stink, if he makes his own mouth the Conduit-pipe of it. But for my own part, I am content to dispense with the *Roman* infirmity of Ben now that time has snowed upon his pericranium. . . . There is another reason that excuseth *Ben*, which is, that if one be allowed to love the natural issue of his Body, why not that of the Brain, which is of a spiritual and more noble extraction? . . .

Thomas Howell to Sir Thomas Hawk, Kt.

'Tis true, dear Ben, thy just chastising hand
Hath fixed upon the sotted age a brand,
To their swollen pride and empty scribbling due;
It can nor judge nor write; and yet 'tis true
Thy comic muse, from the exalted line
Touched by thy *Alchemist*, doth since decline
From that her zenith, and foretells a red
And blushing evening, when she goes to bed;
Yet such as shall outshine the glimmering light
With which all stars shall gild the following night. . . .
    Why should the follies, then, of this dull age
Draw from thy pen such an immodest rage
As seems to blast thy else immortal bays,
When thine own tongue proclaims thy itch of praise? . . .
    Let others glut on the extorted praise
Of vulgar breath; trust thou to after-days.
Thy labored works shall live when time devours
Th' abortive offspring of their hasty hours. . . .
The wiser world doth greater thee confess
Than all men else, than thyself only less.

Thomas Carew: from 'To Ben Jonson'

6 April 📖

1763—Christopher Smart's A Song to David, *the longest pure lyric in English, was first published*

'A SONG TO DAVID, a Poem composed in a Spirit of affection and thankfulness to the great Author of the Book of Gratitude, which is the Psalms of David the King. This song is allowed by Mr. Smart's judicious Friends and Enemies to be the best Piece ever made public by him, its chief fault being the exact Regularity and Method with which it is conducted.'

Advertisement in Poems on Several Occasions, *Nov. 1763*

I have seen his Song to David & from thence conclude him as mad as ever.

William Mason to Thomas Gray, 28 June 1763

I have sent you Smart's *Song to David*, which is a very curious composition, being a strange mixture of *dun obscure* and glowing genius at times. . . . Poor man, he has been relieved from his confinement, but not from his unhappy disorder. However, he has it not in any great height.

James Boswell to Sir David Dalrymple, 30 July 1763

. . . the only great *accomplished* poem of the last century.

Dante Gabriel Rossetti

> A Song where flute-breath silvers trumpet-clang,
> And stations [Smart] for once on either hand
> With Milton and with Keats. . . .
>   Such success
> Befell Smart only out of throngs between
> Milton and Keats that donned the singing-dress –
> Smart, solely of such songmen, pierced the screen
> 'Twixt thing and word, lit language straight from soul, –
> Left no fine film-flake on the naked coal
> Live from the censer – shapely or uncouth,
> Fire-suffused through and through, one blaze of truth
> Undeadened by a lie. . . .

Robert Browning: from Parleyings with Certain People of Importance in Their Day

*   *   *   *   *

For the praise of God can give to a mute fish the notes of a nightingale.

Christopher Smart

1868—Charles Dickens, on a lecture tour in America, reported his regime, and his hopes and fears for success, to his daughter

Boston, Tuesday, Seventh April, 1868

I not only read last Friday, when I was doubtful of being able to do so, but read as I never did before, and astonished the audience quite as much as myself. You never saw or heard such a scene of excitement.

Longfellow and all the Cambridge men urged me to give in. I have been very near doing so, but feel stronger today. I cannot tell whether the catarrh may have done me any lasting injury in the lungs or other breathing organs, until I shall have rested and got home. I hope and believe not. . . .

I cannot eat (to anything like the ordinary extent), and have established this system: At seven in the morning, in bed, a tumbler of new cream and two tablespoonsful of rum. At twelve, a sherry cobbler and a biscuit. At three (dinner time), a pint of champagne. At five minutes to eight, an egg beaten up with a glass of sherry. Between the parts, the strongest beef tea that can be made, drunk hot. At a quarter-past ten, soup, and anything to drink that I can fancy. I don't eat more than half a pound of solid food in the whole twenty-four hours, if so much.

If I hold out, as I hope to do, I shall be greatly pressed in leaving here and getting over to New York before next Saturday's mail from there. . . . Be sure that you shall hear, however, by Saturday's mail, if I should knock up as to reading. I am tremendously 'beat', but I feel really and unaffectedly so much stronger today, both in my body and hopes, that I am much encouraged. I have a fancy that I turned my worst time last night.

Dolby is as tender as a woman and as watchful as a doctor. He never leaves me during the reading now, but sits at the side of the platform and keeps his eye upon me all the time. Ditto George, the gasman, steadiest and most reliable man I ever employed. I am the more hopeful of my not having to relinquish a reading, because last night was 'Copperfield' and 'Bob' – by a quarter of an hour the longest, and, in consideration of the storm, by very much the most trying. Yet I was far fresher afterwards than I have been these three weeks.

Here ends my report. The personal affection of the people in this place is charming to the last.

Ever your affectionate Father.

From Letters of Charles Dickens

1611—George Chapman's translation of the complete Iliad *was entered in the Stationers' Register. Here Chapman gave his readers that 'due praise of your mother tongue above all others' which he had promised in the preface to his version of* Seven Books of the Iliads, *1598*

And for our tongue, that still is so impaired
  By travelling linguists, I can prove it clear
That no tongue hath the Muses' utterance heired
  For verse and that sweet music for the ear
Struck out of rhyme, so naturally as this;
  Our monosyllables so kindly fall
And meet, opposed in rhyme, as they did kiss;
  French and Italian, most immetrical;
Their many syllables, in harsh collision,
  Fall as they brake their necks; their bastard rhymes
Saluting as they justled in transition,
  And set our teeth on edge; nor tunes, nor times
Kept in their falls. And methinks, their long words
  Show in short verse, as in a narrow space
Two opposites should meet, with two-hand swords
  Unwieldy, without or use or grace.

Thus having rid the rubs, and strowed these flowers
  In our thrice-sacred Homer's English way,
What rests to make him yet more worthy yours?
  To cite more praise of him were mere delay
To your glad searches, for what those men found
  That gave his praise, past all, so high a place,
Whose virtues were so many, and so crowned,
  By all consents, divine; that not to grace
Or add increase to them the world doth need
  Another Homer; but even to rehearse
And number them, they did so much exceed;
  Men thought him not a man, but that his verse
Some more celestial nature did adorn.
  And that all may well conclude, it could not be
That for the place where any man was born
  So long and mortally could disagree
So many nations, as for Homer strived,
  Unless his spur in them had been divine.

George Chapman: from 'To the Reader'

1626—Francis Bacon died

It is as natural to die as to be born; and to a little infant, perhaps, the one is as painful as the other. He that dies in an earnest pursuit is like one that is wounded in hot blood; who, for the time, scarce feels the hurt; and therefore a mind fixed and bent upon somewhat that is good doth avert the dolours of death. But above all, believe it, the sweetest canticle is *Nunc dimittis*; when a man hath obtained worthy end and expectations. Death hath this also, that it openeth the gate to good fame, and extinguisheth envy. – *Extinctus amabitur idem.*

Francis Bacon: from Essay II – 'Of Death'

Mr. Hobbes told me that the cause of his lordship's death was trying an experiment: viz., as he was taking the aire in a coach with Dr. Witherborne (a Scotchman, Physitian to the King) towards High-gate, snow lay on the ground, and it came into my lord's thoughts, why flesh might not be preserved in snow, as in salt. They were resolved they would try the experiment presently. They alighted out of the coach, and went into a poore woman's howse at the bottome of High-gate hill, and bought a hen, and made the woman exenterate it, and then stuffed the bodie with snow, and my lord did help to doe it himselfe. The snow so chilled him, that he immediately fell so extremely ill, that he could not returne to his lodgings (I suppose then at Graye's Inne), but went to the earle of Arundell's house at High-gate, where they putt him into a good bed warmed with a panne, but it was a damp bed that had not been layn-in in about a yeare before, which gave him such a cold that in two or three dayes, as I remember he [Hobbes] told me, he dyed of suffocation.

John Aubrey: from Brief Lives

10 April

1798—William Hazlitt spent his twentieth birthday in Wales

It was on the tenth of April, 1798, that I sat down to a volume of the *New Eloise*, at the inn at Llangollen, over a bottle of sherry and a cold chicken. The letter I chose was that in which St. Preux describes his feelings as he first caught a glimpse from the heights of the Jura of the Pays de Vaud, which I had brought with me as a *bon bouche* to crown the evening with. It was my birthday, and I had for the first time come from a place in the neighbourhood to visit this delightful spot. The road to Llangollen turns off between Chirk and Wrexham; and on passing a certain point you come all at once upon the valley, which opens like an amphitheatre, broad, barren hills rising in majestic state on either side, with 'green upland swells that echo to the bleat of flocks' below, and the river Dee babbling over its stony bed in the midst of them. The valley at this time 'glittered green with sunny showers', and a budding ash-tree dipped its tender branches in the chiding stream. How proud, how glad I was to walk along the high road that overlooks the delicious prospect, repeating the lines which I have just quoted from Mr. Coleridge's poems! But besides the prospect which opened beneath my feet, another also opened to my inward sight, a heavenly vision, on which were written, in letters large as Hope could make them, these four words, LIBERTY, GENIUS, LOVE, VIRTUE; which have since faded into the light of common day, or mock my idle gaze.

'The beautiful is vanished, and returns not.'

Still I would return some time or other to this enchanted spot; but I would return to it alone. What other self could I find to share that influx of thoughts, of regret, and delight, the fragments of which I could hardly conjure up to myself, so much have they been broken and defaced. I could stand on some tall rock, and overlook the precipice of years that separates me from what I then was. I was at that time going shortly to visit the poet whom I have above named. Where is he now? Not only I myself have changed; the world which was then new to me has become old and incorrigible. Yet will I turn to thee in thought, O sylvan Dee, in joy, in youth and gladness as thou then wert; and thou shalt always be to me the river of Paradise, where I will drink of the waters of life freely!

William Hazlitt: from 'On Going a Journey'

716—Guthlac, the hermit of the Fens, died in the Abbey he had founded at Croyland ; this day is dedicated to his memory in the Calendar

And so when four and twenty months had run their course during which he lived a life of the greatest self-restraint in the habit of a cleric, he planned to seek the desert with the greatest diligence and the utmost earnestness of mind. For when he read about the solitary life of monks of former days, then his heart was enlightened and burned with an eager desire to make his way to the desert. Briefly, after some days had passed, with the willing consent of the elders, he started out on the path to eternal bliss and proceeded to look for a solitary place. There is in the midland district of Britain a most dismal fen of immense size, which begins at the banks of the river Granta not far from the camp which is called Cambridge and stretches from the south as far north as the sea. It is a very long tract, now consisting of marshes, now of bogs, sometimes of black waters overhung by fog, sometimes studded with wooded islands and traversed by the windings of tortuous streams. So when this man of blessed memory, Guthlac, had learned about the wild places of this vast desert, he made his way thither with divine assistance by the most direct route. . . .

It happened accordingly that when he was questioning those who lived near as to their knowledge of this solitude and they were telling him of many wild places in this far-stretching desert, a certain man among those standing by, whose name was Tatwine, declared that he knew a certain island in the more remote and hidden parts of that desert; many had attempted to dwell there, but had rejected it on account of the unknown portents of the desert and its terrors of various shapes. Guthlac, the man of blessed memory, on hearing this, earnestly besought his informant to show him the place. Tatwine accordingly assented to the commands of the man and, taking a fisherman's skiff, made his way, travelling with Christ, through trackless bogs within the confines of the dismal marsh till he came to the said spot; it is called Crowland, an island in the middle of the marsh which on account of the wildness of this very remote desert had hitherto remained untilled and known to very few. No settler had been able to dwell alone in this place before Guthlac the servant of Christ, on account of the phantoms of demons which haunted it. Here Guthlac, the man of God, despising the enemy, began by divine aid to dwell alone among the shady groves of this solitude. For it happened through the dispensation of divine grace that the blessed Guthlac reached the island of Crowland in the summer time, on the day on which the feast of St. Bartholomew is due to be celebrated. So he began to inhabit the desert with complete confidence in the help of St. Bartholomew. He loved the remoteness of the spot seeing that God had given it him, and vowed with righteous purpose to spend all the days of his life there.

From The Life of Saint Guthlac by Felix, *translated from the Anglo-Saxon by Bertram Colgrave* (*Cambridge University Press, 1956*)

12 April

1709—Sir Richard Steele published the first Tatler

Mr. Bickerstaff issues his proposals

Though the other papers, which are published for the use of the good people of England, have certainly very wholesome effects, and are laudable in their particular kinds, they do not seem to come up the main design of such narrations, which, I humbly presume, should be principally intended for the use of politic persons who are so public-spirited as to neglect their own affairs to look into transactions of state. Now these gentlemen for the most part being persons of strong zeal and weak intellects, it is both a charitable and necessary work to offer something whereby such worthy and well-affected members of the commonwealth may be instructed, after their reading, what to think; which shall be the end and purpose of this my paper, wherein I shall, from time to time, report and consider all matters of what kind soever that shall occur to me, and publish such my advices and reflections every Tuesday, Thursday, and Saturday in the week, for the convenience of the post. I resolve also to have something which may be of entertainment to the fair sex, in honour of whom I have invented the title of this paper. I therefore earnestly desire all persons, without distinction, to take it in for the present gratis, and hereafter at the price of one penny, forbidding all hawkers to take more for it at their peril. And I desire all persons to consider that I am at a very great charge for proper materials for this work, as well as that before I resolved upon it, I had settled a correspondence in all parts of the known and knowing world. And forasmuch as this globe is not trodden upon by mere drudges of business only, but that men of spirit and genius are justly to be esteemed as considerable agents in it, we shall not, upon a dearth of news, present you with musty foreign edits or dull proclamations, but shall divide our relation of the passages which occur in action or discourse throughout the town, as well as elsewhere, under such dates of places as may prepare for the matter you are to expect, in the following manner.

All accounts of gallantry, pleasure, and entertainment shall be under the article of White's chocolate-house; poetry, under that of Will's coffee-house; learning, under the title of the Grecian; foreign and domestic news, you will have from Saint James's coffee-house; and what else I have to offer on any other subject shall be dated from my own apartment.

Richard Steele: The Tatler, *No.* 1

[1923?]—date of the picnic visit to the Marabar Caves in E. M. Forster's A Passage to India, *as given in a dramatization of the novel, made with the author's approval, broadcast by the British Broadcasting Company*

'Do I take you too fast?' inquired Aziz for she had paused, a doubtful expression on her face. The discovery had come so suddenly that she felt like a mountaineer whose rope had broken. Not to love the man one is going to marry! Not to find out till this moment! Not even to have asked oneself the question until now! Something else to think out. . . . 'No, I'm all right, thanks', she said, and, her emotions well under control, resumed the climb, though she felt a bit dashed. Aziz held her hand, the guide adhered to the surface like a lizard and scampered about as if governed by a personal centre of gravity.

'Are you married, Dr. Aziz?' she asked, stopping again, and frowning.

'Yes, indeed, do come and see my wife' – for he felt it more artistic to have his wife alive for a moment.

'Thank you', she said absently.

'She is not at Chandrapore just now.'

'And have you children?'

'Yes, indeed, three', he replied in firmer tones.

'Are they a great pleasure to you?'

'Why, naturally, I adore them', he laughed.

'I suppose so.' What a handsome little Oriental he was, and no doubt his wife and children were beautiful too, for people usually get what they already possess. She did not admire him with any personal warmth, for there was nothing of the vagrant in her blood, but she guessed he might attract women of his own race and rank, and she regretted that neither she nor Ronny had physical charm. It does make a difference in a relationship – beauty, thick hair, a fine skin. Probably this man had several wives – Mohammedans always insist on their full four, according to Mrs. Turton. And having no one else to speak of on that eternal rock, she gave rein to the subject of marriage and said in her honest, decent, inquisitive way: 'Have you one wife or more than one?'

The question shocked the young man very much. It challenged a new conviction of his community, and new convictions are more sensitive than old. If she had said, 'Do you worship one god or several?' he would not have objected. But to ask an educated Indian Moslem how many wives he has – appalling, hideous! He was in trouble how to conceal his confusion. 'One, one in my own particular case', he spluttered, and let go of her hand. Quite a number of caves were at the top of the track, and thinking, 'Damn the English even at their best', he plunged into one of them to recover his balance. She followed at her leisure, quite unconscious that she had said the wrong thing, and not seeing him, she also went into a cave, thinking with half her mind 'sight-seeing bores me', and wondering with the other half about marriage.

E. M. Forster: from A Passage to India

1360—'. . . the 14 day of April . . . King Edward [III] with his host lay before the city of Paris; which day was full dark of mist and hail, and so bitter cold, that many men died on their horsebacks with the cold; wherefore unto this day it hath been called Black Monday'

Stow's Chronicle

[The Lady Meed (Bribery) declares that Black Monday was not her fault; she serves the king more loyally than does Conscience.]

'In Normandy was he not   annoyed for my sake.
But thou thyself soothly   shamedst him oft;
Crept into a cabin   for cold of thy nails,
Weening that winter   would have lasted forever,
And didst dread to be dead   because of the downpour
And hiedest thou homeward   for hunger of guts . . .
While I lingered with my lord   his life to save;
I made his men merry   and mended their mourning.
I patted their backs and   emboldened their hearts
And made them hop for hope of   my help at their will. . . .

'It becometh a king   that keepeth a realm
To give meed to his men   that meekly him serve,
To aliens and to all men   to honour them with gifts.
Meed maketh him loved   and for a man holden.
Emperors and earls   and all manner of lords
For gifts have young men   to run and to ride.
The pope and all prelates   presents accept
And fee men themselves   to maintain their laws.
Sergeants for their service,   we see well the sooth,
Take meed of their masters   as they may agree.
Beggars for their begging   beg of men meed;
And minstrels for their mirth   meed do they ask.
The king hath meed of his men   to make peace in the land;
Men that teach children   crave of them meed;
Priests that preach to the people   for goodness, ask meed
And mass-pence and their meat   at their meal times.
All kinds of craftsmen   crave meed for their prentice;
Merchants and meed   must needs go together.
No wight, as I ween,   without me, Meed, may live.'

Quoth the king to Conscience   'By Christ! as me thinketh
Meed is well worthy   the mastery to have.'

William Langland: from Piers Plowman, *passus iii*

1802—William and Dorothy Wordsworth walked beside Grasmere

[What Dorothy saw]

. . . When we were in the woods beyond Gowbarrow Park we saw a few daffodils close to the waterside. We fancied that the lake had floated the seeds ashore, and that the little colony had so sprung up. But as we went along there were more and yet more; and at last, under the boughs of the trees, we saw that there was a long belt of them along the shore, about the breadth of a country turnpike road. I never saw daffodils so beautiful. They grew among the mossy stones about and about them; some rested their heads upon these stones as on a pillow for weariness; and the rest tossed and reeled and danced, and seemed as if they verily laughed with the wind, that blew upon them over the lake; they looked so gay, ever glancing, ever changing.

[What William 'recollected in tranquility' two years later]

> I wandered lonely as a cloud
> That floats on high o'er vales and hills
> When all at once I saw a crowd,
> A host of golden daffodils;
> Beside the lake, beneath the trees,
> Fluttering and dancing in the breeze.
>
> Continuous as the stars that shine
> And twinkle on the milky way,
> They stretched in never-ending line
> Along the margin of the bay;
> Ten thousand saw I at a glance
> Tossing their heads in sprightly dance.
>
> The waves beside them danced; but they
> Out-did the sparkling waves in glee:
> A poet could not but be gay
> In such a jocund company:
> I gazed – and gazed – but little thought
> What wealth the show to me had brought.
>
> For oft, when on my couch I lie
> In vacant or in pensive mood,
> They flash upon that inward eye
> Which is the bliss of solitude;
> And then my heart with pleasure fills,
> And dances with the daffodils.

1896—A. E. Housman's A Shropshire Lad *was reviewed in* The New Age

'Here at last is a note that has for long been lacking in English poetry – simplicity, to wit. This our time is rife with poets and poetasters, and the most carping critic is compelled to confess that very much of their work is on a very fair level of excellence. But there is so much of it, and it is all so much alike . . .

'The little volume before us contains, on well-nigh every page, essentially and distinctively new poetry. The individual voice rings out true and clear. It is not an inspiring voice; it perhaps speaks not to us of hope in the future, of glory in the past, or of joy in the present. But it says and sings things that have not been sung or said before, and this with a power and directness, and with a heart-penetrating quality for which one may seek in vain through the work of any contemporary lyrist. . . .'

> I hoed and trenched and weeded,
> And took the flowers to fair:
> I brought them home unheeded;
> The hue was not to wear.
>
> So up and down I sow them
> For lads like me to find,
> When I shall lie below them,
> A dead man out of mind.
>
> Some seed the birds devour,
> And some the season mars,
> But here and there will flower
> The solitary stars,
>
> And fields will yearly bear them
> As light-leaved spring comes on,
> And luckless lads will wear them
> When I am dead and gone.

1884—Thomas Hardy wrote the last page of The Mayor of Casterbridge

All was over at last, even her regrets for having misunderstood him on his last visit, for not having searched him out sooner, though these were deep and sharp for a good while. From this time forward, Elizabeth-Jane found herself in a latitude of calm weather, kindly and grateful in itself, and doubly so after the Capharnaum in which some of her preceding years had been spent. As the lively and sparkling emotions of her early married life cohered into an equable serenity, the finer movements of her nature found scope in discovering to the narrow-lived ones around her the secret (as she had once learnt it) of making limited opportunities endurable; which she deemed to consist in the cunning enlargement, by a species of microscopic treatment, of those minute forms of satisfaction that offer themselves to everybody not in positive pain; which, thus handled, have much of the same inspiriting effect upon life as wider interests cursorily embraced.

Her teaching had a reflex action upon herself, insomuch that she thought she could perceive no great personal difference between being respected in the nether parts of Casterbridge and glorified at the uppermost end of the social world. Her position was, indeed, to a marked degree one that, in the common phrase, afforded much to be thankful for. That she was not demonstratively thankful was no fault of hers. Her experience had been of a kind to teach her, rightly or wrongly, that the doubtful honour of a brief transit through a sorry world hardly called for effusiveness, even when the path was suddenly irradiated at some half-way point by daydreams rich as hers. But her strong sense that neither she nor any human being deserved less than was given, did not blind her to the fact that there were others receiving less who had deserved much more. And in being forced to class herself among the fortunate she did not cease to wonder at the persistence of the unforeseen, when the one to whom such unbroken tranquillity had been accorded in the adult stage was she whose youth had seemed to teach that happiness was but the occasional episode in a general drama of pain.

The End.

18 April

1775—Paul Revere rode through the county of Middlesex, Massachusetts, to warn of the coming attack on the illegal arsenals

. . .

It was twelve by the village clock
When he crossed the bridge into Medford town.
He heard the crowing of the cock,
And the barking of the farmer's dog,
And felt the damp of the river fog,
That rises after the sun goes down.

It was one by the village clock
When he galloped into Lexington.
He saw the gilded weathercock
Swim in the moonlight as he pass'd,
And the meeting-house windows, blank and bare,
Gaze at him with a spectral glare,
As if they already stood aghast
At the bloody work they would look upon.

It was two by the village clock
When he came to the bridge in Concord town.
He heard the bleating of the flock,
And the twitter of birds among the trees,
And felt the breath of the morning breeze
Blowing over the meadows brown.

. . .

So through the night rode Paul Revere,
And so through the night went his cry of alarm
To every Middlesex village and farm, –
A cry of defiance, and not of fear,
A voice in the darkness, a knock at the door,
And a word that shall echo for evermore!
For, borne on the night-wind of the Past,
Through all our history, to the last,
In the hour of darkness, and peril, and need,
The people will waken and listen and hear
The hurrying hoof-beats of that steed,
And the midnight message of Paul Revere.

Henry Wadsworth Longfellow, from Paul Revere's
Ride (*like many other of Longfellow's productions,
a poem designed specifically for children*)

1817—Charles Wolfe's 'The Burial of Sir John Moore at Corunna' was first published in the Newry Telegraph (*Ulster*)

Not a drum was heard, not a funeral note,
    As his corpse to the rampart we hurried;
Not a soldier discharged his farewell shot
    O'er the grave where our hero we buried.

We buried him darkly at dead of night,
    The sods with our bayonets turning;
By the struggling moonbeam's misty light
    And the lantern dimly burning.

No useless coffin enclosed his breast,
    Not in sheet nor in shroud we wound him;
But he lay like a warrior taking his rest
    With his martial cloak around him.

Few and short were the prayers we said,
    And we spoke not a word of sorrow:
But we steadfastly gazed on the face that was dead,
    And we bitterly thought of the morrow.

We thought, as we hollowed his narrow bed
    And smoothed down his lonely pillow,
That the foe and the stranger would tread o'er his head,
    And we far away on the billow! . . .

But half of our heavy task was done
    When the clock struck the hour for retiring;
And we heard the distant and random gun
    That the foe was sullenly firing.

Slowly and sadly we laid him down,
    From the field of his fame fresh and gory;
We carved not a line, and we raised not a stone,
    But we left him alone with his glory.

                                        Charles Wolfe

20 April 📖

1567—Arthur Golding finished, at Berwick-on-Tweed, his translation of Ovid's Metamorphosis, *a version which became a storehouse of incident, image, and phrase for later poets*

> *Medea* with hir haire not trust so much as in a lace,
> But flaring on hir shoulders twaine, and barefoote, with hir gowne
> Ungirded, gate hir out of doores and wandred up and downe
> Alone the dead time of the night: both Man, and Beast, and Bird
> Were fast a sleepe: the Serpents lie in trayling forward stird
> So softly as you would have thought they still a sleepe had bene.
> The moysting Ayre was whist: no leafe ye could have moving sene.
> The starres alonly faire and bright did in the welkin shine.
> To which she lifting up hir handes did thrise hirselfe encline,
> And thrice with water of the brooke hir haire besprincled shee:
> And gasping thrise she opte hir mouth: and bowing downe hir knee
> Upon the bare hard ground, she said: O trustie time of night
> Most faithfull unto privities, O golden starres whose light
> Doth jointly with the Moone succeede the beames that blaze by day
> And thou three headed *Hecate* who knowest best the way
> To compasse this our great attempt and art our chiefest stay:
> Ye Charmes and Witchcrafts, and thou Earth which both with herbe and weed
> Of mightie working furnishest the Wizardes at their neede:
> Ye Ayres and Windes: ye Elves of Hilles, of Brookes, of Woods alone,
> Of standing Lakes, and of the Night approche ye everychone.
> Through helpe of whom (her crooked bankes much wondring at the thing)
> I have compelled streames to rune cleane backward to their spring.
> By charmes I make the calme Seas rough, and make the rough Seas plaine
> And cover all the Skie with Cloudes, and chase them thence againe.
> By charmes I rayse and lay the windes, and burst the Vipers jaw,
> And from the bowels of the Earth both stones and trees do drawe.
> Whole Woods and Forestes I remove: I make the Mountaines shake,
> And even the Earth it selfe to grone and fearfully to quake.
> I call up dead men from their graves: and thee o lightsome Moone
> I darken oft, though beaten brasse abate thy perill soone
> Our sorcerie dimmes the Morning faire, and darkes the Sun at Noone.

From The. xv. Bookes of P. Ouidius Naso, entytuled Metamorphosis, translated oute of Latin into English meter, by Arthur Golding Gentleman, A worke very pleasaunt and delectable

1894—Bernard Shaw's Arms and the Man *was first produced by Florence Farr at the Avenue Theatre, in London, and ran for eleven weeks*

One strongly Liberal critic, the late Moy Thomas, who had, in the teeth of a chorus of dissent, received my first play with the most generous encouragement, declared, when Arms and The Man was produced, that I had struck a wanton blow at the cause of liberty in the Balkan Peninsula by mentioning that it was not a matter of course for a Bulgarian in 1885 to wash his hands every day. He no doubt saw soon afterwards the squabble, reported all through Europe, between Stambouloff and an eminent lady of the Bulgarian court who took exception to his neglect of his finger-nails. But it had no bearing on the real issue between my critics and myself, which was, whether the political and religious idealism which had inspired Gladstone to call for the rescue of these Balkan principalities from the despotism of the Turk, and converted miserably enslaved provinces into hopeful and gallant little States, will survive the general onslaught on idealism which is implicit, and indeed explicit, in Arms and The Man and the naturalist plays of the modern school. For my part I hope not; for idealism, which is only a flattering name for romance in politics and morals, is as obnoxious to me as romance in ethics or religion. In spite of a Liberal Revolution or two, I can no longer be satisfied with fictitious morals and fictitious good conduct, shedding fictitious glory on robbery, starvation, disease, crime, drink, war, cruelty, cupidity, and all the other commonplaces of civilization which drive men to the theatre to make foolish pretences that such things are progress, science, morals, religion, patriotism, imperial supremacy, national greatness, and all the other names the newspapers call them. On the other hand, I see plenty of good in the world working itself out as fast as the idealists will allow it; and if they would only let it alone and learn to respect reality, which would include the beneficial exercise of respecting themselves, and incidentally of respecting me, we should all get along much better and faster. At all events, I do not see moral chaos and anarchy as the alternative to romantic convention; and I am not going to pretend I do merely to please the people who are convinced that the world is held together only by the force of unanimous, strenuous, eloquent, trumpet-tongued lying. To me the tragedy and comedy of life lie in the consequences, sometimes terrible, sometimes ludicrous, of our persistent attempts to found our institutions on the ideals suggested to our imaginations by our half-satisfied passions, instead of on a genuinely scientific natural history. And with that hint as to what I am driving at, I withdraw and ring up the curtain.

G. B. Shaw: from 'Preface' to Plays Pleasant

22 April 📖

1930—The Oxford Mail *published the following Obituary on Robert Bridges*

The Poet Laureate, Dr. Robert Bridges, O.M., died yesterday after a short illness at his home, Chilswell House, Boars Hill, Oxford, in his 86th year.

There is a legend that his favourite word was 'damn'. It was not. But he held it in high esteem as an aid to emphatic speech.

When he wished to work, he went to a little summer-house in his garden. It is a remarkable place; by a cunning arrangement of yellow silk hangings and subdued lighting, it is suffused in a golden glow, and in it Dr. Bridges wrote his 'Testament of Beauty'.

When he ventured down the hill to Oxford, he did so in a very old and battered Ford car, which he often drove himself. Mr. John Masefield, driving another car, sometimes raced him down the valley.

The Poet Laureate was sensible to the demands made by the dignity of his office. He dressed the part. Sometimes he wore a cloak. Always he wore a wide sombrero hat beneath which his white hair flowed with careless grace. His wide bow-tie enchanted every undergraduate. It was usually a red tie.

As an undergraduate, he was a notable oarsman, and he was probably the only man who ever refused to stroke the Oxford University boat. This he did on the ground that he could not spare time from the work which he was then doing for his medieval degree.

1564—Presumed birthday of William Shakespeare

Birthdays of this species have a public as well as a private phase. My 'boyhood's home', Dullborough, presents a case in point. An Immortal Somebody was wanted in Dullborough, to dimple for a day the stagnant face of the waters; he was rather wanted by Dullborough generally, and much wanted by the principal hotel-keeper. The County History was looked up for a locally Immortal Somebody, but the registered Dullborough worthies were all Nobodies. In this state of things, it is hardly necessary to record that Dullborough did what every man does when he wants to write a book or deliver a lecture, and is provided with all the materials except a subject. It fell back upon Shakespeare.

No sooner was it resolved to celebrate Shakespeare's birthday in Dullborough, than the popularity of the immortal bard became surprising. You might have supposed the first edition of his works to have been published last week, and enthusiastic Dullborough to have got half through them. (I doubt, by the way, whether it had ever done half that, but this is a private opinion.) A young gentleman with a sonnet, the retention of which for two years had enfeebled his mind and undermined his knees, got the sonnet into the Dullborough Warden, and gained flesh. Portraits of Shakespeare broke out in the bookshop windows, and our principal artist painted a large original portrait in oils for the decoration of the dining-room. It was not in the least like any of the other portraits, and was exceedingly admired, the head being much swollen. . . . Distinguished speakers were invited down, and very nearly came (but not quite). Subscriptions were opened, and committees sat, and it would have been far from a popular measure in the height of the excitement, to have told Dullborough that it wasn't Stratford-upon-Avon. Yet, after all these preparations, when the great festivity took place, and the portrait, elevated aloft, surveyed the company as if it were in danger of springing a mine of intellect and blowing itself up, it did undoubtedly happen, according to the inscrutable mystery of things, that nobody could be induced, not to say to touch upon Shakespeare, but to come within a mile of him, until the crack speaker of Dullborough rose to propose the immortal memory. Which he did with the perplexing and astonishing result that before he had repeated the great name half-a-dozen times, or had been upon his legs as many minutes, he was assailed with a general shout of 'Question'.

Charles Dickens: from The Uncommercial Traveller

1816—Byron was forced to leave England forever, as a result of his incestuous relations with Augusta Leigh

---

MR FLOSKY: [Coleridge]	How can we be cheerful when we are surrounded by a *reading public*, that is growing too wise for its betters?
SCYTHROP: [Shelley]	How can we be cheerful when our great general designs are crossed every moment by our little particular passions?
MR CYPRESS: [Byron]	How can we be cheerful in the midst of disappointment and despair?
MR GLOWRY:	Let us all be unhappy together.
MR HILARY:	Let us sing a catch. . . .
ALL:	A song from Mr Cypress.
MR CYPRESS:	There is a fever of the spirit,

    The brand of Cain's unresting doom,
Which in the lone dark souls that bear it
    Glows like the lamp in Tullia's tomb:
Unlike that lamp, its subtle fire
    Burns, blasts, consumes its cell, the heart,
Till, one by one, hope, joy, desire,
    Like dreams of shadowy smoke depart. . . .

MR GLOWRY:	Admirable. Let us all be unhappy together.
MR HILARY:	Now, I say again, a catch . . .
MR HILARY AND THE REVEREND MR LARYNX:	Seamen three! What men be ye? Gotham's three wise men we be. Whither in your bowl so free?

To rake the moon from out of the sea.
The bowl goes trim. The moon doth shine.
And our ballast is old wine;
And our ballast is old wine. . . .

Mr Cypress, having his ballast on board, stepped, the same evening, into his bowl, or travelling chariot, and departed to rake seas and rivers, lakes and canals, for the moon of ideal beauty.

Thomas Love Peacock: from Nightmare Abbey

1856—Charles Dodgson ('Lewis Carroll') wrote in his diary: 'I mark this day with a white stone': he had met for the first time three-year-old Alice Liddell. Six years later she was to be the 'Secunda' of the boating-picnic party to whom he began to tell the story of Alice's Adventures in Wonderland

All in the golden afternoon
　　Full leisurely we glide;
For both our oars, with little skill,
　　By little arms are plied,
While little hands make vain pretence
　　Our wanderings to guide.

Ah, cruel Three! In such an hour,
　　Beneath such dreamy weather,
To beg a tale of breath too weak
　　To stir the tiniest feather!
Yet what can one poor voice avail
　　Against three tongues together?

Imperious Prima flashes forth
　　Her edict 'to begin it' –
In gentler tone Secunda hopes
　　'There will be nonsense in it!'
While Tertia interrupts the tale
　　Not *more* than once a minute.

Anon, to sudden silence won,
　　In fancy they pursue
The dream-child moving through a land
　　Of wonders wild and new,
In friendly chat with bird or beast –
　　And half believe it true. . . .

Thus grew the tale of Wonderland:
　　Thus slowly, one by one,
Its quaint events were hammered out –
　　And now the tale is done;
And home we steer, a merry crew,
　　Beneath the setting sun. . . .

　　　　　　Lewis Carroll: Introductory Verses to Alice's
　　　　　　Adventures in Wonderland

1862—Emily Dickinson wrote a second time to Thomas Wentworth Higginson

---

Mr. Higginson, – Your kindness claimed earlier gratitude, but I was ill, and write today from my pillow.

Thank you for the surgery; it was not so painful as I supposed. I bring you others, as you ask, though they might not differ. While my thought is undressed, I can make no distinction; but when I put them in the gown, they look alike and numb.

You ask how old I was? I made no verse, but one or two, until this winter, sir.

I had a terror since September, I could tell to none; and so I sing, as the boy does of the burying ground, because I am afraid.

You inquire my books. For poets, I have Keats, and Mr. and Mrs. Browning. For prose, Mr. Ruskin, Sir Thomas Browne, and the 'Revelations'! I went to school, but in your manner of the phrase had no education. When a little girl, I had a friend who taught me Immortality; but venturing too near, himself, he never returned. Soon after my tutor died, and for several years my lexicon was my only companion. Then I found one more, but he was not contented I be his scholar, so he left the land. . . .

I have a brother and sister; my mother does not care for thought; and father, too busy with his briefs to notice what we do. He buys me many books, but begs me not to read them, because he fears they joggle the mind. They are religious, except me, and address an eclipse, every morning, whom they call their 'Father'.

But I fear my story fatigues you. I would like to learn. Could you tell me how to grow, or is it unconveyed, like melody or witchcraft?

You speak of Mr. Whitman. I never read his book, but was told that it was disgraceful.

I read Miss Prescott's 'Circumstance', but it followed me in the dark, so I avoided her.

Two editors of journals came to my father's house this winter, and asked me for my mind, and when I asked them 'why' they said I was penurious, and they would use it for the world.

I could not weigh myself, myself. My size felt small to me. I read your chapters in the 'Atlantic', and experienced honor for you. I was sure you would not reject a confiding question.

Is this, sir, what you asked me to tell you?

Your friend,

Emily Dickinson

1932—Hart Crane committed suicide by leaping from the s.s. Orizaba *into the sea, about three hundred miles north of Havana*

Voyages II.

– – And yet this great wink of eternity,
Of rimless floods, unfettered leewardings,
Samite sheeted and processioned where
Her undinal vast belly moonward bends,
Laughing the wrapt inflections of our love;

Take this Sea, whose diapason knells
On scrolls of silver snowy sentences,
The sceptred terror of whose sessions rends
As her demeanors motion well or ill,
All but the pieties of lovers' hands.

And onward, as bells off San Salvador
Salute the crocus lustres of the stars,
In these poinsettia meadows of her tides, –
Adagios of islands, O my Prodigal,
Complete the dark confessions her veins spell.

Mark how her turning shoulders wind the hours,
And hasten while her penniless rich palms
Pass superscription of bent foam and wave, –
Hasten, while they are true, – sleep, death, desire,
Close round one instant in one floating flower.

Bind us in time, O Seasons clear, and awe.
O minstrel galleons of Carib fire,
Bequeath us to no earthly shore until
Is answered in the vortex of our grave
The seal's wide spindrift gaze toward paradise.

Hart Crane

Felix Randal

Felix Randal the farrier, O is he dead then? my duty all ended,
Who have watched his mould of man, big-boned and hardy-handsome
Pining, pining, till time when reason rambled in it and some
Fatal four disorders, fleshed there, all contended?

Sickness broke him. Impatient he cursed at first, but mended
Being anointed and all; though a heavenlier heart began some
Months earlier, since I had our sweet reprieve and ransom
Tendered to him. Ah well, God rest him all road ever he offended!

This seeing the sick endears them to us, us too it endears.
My tongue had taught thee comfort, touch had quenched thy tears,
Thy tears that touched my heart, child, Felix, poor Felix Randal;

How far from then forethought of, all thy more boisterous years,
When thou at the random grim forge, powerful amidst peers,
Didst fettle for the great grey drayhorse his bright and battering sandal!

G. M. Hopkins

1752—Adam Smith was moved from the chair of logic to that of moral philosophy at the University of Glasgow

Consumption is the sole end and purpose of all production; and the interest of the producer ought to be attended to only so far as it may be necessary for promoting that of the consumer. The maxim is so perfectly self-evident that it would be absurd to attempt to prove it. But in the mercantile system the interest of the consumer is almost constantly sacrificed to that of the producer; and it seems to consider production, and not consumption, as the ultimate end and object of all industry and commerce. . . .

But in the system of laws which has been established for the management of our American and West Indian colonies, the interest of the home consumer has been sacrificed to that of the producer with a more extravagant profusion than in all our other commercial regulations. A great empire has been established for the sole purpose of raising up a nation of customers who should be obliged to buy from the shops of our different producers all the goods with which these could supply them. For the sake of that little enhancement of price which this monopoly might afford our producers, the home consumers have been burdened with the whole expense of maintaining and defending that empire. . . .

It cannot be very difficult to determine who have been the contrivers of this whole mercantile system; not the consumers, we may believe, whose interest has been entirely neglected; but the producers, whose interest has been so carefully attended to; and among this latter class our merchants and manufacturers have been by far the principal architects. . . .

> *Adam Smith: from* The Wealth of Nations
> (*1776–8*)

1642—Richard Lovelace, on the King's behalf, presented to Parliament the Kentish Petition in favour of the Bishops and of the liturgy and common prayer ; for this, he was imprisoned for seven weeks in the Gate House, Westminster, where he wrote the lines, 'To Althea, from prison'

When love with unconfinëd wings
    Hovers within my gates,
And my divine Althea brings
    To whisper at the grates;
When I lie tangled in her hair,
    And fettered to her eye,
The gods that wanton in the air
    Know no such liberty.

When flowing cups run swiftly round
    With no allaying Thames,
Our careless heads with roses bound,
    Our hearts with loyal flames;
When thirsty grief in wine we steep,
    When healths and draughts go free,
Fishes that tipple in the deep
    Know no such liberty.

When, like committed linnets, I
    With shriller throat shall sing
The sweetness, mercy, majesty
    And glories of my King;
When I shall voice aloud how good
    He is, how great should be,
Enlargëd winds that curl the flood
    Know no such liberty.

Stone walls do not a prison make,
    Nor iron bars a cage;
Minds innocent and quiet take
    That for an hermitage;
If I have freedom in my love,
    And in my soul am free,
Angels alone that soar above
    Enjoy such liberty.

Richard Lovelace: 'To Althea'

Maye.

Hymn XIII

St. Philip and St. James

Now the winds are all composure,
    But the breath upon the bloom,
Blowing sweet o'er each enclosure
    Grateful off'rings of perfume.

Tansy, calaminth, and daisies,
    On the river's margin thrive;
And accompany the mazes
    Of the stream that leaps alive. . . .

Beeches, without order seemly,
    Shade the flow'rs of annual birth,
And the lily smiles supremely
    Mention'd by the Lord on earth.

Cowslips seize upon the fallow,
    And the cardamine in white,
Where the corn-flow'rs join the mallow,
    Joy and health, and thrift unite. . . .

Hark! aloud, the black-bird whistles,
    With surrounding fragrance blest,
And the goldfinch in the thistles
    Makes provision for her nest.

Ev'n the hornet hives his honey,
    Bluecap builds his stately dome,
And the rocks supply the coney
    With a fortress and a home.

But the servants of their Saviour,
    Which with gospel-peace are shod,
Have no bed but what the paviour
    Makes them in the porch of God. . . .

Christopher Smart: from Hymns and Spiritual
Songs for the Fasts and Festivals of the Church
of England (*1765*)

1850—John Greenleaf Whittier's 'Ichabod' written in anger and despair over Daniel Webster's 'betrayal' of the Abolitionist cause in his 'Seventh of March' speech, was published in The National Era. *The name 'Ichabod', which means 'the glory is departed' had been applied to Webster by Oliver Wendell Holmes*

So fallen! so lost! the light withdrawn
    Which once he wore!
The glory from his grey hairs gone
    Forevermore!

Revile him not, the Tempter hath
    A snare for all;
And pitying tears, not scorn and wrath
    Befit his fall!

Oh, dumb be passion's stormy rage,
    When he who might
Have lighted up and led his age,
    Falls back in night.

Scorn! would the angels laugh, to mark
    A bright soul driven,
Fiend-goaded, down the endless dark
    From hope and heaven! . . .

Of all we loved and honored, naught
    Save power remains;
A fallen angel's pride of thought,
    Still strong in chains.

All else is gone; from those great eyes
    The soul has fled:
When faith is lost, when honor dies,
    The man is dead!

Then, pay the reverence of old days
    To his dead fame;
Walk backward, with averted gaze,
    And hide the shame!

1810—Lord Byron, accompanied by Lt Ekenhead, swam across the Hellespont

If, in the month of dark December,
  Leander, who was nightly wont
(What maid will not the tale remember?)
  To cross thy stream, broad Hellespont!

If, when the wintry tempest roared,
  He sped to Hero, nothing loth,
And thus of old thy current poured,
  Fair Venus, how I pity both!

For *me*, degenerate modern wretch,
  Though in the genial month of May,
My dripping limbs I faintly stretch,
  And think I've done a feat today.

But since he crossed the rapid tide,
  According to the doubtful story,
To woo – and – Lord knows what beside,
  And swam for Love, as I for Glory;

'Twere hard to say who fared the best;
  Sad mortals! thus the gods still plague you!
He lost his labour, I my jest;
  For he was drowned, and I've the ague.

*George Gordon, Lord Byron: 'Written after
Swimming from Sestos to Abydos'*

4 May 📖

1862(?)—*'A Mad Tea-Party'*

('. . . perhaps, as this is May, *it won't be raving mad—at least not so mad as it was in* March')

The Hatter was the first to break the silence. 'What day of the month is it?' he said, turning to Alice; he had taken his watch out of his pocket, and was looking at it uneasily, shaking it every now and then, and holding it to his ear.

Alice considered a little, and then said, 'The fourth.'

'Two days wrong!' sighed the Hatter. 'I told you butter wouldn't suit the works!' he added, looking angrily at the March Hare.

'It was the *best* butter', the March Hare meekly replied. . . .

Alice had been looking over his shoulder with some curiosity. 'What a funny watch!' she remarked. 'It tells the day of the month, and doesn't tell what o'clock it is!'

'Why should it?' muttered the Hatter. 'Does *your* watch tell you what year it is?'

'Of course not', Alice replied very readily. 'But that's because it stays the same year for such a long time together.'

'Which is just the same with *mine*', said the Hatter.

Alice felt dreadfully puzzled. . . .

'Have you guessed the riddle yet?' the Hatter said, turning to Alice again.

'No, I give up', Alice replied: 'what's the answer?'

'I haven't the slightest idea', said the Hatter.

'Nor I', said the March Hare.

Alice sighed wearily. 'I think you might do something better with time', she said, 'than waste it asking riddles with no answers.'

'If you knew Time as well as I do', said the Hatter, 'you wouldn't talk about wasting *it*. It's *him*.'

'I don't know what you mean', said Alice.

'Of course you don't!' the Hatter said, tossing his head contemptuously. 'I dare say you never even spoke to Time!'

'Perhaps not', Alice cuatiously replied; 'but I know I have to beat time when I learn music.'

'Ah! that accounts for it', said the Hatter. 'He won't stand beating. Now, if you only kept on good terms with him, he'd do almost anything you liked with the clock.'

Lewis Carroll: from Alice's Adventures in Wonderland

1640—Thomas Hobbes discovered that his Elements of Law, Natural and Politic *had 'occasioned much talk of the author, and had not his majesty dissolved the parliament, it had brought him into the danger of his life'*

... the greatest inconvenience that can happen to a commonwealth, is the aptitude to dissolve into civil war; and to this are the monarchies much less subject, than any other governments. For where the union, or band of a commonwealth, is one man, there is no distraction; whereas in assemblies, those that are of different opinions, are apt to fall out among themselves, and to cross the designs of commonwealth for one another's sake: and when they cannot have the honour of making good their own devices, they yet seek the honour to make the counsels of their adversaries to prove vain. And in this contention, when the opposite factions happen to be anything equal in strength, they presently fall to war. Wherein necessity teacheth both sides, that an absolute monarch, (viz.) a general, is necessary both for their defence against one another, and also for the peace of each faction within itself. ...

For maintaining of peace at home ... there ought to be some means for keeping under of those, that are disposed to rebellion by ambition. ... Another thing necessary, is the rooting out from the consciences of men all those opinions which seem to justify, and give pretence of right to rebellious actions; such as are: the opinion, that a man can do nothing lawfully against his private conscience; that they who have the sovereignty, are subject to the civil laws; that there is any authority of subjects, whose negative may hinder the affirmative of the sovereign power; that any subject hath a propriety distinct from the dominion of the commonwealth; that there is a body of the people without him or them that have the sovereign power; and that any lawful sovereign may be resisted under the name of tyrant. ...

And because opinions which are gotten by education, and in length of time are made habitual, cannot be taken away by force, and upon the sudden: they must therefore be taken away also, by time and education. And seeing the said opinions have proceeded from private and public teaching, and those teachers have received them from grounds and principles, which they have learned in the Universities, from the doctrine of Aristotle, and others (who have delivered nothing concerning morality and policy demonstratively; but being passionately addicted to popular government, have insinuated their opinions, by eloquent sophistry): there is no doubt, if the true doctrine concerning the law of nature, and the properties of a body politic ... were perspicuously set down and taught in the Universities, but that young men, who come thither void of prejudice ... would more easily receive the same, and afterwards teach the people.

1687—'Your discourse about the liberty of conscience [Locke's Letter Concerning Toleration] *would not be amiss now, to dispose people's minds to pass it into law whenever the Parliament sits . . .'*

Tyrell to John Locke, 6 May 1687

Every man has an immortal soul, capable of eternal happiness or misery, whose happiness depending upon his believing and doing those things in his life which are necessary to the obtaining of God's favour, and are prescribed by God to that end. It follows from thence first, that the observance of these things is the highest obligation that lies upon mankind, and that our utmost care, application, and diligence ought to be exercised in the search and performance of them; because there is nothing in this world that is of any consideration in comparison with eternity. Secondly, that seeing one man does not violate the right of another by his erroneous opinions and undue manner or worship, nor is his perdition any prejudice to another man's affairs, therefore, the care of each man's salvation belongs only to himself. . . . Anyone may employ as many exhortations and arguments as he pleases, toward the promoting of another man's salvation. But all force and compulsion are to be forborne. . . .

But besides their souls, which are immortal, men have also their temporal lives here upon earth; the state whereof being frail and fleeting, and the duration uncertain, they have need of several outward conveniences to the support thereof, which are to be procured or preserved by pains and industry. . . . But the pravity of mankind being such that they had rather injuriously prey upon the fruits of other men's labours than take pains to provide for themselves, the necessity of preserving men in the possession of what honest industry has already acquired, and also of preserving their liberty and strength, whereby they may acquire what they further want, obliges men to enter into society with one another, that by mutual assistance and joint force they may secure unto each other their properties, in the things that contribute to the comfort and happiness of this life, leaving in the meanwhile to every man the care of his own eternal happiness, the attainment of which can neither be facilitated by another man's industry, nor can the loss of it turn to another man's prejudice. . . . This is the original, this is the use, and these are the bounds of the legislative (which is the supreme) power in every commonwealth. . . .

These things being thus explained, it is easy to understand to what end the legislative power ought to be directed, and by what means regulated; and that it is the temporal good and outward prosperity of the society, which is the sole reason of men's entering into society, and the only thing they seek and aim at in it. And it is also evident what liberty remains to men in reference to their eternal salvation. . . . For obedience is due, in the first place, to God, and afterwards to the laws.

John Locke: from A Letter Concerning Toleration

A.D. 878—King Alfred won a victory over the Danes in the Battle of Ethandune (at the Hill of the White Horse)

The Northmen came about our land,
    A Christless chivalry,
Who knew not of the arch or pen:
Great, beautiful half-witted men
    From the sunrise and the sea.

Misshapen ships stood on the deep
    Full of strange gold and fire,
And hairy men, as huge as sin,
With horned heads, came wading in
    Through the long, low sea-mire. . . .

Then Alfred, King of England,
    Bade blow the horns of war,
And fling the Golden Dragon out,
With crackle and acclaim and shout,
    Scrolled and aflame and far.

And under the Golden Dragon
    Went Wessex all along,
Past the sharp point of the cloven ways,
Out from the black wood into the blaze
    Of sun and steel and song.

And when they came to the open land
    They wheeled, deployed, and stood;
Midmost were Marcus and the King,
And Eldred on the right-hand wing,
And leftwards Colan darkling,
    In the last shade of the wood.

But the Earls of the Great Army
    Lay like a long half moon,
Ten poles before their palisades,
With wide-winged helms and runic blades,
Red giants of an age of raids,
    In the thornland of Ethandune.

G. K. Chesterton: from 'The Ballad of the White Horse'

1373—Juliana of Norwich received her revelation that 'all shall be well, and all shall be well, and all manner of thing shall be well'

This is a Revelation of Love that Jesus Christ, our endless bliss, made in Sixteen Shewings, or Revelations particular. . . . These Revelations were shewed to a simple creature unlettered, the year of our Lord 1373, the Eighth day of May. . . .

And when I was thirty years old and a half, God sent me a bodily sickness, in which I lay three days and three nights; and on the fourth night I took all my rites of Holy Church, and weened not to have lived till day. And after this I languored forth two days and two nights, and on the third night I weened oftentimes to have passed, and so weened they that were with me.

And being in youth as yet, I thought it great sorrow to die; – but for nothing that was in earth that meliked to live for, nor for no pain that I had fear of; for I trusted in God of His mercy. But it was to have lived that I might have loved God better, and longer time, that I might have the more knowing and loving of God in bliss of heaven. . . . And I understood by my reason and by my feeling of my pains that I should die. . . .

After this my sight began to fail, and it was all dark about me in the chamber, as if it had been night, save in the Image of the Cross, whereon I beheld a common light; and I wist not how. . . . After this the upper part of my body began to die, so far forth that scarcely I had any feeling; – with shortness of breath. And then I weened in sooth to have passed.

And in this moment suddenly all my pain was taken from me, and I was as whole (and specially in the upper part of my body) as ever I was afore. . . . Then came suddenly to my mind that I should desire the second wound of our Lord's gracious gift. . . . But in this I desired never bodily sight nor shewing of God, but compassion such as a kind soul might have with our Lord Jesus, that for love would be a mortal man: and therefore I desired to suffer with him.

The First Revelation

In this moment suddenly I saw the red blood trickle down from under the Garland hot and freshly and right plenteously, as it were in the time of His Passion when the Garland of Thorns was pressed on His blessed head who was both God and Man. . . .

And in the same Shewing suddenly the Trinity fulfilled my heart most of joy. And so I understood it shall be in heaven without end to all that shall come there. . . . And I said, 'Benedicite Domine!'

Juliana of Norwich: from Revelations of Divine Love (*ed. Grace Warrack*)

1839—Emily Jane Brontë wrote the poem which Fannie E. Ratchford has shown to be intended as the lament of 'Augusta Geraldine Almeda' (the heroine of Emily and Ann Brontë's 'Gondal' stories) on the death of her child

A. G. A.   To the Bluebell   E.   May 9, 1839

Sacred watcher, wave thy bells!
Fair hill flower and woodland child!
Dear to me in deep green dells –
Dearest on the mountains wild.

Bluebell, even as all divine
I have seen my darling shine –
Bluebell, even as wan and frail
I have seen my darling fail –
Thou hast found a voice for me,
And soothing words are breathed by thee.

Thus they murmur, 'Summer's sun
Warms me till my life is done.
Would I rather choose to die
Under winter's ruthless sky?

'Glad I bloom and calm I fade;
Weeping twilight dews my bed;
Mourner, mourner, dry thy tears –
Sorrow comes with lengthened years!'

From The Complete Poems of Emily Jane Brontë, *edited from the manuscripts by C. W. Hatfield, N. Y. (Columbia University Press), 1941, 1947.*

10 May

1762—David Hume thanked Benjamin Franklin for the invention of the lightning-rod

Dear Sir

I have a great many Thanks to give you for your Goodness in remembering my Request, and for the exact Description, which you sent me of your Method of preserving Houses from Thunder. I communicated it to our philosophical Society, as you gave me Permission; and they desire me to tell you that they claim it as their own, and intend to enrich with it the first Collection, which they may publish. The establish'd Rule of our Society is, that, after a paper is read to them, it is delivered by them to some Member, who is oblig'd, in a subsequent Meeting, to read some Paper of Remarks upon it. It was communicated to our Friend, Mr Russel; who is not very expeditious in finishing any Undertaking; and he did not read his Remarks, till the last Week, which is the Reason, why I have been so late in acknowledging your Favour. Mr Russel's Remarks, besides the just Praises of your Invention, contain'd only two Proposals for improving it: One was, that in Houses, where the Rain Water is carry'd off the Roof by a lead Pipe, this metallic Body might be employd as a Conductor to the electric Fire, and save the Expence of a new Apparatus: Another was, that the Wire might be carry'd down to the Foundation of the House, and be thence convey'd below Ground to the requisite Distance, which would better secure it against Accidents. I thought it proper to convey to you these two Ideas of so ingenious a Man, that you might adopt them, if they appear to you well founded.

I have sent off your Letter to Lord Mareschal, who will consider himself as much beholden to you. His Lordship is at present very much employ'd in settling the Controversy about the Eternity of Hell-Torments, which has set the little Republic of Neuf-chatel in Combustion. I have ventur'd to recommend to his Lordship the abridging these Torments as much as possible, and I have told him, that, as we have taken so much Pains to preserve him & his Subjects from the Fires of Heaven, they cannot do less than to guard us from the Fires of Hell. . . .

I am very sorry, that you intend soon to leave our Hemisphere. America has sent us many good things, Gold, Silver, Sugar, Tobacco, Indigo, &c: But you are the first Philosopher, and indeed the first Great Man of Letters for whom we are beholden to her: It is our own Fault, that we have not kept him: Whence it appears, that we do not agree with Solomon, that Wisdom is above Gold: For we take care never to send back an Ounce of the latter, which we once lay our Fingers upon.

I saw yesterday our Friend Sir Alexander Dick, who desir'd me to present his Compliments to you. We are all very unwilling to think of your settling in America, and that there is some Chance of our never seeing you again: But no-one regrets it more than does

Dear Sir
Your most affectionate humble servant

David Hume

Edinburgh
10 May 1762

1869—'I think on the back should be put, on one panel, Matthew Arnold's Poems *... It must not be* Arnold's Poems *because the Arnolds are legion ...'*

M.A. to his publisher, Frederick Macmillan

The sea is calm tonight.
The tide is full, the moon lies fair
Upon the straits; – on the French coast the light
Gleams and is gone; the cliffs of England stand,
Glimmering and vast, out in the tranquil bay.
Come to the window, sweet is the night-air!

Only, from the long line of spray
Where the sea meets the moon-blanch'd land,
Listen! you hear the grating roar
Of pebbles which the waves draw back, and fling,
At their return, up the high strand,
Begin, and cease, and then again begin,
With tremulous cadence slow, and bring
The eternal note of sadness in. . . .

The Sea of Faith
Was once, too, at the full, and round earth's shore
Lay like the folds of a bright girdle furl'd.
But now I only hear
Its melancholy, long, withdrawing roar,
Retreating, to the breath
Of the night-wind, down the vast edges drear
And naked shingles of the world.

Ah, love, let us be true
To one another! for the world, which seems
To lie before us like a land of dreams,
So various, so beautiful, so new,
Hath really neither joy, nor love, nor light,
Nor certitude, nor peace, nor help for pain;
And we are here as on a darkling plain
Swept with confused alarms of struggle and flight,
Where ignorant armies clash by night.

Matthew Arnold: from 'Dover Beach'

1515—Sir Thomas More left England as Henry VIII's ambassador to Flanders. It was during this assignment (before December 1516) that he wrote his Utopia

I never saw a clearer instance of the different impressions that different customs make on people, than I observed in the ambassadors of the Anemolians who came to Amaurot when I was there . . . they being a vainglorious, rather than a wise people, resolved to set themselves out with so much pomp, that they should look like gods, and so strike the eyes of the poor Utopians with their splendour. Thus three ambassadors made their entry with an hundred attendants, that were all clad in garments of different colours, and the greater part in silk; the ambassadors themselves, who were of the nobility of their country, were in cloth of gold, and adorned with massy chains, ear-rings, and rings of gold: their caps were covered with bracelets set full of pearls and other gems: in a word, they were set out with all those things, that among the Utopians were either the badges of slavery, the marks of infamy or children's rattles.

It was not unpleasant to see on the one side how they looked big, when they compared their rich habits with the plain clothes of the Utopians, who were come out in great numbers to see them make their entry: and on the other side, to observe how much they were mistaken in the impression which they hoped this pomp would have made on them: it appeared so ridiculous a show to all that had never stirred out of their country, and so had not seen the customs of other nations, that though they paid some reverence to those that were the most meanly clad, as if they had been the ambassadors, yet when they saw the ambassadors themselves so full of gold chains, they looking upon them as slaves, made them no reverence at all. You might have seen their children, who were grown up to that bigness that they had thrown away their jewels, call to their mothers, and push them gently, and cry out, See that great fool that wears pearls and gems, as if he were yet a child. And their mothers answered them in good earnest, Hold your peace, this is, I believe, one of the ambassador's fools. . . .

The Utopians wonder how any man should be so much taken with the glaring doubtful lustre of a jewel or stone, that can look up to a star, or to the sun himself; or how any should value himself because his cloth is made of a finer thread: for how fine soever that thread may be, it was once no better than the fleece of a sheep, and that sheep was a sheep still for all its wearing it. They wonder much to hear that gold, which in itself is so useless a thing, should be everywhere so much esteemed, that even men for whom it was made, and by whom it has its value, should yet be thought of less value than it is: so that a man of lead, who has no more sense than a log of wood, and is as bad as he is foolish, should have many wise and good men serving him, only because he has a great heap of that metal. . . .

Thomas More: from Utopia

1933—The Burning of the Books in Nazi Germany

It is important to remember that Germany had to make war on her own people before she could attack Europe. So much has been happening lately that we sometimes forget that during the past seven years she robbed and tortured and interned and expelled and killed thousands and thousands of her own citizens. When she got rid of them, and not until then, she was in a position to transfer operations, and start against France and England. . . .

Now for literature. Let me recall that famous burning of the books, for it illustrates better than any single event can the way in which Germany has been behaving to Germans. The Nazis wished it to symbolize their cultural outlook, and it will. It took place on 13 May 1933. That night twenty-five thousand volumes were destroyed outside the University of Berlin, in the presence of forty thousand people. Most people enjoy a blaze, and we are told that the applause was tremendous. Some of the books were by Jews, others communist, others liberal, others 'unscientific', and all of them were 'un-German'. It was for the government to decide what was un-German. There was an elaborate ritual. Nine heralds came forward in turn, and consigned an author with incantations to the flames. . . . There were holocausts in the provinces, too, and students were instructed to erect 'pillars of infamy' outside their universities; the pillar should be 'a thick tree-trunk, somewhat above the height of a man', to which were to be nailed 'the utterances of those who, by their participation in activities defamatory of character, have forfeited their membership in the German nation'. Note the reference to 'character', it is significant. 'Character', like the 'soul', is always an opportunity for brutality. The Burning of the Books was followed by a systematic control of literature. A bureau was created to look after public libraries, second-hand shops were purged, books may not be published without licence, and a licence is also required for commenting.

Unfortunately for the Nazis, not all books are modern books. Germany has had a great literature in the past, and they have had to do something about that. They have been especially troubled by Goethe and Heine. Over Heine they have taken a strong line, since he was a Jew; they have denounced him as 'the most baneful fellow that has ever passed through German life, soul-devastating, soul-poisoning' (notice again the 'soul'), and have banned his works. Goethe had to be treated with more respect – so far as I know, they have not banned Goethe. But they rightly consider him their arch-enemy. For Goethe believed in toleration, he was the nationalist who is ripe for super-nationalism, he was the German who was wanting Germany's genius to enrich the whole world. His spirit will re-arise when this madness and cruelty have passed.

E. M. Forster : 'What has Germany done to the Germans ?', the second of three broadcasts in 1940 (reprinted in Two Cheers for Democracy, *1951)*

1945—Dylan Thomas's 'A Refusal to Mourn the Death, by Fire, of a Child in London' was first published in The New Republic

Never until the mankind making
Bird beast and flower
Fathering and all humbling darkness
Tells with silence the last light breaking
And the still hour
Is come of the sea tumbling in harness

And I must enter again the round
Zion of the water bead
And the synagogue of the ear of corn
Shall I let pray the shadow of a sound
Or sow my salt seed
In the least valley of sackcloth to mourn

The majesty and burning of the child's death.
I shall not murder
The mankind of her going with a grave truth
Nor blaspheme down the stations of the breath
With any further
Elegy of innocence and youth.

Deep with the first dead lies London's daughter,
Robed in the long friends,
The grains beyond age, the dark veins of her mother,
Secret by the unmourning water
Of the riding Thames.
After the first death, there is no other.

1711—Jacob Tonson published the first edition of Alexander Pope's Essay on Criticism

But most by numbers judge a poet's song,
And smooth or rough, with them, is right or wrong:
In the bright muse, though thousand charms conspire,
Her voice is all these tuneful fools admire;
Who haunt Parnassus but to please their ear,
Not mend their minds; as some to church repair,
Not for the doctrine, but the music there.
These equal syllables alone require,
Though oft the ear the open vowels tire;
While expletives their feeble aid do join,
And ten low words oft creep in one dull line:
While they ring round the same unvaried chimes,
With sure return of still expected rhymes;
Where'er you find 'the cooling western breeze',
In the next line, it 'whispers through the trees':
If crystal streams 'with pleasing murmurs creep',
The reader's threaten'd (not in vain) with 'sleep'.
Then, at the last and only couplet fraught
With some unmeaning thing they call a thought,
A needless Alexandrine ends the song,
That, like a wounded snake, drags its slow length along.
    Leave such to tune their own dull rhymes, and know
What's roundly smooth, or languishingly slow;
And praise the easy vigour of a line
Where Denham's strength and Waller's sweetness join.
    True ease in writing comes from art, not chance,
As those move easiest who have learn'd to dance.
'Tis not enough no harshness gives offense;
The sound must seem an echo to the sense:
Soft is the strain when Zephyr gently blows,
And the smooth stream in smoother numbers flows;
But when loud surges lash the sounding shore,
The hoarse, rough verse should, like the torrent, roar.
When Ajax strives some rock's vast weight to throw,
The line, too, labours, and the words move slow:
Not so, when swift Camilla scours the plain,
Flies o'er th' unbending corn, and skims along the main.

An Essay on Criticism, *II, 337–373*

16 May

At last, on Monday the 16th of May, when I was sitting in Mr. Davies's back-parlour, after having drunk tea with him and Mrs. Davies, Johnson unexpectedly came into the shop; and Mr. Davies having perceived him through the glass-door in the room in which we were sitting, advancing towards us, – he announced his awful approach to me, somewhat in the manner of an actor in the part of Horatio, when he addresses Hamlet on the appearance of his father's ghost, 'Look, my lord, it comes.' I found that I had a very perfect idea of Johnson's figure, from the portrait of him painted by Sir Joshua Reynolds . . . Mr. Davies mentioned my name, and respectfully introduced me to him. I was much agitated; and recollecting his prejudice against the Scotch, of which I had heard much, I said to Davies, 'Don't tell where I come from.' – 'From Scotland', cried Davies, roguishly. 'Mr. Johnson, (said I) I do indeed come from Scotland, but I cannot help it.' I am willing to flatter myself that I meant this as light pleasantry to soothe and conciliate him, and not as an humiliating abasement at the expense of my country. But however that might be, this speech was somewhat unlucky; for with that quickness of wit for which he was so remarkable, he seized the expression 'come from Scotland', which I used in the sense of being of that country; and, as if I had said that I had come away from it, or left it, retorted, 'That, Sir, I find, is what a very great many of your countrymen cannot help.' This stroke stunned me a great deal; and when we had sat down, I felt myself not a little embarrassed, and apprehensive of what might come next. He then addressed himself to Davies: 'What do you think of Garrick? He has refused me an order for the play for Miss Williams, because he knows the house will be full, and that an order would be worth three shillings.' Eager to take any opening to get into conversation with him, I ventured to say, 'O, Sir, I cannot think Mr. Garrick would grudge such a trifle to you.' 'Sir, (said he, with a stern look,) I have known David Garrick longer than you have done: and I know no right you have to talk to me on the subject.' Perhaps I deserved this check; for it was rather presumptuous in me, an entire stranger, to express any doubt of the justice of his animadversion upon his old acquaintance and pupil. I now felt myself much mortified, and began to think, that the hope which I had long indulged of obtaining his acquaintance was blasted. And, in truth, had not my ardour been uncommonly strong, and my resolution uncommonly persevering, so rough a reception might have deterred me for ever from making any further attempts. Fortunately, however, I remained upon the field not wholly discomfited; and was soon rewarded by hearing some of his conversation.

James Boswell: from The Life of Johnson

1763—Horace Walpole entertained two Continental visitors to his 'stately home' at Strawberry Hill with some products of his famous private press

The French do not come hither *to see*. *A l'angloise* happened to be the word in fashion; and half a dozen of the most fashionable people have been the dupes of it. I take for granted that their next mode will be *a l'iroquoise*, that they may be under no obligation of realizing their pretensions. Madame de Boufflers I think will die a martyr to a taste, which she fancied she had, and finds she has not. Never having stirred ten miles from Paris, and having only rolled in an easy coach from one hotel to another on a gliding pavement, she is already worn out with being hurried from morning to night from one sight to another. She rises every morning so fatigued with the toils of the preceding day, that she has not strength, if she had inclination, to observe the least, or the finest thing she sees! She came hither today to a great breakfast I made for her, with her eyes a foot deep in her head, her hands dangling, and scarce able to support her knotting-bag. She had been yesterday to see a ship launched, and went from Greenwich by water to Ranelagh. Madame Dusson, who is Dutch-built, and whose muscles are pleasure-proof, came with her. . . . We break-fasted in the great parlour, and I had filled the hall and large cloister by turns with French horns and clarionets. As the French ladies had never seen a printing-house, I carried them into mine; they found something ready set, and desiring to see what it was, it proved as follows: –

> For Madame de Boufflers.
> The graceful fair, who loves to know,
> Nor dreads the north's inclement show;
> Who bids her polish'd accent wear
> The British diction's harsher air:
> Shall read her praise in every clime
> Where types can speak or poets rhyme.

> For Madame Dusson.
> Feign not an ignorance of what I speak;
> You could not miss my meaning were it Greek.
> 'Tis the same language Belgium utter'd first,
> The same which from admiring Gallia burst.
> True sentiment a like expression pours;
> Each country says the same to eyes like yours.

. . . This little *gentillesse* pleased, and atoned for the popery of my house, which was not serious enough for Madame de Boufflers, who is Montmorency, *et du sang du premier Chretien*; and too serious for Madame Dusson, who is a Dutch Calvinist.

Horace Walpole : from a letter to George Montagu

18 May

1593—The Privy Council issued a warrant to Henry Maunder 'to repair to the house of Mr. Thomas Walsingham in Kent, or to any other place where he shall understand Christopher Marlowe to be remaining, and by virtue thereof to bring him to the Court in his company' to answer charges of having expressed 'blasphemous and damnable opinions'

FAU: Stand stil you euer moouing spheres of heauen,
        That time may cease, and midnight neuer come;
        Faire Natures eie, rise, rise againe, and make
        Perpetuall day, or let this houre be but
        A yeere, a moneth, a weeke, a naturall day,
        That Faustus may repent, and saue his soule,
        O lente, lente currite noctis equi:
        The starres mooue stil, time runs, the clocke wil strike,
        The diuel wil come, and Faustus must be damnd.
        O Ile leape vp to my God: who pulles me downe?
        See where Christs blood streames in the firmament.
        One drop would saue my soule, halfe a drop, ah my Christ.
        Ah rend not my heart for naming of my Christ.
        Yet wil I call on him: oh spare me *Lucifer!* . . .

        O it strikes, it strikes: now body turne to ayre,   [*Thunder and lightning*]
        Or *Lucifer* wil beare thee quicke to hel:
        O soule, be changde into little water drops,
        And fal into the *Ocean*, nere be found:
        My God, my God, looke not so fierce on me: [*Enter diuels*]
        Adders and Serpents, let me breathe a while:
        Vgly hell gape not, come not *Lucifer*,
        Ile burne my bookes, ah *Mephistophilis*.   [*Exeunt with him*]

Enter Chorus

CHOR: Cut is the branch that might haue growne ful straight,
        And burned is *Apolloes* Laurel bough,
        That sometime grew within this learned man:
        Faustus is gone, regard his hellish fall,
        Whose fiendful fortune may exhort the wise,
        Onely to wonder at vnlawful things,
        Whose deepnesse doth intise such forward wits,
        To practise more than heauenly power permits.

Christopher Marlowe: *from* The Tragical History of Dr. Faustus

1897—Oscar Wilde was released from prison, where he had written the 'letter' entitled De Profundis, *which he had sent for publication to his friend, Robert Ross*

I don't defend my conduct. I explain it. Also there are in my letter certain passages which deal with my mental development in prison, and the inevitable evolution of my character and intellectual attitude towards life that has taken place; and I want you and others who still stand by me and have affection for me to know exactly in what mood and manner I hope to face the world. Of course, from one point of view, I know that on the day of my release I shall be merely passing from one prison into another, and there are times when the whole world seems to me no larger than my cell, and as full of terror for me. Still I believe that at the beginning God made a world for each separate man, and in that world, which is within us, one should seek to live. At any rate, you will read those parts of my letter with less pain than the others. Of course I need not remind you how fluid a thing thought is with me – with us all – and of what an evanescent substance are our emotions made. Still I do see a sort of possible goal towards which, through art, I may progress.

Prison life makes one see people and things as they really are. That is why it turns one to stone. It is the people outside who are deceived by the illusions of a life in constant motion. They revolve with life and contribute to its unreality. We who are immobile both see and know.

Whether or not the letter does good to narrow natures and hectic brains, to me it has done good. I have 'cleansed my bosom of much perilous stuff'. I need not remind you that mere expression is to an artist the supreme and only mode of life. It is by utterance that we live. Of the many, many things for which I have to thank the Governor there is none for which I am more grateful than for his permission to write fully to you, and at as great a length as I desire. For nearly two years I had had within a growing burden of bitterness, of much of which I have now got rid. On the other side of the prison wall there are some poor black soot-besmirched trees which are just breaking out into buds of an almost shrill green. I know quite well what they are going through. They are finding expression.

Oscar Wilde, as quoted in Robert Ross's 'Preface'
to De Profundis

1608—Shakespeare's Antony and Cleopatra *was entered in the Stationer's Register to Edward Blount*

ENOBARBUS: The barge she sat in, like a burnished throne,
Burned on the water; the poop was beaten gold,
Purple the sails, and so perfumed that
The winds were love-sick with them; the oars were silver,
Which to the tune of flutes kept stroke, and made
The water which they beat to follow faster,
As amourous of their strokes. For her own person,
It beggared all description: she did lie
In her pavilion, cloth-of-gold, of tissue,
O'er-picturing that Venus where we see
The fancy outwork nature. On each side her,
Stood pretty dimpled boys, like smiling Cupids,
With divers coloured fans, whose wind did seem
To glow the delicate cheeks which they did cool,
And what they undid did.
  . . .
Her gentlewomen, like the Nereides,
So many mermaids, tended her i' th' eyes,
And made their bends adornings. At the helm,
A seeming mermaid steers. The silken tackle
Swell with the touches of those flower-soft hands,
That yarely frame the office. From the barge
A strange invisible perfume hits the sense
Of the adjacent wharfs. The city cast
Her people out upon her; and Antony,
Enthron'd i' th' market place, did sit alone,
Whistling to th' air; which, but for vacancy,
Had gone to gaze on Cleopatra too,
And made a gap in nature.
  . . .

MAECENAS: Now Antony must leave her utterly.
ENOBARBUS: Never! He will not.
Age cannot wither her, nor custom stale
Her infinite variety. Other women cloy
The appetites they feed, but she makes hungry
Where most she satisfies; for vilest things
Become themselves in her, that the holy priests
Bless her when she is riggish.

> *William Shakespeare: from* Antony and Cleo-
> patra, *Act II, scene 2*

1898—George Bernard Shaw published his 'Valedictory' at the conclusion of his career as a professional drama critic, to be succeeded by Max Beerbohm

As I lie here, helpless and disabled, or, at best, nailed by one foot to the floor like a doomed Strasburg goose, a sense of injury grows on me. For nearly four years – to be precise, since New Year 1895 – I have been the slave of the theatre. It has tethered me to the mile radius of foul and sooty air which has its centre in the Strand, as a goat is tethered in the little circle of cropped and trampled grass that makes the meadow ashamed. Every week it clamors for its tale of written words; so that I am like a man fighting a windmill. . . .The English do not know what to think until they are coached, laboriously and insistently for years, in the proper and becoming opinion. For ten years past, with an unprecedented pertinacity and obstination, I have been dinning into the public head that I am an extraordinarily witty, brilliant, and clever man. That is now part of the public opinion of England; and no power in heaven or on earth will ever change it. I may dodder and dote; I may potboil and platitudinize; I may become the butt and chopping-block of all the bright, original spirits of the rising generation; but my reputation shall not suffer; it is built up fast and solid, like Shakespeare's, on an impregnable basis of dogmatic reiteration.

When a man of normal habits is ill, every one hastens to assure him that he is going to recover. When a Vegetarian is ill (which fortunately very seldom happens), every one assures him that he is going to die, and that they told him so, and that it serves him right. They implore him to take at least a little gravy, so as to give himself a chance of lasting out the night. They tell him awful stories of cases just like his own which ended fatally after indescribable torments; and when he tremblingly inquires whether the victims were not hardened meat-eaters, they tell him he must not talk, as it is not good for him. Ten times a day I am compelled to reflect on my past life, and on the limited prospect of three weeks or so of lingering moribundity which is held up to me as my probable future, with the intensity of a drowning man. And I can never justify to myself the spending of four years on dramatic criticism. I have sworn an oath to endure no more of it. Never again will I cross the threshold of a theatre. The subject is exhausted; and so am I.

Still, the gaiety of nations must not be eclipsed. . . . The younger generation is knocking at the door; and as I open it there steps spritely in the incomparable Max.

For the rest, let Max speak for himself. I am off duty for ever, and am going to sleep.

G. B. Shaw: from Dramatic Opinions and Essays

22 May 🔲

Epilogue

And how, and how, in faith – a pretty plot;
And smartly carried through too, was it not?
And the devils, how? well; and the fighting?
Well too; – a fool, and't had been just old writing.
O, what a monster-wit must that man have,
That could please all, which now their twelvepence gave!
High characters (cries one), and he would see
Things that ne'er were, nor are, nor ne'er will be.
Romances, cry easy souls; and then they swear
The play's well-writ, though scarce a good line's there.
The woman – O, if Stephen should be kill'd,
Or miss the lady, how the plot is spill'd!
And into how many pieces a poor play.
Is taken still before the second day!
Like a strange beauty newly come to court;
And to say truth, good faith, 'tis all in sport.
One will like all the ill things in a play,
Another some o' the good, but the wrong way;
So that from one poor play there comes to rise
At several tables several comedies.
The ill is only here, that 't may fall out
In plays as faces; and who goes about
To take asunder, oft destroys (we know)
What all together made a pretty show.

Sir John Suckling's original answer to such critics of The Goblins *as Pepys*

1829—John Greenleaf Whittier acknowledged the hopelessness of his love for Mary Emerson Smith

---

Boston, 23d, 5th month, 1829

Miss Smith:

This is not the first time I have attempted to write you. I have written and rewritten and as often destroyed my fruitless efforts. Why, you will ask me, was this? Simply because I was afraid you had ceased to be the good kind-hearted girl, the generous friend and confidant which you once were. I have always esteemed you highly; fondly perhaps; but let that pass, *you* have forgotten 'Auld Lang Syne', and why should I be foolish enough to cherish an idle dream of my boyhood, a yearning for that confidence and friendship which I fear has no existence in real life. No! I have shaken off every feeling of a tender nature, and I would ask nothing more than the friendship of the cold-hearted world. Can you deny me this? Enough of sentimentality, I have done with it.

The blessed hopes I have cherished have gone; all gone; and memory treasures up with a miserly fondness the bright things of the past. Do you suppose you are not included among them? Depend upon it you are among the foremost.

They say, and I listen to it with a mingled feeling of pleasure and pain, that your hand has been plighted to another; to a worthy and deserving gentlemen. God grant that happiness may attend you both, but it is idle, perfectly so, for those who know so much of each other as we do, to affect to misunderstand each other. Mary! I have loved you passionately; deeply; and you, if there is any faith in woman's words, you have not *hated* me.

Do you remember that last walk we had on the banks of the Merrimac when the moon was looking down upon us? Ay! and on a hundred others. They are living in *my* memory, every clasp of the hand, every look of kindness is remembered, cherished.
. . .

I need not repeat that I value your friendship, admire your disposition, and love you as a brother should love his sister; you know all this; you have known my devotion and such, too, as none other will ever exact of me; you are the beau ideal of my imagination, and yet I ask nothing of you but your friendship, nothing more. Whatever may be our situation in life, in weal or woe, nothing shall interrupt it on my part, and from what I know of you I am sure that you will not forget an old friend. . . .

John G. Whittier

24 May

1902—'Empire Day' was first celebrated (on the eighty-third anniversary of Queen Victoria's birthday). In 1959 it was re-named 'Commonwealth Day'

Recessional

God of our fathers, known of old –
    Lord of our far-flung battle-line –
Beneath whose awful Hand we hold
    Dominion over palm and pine –
Lord God of Hosts, be with us yet,
Lest we forget, lest we forget!

The tumult and the shouting dies –
    The captains and the kings depart –
Still stand Thine ancient sacrifice,
    An humble and a contrite heart.
Lord God of Hosts, be with us yet,
Lest we forget, lest we forget!

Far-called our navies melt away –
    On dune and headland sinks the fire –
Lo, all our pomp of yesterday
    Is one with Nineveh and Tyre!
Judge of the Nations, spare us yet,
Lest we forget, lest we forget!

If, drunk with sight of power, we loose
    Wild tongues that have not Thee in awe –
Such boastings as the Gentiles use,
    Or lesser breeds without the Law –
Lord God of Hosts, be with us yet,
Lest we forget, lest we forget!

For heathen heart that puts her trust
    In reeking tube and iron shard –
All valiant dust that builds on dust,
    And guarding calls not Thee to guard –
For frantic boast and foolish word,
Thy mercy on Thy People, Lord!

Rudyard Kipling

A.D. 735—The Venerable Bede died

For nearly a fortnight before the Feast of our Lord's Resurrection he was troubled by weakness and breathed with great difficulty . . . During these days, in addition to the daily instruction that he gave us and his recitation of the psalter, he was working to complete two books worthy of mention. For he translated the Gospel of Saint John into our own language for the benefit of the Church of God as far as the words 'but what are these among so many'. He also made some extracts from the works of Bishop Isidore, saying 'I do not wish my sons to read anything untrue, or to labour unprofitably after my death.' But on the Tuesday before Our Lord's Ascension his breathing became increasingly laboured, and his feet began to swell. Despite this he continued cheerfully to teach and dictate all day, saying from time to time, 'Learn quickly. I do not know how long I can continue, for my Lord may call me in a short while.' . . .

When dawn broke on Wednesday, he told us to write diligently what we had begun, and we did this until Terce. After Terce we walked in procession with the relics of the Saints as the customs of the day required, but one of us remained with him, who said, 'There is still one chapter missing in the book that you have been dictating; but it seems hard that I should trouble you any further.' 'It is no trouble', he answered: 'Take your pen and sharpen it, and write quickly.' And he did so.

But at None he said to me, 'I have a few articles of value in my casket, such as pepper, linen, and incense. Run quickly and fetch the priests of the monastery, so that I may distribute among them the gifts that God has given me.' In great distress I did as he bid me. And when they arrived, he spoke to each of them in turn, requesting and reminding them diligently to offer Masses and prayers for him. . . . He also told us many other edifying things, and passed his last day happily until evening.

Then the same lad, named Wilbert, said again: 'Dear master, there is one sentence still unfinished.' 'Very well', he replied: 'write it down.' After a short while the lad said, 'Now it is finished.' 'You have spoken truly', he replied: 'It is well finished. Now raise my head in your hands, for it would give me great joy to sit facing the holy place where I used to pray, so that I may sit and call on my Father.' And thus, on the floor of his cell, he chanted 'Glory be to the Father, and to the Son, and to the Holy Spirit' to its ending, and breathed his last.

> *'To his fellow teacher Cuthwin, most beloved in Christ, from his school-friend Cuthbert', as quoted by Leo Sherley-Price in his translation of Bede's* History of the English Church and People, *London (Penguin) 1955*

26 May 📖

1770—Oliver Goldsmith published, in The Deserted Village, *his exposure of the bitter realities of an 'affluent society' produced, in this instance, by the enclosure of common lands*

'I expect the shout of modern politicians against me. . . . Still, however, I must . . . continue to think those luxuries prejudicial to states, by which so many vices are introduced, and so many kingdoms have been undone.'

From the prose 'Dedication'

> Sweet smiling village, loveliest of the lawn,
> Thy sports are fled, and all thy charms withdrawn;
> Amidst thy bowers the tyrant's hand is seen,
> And desolation saddens all thy green;
> One only master grasps the whole domain,
> And half a tillage stints thy smiling plain.
> No more thy glassy brook reflects the day,
> But, choked with sedges, works its weedy way;
> Along the glades, a solitary guest,
> The hollow sounding bittern guards its nest;
> Amidst thy desert walks the lapwing flies,
> And tires their echoes with unvaried cries.
> Sunk are thy bowers in shapeless ruin all,
> And the long grass o'ertops the mouldring wall;
> And trembling, shrinking from the spoiler's hand,
> Far, far away thy children leave the land.
>
> Ill fares the land, to hastening ills a prey,
> Where wealth accumulates, and men decay.
> Princes and lords may flourish, or may fade;
> A breath can make them, as a breath has made;
> But a bold peasantry, their country's pride,
> When once destroyed, can never be supplied. . . .
>
> O luxury! thou cursed by Heaven's decree,
> How ill exchanged are things like these for thee! . . .
> Kingdoms by thee, to sickly greatness grown,
> Boast of a florid vigour not their own.
> At every draft more large and large they grow,
> A bloated mass of rank, unwieldy woe;
> Till sapped their strength, and every part unsound,
> Down, down they sink, and spread a ruin around.

Oliver Goldsmith: from The Deserted Village

1732—William Hogarth, at one o'clock in the morning, set off with four of his tavern companions on the 'Five Days' Peregrination', which resulted in their amusing book published later in the year, written by Forrest and enlivened with a map drawn by Thornhill and sketches by Scott and Hogarth

Saturday, May the 27th, we set out with the morning, and took our departure from the Bedford Arms Tavern in Covent Garden, to the tune of 'Why should we quarrel for riches?' The first land we made was Billingsgate, where we dropped anchor at the Dark Horse. There Hogarth made a Caricature of a Porter, who called himself 'the Duke of Puddle Dock'. The drawing was (by his Grace) pasted on the cellar-door. We were agreeably entertained with the humours of the place, particularly with an explanation of a Gaffer and a Gammer, a little obscene, though in the presence of two of the fair sex. Here we continued till the clock struck one.

Then set sail in a Gravesend-boat we had hired for ourselves. Straw was our bed and a tilt our covering. The wind blew hard S.E. by E. We had much rain, and no sleep, for about three hours. At Cuckold's Point we sung 'St. John-at-Deptford Pishoken'; and in Blackwall Reach eat hung beef and biscuit, and drank right *Hollands.* . . .

At ten we walked on, and calling a council among ourselves, it was proposed that, if any one was dissatisfied with our past proceedings, or intended progress, he might depatriate, and be allowed money to bear his charges. It was unanimously rejected, and resolved to proceed to Upnor. We viewed, and Hogarth made a drawing of the Castle, and Scott of some Shipping riding near it.

The Castle is not very large, but strong; garrisoned with twenty-four men, and the like number of guns, though no more than eight are mounted. I went and bought cockles of an old blind man and woman, who were in a little cock-boat on the River. We made a hurry-scurry dinner at the *Smack* at the ten-gun battery, and had a battle-royal with sticks, pebbles, and hog's dung. In this fight Tothall was the greatest sufferer, and his cloaths carried the marks of his digrace. Some time this occasioned much laughter, and we marched on to the Birds'-nest battery, and, keeping the river and shipping still in view, passed over the hills and came to Hoo Church-yard, where on a wooden rail over a grave, is an epitaph, supposed to be wrote by a servant-maid on her master, which being something extraordinary, I shall transcribe *verbatim*:

> And. wHen. he. Died you. plainLy see.
> He. freely. gave. al. to. Sara. passa. Wee.
> And. in. Doing. so. it. DoTh. prevail.
> that Ion. him. can. Well. besTow. this. Rayel.
> On. Year. I. sarved. him. it. is. well. None.
> BuT. Thanks. beto. God. it. is. al. my. One.

From An Account of What Seemed Most Remarkable in the FIVE DAYS' PEREGRIN-ATION . . ., *etc. London, Published in 1732*

The actors in the old tragedies, as we read, piped their iambics to a tune, speaking from under a mask, and wearing stilts and a great head-dress. 'Twas thought the dignity of the Tragic Muse required these appurtenances, and that she was not to move except to a measure and a cadence. So Queen Medea slew her children to a slow music: and King Agamemnon perished in a dying fall (to use Mr. Dryden's words): the Chorus standing by in a set attitude, and rhythmically and decorously bewailing the fates of those great crowned persons. The Muse of History hath encumbered herself with ceremony as well as her Sister of the Theatre. She too wears the mask and the cothurnus, and speaks to measure. She too, in our age, busies herself with the affairs only of kings; waiting on them obsequiously and stately, as if she were but a mistress of court ceremonies, and had nothing to do with the registering of the affairs of the common people. I have seen in his very old age and decrepitude the old French King Lewis the Fourteenth, the type and model of kinghood – who never moved but to measure, who lived and died according to the laws of his Court-marshal, persisting in enacting through life the part of Hero; and, divested of poetry, this was but a little wrinkled old man, pock-marked, and with a great periwig and red heels to make him look tall – a hero for a book if you like, or for a brass statue or a painted ceiling, a god in Roman shape; but what more than a man for Madame Maintenon, or the barber who shaved him, or Monsieur Fagon, his surgeon? I wonder shall History ever pull off her periwig and cease to be court-ridden? Shall we see something of France and England besides Versailles and Windsor? I saw Queen Anne at the latter place tearing down the Park slopes after her stag-hounds, and driving her one-horse chaise – a hot, redfaced woman, not in the least resembling that statue of her which turns its stone back upon St. Paul's, and faces the coaches struggling up Ludgate Hill. She was neither better bred nor wiser than you and me, though we knelt to hand her a letter or a wash-hand basin. Why shall History go on kneeling to the end of time? I am for having her rise up off her knees and take a natural posture: not to be for ever performing cringes and congees like a court-chamberlain, and shuffling backwards out of doors in the presence of the sovereign. In a word, I would have history familiar rather than heroic; and I think that Mr. Hogarth and Mr. Fielding will give our children a much better idea of the manners of the present age than the *Court Gazette* and the newspapers which we get thence.

> *William Makepeace Thackeray: from* Henry
> Esmond, '*Early Youth*'

1819—Shelley dedicated The Cenci *to Leigh Hunt*

My dear friend,

I inscribe with your name, from a distant country, and after an absence whose months have seemed years, this the latest of my literary efforts.

Those writings which I have hitherto published, have been little else than visions which impersonate my own apprehensions of the beautiful and the just. I can also perceive in them the literary defects incidental to youth and impatience; they are dreams of what ought to be, or may be. The drama which I now present to you is a sad reality. I lay aside the presumptuous attitude of an instructor, and am content to paint, with such colours as my own heart furnishes, that which has been.

Had I known a person more highly endowed than yourself with all that it becomes a man to possess, I had solicited for this work the ornament of his name. One more gentle, honourable, innocent, and brave; one of more exalted toleration for all who do and think evil, and yet himself more free from evil; one who knows better how to receive, and how to confer a benefit, though he must ever confer far more than he can receive; one of simpler, and, in the highest sense of the word, of purer life and manners, I never knew: and I had already been fortunate in friendships when your name was added to the list.

In that patient and irreconcilable enmity with domestic and political tyranny and imposture, which the tenor of your life has illustrated, and which, had I health and talents, should illustrate mine, let us, comforting each other in our task, live and die.

All happiness attend you!

Your affectionate friend,

Percy B. Shelley

Rome, May 29, 1819

1874—George Eliot, having read James Thomson's The City of Dreadful
Night, *undertook to persuade its tortured author to a more 'liberal' view of
Victorian London and to some glimpse of the 'sublimity' of its social order*

The Priory, 21, North Bank, Regent's Park
May 30, 1874

DEAR POET, – I cannot rest satisfied without telling you that my mind responds
with admiration to the distinct vision and grand utterance in the poem which you
have been so good as to send me.

Also, I trust that an intellect formed by so much passionate energy as yours will
soon give us more heroic strains with a wider embrace of human fellowship in them –
such as will be to the labourers of the world what the odes of Tyrtaeus were to the
Spartans, thrilling them with the sublimity of the social order and the courage of
resistance to all that would dissolve it. To accept life and write much fine poetry
is to take a very large share in the quantum of human good, and seems to draw with
it necessarily some recognition, affectionate and even joyful, of the manifold willing
labours which have made such a lot possible. –

Yours sincerely,

M. E. Lewes

Lo, thus, as prostrate, 'In the dust I write
    My heart's deep languor and my soul's sad tears.'
Yet why evoke the spectres of black night
    To blot the sunshine of exultant years?
Why disinter dead faith from mouldering hidden?
Why break the seals of mute despair unbidden,
    And wail life's discords into careless ears?

Because a cold rage seizes one at whiles
    To show the bitter old and wrinkled truth
Stripped naked of all vesture that beguiles,
    False dreams, false hopes, false masks and modes of youth;
Because it gives some sense of power and passion
In helpless ignorance to try to fashion
    Our woe in living words howe'er uncouth.

James Thomson: from the 'Proem' to The City
of Dreadful Night

1812—Henry Crabb Robinson spent 'a day of great enjoyment' in the company of William Wordsworth

... At Hammond's found Wordsworth demonstrating ... some of his philosophical theory. Speaking of his own poems, Wordsworth said he principally valued them as being *a new power* in the literary world. Hammond's friend, Miller, esteemed Wordsworth for the pure morality of his works. Wordsworth said he himself looked to the powers of the mind his poems call forth, and the energies they presuppose and excite, as the standard by which they are to be estimated. ... *The Kitten and the Falling Leaves* he spoke of [as] merely fanciful, *The Highland Girl* as of the highest kind being imaginative, *The Happy Warrior* as appertaining to reflection. In illustration of his principle of imaginative power he quoted his *Cuckoo*, and in particular the 'wandering voice', as giving local habitation to an abstraction. ...

Wordsworth spoke with great contempt of Campbell as a poet, and illustrated his want of truth and poetic sense in his imagery by a close analysis of a celebrated passage in *The Pleasures of Hope*:

> Where Andes, giant of the Western star,
> [With meteor-standard to the winds unfurl'd,
> Looks from his throne of clouds o'er half the world.]

showing the whole to be a mere jumble of discordant images, meaning, in fact, nothing, nor conveying very distinct impression, it being first uncertain who or what is the giant, and who or what is the star. Then the giant is made to hold a meteor-standard and to sit on a throne of clouds and look (it is not apparent for what) on half the world. Gray's line, speaking of the bard's beard which 'stream'd like a meteor to the troubled air', Wordsworth also considered as ridiculous, and both passages he represented to be unmeaningly stolen from a fine line by Milton. ...

Wordsworth spoke with great feeling of the present state of the country. He considers the combinations among journeymen, and even the Benefit Societies and all associations of men, apparently for the best purposes, as very alarming: he contemplates a renovation of all the horrors of a war between the poor and the rich, a conflict of property with no property. ... Wordsworth spoke in defence of the Church establishment, and on the usual grounds said he would shed his blood for it. ... Confessed he knew not when he had been in church at home – 'All our ministers are such vile creatures' – and he allowed us to laugh at this droll concession from a staunch advocate for the establishment. The mischief of making the clergy depend on the caprice or fashion of the mob he considered as more than counterbalancing all other evils. And I agree with him.

From The Diary of Henry Crabb Robinson

June.

1599—Satires by Joseph Hall and John Marston, and Epigrams *and* Elegies *by Christopher Marlowe and Sir John Davies, were publicly burned in front of St Paul's Cathedral by order of Archbishop Whitgift – an act already seemingly commented on in the offending documents*

To *Detraction* I present my *Poesie*

Foule canker of faire vertuous action,
Vile blaster of the freshest bloomes on earth,
Envies abhorred childe *Detraction*,
I heare expose, to thy al-taynting breath
    The issue of my braine: snarle, raile, barke, bite;
    Know that my spirit scornes *Detractions* spight.

Know that the *Genius*, which attendeth on,
And guides my powers intellectuall,
Holds in all vile repute *Detraction*,
My soule an essence metaphysicall,
    That in the basest sort scornes *Critickes* rage
    Because he knows his sacred parentage. . . .

A partiall prayse shall never elevate
My setled censure, of mine owne esteeme.
A cankered verdict of malignant Hate
Shall nere provoke me, worse my selfe to deeme.
    Spight of despight, and rancors villanie,
    I am my selfe, so is my poesie.

John Marston: from The Scourge of Villainie

Since Saint Iohn Baptist lost his holy head
For telling Herod of his cursèd crime,
No one with kings will find fault in his steede
But all doe seeke to sooth the kings and time.
So they that haue authorite, may sinne
As if they sinnèd by authority:
Then king's high-waies haue lowest falls therein,
If to their stepps themselues haue not an eye:
    Therefore O kings (whose waies are smoth'd of all)
    Looke to your selues if you will neuer fall.

Sir John Davies of Hereford: The Scourge of
Folly, *Epigram* 193

1753—Samuel Richardson answered the request of his Dutch translator for some information about his career as a pioneer novelist

As a bashful & not forward Boy, I was an early Favourite with all the young Women of Taste & Reading in the Neighbourhood. Half a dozen of them when met to Work with their Needles, used, when they got a Book they liked, & thought I should, to borrow me to read to them; their Mothers sometimes with them; & both Mothers and Daughters used to be pleased with the Observations they put me upon making.

I was not more than Thirteen, when three of these young Women, unknown to each other, having an high Opinion of my Taciturnity, revealed to me their Love Secrets, in order to induce me to give them Copies to write after, or correct, for Answers to their Lovers Letters: Nor did any of them ever know, that I was the Secretary to the others. I have been directed to chide, & even repulse, when an Offense was either taken or given, at the very time that the Heart of the Chider or Repulser was open before me, overflowing with Esteem & Affection; & the fair Repulser dreading to be taken at her Word; directing *this* Word, or *that* Expression, to be softened or changed. One, highly gratified with her Lover's Fervour, & Vows of everlasting Love, has said, when I asked her Direction; 'I cannot tell you what to write; But (her Heart on her Lips) you cannot write too kindly:' All her Fear only, that she shd incurr Slight for her Kindness.

I recollect, that I was early noted for having Invention. I was not fond of Play, as other Boys: My Schoolfellows used to call me *Serious* and *Gravity*: and five of them particularly delighted to single me out, either for a Walk, or at their Father's Houses or at mine, to tell them Stories, as they phrased it. Some I told them from my Reading as true; others from my Head, as mere Invention; of which they would be most fond: & often were affected by them. One of them, particularly, I remember, was for putting me to write a History, as he called it, on the Model of Tommy Potts; I now forget what it was; only, that it was of a Servant-Man preferred by a fine young Lady (for his Goodness) to a Lord, who was a Libertine. All my Stories carried with them, I am bold to say, an useful Moral.

I am ashamed of these Puerilities: But thus, Sir, when I have been asked a like Question by others, to that you put, have I accounted for a kind of Talent; which I little thought of resuming; or thinking it worthwhile to resume. As a Proof of this, let me say, that when I had written the two first Vols. of Pamela, & was urged by a Particular Friend to put it to the Press, I accepted of 20 Guineas for two Thirds of the Copy-Right; reserving to myself only one Third.

Samuel Richardson to Johannes Stinstra, 2 June
1753

1895—'. . . there is no preface to Chaucer, and no introduction, and no essay on his position as a poet, and no notes, and no glossary ; so that all is prepared for you to enjoy him thoroughly'

> *Sir Edward Burne-Jones to his daughter,*
> *with his copy of the Kelmscott Chaucer,*
> *published this day, as her birthday present*

Whan that Aprille with his shoures soote
The droghte of Merche hath perced to the roote,
And bathed every veyne in swich licour
Of which vertu engendred is the flour;
Whan Zephyrus eek with his swete breeth
Inspired hath in every holt and heeth
The tendre croppes, and the yong sonne
Hath in the Ram his halve cours y-ronne,
And smale fowles maken melodye
That slepen al the nyght with open ye
(So priketh hem nature in hir corages):
Than longen folk to goon on pilgrimages . . .
And specially, from every shires ende
Of Engelonde, to Caunterbury they wende,
The holy blisful martir for to seke
That hem hath holpen, whan that they were seke.
  Bifel that in that sesoun on a day
In Southwerk at the Tabard as I lay
Redy to wenden on my pilgrimage
To Caunterbury with ful devout corage,
At nyght was come in-to that hostelrye
Wel nyne and twenty in a compaignye
Of sondry folk, by aventure y-falle
In felawshipe, and pilgrims were they alle
That toward Caunterbury wolden ryde;
The chambres and the stables weren wyde,
And wel we weren esed atte beste.
And shortly, whan the sonne was to reste,
So had I spoken with hem everichon,
That I was of hir felawshipe anon,
And made forward erly for to ryse
To take our wey, ther as I yow devyse.

> *Geoffrey Chaucer: from the Prologue to* The
> Canterbury Tales

4 June

1555—The Fall of Princes, later known as The Mirror for Magistrates ('gathered by John Bochas, translated by John Lidgate, Monk of Bury'), was published

And sorrowing I to see the summer flowers,
The lively green, the lusty leas forlorn,
The sturdy trees so shattered with the showers,
The fields so fade that flourished so beforn
It taught me well all earthly things be born
    To die the death, for nought long time may last;
    The summer's beauty yields to winter's blast.

Then looking upward to the heaven's leams,
With nightès stars thick powdered everywhere,
Which erst so glistened with the golden streams
That cheerful Phoebus spread down from his sphere,
Beholding dark oppressing day so near;
    The sudden sight reducèd to my mind
    The sundry changes that in earth we find.

That musing on this worldly wealth in thought,
Which comes and goes more faster than we see
The flickering flame that with the fire is wrought,
My busy mind presented unto me
Such fall of peers as in this realm had be
    That oft I wished some would their woes descrive,
    To warn the rest whom fortune left alive. . . .

Whence come I am, the dreary destiny
Ahd luckless lot for to bemoan of those
Whom fortune, in this maze of misery,
Of wretched chance, most woeful mirrors chose;
That when thou seest how lightly they did lose
    Their pomp, their power, and that they thought most sure,
    Thou mayst soon deem no earthly joy may dure.

From Thomas Sackville's 'Induction' which was added to the Mirror for Magistrates *in the edition of* 1563

1851—Harriet Beecher Stowe published, in the Abolitionist journal, The National Era, *the first instalment of* Uncle Tom's Cabin

---

I have been the mother of seven children, the most beautiful and the most loved of whom lies buried near my Cincinnatti residence. It was at his dying bed and at his grave that I learned what a poor slave mother may feel when her child is torn away from her. In those depths of sorrow which seemed to me immeasurable, it was my only prayer to God that such anguish might not be suffered in vain . . . that this crushing of my own heart might enable me to work out some great good to others. . . . I have often felt that much that is in that book had its roots in the awful scenes and bitter sorrows of that summer. . . .

My cook, poor Eliza Buck . . . was a regular epitome of slave life in herself; fat, gentle, easy, loving and lovable, always calling my very modest house and dooryard 'The Place', as if it had been a plantation with seven hundred hands on it. She had lived through the whole sad story of a Virginia-raised slave's life . . . She was raised in a good family as a nurse and seamstress. When the family became embarrassed, she was suddenly sold on to a plantation in Louisiana. She has often told me how, without any warning, she was suddenly forced into a carriage, and saw her little mistress screaming and stretching her arms from the window towards her as she was driven away. She has told me of scenes on the Louisiana plantation, and she has often been out at night by stealth administering to poor slaves who had been mangled and lacerated by the lash. Hence she was sold to Kentucky, and her last master was the father of all her children. On this point she ever maintained a reserve that always appeared to me remarkable. She always called him her husband; and it was not till after she had lived with me for some years that I discovered the real nature of the connection. I shall never forget how sorry I felt for her, nor my feelings at her humble apology, 'You know, Mrs. Stowe, slave women cannot help themselves.' She had two very pretty quadroon daughters, with her beautiful hair and eyes, interesting children, whom I had instructed in the family school with my children.

Time would fail to tell you all that I learned incidentally of the slave system in the history of various slaves who came into my family, and of the underground railroad which, I may say, ran through our house. . . . The law records of courts and judicial proceedings are so incredible as to fill me with amazement whenever I think of them. . . .

I suffer exquisitely in writing these things. It may be truly said that I write with my heart's blood. Many times in writing 'Uncle Tom's Cabin' I thought my health would fail utterly; but I prayed earnestly that God would help me till I got through, and still am pressed beyond measure and above strength.

Harriet Beecher Stowe: from a letter to Mrs. Follen

6 June 🔖

1905—John Galsworthy, having finished A Man of Property, *sought Edward Garnett's advice as to whether he should develop in a trilogy the great theme he had recognized in it (instead of the watered-down* Forsyte Saga *he made of it ten years later)*

At the very back of my mind, in the writing of this book (and indeed of *The Island Pharisees*, but put that aside) there has always been the feeling of the utter disharmony of the Christian religion with the English character; the cant and humbug of our professing it as a *national* religion. Not an original idea this, but a broad enough theme to carry any amount of character study. I've got it in my mind now to carry on this idea for at least two more volumes. Just as the theme of the first book is the sense of property, the themes of the next (or rather the national traits dealt with) are (1) the reforming spirit, (2) the fighting spirit – done of course through story and definite character study. The theme of the third book would be the spirit of advertisement, self-glorification, and impossibility of seeing ourselves in the wrong, and it would deal with the Boer War (of course only in character, not in story). I call the second book *Danaë* and the third *The Mouth of Brass*. Six years elapse between each book, and I carry young Jolyon through all three as a commentator. I have my figures for the second book, but only the idea for the third.

Now what I want to ask you is this. Is it worth while to put after the title of *The Man of Property*, etc., some such addition as this:

> National Ethics – I
> or   Christian Ethics – I
> or   Tales of a Christian People – I

in other words to foreshadow a series upon that central idea?

My intention is to make that central idea plainer in Vol. II and absolutely patent in Vol. III, without I hope transgressing against Art. It has become obvious to me, and I expect to you, that my strength, if any, lies in writing to a polemical strain through character; and I find it natural to think of life in my fiction in a sort of string, a sort of second world peopled by my own people. One person makes another in fact, and it all comes into a sort of mould gradually that way. So that if I live, and don't collapse, I ought to be able to carry out my intention; and with regard to the third book, by the time it comes out the public would be able to look on at an analysis of our attitude to the Boer war without blood in the eyes.

However, if you say it is unwise to commit myself thus, I will take your advice.

Our best love,
Ever yours,
John Galsworthy

1780—The Gordon Riots were at their height

During the whole of this day, every regiment in or near the metropolis was on duty in one or other part of the town; and the regulars and militia, in obedience to the orders which were sent to every barrack and station within twenty-four hours' journey, began to pour in by all the roads. But the disturbance had attained to such a formidable height, and the rioters had grown, with impunity, to be so audacious, that the sight of this great force, continually augmented by new arrivals, instead of operating as a check, stimulated them to outrages of greater hardihood than any they had yet committed; and helped to kindle a flame in London, the like of which had never been beheld, even in its ancient and rebellious times.

All yesterday, and on this day likewise, the commander-in-chief endeavoured to arouse the magistrates to a sense of their duty, and in particular the Lord Mayor, who was the faintest-hearted and most timid of them all. With this object, large bodies of the soldiery were several times despatched to the Mansion House to await his orders: but as he could, by no threats or persuasions, be induced to give any, and as the men remained in the open street, fruitlessly for any good purpose, and thrivingly for a very bad one; these laudable attempts did harm rather than good. For the crowd, becoming speedily acquainted with the Lord Mayor's temper, did not fail to take advantage of it by boasting that even the civil authorities were opposed to the Papists, and could not find in their hearts to molest those who were guilty of no other offence. . . .

By this time, the crowd was everywhere; all concealment and disguise were laid aside, and they pervaded the whole town. If any man among them wanted money, he had but to knock at the door of a dwelling-house, or walk into a shop, and demand it in the rioters' name; and his demand was instantly complied with. The peacable citizens being afraid to lay hand upon them, singly and alone, it may be easily supposed that when gathered together in bodies, they were perfectly secure from interruption. They assembled in the streets, traversed them at their will and pleasure, and publicly concerted their plans. Business was quite suspended; the greater part of the shops were closed; most of the houses displayed a blue flag in token of their adherence to the popular side; and even the Jews in Houndsditch, Whitechapel, and those quarters, wrote upon their doors or window-shutters 'This House is a True Protestant.' The crowd was the law, and never was the law held in greater dread, or more implicitly obeyed.

Charles Dickens: from Barnaby Rudge, *Chapter 63*

8 June

1689—'I sat for my picture to Mr Kneller, for Mr Pepys, late Secretary of the Admiralty, holding my "Silva" in my right hand'

—*John Evelyn:* Diary

After what the Frontispiece and Porch of this Wooden Edifice presents you, I shall need no farther to repeat the Occasion of this following Discourse; I am only to acquaint you, That as it was delivered to the Royal Society by an unworthy Member thereof, in Obedience to their Commands; by the same it is now Re-publish'd without any farther Prospect: . . . it is only for the encouragement of an Industry, and worthy Labour, much in our days neglected, as haply reputed a Consideration of too sordid and vulgar a nature for Noble Persons, and Gentlemen to busie themselves withal, and who oftner find out occasions to Fell-down, and Destroy their Woods and Plantations, than either to repair or improve them.

But we are not without hopes of taking off these Prejudices, and of reconciling them to a Subject and an Industry which has been consecrated (as I may say) by as good, and as great Persons, as any the World has produced; . . . But since these may suffice after due reproofs of the late impolitique Wast, and universal sloth amongst us; we should now turn our Indignation into Prayers, and address ourselves to our better-natur'd Countrymen; that such Woods as do yet remain intire, might be carefully preserv'd, and such as are destroy'd, sedulously repaired: It is what all Persons who are Owners of Land may contribute to, and with infinite delight, as well as profit, who are touch'd with that laudable Ambition of imitating their Illustrious Ancestors, and of worthily serving their Generation. To these my earnest and humble Advice should be, That at their very first coming into their Estates, and as soon as they get Children, they would seriously think of this Work of Propagation also: For I observe there is no part of Husbandry, which Men commonly more fail in, neglect, and have cause to repent of, than that they did not begin Planting betimes, without which, they can expect neither Fruit, Ornament, or Delight from their Labours: Men seldom plant Trees till they begin to be Wise, that is, till they grow Old, and find by Experience the prudence and Necessity of it. When Ulysses, after a ten-years Absence, was return'd from Troy, and coming home, found his aged Father in the Field planting of Trees, He asked him, why (being so far advanc'd in Years) he would put himself to the Fatigue and Labour of Planting, that which he was never likely to enjoy the Fruits of? The good old Man (taking him for a Stranger) gently reply'd; *I plant* (says he) *against my Son Ulysses comes home.* The Application is Obvious and Instructive for both Old and Young.

> *John Evelyn:* Silva, or a Discourse of Forest-Trees, and the Propagation of Timber . . ., *from 'To the Reader'*

1862—'The notices that have appeared [reviews of Modern Love, and Poems *of the English Roadsides] fix favourably on the Roadside poems, but discard 'Modern Love', which, I admit, requires thought, and discernment, and reading more than once.... I find, to my annoyance, that I am susceptible to remarks on my poems....'*

George Meredith to Captain Maxse

In our old shipwrecked days there was an hour,
When in the firelight steadily aglow,
Joined slackly, we beheld the red chasm grow
Among the clicking coals. Our library-bower
That eve was left to us: and hushed we sat
As lovers to whom Time was whispering.
From sudden-opened doors we heard them sing:
The nodding elders mixed good wine with chat.
Well knew we that Life's greatest treasure lay
With us, and of it was our talk. 'Ah, yes!
Love dies!' I said: I never thought it less.
She yearned to me that sentence to unsay.
Then when the fire domed blackening, I found
Her cheek was salt against my kiss, and swift
Up the sharp scale of sobs her breast did lift: –
Now am I haunted by that taste! that sound!

. . .

Thus piteously Love closed what he begat:
The union of this ever-diverse pair!
These two were rapid falcons in a snare,
Condemn'd to do the flitting of the bat.
Lovers beneath the singing sky of May,
They wander'd once; clear as the dew on flowers:
But they fed not on the advancing hours;
Their hearts held cravings for the buried day.
Then each applied to each that fatal knife,
Deep questioning, which probes to endless dole.
Ah, what a dusty answer gets the soul
When hot for certainties in this our life! –
In tragic hints here see what evermore
Moves dark as yonder midnight ocean's force,
Thundering like ramping hosts of warrior horse,
To throw that faint thin line upon the shore!

George Meredith: Two stanzas from Modern Love

10 June 𝕨

1902—Joseph Conrad, in one of his self-deprecatory moods, confessed to Edward Garnett that he felt himself near the end of his tether

Dearest Edward,

In so far as writing is concerned I hardly dare look you in the face. Why do you introduce the name of Pinker into your letter? It is almost indelicate on your part. The times indeed are changed – and all my art has become artfulness in exploiting agents and publishers.

I am simply afraid to show you my work; and as to writing about it – this I can't do. I have now lost utterly all faith in myself, all sense of style, all belief in my power of telling the simplest fact in a simple way. For no other way do I care now. It is an unattainable way. My expression has become utterly worthless: it is time for the money to come rolling in.

The Blackwood vol: shall be coming out in two three months: *Youth Heart of Dark*ss and a thing I am trying to write now called the *End of the Tether* – an inept title to heartbreaking bosh. Pawling's vol. shall follow at a decent interval; four stories of which Typhoon is first and best. I am ashamed of them all; I don't believe either in their popularity or in their merit. Strangely enough it is yet my share of *Romance* (collab°n stuff with Ford) that fills me with the least dismay. My mind is becoming base, my hand heavy, my tongue thick – as though I had drunk some subtle poison, some slow poison that will make me die, die as it were without an echo. You understand?

I am always coming to you and some day I shall appear. I don't suppose you are angry with me; for in truth where would be the sense of expending your find stock of indignation upon such a base wretch.

The other day I ran into Duckth to try and see you. No luck.

Remember me affectionately to your wife whose trans of Karenina is splendid. Of the thing itself I think but little, so that her merit shines with the greater lustre. Jessie joins me in our love to you all, We talk of your boy very often. Oh! my dear dear fellow I am so very disgusted with my mental impotence, so afraid of my hollowness – so weary – deadly weary of writing!

Ever yours

JOSEPH CONRAD

1594—Edmund Spenser married Elizabeth Boyle

What guile is this, that those her golden tresses
 She doth attire under a net of gold;
 And with sly skill so cunningly them dresses,
 That which is gold, or hair, may scarce be told?
Is it that men's frail eyes, which gaze too bold,
 She may entangle in that golden snare;
 And being caught, may craftily enfold
 Their weaker hearts, which are not well aware?
Take heed, therefore, mine eyes, how ye do stare
 Henceforth too rashly on that guileful net,
 In which, if ever ye entrappéd are,
 Out of her hand ye by no means shall get.
Fondness it were for any, being free
 To covet fetters, though they golden be!

  .   .   .   .   .

After long stormes and tempests sad assay,
 Which hardly I enduréd heretofore;
 In dread of death and daungerous dismay,
 With which my silly barke was tosséd sore:
I doe at length descry the happy shore,
 In which I hope ere long for to arryve;
 Fayre soyle it seemes from far and fraught with store
 Of all that deare and daynty is alyve.
Most happy he that can at last atchyve
 The joyous safety of so sweet a rest;
 Whose least delight suthceth to deprive
 Remembrance of all paines which him opprest.
All paines are nothing in respect of this,
 All sorrowes short that gaine eternall blisse.

Spenser: two sonnets from Amoretti

12 June 🕮

1381—John Ball preached, for the last time, to the serfs assembled on Blackheath during the Peasants' Revolt, from his own text: 'When Adam delved and Eva span, | Who was then the gentleman?'

These unhappy people . . . began to styrre, bycause they sayde they were kept in great servage; and in the begynning of the worlde they sayd there were no bonde men. Wherefore . . . they sayd they wold no lengar suffre, for they wolde be all one; and if they labored or dyd any thyng for theyr lordes, they wold have wages therfor as well as other. And of this imaginacion was a folisshe preest in the countre of Kent, called Johan Ball, for the which folysshe wordes he had ben thre tymes in the bysshop of Canterburies prison. For this preest used often tymes on the Sondayes after masse, whanne the people were goynge out of the mynster, to go into the cloyster and preche, and made the people to assemble about hym, and wolde say thus:

'A ye good people, the maters gothe nat well to passe in Englande, nor shall nat do tyll every thyng be common; and that there be no villayns nor gentylmen, but that we may be all unyed toguyder, and that the lordes be no greatter maisters than we be. What have we deserved, or why shulde we be kept thus in servage? We be all come fro one father and one mother, Adam and Eve: wherby can they say or shewe that they be gretter lordes than we be? Savynge by that they cause us to wyn and labour for that they dispende. They ar clothed in velvet and chamlet furred with grise, and we be vestured with pore clothe; they have their wynes, spyces, and good breed, and we have the drawyng out of the chaffe, and drinke water; they dwell in fayre houses, and we have the payne and traveyle, rayne, and wynde in the feldes; and by that that cometh of our labours they kepe and maynteyne their estates: we be called their bondmen, and without we do redilye them servyce, we be beaten; and we have no soverayne to whom we may complayne, nor that wyll here us nor do us right. Lette us go to the kyng, he is yonge, and shewe hym what servage we be in, and shewe him howe we wyll have it otherwyse, or els we wyll provyde us of some remedy. And if we go togyder, all maner of people that be nowe in any bondage wyll folowe us, to thentent to be made fre; and whan the kyng seyth us, we shall have some remedy, outher by fayrnesse or otherwyse.'

Thus John Ball sayd on Sondayes whan the people issued out of the churches in the vyllages; wherfore many of the meane people loved him, and suche as entended to no goodnesse sayde howe he sayd trouth. And so they wolde murmure one with another in the feldes and in the wayes as they went togyder, affermyng howe Johan Ball sayde trouthe.

From: The Cronycle of Syr John Froissart, *translated out of the French by Sir John Bourchier, Lord Berners (c. 1525)*

1863—'The first part of Erewhon *written was an article headed 'Darwin Among the Machines' and signed 'Cellarius'. It was written in the Upper Rangitata district of Canterbury Province (as it then was) of New Zealand, and appeared at Christchurch in the Press newspaper, June 13, 1863'*

Samuel Butler in the preface to a revised edition of Erewhon, *1901*

We refer to the question: What sort of creature is man's next successor in the supremacy of the earth likely to be? We have often heard this debated; but it appears to us that we are ourselves creating our own successors; we are daily adding to the beauty and delicacy of their physical organisation; we are daily giving them greater power and supplying, by all sorts of ingenious contrivances, that self-regulating, self-acting power which will be to them what intellect has been to the human race. In the course of ages we shall find ourselves the inferior race. Inferior in power, inferior in that moral quality of self-control, we shall look up to them as the acme of all that the best and wisest man can ever dare to aim at. No evil passions, no jealousy, no avarice, no impure desires will disturb the serene might of those glorious creatures. Sin, shame and sorrow will have no place among them. Their minds will be in a state of perpetual calm, the contentment of a spirit that knows no wants, is disturbed by no regrets. Ambition will never torture them. Ingratitude will never cause them the uneasiness of a moment. The guilty conscience, the hope deferred, the pains of exile, the insolence of office and the spurns that patient merit of the unworthy takes – these will be entirely unknown to them. If they want 'feeding' (by the use of which very word we betray our recognition of them as living organism) they will be attended by patient slaves whose business and interest it will be to see that they shall want for nothing. If they are out of order they will be promptly attended to by physicians who are thoroughly acquainted with their constitutions; if they die, for even these glorious animals will not be exempt from that necessary and universal consummation, they will immediately enter into a new phase of existence, for what machine dies entirely in every part at one and the same instant?

We take it that when the state of things shall have arrived which we have above been attempting to describe, man will have become to the machine what the horse and the dog are to man. He will continue to exist, nay even to improve, and will be probably better off in his state of domestication than he is in his present wild state. We treat our horses, dogs, cattle and sheep, on the whole, with great kindness, we give them whatever experience teaches us to be best for them, and there can be no doubt that our use of meat has added to the happiness of the lower animals far more than it has detracted from it; in like manner it is reasonable to suppose that the machines will treat us kindly, for their existence is as dependent upon ours as ours is upon the lower animals.

Samuel Butler: from 'Darwin among the Machines'

14 June

1643—Parliament issued the Order for licensing of books, the act against which Milton's Areopagitica *was directed*

Lords and Commons of England, consider what nation it is whereof ye are the governors: a nation not slow and dull, but of a quick, ingenious and piercing spirit, acute to invent, subtle and sinewy to discourse, not beneath the reach of any point the highest that human capacity can soar to. . . . Behold now this vast city: a city of refuge, the mansion house of liberty, encompassed and surrounded with his protection; the shop of war hath not there more anvils and hammers waking, to fashion out the plates and instruments of armed justice in defence of beleaguered truth, than there be pens and heads there, sitting by their studious lamps, musing, searching, revolving new notions and ideas wherewith to present, as with their homage and their fealty, the approaching Reformation; others as fast reading, trying all things, assenting to the force of reason and convincement. . . .

What some lament of, we rather should rejoice at, should rather praise this pious forwardness among men, to reassume the ill-deputed care of their religion into their own hands again. A little generous prudence, a little forbearance of one another, and some grain of charity might win all these diligences to join, and unite into one general and brotherly search after truth; could we but forego this prelatical tradition of crowding free consciences and Christian liberties into canons and precept of men. . . . Yet these are the men cried out against for schismatics and sectaries, as if, while the temple of the Lord was building, some cutting some squaring the marble, others hewing the cedars, there should be a sort of irrational men, who could not consider there must be many schisms and many dissections made in the quarry and in the timber, ere God's house can be built. And when every stone is laid artfully together, it cannot be united into a continuity, it can but be contiguous in this world; neither can every piece of the building be of one form; nay rather the perfection consists in this, that out of many moderate varieties and brotherly dissimilitudes that are not vastly disproportional, arises the goodly and graceful structure that commends the whole pile and structure. Let us therefore be more considerate builders, more wise in spiritual architecture, when great reformation is expected.

John Milton: from Areopagitica

1215—King John sealed Magna Carta *'in the meadow called Ronimed between Windsor and Staines on the fifteenth day of June in the seventeenth year of our reign'*

My eye descending from the Hill, surveys
Where Thames amongst the wanton vallies strays.
Thames, the most loved of all the ocean's sons
By his old sire, to his embraces runs,
Hasting to pay his tribute to the sea,
Like mortal life to meet eternity.
Though with those streams he no resemblance hold
Whose foam is amber, and their gravel gold,
His genuine and less guilty wealth t' explore,
Search not his bottom, but survey his shore,
O'er which he kindly spreads his spacious wing
And hatches plenty for th' ensuing spring;
Nor then destroys it with too fond a stay,
Like mothers which their infants overlay;
Nor with a sudden and impetuous wave,
Like profuse kings, resumes the wealth he gave.
No unexpected inundations spoil
The mower's hopes, nor mock the plowman's toil;
But godlike his unwearied bounty flows,
First loves to do, then loves the good he does. . . .
Oh, could I flow like thee, and make thy stream
My great example, as it is my theme!
Though deep, yet clear; though gentle, yet not dull;
Strong without rage, without o'erflowing full.
    . . .
Low at his foot a spacious plain is placed,
Between the mountain and the stream embraced,
Which shade and shelter from the hill derives,
While the kind river wealth and beauty gives,
And in the mixture of all these appears
Variety, which all the rest endears. . . .
Here was that Charter seal'd, wherein the Crown
All marks of arbitrary power lays down:
Tyrant and slave, those names of hate and fear,
The happier stile of King and Subject bear:
Happy, when both to the same Center move,
When Kings give liberty, and Subjects love.

Sir John Denham: from 'Cooper's Hill'

16 June

The day on which everything happens in James Joyce's novel Ulysses

At Inisfail the fair there lies a land, the land of holy Michan. There rises a watch-tower beheld of men afar. There sleep the mighty dead as in life they slept, warriors and princes of high renown. A pleasant land it is in sooth of murmuring waters, fishful streams where sport the gunnard, the plaice, the roach, the halibut, the gibbed haddock, the grilse, the dab, the brill, the flounder, the mixed coarse fish generally and other denizens of the aqueous kingdom too numerous to be enumerated. In the mild breezes of the west and of the east the lofty trees wave in different directions their first class foliage, the wafty sycamore, the Lebanonian cedar, the exalted plane-tree, the eugenic eucalyptus and other ornaments of the arboreal world with which that region is thoroughly well supplied. Lovely maidens sit in close proximity to the roots of the lovely trees singing the most lovely songs while they play with all kinds of lovely objects, as for example golden ingots, silvery fishes, crans of herrings, drafts of eels, codlings, creels of fingerlings, purple seagems and playful insects. And heroes voyage from afar to woo them, from Eblana to Slievemargy, the peerless princes of unfettered Munster and of Connacht the just and of smooth sleek Leinster and of Crauachan's land and of Armagh the splendid and of the noble district of Boyle, princes, the sons of kings.

And there rises a shining palace whose crystal glittering roof is seen by mariners who traverse the extensive sea in barks built expressly for that purpose and thither come all herds and fatlings and first fruits of that land for O'Connell Fitzsimon takes toll of them, a chieftain descended from chieftains. Thither the extremely large wains bring foison of the fields, flaskets of cauliflowers, floats of spinach, pineapple chunks, Rangoon beans. . . . And by that way wend the herds innumerable of bellwethers and flushed ewes and shearling rams and lambs and stubble geese and roaring mares and polled calves and longwools and Cuffe's prime springers and culls and sowpigs and baconhogs and the various different varieties of highly distinguished swine and Angus heifers and polly bullocks of immaculate pedigree together with prime premiated milchcows and beeves; and there is ever heard a trampling, cackling, roaring, lowing, bleating, rumbling, grunting, champing, chewing, of sheep and pigs and heavyhooved kine from pasturelands of Lush and Rush and Carrickmines and from the streamy vales of Thomond . . . and from the gentle declivities of the place of the race of Kiar, their udders distended with superabundance of milk and butts of butter and rennets of cheese and farmer's firkins and targets of lamb and crannocks of corn and oblong eggs, in great hundreds, various in size, the agate with the sun.

So we turned into Barney Kiernan's and there sure enough was the citizen up in the corner having a great confab with himself and that bloody mangy mongrel, Garryowen, and he waiting for what the sky would drop in the way of drink. . . .

James Joyce: from Ulysses

1391—Geoffrey Chaucer was dismissed from his job as Richard II's Clerk of the Works. It is generally thought that his 'Complaint' was written soon after, though the envoy was added when Chaucer re-presented it to Henry IV in 1399

To yow, my purse, and to noon other wight
Complayne I, for ye be my lady dere!
I am so sory, now that ye been lyght;
For certes, but ye make me hevy chere,
Me were as leef be layd upon my bere;
For which unto your mercy thus I crye:
Beth hevy ageyn, or elles mot I dye!

Now voucheth sauf this day, or yt be nyght,
That I of yow the blisful soun may here,
Or see your colour lyk the sonne bryght,
That of yelownesse hadde never pere.
Ye be my lyf, ye be myn hertes stere,
Quene of comfort and of good companye:
Beth hevy ageyn, or elles moote I dye!

Now purse, that ben to me my lyves lyght
And saveour, as doun in this world here,
Out of this toune helpe me thurgh your myght,
Syn that ye wole nat ben my tresorere;
For I am shave as nye as any frere.
But yet I pray unto your coutesye:
Beth hevy agen, or elles moote I dye!

Lenvoy de Chaucer

O conquerour of Brutes Albyon,
Which that by lyne and free eleccion
Been verray kyng, this song to yow I sende;
And ye, that mowen alle oure harmes amende,
Have mynde upon my supplicacion!

Geoffrey Chaucer: 'The Complaint to His Purse'

18 June 📖

1799—Fictional date of the opening scene in George Eliot's novel, Adam Bede

With a single drop of ink for a mirror, the Egyptian sorcerer undertakes to reveal to any chance-comer far-reaching visions of the past. With this drop of ink at the end of my pen, I will show you the roomy workshop of Mr. Jonathan Burge, carpenter and builder, in the village of Hayslope, as it appeared on the eighteenth of June, in the year of our Lord 1799.

The afternoon sun was warm on the five workmen there, busy upon doors and window-frames and wainscoting. . . . A rough grey shepherd-dog . . . was lying with his nose between his forepaws, occasionally wrinkling his brows to cast a glance at the tallest of the five workmen, who was carving a shield in the centre of a wooden mantel-piece. It was to this workman that the strong baritone belonged which was heard above the sound of plane and hammer singing –

> 'Awake, my soul, and with the sun
> Thy daily stage of duty run;
> Shake off dull sloth . . .'

Such a voice could only come from a broad chest, and the broad chest belonged to a large-boned muscular man nearly six feet high, with a back so flat and a head so well poised that when he drew himself up to take a more distant survey of his work, he had the air of a soldier standing at ease. . . . In his tall swartness Adam Bede was a Saxon, and justified his name; but the jet-black hair made the more noticeable by its contrast with the light paper cap, and the keen glance of the dark eyes that shone from under strongly marked, prominent and mobile eyebrows, indicated a mixture of Celtic blood. The face was large and roughly hewn, and when in repose had no other beauty than such as belongs to an expression of good humoured honest intelligence. . . .

The concert of the tools and Adam's voice was at last broken by Seth, who, lifting the door at which he had been working intently, placed it against the wall, and said –

'There! I've finished my door today, anyhow.'

The workmen all looked up; Jim Salt, a burly red-haired man, known as Sandy Jim, paused from his planing, and Adam said to Seth, with a sharp glance of surprise –

'What! dost think thee'st finished the door?'

'Ay, sure,' said Seth, with answering surprise, 'what's awanting to 't?'

A loud roar of laughter from the other three workmen made Seth look round confusedly. Adam did not join in the laughter, but there was a slight smile on his face, as he said, in a gentler tone than before –

'Why, thee'st forgot the panels.'

George Eliot : from Adam Bede

1312—King Edward II's favourite, Piers Gaveston, was killed on Blacklow Hill by rebellious lords

---

MORTIMER SENIOR: Nephue, I must to Scotland, thou staiest here,
Leaue now to oppose thy selfe against the king.
Thou seest by nature he is milde and calme,
And seeing his mind so dotes on *Gaueston*,
Let him without controulement haue his will.
The mightiest kings haue had their minions,
Great *Alexander* loude *Ephestion*,
The conquering *Hercules* for *Hylas* wept,
And for *Patroclus* sterne *Achillis* droopt:
And not kings onelie, but the wisest men,
The Romaine *Tullie* loued *Octauius*,
Graue *Socrates*, wilde *Alcibiades*:
Then let his grace, whose youth is flexible,
And promiseth as much as we can wish,
Freely enjoy that vaine light-headed earle,
For riper yeares will weane him from such toyes.

MORTIMER IUNIOR: Vnckle, his wanton humor greeues not me,
But this I scorne, that one so baselie borne
Should by his soueraignes fauour grow so pert,
And riote with the treasure of the realme.
While souldiers mutinie for want of paie,
He weares a lords reuenewe on his back,
And *Midas* like he iets it in the court,
With base outlandish cullions at his heeles,
Whose proud fantastick liveries make such show,
As if that *Proteus* god of shapes appearde.
I haue not seene a dapper iack so briske;
He weares a short Italian hooded cloake,
Larded with pearle, and in his tuskan cap
A iewell of more value then the crowne:
Whiles other walke below, the king and he
From out a window laugh at such as we,
And floute our traine, and iest at our attire:
Vnckle, tis this that makes me impatient.

Christopher Marlowe: from Edward the Second,
Act I, Sc. iv

1832—John Clare wrote his poem 'The Flitting' ('I've left my own old Home of Homes') at Northborough

Give me no high-flown fangled things,
    No haughty pomp in marching chime,
Where muses play on golden strings
    And splendour passes for sublime,
Where cities stretch as far as fame
    And fancy's straining eye can go,
And piled until the sky for shame
    Is stooping far away below.

I love the verse that mild and bland
    Breathes of green fields and open sky,
I love the muse that in her hand
    Bears flowers of native poesy;
Who walks nor skips the pasture brook
    In scorn, but by the drinking horse
Leans oer its little brig to look
    How far the sallows lean across.

And feels a rapture in her breast
    Upon their root-fringed grains to mark
A hermit morehen's sedgy nest
    Just like a naiad's summer bark.
She counts the eggs she cannot reach
    Admires the spot and loves it well,
And yearns, so nature's lessons teach,
    Amid such neighbourhoods to dwell.

Een here my simple feelings nurse
    A love for every simple weed,
And een this little shepherd's purse
    Grieves me to cut it up; indeed
I feel at times a love and joy
    For every weed and every thing,
A feeling kindred from a boy,
    A feeling brought with every Spring . . .

John Clare : from 'The Flitting'

1890—Rudyard Kipling's 'Mandalay' was first published in W. E. Henley's periodical, The Scots Observer

By the old Moulmein Pagoda, lookin' eastward to the sea,
There's a Burma girl a-settin', and I know she thinks o' me;
For the wind is in the palm-trees, and the temple-bells they say:
'Come you back, you British soldier; come you back to Mandalay!'
      Come you back to Mandalay
      Where the old Flotilla lay:
Can't you 'ear their paddles chunkin' from Rangoon to Mandalay?
      On the road to Mandalay,
      Where the flyin'-fishes play,
And the dawn comes up like thunder outer China 'crost the Bay!

'Er petticoat was yaller an' 'er little cap was green,
An' 'er name was Supi-yaw-lat – jes' the same as Theebaw's Queen,
An' I seed 'er first a-smokin' of a whackin' white cheeroot,
An' a'wastin' Christian kisses on an 'eathen idol's foot:
      Bloomin' idol made o' mud –
      Wot they called the Great Gawd Budd –
Plucky lot she cared for idols when I kissed 'er where she stud!
      On the road to Mandalay . . .

When the mist was on the rice-fields an' the sun was droppin' slow,
She'd git 'er little banjo an' she'd sing 'Kulla-lo-lo!'
With 'er arm upon my shoulder an' 'er cheek agin my cheek
We useter watch the steamers an' the hathis pilin' teak.
      Elephints a-pilin' teak
      In the sludgy, squdgy creek,
Where the silence 'ung that 'eavy you was 'arf afraid to speak!
      On the road to Mandalay . . .

Ship me somewhere east of Suez, where the best is like the worst,
Where there aren't no Ten Commandments an' a man can raise a thirst;
For the temple-bells are callin', an' it's there that I would be –
By the old Moulmein Pagoda, lookin' lazy at the sea;
      On the road to Mandalay . . .

22 June

303(?)—Alban, the Roman soldier who became the first Christian martyr in Britain, was executed on the spot where St Alban's Cathedral now stands

When the judge perceived that he was not to be overcome by tortures, or withdrawn from the exercise of the Christian religion, he ordered him to be put to death. Being led to execution, he came to a river which, with most rapid course, ran between the wall of the town and the arena where he was to be executed. He there saw a multitude of people of both sexes, and of several ages and conditions, which was doubtless assembled by Divine instinct, to attend the most blessed confessor and martyr, and had so taken up the bridge on the river, that he could scarce pass over that evening. In short, almost all had gone out, so that the judge remained in the city without attendance. St. Alban, therefore, urged by an ardent and devout wish to arrive quickly at martyrdom, drew near to the stream, and on lifting up his eyes to heaven, the channel was immediately dried up, and he perceived that the water had departed and made way for him to pass. Among the rest, the executioner who was to have put him to death, observing this, moved by Divine inspiration, hastened to meet him at the place of execution, and casting down the sword which he had carried ready drawn, fell at his feet, earnestly praying that he might suffer with, or for, the martyr, whom he was ordered to execute. Whilst he thus from a persecutor was become a companion in the faith, and the other executioners hesitated to take up the sword which was lying on the ground, the reverend confessor, accompanied by the multitude, ascended a hill, about 500 paces from the place, adorned, or rather clothed with all kinds of flowers, having the sides neither perpendicular, nor even craggy, but sloping down into a most beautiful plain, worthy from its lovely appearance to be the scene of a martyr's suffering. On the top of this hill, St. Alban prayed that God would give him water, and immediately a living spring broke out before his feet. ... Here, therefore, the head of our most courageous martyr was struck off, and here he received the crown of life, which God has promised those who love him. But he who gave the wicked stroke was not permitted to rejoice over the deceased, for his eyes dropped upon the ground together with the blessed martyr's head.

Bede: from Ecclesiastical History, *translated by J. A. Giles (1840)*

Midsummer Night

HIPPOLYTA: 'Tis strange, my Theseus, that these lovers speak of.

THESEUS: More strange than true. I never may believe
These antique fables, nor these fairy toys.
Lovers and madmen have such seething brains,
Such shaping fantasies, that apprehend
More than cool reason ever comprehends.
The lunatic, the lover, and the poet,
Are of imagination all compact:
One sees more devils than vast hell can hold,
That is, the madman; the lover, all as frantic,
Sees Helen's beauty in a brow of Egypt;
The poet's eye, in a fine frenzy rolling,
Doth glance from heaven to earth, from earth to heaven;
And, as imagination bodies forth
The forms of things unknown, the poet's pen
Turns them to shapes, and gives to airy nothing
A local habitation and a name.
Such tricks hath strong imagination,
That, if it would but apprehend some joy,
It comprehends some bringer of that joy;
Or in the night, imagining some fear,
How easy is a bush suppos'd a bear!

HIPPOLYTA: But all the story of the night told over,
And all their minds transfigur'd so together,
More witnesseth than fancy's images,
And grows to something of great constancy,
But, howsoever, strange and admirable.

William Shakespeare: from A Midsummer
Night's Dream, *Act V, sc. 1, 1–27*

24 June

1314—The Scots under Robert Bruce won a great victory over the English at Bannockburn

At Bannockburn the English lay, –
The Scots they were na far away,
But waited for the break o' day
    That glinted in the east.

But soon the sun broke through the heath
And lighted up that field o' death,
When Bruce, wi' soul-inspiring breath,
    His heralds thus addressed: –

Scots, wha hae wi' Wallace bled,
Scots, wham Bruce has aften led;
Welcome to your gory bed,
    Or to victory.

Now's the day, and now's the hour;
See the front o' battle lour:
See approach proud Edward's power, –
    Chains and slaverie!

Wha will be a traitor knave?
Wha can fill a coward's grave?
Wha sae base as be a slave?
    Let him turn and flee!

Wha for Scotland's king and law
Freedom's sword will strongly draw,
Freeman stand, or freeman fa'?
    Let him follow me!

Lay the proud usurpers low!
Tyrants fall in every foe!
Liberty's in every blow!
    Let us do, or die!

                  Robert Burns

1680—John Wilmot, Earl of Rochester, in his last illness, sent for Bishop Gilbert Burnet. They spent the last four days of Rochester's life in spiritual discourse ; Burnet later made these conversations the basis of his Life of Rochester

Were I (who to my cost already am
One of those strange prodigious Creatures *Man*)
A Spirit free to choose for my own share,
What Case of Flesh and Blood, I pleas'd to weare,
I'd be a *Dog*, a *Monkey*, or a *Bear*;
Or any thing but that vain *Animal*
Who is so proud of being rational.
The senses are too gross, and he'll contrive
A Sixth, to contradict the other Five;
And before certain instinct, will preferr
Reason, which Fifty times for one does err.
Reason, an *Ignis fatuus* in the Mind,
Which leaving light of *Nature*, sense, behind,
Pathless and dang'rous wandring ways it takes,
Through error's Fenny-*Boggs*, and Thorny *Brakes*;
Whilst the misguided follower climbs with pain,
Mountains of Whimseys, heap'd in his own *Brain*:
Stumbling from thought to thought, falls head long down,
Into doubt's boundless Sea, where like to drown,
Books bear him up awhile, and makes him try
To swim with Bladders of *Philosophy*;
In hopes still t'oretake th'escaping light,
The *Vapour* dances in his dazled sight,
Till spent, it leaves him to eternal Night.
Then Old Age, and experience, hand in hand,
Lead him to death, and make him understand,
After a search so painful, and so long,
That all his Life he has been in the wrong:
Hudled in dirt, the reas'ning *Engine* lyes,
Who was so proud, so witty, and so wise.

Rochester: from Satyr Against Reason and Mankind

26 June

1853—'at Dessein's Hotel in Sterne's Room! . . . *Sterne's picture is looking down on me from the chimney piece at which he warmed his lean old shanks ninety years ago. He seems to say, "You are right. I was a humbug : and you, my lad, are you not as great?"* '

Thackeray to 'Miss Sarah'?, Letters

'I remember him [King George IV] in his cradle at St. James's . . . I was in London the year he was born. . . . I did not become the fashion until two years later, when my 'Tristram' made his appearance, who has held his own for a hundred years. By the way, mon bon monsieur, how many authors of your present time will last till the next century? Do you think Brown will? . . .

'Brown!' I roared. 'One of the most overrated men that ever put pen to paper!' . . .

'Ah! I see you men of letters have your cabals and jealousies, as we had in my time. There was an Irish fellow by the name of Goldsmith, who used to abuse me; but he went into no genteel company – and faith! it mattered little, his praise or abuse. I never was more surprised than when I heard that Mr. Irving, an American gentleman of parts and elegance, had wrote the fellow's life. To make a hero of that man, my dear sir, 'twas ridiculous! You followed in the fashion, I hear, and chose to lay a wreath before this queer little idol. Preposterous! A pretty writer, who has turned some neat couplets. Bah! I have no patience with Master Posterity, that has chosen to take up this fellow, and make a hero of him! And there was another gentleman of my time, Mr. Thiefcatcher Fielding, forsooth! a fellow with the strength, and the tastes, and the manners of a porter! What madness has possessed you all to bow before that Calvert Butt of a man? The dog has spirits, certainly. I remember my lord Bathurst praising them: but as for reading his books – *ma foi*, I would as lief go and dive for tripe in a cellar. The man's vulgarity stifles me. He wafts me whiffs of gin. Tobacco and onions are in his great coarse laugh, which choke me, *pardi*; and I don't think much better of the other fellow – the Scots' gallipot purveyor – Peregrine Clinker, Humphrey Random – how did the fellow call his rubbish? Neither of these men had the *bel air*, the *bon ton*, the *je ne sais quoy*. Pah! If I meet them in my walks by our Stygian river, I give them a wide berth, as that hybrid apothecary fellow would say. An ounce of civet, good apothecary: horrible, horrible! The mere thought of the coarseness of those men gives me the *chair de poule*. Mr. Fielding, especially, has no more sensibility than a butcher in Fleet Market. He takes his heroes out of ale-house kitchens, or worse places still. And this is the person whom Posterity has chosen to honour along with me – *me*! Faith, Monsieur Posterity, you have put me in pretty company, and I see you are no wiser than we were in our time.'

'And so', I said, turning round to Mr. Sterne, 'you are actually jealous of Mr. Fielding? Oh, you men of letters, you men of letters! Is not the world (your world I mean) big enough for all of you?'

William Makepeace Thackeray: from Round-about Papers (*the essay entitled 'Dessein's'*)

1787—Edward Gibbon finished his Decline and Fall of the Roman Empire

My transmigration from London to Lausanne could not be effected without interrupting the course of my historical labours. The hurry of my departure, the joy of my arrival, the delay of my tools, suspended their progress, and a full twelvemonth was lost before I could resume the thread of regular and daily industry. . . . Happily for my eyes, I have always closed my studies with the day, and commonly with the morning, and a long but temperate labour has been accomplished without fatiguing either the mind or body. But when I computed the remainder of my time and my task, it was apparent that, according to the season of publication, the delay of a month would be productive of that of a year. I was now straining for the goal, and in the last winter many evenings were borrowed from the social pleasures of Lausanne. I could now wish that a pause, an interval, had been allowed for a serious revisal.

I have presumed to mark the moment of conception [cf. October 15]; I shall now commemorate the hour of my final deliverance. It was on the day, or rather the night, of the 27th of June, 1787, between the hours of eleven and twelve, that I wrote the last lines of the last page in a summer-house in my garden. After laying down my pen I took several turns in a *berceau*, or covered walk of Acacias, which commands a prospect of the country, the lake, and the mountains. The air was temperate, the sky was serene, the silver orb of the moon was reflected from the waters, and all Nature was silent. I will not dissemble the first emotions of joy on the recovery of my freedom, and perhaps the establishment of my fame. But my pride was soon humbled, and a sober melancholy was spread over my mind by the idea that I had taken an everlasting leave of an old and agreeable companion, and that, whatever might be the future date of my history, the life of the historian must be short and precarious. I will add two facts which have seldom occurred in the composition of six, or at least five, quartos. 1. My first rough manuscript, without any intermediate Copy, has been sent to the press. 2. Not a sheet has been seen by any human eyes except those of the Author and the printer: the faults and the merits are exclusively my own.

From The Autobiographies of Edward Gibbon

28 June

1709—'Mr. Bickerstaff has been working certain wonderful effects by prescribing his circumspection-water, which has cured Mrs. Spy of rolling her eyes about in public places. Lady Petulant has made use of it to cure her husband's jealousy, and Lady Gad has cured a whole neighbourhood of detraction'

'The fame of these things,' continues the Censor-General, 'added to my being an old fellow, makes me extremely acceptable to the fair sex. You would hardly believe me when I tell you there is not a man in town so much their delight as myself. They make no more of visiting me than going to Madam Despingle's; there were two of them, namely, Dainia and Clidamira (I assure you women of distinction), who came to see me this morning, in their way to prayers, and being in a very diverting humour (as innocence always makes people cheerful) they would needs have me, according to the distinction of pretty and very pretty fellows, inform them if I thought either of them had a title to the very pretty among those of their sex; and if I did, which was the most deserving of the two?

'To put them on trial, "look ye", said I, "I must not rashly give my judgment in matters of this importance; pray let me see you dance; I play upon the kit." They immediately fell back to the lower end of the room (you may be sure they curtsied low enough to me), and began. Never were two in the world so equally matched. . . . Never was man in so dangerous a condition as myself, when they began to expand their charms. "O! ladies, ladies", cried I; "not half that air; you will fire the house!" Both smiled, for, by-the-bye, there is no carrying a metaphor too far when a lady's charms are spoken of. Somebody, I think, has called a fine woman dancing "a brandished torch of beauty". These rivals moved with such an agreeable freedom that you would believe their gesture was the necessary effect of the music, and not the product of skill and practise. Now Clidamira came on with a crowd of graces, and demanded my judgment with so sweet an air – and she had no sooner carried it, but Dainia made her utterly forgot, by a gentle sinking and rigadoon step. The contest held a full half hour; and, I protest, I saw no manner of difference in their perfections until they came up together and expected sentence. "Look ye, ladies", said I, "I see no difference in the least in your performances; but you, Clidamira, seem to be so well satisfied that I should determine for you, that I must give it to Dainia, who stands with so much diffidence and fear, after showing an equal merit to what she pretends to. Therefore, Clidamira, you are a pretty, but, Dainia, you are a very pretty lady; for", said I, "beauty loses its force if not accompanied with modesty. She that hath an humble opinion of herself, will have everybody's applause, because she does not expect it; while the vain creature loses approbation through too great a sense of deserving it." '

Sir Richard Steele: from The Tatler, *No. 34*

1854—Charlotte Brontë was married to the Rev. Arthur Nicholls

It was fixed that the marriage was to take place on the 29th of June. Her two friends arrived at Haworth Parsonage the day before; and the long summer afternoon and evening were spent by Charlotte in thoughtful arrangements for the morrow, and for her father's comfort during her absence from home. When all was finished – the trunk packed, the morning's breakfast arranged, the wedding-dress laid out, – just at bedtime, Mr. Brontë announced his intention of stopping at home while the others went to church. What was to be done? Who was to give the bride away? There were only to be the officiating clergyman, the bride and bridegroom, the brides-maid, and Miss Wooler present. The Prayer-book was referred to; and there it was seen that the Rubric enjoins that the Minister shall receive 'the woman from her father's or *friend's* hands', and that nothing is specified as to the sex of the 'friend'. So Miss Wooler, ever kind in emergency, volunteered to give her old pupil away.

The news of the wedding had slipt abroad before the little party came out of the church, and many old and humble friends were there, seeing her look 'like a snow-drop', as they say. Her dress was white embroidered muslin, with a lace mantle, and white bonnet trimmed with green leaves, which perhaps might suggest the resemblance to the pale wintry flower.

Mr. Nicholls and she went to visit his friends and relations in Ireland; and made a tour by Killarney, Glengariff, Tarbert, Tralee, and Cork, seeing scenery, of which she says, 'some parts exceeded all I had ever imagined'. . . . 'I must say I like my new relations. My dear husband, too, appears in a new light in his own country. More than once I have had deep pleasure in hearing his praises on all sides. Some of the old servants and followers of the family tell me I am a most fortunate person; for that I have got one of the best gentlemen in the country. . . . I trust I feel thankful to God for having enabled me to make what seems a right choice; and I pray to be enabled to repay as I ought the affectionate devotion of a truthful, honourable man.'

Elizabeth Cleghorn Gaskell: from The Life of Charlotte Brontë

1688—The Seven Bishops, one of whom was the Cornishman, Trelawney, were acquitted after a trial that had roused popular wrath all over the country

The Song of the Western Men

A good sword and a trusty hand!
    A merry heart and true!
King James's men shall understand
    What Cornish lads can do!

And have they fix'd the where and when?
    And shall Trelawney die?
Here's twenty thousand Cornish men
    Will see the reason why!

Out spake their captain brave and bold,
    A merry wight was he:
'If London Tower were Michael's hold,
    We'll set Trelawney free!

We'll cross the Tamar, land to land,
    The Severn is no stay, –
All side by side, and hand to hand,
    And who shall bid us nay!

'And when we come to London Wall,
    A pleasant sight to view,
Come forth! come forth! ye Cowards all,
    To better men than you!

'Trelawney he's in keep and hold,
    Trelawney he may die,
But here's twenty thousand Cornish bold
    Will see the reason why!'

Robert Stephen Hawker

Iulye.

1858—Charles Darwin sent to the Linnaean Society his first communication on the theory he was to develop in The Origin of Species

De Candolle, in an eloquent passage, has declared that all nature is at war, one organism with another, or with external nature. Seeing the contented face of nature, this may at first well be doubted; but reflection will inevitably prove it to be true. The war, however, is not constant, but recurrent in a slight degree at short periods, and more severely at occasional more distant periods; and hence its effects are easily overlooked. It is the doctrine of Malthus applied in most cases with tenfold force. As in every climate there are seasons, for each of its inhabitants, of greater and less abundance, so all annually breed; and the moral restraint which in some small degree checks the increase of mankind is entirely lost. Even slow-breeding mankind has doubled in twenty-five years; and if he could increase his food with greater ease, he would double in less time. But for animals without artificial means, the amount of food for each species must, *on an average*, be constant, whereas the increase of all organisms tends to be geometrical, and in a vast majority of cases at an enormous ratio. Suppose in a certain spot there are eight pairs of birds, and that *only* four pairs of them annually (including double hatches) rear only four young, and that these go on rearing their young at the same rate, then at the end of seven years (a short life, excluding violent deaths, for any bird), there will be 2048 birds, instead of the original sixteen. As this increase is quite impossible, we must conclude either that birds do not rear nearly half their young, or that the average life of a bird is, from accident, not nearly seven years. . . .

But let the external conditions of a country alter . . . let the change of conditions continue progressing (forming new stations), in such a case the original inhabitants must cease to be as perfectly adapted to the changed conditions as they were originally. . . . Now, can it be doubted, from the struggle each individual has to obtain subsistence, that any minute variation in structure, habits, or instincts, adapting that individual better to the new conditions, would tell upon its vigour and health? In the struggle it would have a better *chance* of surviving; and those of its offspring which inherited the variation, be it ever so slight, would also have a better *chance*. Yearly more are bred than can survive; the smallest grain in the balance, in the long run, must tell on which death shall fall, and which shall survive. Let this work of selection on the one hand, and death on the other, go on for a thousand generations, who will pretend to affirm that it would produce no effect, when we remember what, in a few years, Bakewell effected in cattle, and Western in sheep, by this identical principle of selection?

1681—The Earl of Shaftesbury ('Achitophel') was arrested on charges of high treason in connection with his role in Monmouth's Rebellion

Of these the false Achitophel was first;
A name to all succeeding ages cursed:
For close designs, and crooked counsels fit;
Sagacious, bold, and turbulent of wit;
Restless, unfixed in principles and place;
In power unpleased, impatient of disgrace:
A fiery soul, which, working out its way,
Fretted the pygmy body to decay,
And o'er-informed the tenement of clay.
A daring pilot in extremity;
Pleased with the danger, when the waves went high,
He sought the storms; but, for the calm unfit,
Would steer too nigh the sands, to boast his wit.
Great wits are sure to madness near allied,
And thin partitions do their bounds divide;
Else why should he, with wealth and honor blest,
Refuse his age the needful hours of rest?
Punish a body which he could not please;
Bankrupt of life, yet prodigal of ease?
And all to leave what with his toil he won
To that unfeathered two-legged thing, a son;
Got while his soul did huddled notions try,
And born a shapeless lump, like anarchy.

In friendship false, implacable in hate,
Resolved to ruin or to rule the state.
To compass this the triple bond he broke,
The pillars of the public safety shook,
And fitted Israel for a foreign yoke;
Then seized with fear, yet still affecting fame,
Usurped a patriot's all-atoning name.
So easy still it proves in factious times,
With public zeal to cancel private crimes.
How safe is treason, and how sacred ill,
Where none can sin against the people's will!

John Dryden: from Absalom and Achitophel

1851—William Makepeace Thackeray delivered the last of his lectures on the English humourists at Willis's Rooms in London, and took the occasion to assure his fashionable audience that their attitude towards literature and literary men was fitting and proper in the best of Victorian worlds

Does society look down on a man because he is an author? . . . He is not fair to society if he enters it with this suspicion hankering about him; if he is doubtful about his reception, how hold up his head honestly, and look frankly in the face of that world. . . ? Is he place-hunting, and thinking in his mind that he ought to be made an Ambassador, like Prior, or a Secretary of State, like Addison? his pretence of equality falls to the ground at once: he is scheming for a patron, not shaking the hand of a friend, when he meets the world.

Treat such a man as he deserves; laugh at his buffoonery, and give him a dinner and a *bon jour*; laugh at his self-sufficiency and absurd assumptions of superiority, and his equally ludicrous airs of martydom: laugh at his flattery and his scheming, and buy it, if it's worth the having. Let the wag have his dinner and the hireling his pay, if you want him, and make a profound bow to the *grand homme incompris*, and the boisterous martyr, and show him the door.

The great world, the great aggregate experience, has its good sense, as it has its good humour. It detects a pretender, as it trusts a loyal heart. It is kind in the main: how should it be otherwise than kind, when it is so wise and clear-headed? To any literary man who says, 'It despises my profession', I say, with all my might – no, no, no. It may pass over your individual case – how many a brave fellow has failed in the race, and perished unknown in the struggle? – but it treats you as you merit in the main. If you serve it, it is not unthankful; if you please it, it is pleased; if you cringe to it, it detects you, and scorns you if you are mean; returns your cheerfulness with its good humour; it deals not ungenerously with your weaknesses; it recognizes most kindly your merits; it gives you a fair place and fair play. To any one of those men of whom we have spoken was it in the main ungrateful? A king might refuse Goldsmith a pension, as a publisher might keep his masterpiece and the delight of all the world in his desk for two years; but it was a mistake, and not ill-will. Noble and illustrious names of Swift, and Pope, and Addison! dear and honoured memories of Goldsmith and Fielding! kind friends, teachers, benefactors! who shall say that our country, which continues to bring you such unceasing tribute of applause, admiration, love, sympathy, does not do honour to the literary calling which it bestows upon *you*!

Wm. Makepeace Thackeray: from The English Humourists of the Eighteenth Century

I celebrate myself, and sing myself,
And what I assume you shall assume,
For every atom belonging to me as good belongs to you.

I loafe and invite my soul,
I lean and loaf at my ease observing a spear of summer grass.

My tongue, every atom of my blood, form'd from this soil, this air,
Born here of parents born here from parents the same, and their parents the same,
I, now thirty-seven years old in perfect health begin,
Hoping to cease not till death.

. . .

The spotted hawk swoops by and accuses me, he complains of my gab and loitering.
I too am not a bit tamed, I too am untranslatable,
I sound my barbaric yawp over the roofs of the world.

The last scud of day holds back for me,
It flings my likeness after the rest and true as any on the shadow'd wilds,
It coaxes me to the vapor and the dusk.

I depart as air, I shake my white locks at the runaway sun,
I effuse my flesh in eddies, and drift it in lacy jags.

I bequeath myself to the dirt to grow from the grass I love,
If you want me again look for me under your boot-soles.

You will hardly know who I am or what I mean,
But I shall be good health to you nevertheless,
And filter and fibre your blood.

Failing to fetch me at first keep encouraged,
Missing me one place search another,
I stop somewhere waiting for you.

1535—Sir Thomas More, shortly before his execution, sent his last letter ('written with a coal') to his daughter, Margaret Roper

Our Lord bless you, good daughter, and your good husband, and your little boy, and all yours, and all my children, and all my godchildren and all our friends. Recommend me when ye may to my good daughter Cicely, whom I beseech our Lord to comfort. And I send her my blessing, and to all her children, and pray her to pray for me. I send her a handkerchief: and God comfort my good son her husband. My good daughter Dauncey hath the picture in parchment that you delivered me from my Lady Coniers, her name is on the backside. Shew her that I heartily pray her that you may send it in my name to her again, for a token from me to pray for me. I like special well Dorothy Colly, I pray you be good unto her. I would wit whether this be she that you wrote me of. If not, yet I pray you be good to the other as you may in her affliction, and to my good daughter Joan Aleyn too. Give her, I pray you, some kind answer, for she sued hither to me this day to pray you be good to her. I cumber you, good Margaret, much, but I would be sorry if it should be any longer than tomorrow. For it is Saint Thomas' even and the Utas of Saint Peter; and therefore tomorrow long I to go to God: it were day very meet and convenient for me. I never liked your manner toward me better than when you kissed me last: for I love when daughterly love and dear charity hath no leisure to look to worldly courtesy. Farewell, my dear child, and pray for me, and I shall for you and all your friends, that we may merrily meet in Heaven. I thank you for your great cost. I send now to my good daughter Clement her algorism stone, and I send her and my godson, and all hers, God's blessing and mine. I pray you at time convenient recommend me to my good son John More. I liked well his natural fashion. Our Lord bless him and his good wife my loving daughter, to whom I pray him be good as he hath great cause: and that if the land of mine come to his hand he break not my will concerning his sister Dauncey. And our Lord bless Thomas and Austen and all that they shall have.

6 July

Sir Thomas Browne received his diploma as socius honorarius *of the College of Physicians*

For my Religion, though there be severall circumstances that might perswade the world I have none at all, as the generall scandal of my profession, the naturall course of my studies, the indifferency of my behaviour, and discourse in matters of Religion, neither violently defending one, nor with that common ardour and contention opposing another; yet in despight thereof I dare, without usurpation, assume the honorable stile of a Christian: not that I merely owe this title to the Font, my education, or Clime wherein I was borne, as being bred up either to confirme those principles my Parents instilled into my unwary understanding; or by a generall consent proceed in the Religion of my Countrey: But that having, in my riper yeares, and confirmed judgement, seene and examined all, I finde my selfe obliged by the principles of Grace, and the law of mine owne reason, to embrace no other name than this; neither doth herein my zeale so farre make me forget the generall charitie I owe unto humanity, as rather to hate then pity Turkes, Infidels, and (what is worse) the Jewes, rather contenting my selfe to enjoy that happy stile, then maligning those who refuse so glorious a title.

. . . I confesse every Countrey hath its Machiavell, every age its Lucian, whereof common heads must not heare, nor more advanced judgements too rashly venture on: 'tis the Rhetorick of Satan, and may pervert a loose or prejudicate beleefe.

I confesse I have perused them all, and can discover nothing that may startle a discreet beliefe: . . . I confesse there are in Scripture stories that doe exceed the fables of Poets, and to a captious Reader sound like *Gargantua* or *Bevis*: Search all the Legends of times past, and the fabulous conceits of these present, and 'twill be hard to find one that deserves to carry the buckler unto *Sampson*, . . . Myselfe could shewe a catalogue of doubts. . . . Whether *Eve* was framed out of the left side of *Adam*, I dispute not; because I stand not yet assured which is the right side of a man, or whether there be any such distinction in Nature: that she was edified out of the ribbe of *Adam* I believe, yet raise no question who shall arise with that ribbe at the Resurrection. . . . There are a bundle of Curiosities, not onely in Philosophy but in Divinity, proposed and discussed by men of the most supposed abilities, which indeed are not worthy our vacant hours, much lesse our more serious studies.

Sir Thomas Browne: from Religio Medici

1757—Benjamin Franklin published Poor Richard Improved, Being an Almanac &c. for the year of Our Lord, 1758

I stopped my horse lately, where a great number of people were collected at a Vendue of Merchant's goods. The hour of sale not being come, they were conversing on the badness of the Times: and one of the company called to a clean old man, with white locks, 'Pray, Father ABRAHAM! what do you think of the Times? Won't these heavy taxes quite ruin the country? How shall we ever be able to pay them? What would you advise us to?'

Father ABRAHAM stood up, and replied, 'If you would have my advice; I will give it you, in short; for *a word to the wise is enough*, and *many words won't fill a bushel*, as *Poor* RICHARD says.'

They all joined, desiring him to speak his mind; and gathering round him, he proceeded as follows:

'Friends' says he, 'and neighbours! The taxes are indeed very heavy; and if those laid on by the Government were the only ones we had to pay, we might the more easily discharge them: but we have many others, and much more grievous to some of us. We are taxed twice as much by our IDLENESS, three times as much by our PRIDE, and four times as much by our FOLLY: and from these taxes, the Commissioners cannot ease, or deliver us by allowing an abatement. However let us hearken to good advice, and something may be done for us. *GOD helps them that help themselves*, as *Poor* RICHARD says in his *Almanac* of 1733.

It would be thought a hard Government that should tax its people One-tenth part of their TIME, to be employed in its service. But Idleness taxes many of us much more; if we reckon all that is spent in absolute sloth, or doing of nothing; with that which is spent in idle employments or amusements that amount to nothing. Sloth, by bringing on diseases, absolutely shortens life. *Sloth, like Rust, consumes faster than Labour wears; while the used key is always bright,* as *Poor* RICHARD says. But *dost thou love Life? Then do not squander time! for that's the stuff Life is made of,* as *Poor* RICHARD says. . . .

If Time be of all things the most precious, *Wasting of Time must be* (as *Poor* RICHARD says) *the greatest prodigality*; since, as he elsewhere tells us, *Lost time is never found again* . . . and *He that riseth late, must trot all day; and shall scarce overtake his business at night*. While *Laziness travels so slowly, that Poverty soon overtakes him*, as we read in *Poor* RICHARD; who adds, *Drive thy business! Let not that drive thee!* and

> *Early to bed, and early to rise,*
> *Makes a man healthy, wealthy, and wise.*

> From Poor Richard Improved (*by 'Richard Saunders'*)

8 July 📖

Your wickedness makes you, as it were, heavy as lead, and to tend downward with great weight and pressure toward hell; and if God should let you go you would immediately sink and swiftly descend and plunge into the bottomless gulf, and your healthy constitution, and your own care and prudence, and best contrivance, and all your righteousness, would have no more influence to uphold you and keep you out of hell than a spider's web would have to stop a falling rock. Were it not that so is the sovereign pleasure of God, the earth would not bear you one moment; for you are a burden to it; the creation groans with you; the creature is made subject to the bondage of your corruption, not willingly; the sun does not willingly shine upon you to give you light to serve sin and Satan; the earth does not willingly yield her increase to satisfy your lusts; nor is it willingly a stage for your wickedness to be acted upon; the air does not willingly serve you for breath to maintain the flame of life in your vitals, while you spend your life in the service of God's enemies. God's creatures are good, and were made for man to serve God with, and do not willingly subserve to any other purpose, and groan when they are abused to purposes so directly contrary to their nature and end. And the world would spew you out, were it not for the sovereign hand of Him who hath subjected it in hope. . . .

The wrath of God is like great waters that are dammed up for the present; they increase more and more, and rise higher and higher, till an outlet is given; and the longer the stream is stopped the more rapid and mighty its course, when once it is let loose. It is true, that judgment against your evil work has not been executed hitherto; the floods of God's vengeance have been withheld; but your guilt in the meantime is constantly increasing, and you are every day treasuring up more wrath; the waters are continually rising, and waxing more and more mighty. . . . If God should only withdraw His hand from the flood-gate, it would immediately fly open, and the fiery floods of the fierceness and wrath of God would rush forth with inconceivable fury, and would come upon you with omnipotent power; . . .

O sinner! consider the fearful danger you are in: it is a great furnace of wrath, a wide and bottomless pit, full of the fire of wrath, that you are held over in the hands of that God whose wrath is provoked . . . you hang by a slender thread, with the flames of Divine wrath flashing about it and ready every moment to singe it, and burn it asunder. . . .

1859—George Meredith's novel The Ordeal of Richard Feverel *was reviewed in* The Athenaeum

. . . The reader feels that none of the characters are real, live human beings; but then they are all so like life, their conversation is so bright and spirited, that it affects the reader like a painful reality to see such cruelty and blindness and blundering, such child's play with the most sacred mysteries of life, even though he is quite aware of the fiction that lies at the root of this 'seeming show'. The story of 'The Ordeal of Richard Feverel' is brief enough as regards facts. Sir Austen Feverel is a baronet who has been bitterly wronged in life; a faithless wife and a treacherous friend round the story of his griefs. Being very proud, very sensitive, with a great leaven of insane philosophy, he resolves that his only son shall be brought up on a system of art and nature which shall train him to be superior to the strokes of fate, and to be, moreover, all that the most perfect human being was ever intended by nature to be, both in mind and body. This 'system' he follows rigidly, with blind despotism, and though a good man, full of generous and noble instincts, this 'system' makes him cruel, hard, relentless, in all that relates to its requisitions. His son grows up to be a very fine young man, but his father cannot recognize where the 'system' which had worked well on the youth should give way to common sense when he grows to the age of a reasonable, rational, responsible human being . . . The misery, sin and sorrow that ensue . . . concur to strengthen all that is wrong and perverse, – and how the only blameless creature, the one thoroughly good, gentle, unselfish being, who would have retrieved and redeemed all – the one good angel thrown into the strife – is the one who falls the victim, and in death, although she could not do it in life, brings all the long ordeal to a solution, leaving the actors, not to grief and tears, the tumult of a grief with hope in it, but to cold despair and the silence of eternal regret, making a sort of modern adaptation of the old Greek tragedy, which is what we suppose the author intended. The only comfort the reader can find on closing the book is, – that it is not true. We hope the author will use his great ability to produce something pleasanter next time.

10 July

1666—Fire destroyed the home of Anne Bradstreet, the first American poet to win general recognition

In silent night when rest I took,
For sorrow near I did not look,
I waken'd was with thundring noise
And piteous shreiks of dreadfull voice.
That fearfull sound of 'Fire!' and 'Fire!'
Let no man know is my Desire.
I, starting up, the light did spye,
And to my God my heart did cry
To strengthen me in my Distresse,
And not to leave me succourlesse.
Then coming out, beheld apace
The flame consume my dwelling place. . . .

When by the Ruines oft I past,
My sorrowing eyes aside did cast,
And here and there the places spye
Where oft I sate, and long did lye.
Here stood that Trunk, and there that chest;
There lay that store I counted best:
My pleasant things in ashes lye,
And them behold no more shall I.
Under thy roof no guest shall sitt,
Nor at thy Table eat a bitt.
No pleasant tale shall e'er be told,
Nor things recounted done of old.
No Candle e'er shall shine in Thee,
Nor bridegroom's voice e'er heard shall bee.
In silence ever shalt thou lye;
Adeiu, Adeiu; All's vanity.

Then streight I 'gan my heart to chide:
And did thy wealth on earth abide? . . .
Raise up thy thoughts above the skye,
That dunghill mists away may flie. . . .
There's wealth enough, I need no more;
Farewell my Pelf, farewell my Store.
The world no longer let me Love,
My hope and Treasure lyes Above.

Ann Bradstreet: 'Upon the Burning of our
House, July 10th, 1666'

1723—'in the Evening-Post . . . a Presentment was inserted of the Grand Jury of Middlesex, against the publisher of a Book, entitled, The Fable of the Bees; or, Private Vices Publick Benefits', *for 'labouring to subvert and ruin our Constitution, under a specious Pretense of defending it'.*

. . . But it is ridiculous for Men to meddle with Books above their Sphere. The *Fable of the Bees* was design'd for the Entertainment of People of Knowledge and Education, when they have an idle Hour which they know not how to spend better: It is a Book of severe and exalted Morality, that contains a strict Test of Vertue, an infallible Touch-stone to distinguish the real from the counterfeited, and shews many Actions to be faulty that are pawm'd upon the World for good ones: It describes the Nature and Symptoms of human Passions, detects their Force, and disguises and traces Self Love in its darkest Recesses; I might safely add, beyond any other System of Ethicks: The Whole is a Rhapsody void of Order or Method, but no Part of it has any thing in it that is sour or pedantick; the Style I confess is very unequal, sometimes very high and rhetorical, and sometimes very low and even very trivial; such as it is, I am satisfied that it has diverted Persons of great Probity and Virtue, and unquestionable good Sense; and I am in no fear that it will ever cease to do so whilst it is read by such. Whoever has seen the violent Charge against this Book, will pardon me for saying more in Commendation of it, than a Man not labouring under the same Necessity would do of his own Work on any other Occasion.

The Encomiums upon Stews complain'd of in the Presentment are no where in the Book. What might give a Handle to this Charge, must be a Political Dissertation concerning the best Method to guard and preserve Women of Honour and Virtue from the Insults of dissolute Men, whose Passions are often ungovernable: As in this there is a Dilemma between two Evils, which it is impracticable to shun both, so I have treated it with the utmost Caution, and begin thus: *I am far from encouraging Vice, and should think it unspeakable Felicity for a State, if the Sin of Uncleanness could be utterly banish'd from it; but I am afraid it is impossible.* I give my Reasons why I think it so; and speaking occasionally of the Musick-houses at *Amsterdam,* I give a short account of them, than which nothing could be more harmless; and I appeal to all impartial Judges, whether what I have said of them is not ten times more proper to give Men (even the voluptuous of any Taste) a Disgust and Aversion against them, than it is to raise any criminal Desire. I am sorry the Grand-Jury should conceive that I publish'd this with a design to debauch the Nation, without considering. . . that the Matter complain'd of is manifestly address'd to Magistrates and Politicians, or at least the more serious and thinking Part of Mankind; whereas a general Corruption of Manners as to Lewdness, to be produced by reading, can only be apprehended from Obscenities easily purchas'd, and every Way adapted to the Tastes and Capacities of the heedless Multitude. . . .

Bernard de Mandeville: from 'A Vindication of the Book call'd, The Fable of the Bees', London Journal, *3 August, 1723*

True it was that I, Sir John Froissart, had great affection to go and see the realm of England . . . because in my youth I had been brought up in the court of the noble King Edward the Third . . . for I had not been there twenty-seven years before, and I thought, though I saw not those lords that I left alive there, yet at the least I should see their heirs, the which should do me much good to see, and also to justify the histories and matters that I had written of them. . . . I had engrossed in a fair book well enlumined all the matters of amours and moralities, that in four and twenty years before I had made and compiled, which greatly quickened my desire to go into England to see King Richard, who was son to the noble Prince of Wales and of Aquitaine, for I had not seen this King Richard since he was christened in the cathedral church of Bourdeaux, at which time I was there. . . .

For these causes and other I had great desire to go into England to see the king and his uncles. Also I had this said fair book well covered with velvet garnished with clasps of silver and gilt, thereof to make a present to the king on my first coming to his presence; I had such desire to go this voyage that the pain and travail grieved me nothing. Thus provided of horses and other necessaries,I passed the sea at Calais, and came to Dover, the twelfth day of the month of July. When I came there I found no man of my knowledge, it was so long sith I had been in England, and the houses were all newly changed, and young children were become men and the women knew me not nor I them: so I abode half a day and all a night at Dover: it was on a Tuesday, and the next day by nine of the clock I came to Canterbury, to Saint Thomas's Shrine, and to the Tomb of the noble prince of Wales who is there interred right richly: there I heard mass, and made mine offering to the Holy Saint, and then dined at my lodging: and there I was informed how King Richard should be there the next day on pilgrimage, which was after his return out of Ireland where he had been the space of nine months or there about: the king had a devotion to visit St. Thomas's Shrine, and also because the prince his father was there buried. Then I thought to abide the king there, and so I did; and the next day the king came thither with a noble company of lords, ladies, and damoselles: and when I was among them they seemed to me all new folks, I knew no person: the time was sore changed in twenty-eight years, and with the king as then was none of his uncles; the duke of Lancaster was in Aquitaine, and the dukes of York and Gloucester were in other business, so that I was at the first all abashed, for if I had seen any ancient knight that had been with King Edward or with the prince I had been well recomforted and would have gone to him, but I could see none such.

Froissart's Chronicles, *as translated by Lord Berners*

1798—William Wordsworth wrote, entirely 'in his head', the 'Lines Composed a few miles above Tintern Abbey ...'

'No poem of mine was composed under circumstances more pleasant for me to remember than this. I began it upon leaving Tintern, after crossing the Wye, and concluded it just as I was entering Bristol in the evening, after a ramble of four or five days with my sister. Not a word of it was altered, and not any part of it was written down till I had reached Bristol.'

> ... For I have learned
> To look on nature, not as in the hour
> Of thoughtless youth; but hearing oftentimes
> The still, sad music of humanity,
> Nor harsh nor grating, though of ample power
> To chasten and subdue. And I have felt
> A presence that disturbs me with the joy
> Of elevated thoughts; a sense sublime
> Of something far more deeply interfused,
> Whose dwelling is the light of setting suns,
> And the round ocean and the living air,
> And the blue sky, and in the mind of man:
> A motion and a spirit, that impels
> All thinking things, all objects of all thought,
> And rolls through all things. Therefore am I still
> A lover of the meadows and the woods,
> And mountains; and of all that we behold
> From this green earth; of all the mighty world
> Of eye, and ear, – both what they half create,
> And what perceive; well pleased to recognize
> In nature and the language of the sense,
> The anchor of my purest thoughts, the nurse,
> The guide, the guardian of my heart, and soul
> Of all my moral being. ...
> That neither evil tongues,
> Rash judgments, nor the sneers of selfish men,
> Nor greetings where no kindness is, nor all
> The dreary intercourse of daily life,
> Shall e'er prevail against us, or disturb
> Our cheerful faith, that all which we behold
> Is full of blessings. ...

William Wordsworth

14 July 🕮

1842—Herman Melville and 'Toby' arrived among the cannibals in the Valley of Typee

Various and conflicting were the thoughts which oppressed me during the silent hours that followed the events related in the preceding chapter. Toby, wearied with the fatigues of the day, slumbered heavily by my side; but the pain under which I was suffering eventually prevented my sleeping, and I remained distressingly alive to all the fearful circumstances of our present situation. Was it possible that, after all our vicissitudes, we were really in the terrible valley of Typee, and at the mercy of its inmates, a fierce and unrelenting tribe of savages?

Typee or Happar? I shuddered when I reflected that there was no longer any room for doubt; and that, beyond all hope of escape, we were now placed in those very circumstances from the bare thought of which I had recoiled with such abhorrence but a few days before. What might not be our fearful destiny? To be sure, as yet we had been treated with no violence; nay, had been even kindly and hospitably entertained. But what dependence could be placed upon the fickle passions which sway the bosom of a savage?. . .

From the excitement of these fearful thoughts I sank towards morning into an uneasy slumber; and on awaking, with a start, in the midst of an appalling dream, looked up into the eager countenances of a number of the natives, who were bending over me.

It was broad day; and the house was nearly filled with young females, fancifully decorated with flowers, who gazed upon me as I rose with faces in which childish delight and curiosity were vividly portrayed. After waking Toby, they seated themselves round us on the mats, and gave full play to that prying inquisitiveness which time out of mind has been attributed to the adorable sex.

As these unsophisticated young creatures were attended by no jealous duennas, their proceedings were altogether informal, and void of artificial restraint. Long and minute was the investigation with which they honoured us, and so uproarious their mirth, that I felt infinitely sheepish; and Toby was immeasurably outraged at their familiarity.

These lively young ladies were at the same time wonderfully polite and humane; fanning aside the insects that occasionally lighted on our brows; presenting us with food; and compassionately regarding me in the midst of my afflictions. But in spite of all their blandishments, my feelings of propriety were exceedingly shocked, for I could not but consider them as having overstepped the due limits of female decorum.

Herman Melville: from Typee (*his first book, published in 1846), Chapter XI.*

1881—Wm. H. Bonney ('Billy the Kid') was killed at Ft. Sumner, N. M.

Billy the Kid

I'll tell you the story of Billy the Kid,
I'll sing of the desperate deeds that he did
'Way out in New Mexico long, long ago,
When a man's only friend was his own forty-four.

When Billy the Kid was a very young lad,
In old Silver City he went to the bad;
Way out in the West with a gun in his hand
At the age of twelve years he killed his first man.

Fair Mexican maidens strum guitars and sing
A song about Billy, their boy bandit king,
How ere his young manhood had reached its sad end
Had a notch on his pistol for twenty-one men.

'Twas on the same night when poor Billy died
He said to his friends: 'I am not satisfied;
There's twenty-one men I have put bullets through
And Sheriff Pat Garrett must make twenty-two.'

Now, this is how Billy the Kid met his fate:
The moon was a-shining, the hour was late,
Shot down by Pat Garrett, who once was his friend,
The young outlaw's life had now come to its end.

There's many a man with a face fine and fair
Who starts out in life with a chance to be square,
But just like poor Billy he wanders astray
And loses his life in the very same way.

Anon

16 July 📖

1557—Sir John Cheke, sometime tutor to Edward VI and Regius Professor of Greek at Cambridge, thanked Sir Thomas Hoby, the translator of Castiglione's The Courtier, *for 'submitting your doings to my judgement', and took the occasion to warn English writers against Latinate words and outlandish constructions*

For your opinion of my good will unto you as you write, you cannot be deceived: for submitting your doings to my judgment, I thank you: for taking this pain of your translation, you worthily deserve great thanks of all sorts. I have taken some pain at your request chiefly in your preface, not in the reading of it for that was pleasant unto me both for the roundness of your sayings and well-speakings of the same, but in changing certain words which might very well be let alone, but that I am very curious in my friend's matters, not to determine, but to debate what is best. Wherein, I seek not the best happily by truth, but by mine own fancy, and show of goodness.

I am of this opinion that our own tongue should be written clean and pure, unmixed and unmangled with borrowing of other tongues, wherein if we take not heed by time, ever borrowing and never paying, she shall be fain to keep her house as bankrupt. For then doth our tongue naturally and praisably utter her meaning, when she borroweth no counterfeitness of other tongues to attire herself withal, but useth plainly her own, with such shift as nature, craft, experience and following of other excellent [guides] doth lead her unto, and if she want at any time (as being unperfight she must) yet let her borrow with such bashfulness that it may appear that if either the mould of our own tongue could serve us to fashion a word of our own, or if the old denisoned words could content and ease this need, we would not boldly venture of unknown words. This I say not for reproof of you, who have scarcely and necessarily used where occasion serveth a strange word so, as it seemeth to grow out of the matter and not to be sought for; but for mine own defense, who might be counted over-straight a deemer of things, if I gave not this account to you, my friend and wise, of my marring this your handiwork. But I am called away, I pray you pardon my shortness, the rest of my sayings should be but praise and exhortation in this your doings, which at more leisure I should do better.

From my house in Woodstreet the 16. of July, 1557.

Yours assured   John Cheke

As quoted in the Preface to Sir Thomas Hoby's translation of Castiglione's The Courtier, *1561*

1660—Robinson Crusoe found himself 'monarch of all he surveyed', and immediately discovered some of the difficulties inherent in imperial possession

The next day, the 16th, I went up the same way again . . . something further than I had gone the day before. . . . In this part I found different fruits, and particularly I found melons upon the ground, in great abundance, and grapes . . . the vines had spread indeed over the trees, and the clusters of grapes were just now in their prime, very ripe and rich. . . .

I spent all that evening there . . . and got up into a tree, where I slept well; and next morning proceeded upon my discovery, travelling nearly four miles . . . At the end of this march I came to an opening, where the country seemed to descend to the west; and a little spring of fresh water, which issued out of the side of the hill by me, ran the other way, that is, due east; and the country appeared so fresh, so green, so flourishing, everything being in a constant verdue, or flourish of spring, that it looked like a planted garden. I descended a little on the side of that delicious valley, surveying it with a secret kind of pleasure, though mixed with other afflicting thoughts, to think that this was all my own; that I was king and lord of all this country indefeasibly, and had a right of possession; and, if I could convey it, I might have had it in inheritance as completely as any lord of a manor in England. I saw here abundance of cocoa-trees, orange and lemon, and citron-trees; but all wild, and few bearing any fruit, at least not then. However, the green limes that I gathered were not only pleasant to eat, but very wholesome; and I mixed their juice afterwards with water, which made it very wholesome, and very cool and refreshing.

I found now I had business enough to gather and carry home; and I resolved to lay up a store, as well of grapes as limes and lemons, to furnish myself for the wet season, which I knew was approaching. In order to do this, I gathered a great heap of grapes in one place, a lesser heap in another place, and a great parcel of limes and lemons in another place; and taking a few of each with me, I travelled homeward, and resolved to come again, and bring a bag or sack, or what I could make, to carry the rest home. Accordingly, having spent three days in this journey, I came home (so I must now call my tent and my cave); but before I got thither, the grapes were spoiled; the richness of the fruit, and the weight of the juice, having broken them and bruised them, they were good for little or nothing: as to the limes, they were good, but I could bring but few.

Daniel Defoe: from The Life and Strange Surprizing Adventures of Robinson Crusoe

18 July ⚏

1837—Captain Frederick Marryat discovered the perfidy of some American publishers in the bad old days before the Copyright Union, and the irony of some American journalists

The following just and eloquent epistle will be perused with sorrow and chagrin by the admirers of the author of *Peter Simple*, and with a feeling of indignant pleasure by each true partisan of our patriotic 'book manafacturers'. . . .

Cincinnati, July 18, 1837

Messre. Carey and Hart:

Gentlemen, – Yours, through Mr. L. Johnson, reached us some time since we will sell you our plates for Snarleyyow. at 80 cts per 1000. ms. at 6 mos. and will not Publish the Balance of it, we have all the information in Point of LAW. to satisfy us that Capt. Marryatt has no more right to this work than we have, the case is a peculiar one and we think our Business will not be injured by a Foreigner attempting to Prevent us from manufacturing Books that are and have been considered and acted upon as common Property, the western People see the necessity of our manufacturing for ourselves, and any forcible attempt by Foreign or Eastern capitalist to run down our manufactories, and thereby take the living from our Laboring class of society will not be popular to say the least of it. We are not disposed to take any work that Justly belongs to another, and if you will take our plates we will go no further in this matter if not we will finish it and any other of his works that may be to our interest to do. an answer by return of mail will oblige   yours Resp.

J. A. JAMES AND CO.

Now, can anything be more conclusive than this argument of the patriotic and intelligent Messrs. J. A. James and Co., of Cincinnati? . . . 'Captain Marryat has no more right to this work than we have!' Most assuredly not. His literary property in this country is outlawed by the Act upon our statute-books; and as the law thus refuses to protect him, it is the duty of every good man to seize upon and spoil one who can thus assert no legal right to the produce of his labors. . . . Let us kindle our torches at the same holy altar, and raise an intellectual blaze that will consume these foreign authors, and make dim those dull fires which dotard Europe expects us to help her in feeding. . . . let us still practise our natural right of despoiling others of their property; let us go on in the so-called piratical traffic of human intellect. Let us steal and sell the *Peter Simples*, the *Japhets*, the *Jacob Faithfuls*, and all other ideal persons of whom American law takes no cognizance; and let us resist every attempt to repeal this most profitable kind of slave-trade, as an aggression upon the rights of freedom!

The New York Mirror, *as quoted in* Life and Letters of Captain Marryat, *by Florence Marryat*

1333—Battle of Halidon Hill, in which the English took their revenge for the terrible defeat at Bannockburn nineteen years before (see 24 June)

Scots from Berwick and Aberdeen,
At Bannockburn so fierce and keen,
You killed the innocent, as was seen;
But now King Edward's avenged it clean:
    Avenged it clean, and well worth while.
    But watch the Scots, they're full of guile. . . .

The Scots of Stirling were stern and proud;
Nor God nor good men had them cowed.
The robbers, they raided round about,
But in the end Edward put them to rout.
    He puts them to rout, and well worth while:
    They'll always lose, though full of guile.

You clumping brogue, now kindles your care!
You boasting bagman, your bothy's bare!
You wily traitor, where now? Where?
Go back to Bruges, and bed down there!
    Yes, there, and waste a weary while!
    Your Dundee dwelling's down through your guile.

The Scot goes to Bruges, and strolls the streets;
He plans for England heavy defeats;
He promptly complains to people he greets,
But few to cure his cares he meets.
    Few cure his cares, and well worth while:
    He threatens with traitor's tricks and guile.

But many threaten and utter ill
Who were better silent, standing stone-still.
The Scot has wind and spare to spill,
But in the end Edward shall have his will.
    He had his will at Berwick, and well worth while:
    Scots gave up the keys; yet guard against their guile!

Laurence Minot (from Medieval English Verse,
translated by Brian Stone, Penguin, 1964)

1711—Sir Roger de Coverley approved the transformation of his portrait into a 'Saracen's Head'

In our return home we met with a very odd accident; which I cannot forbear relating, because it shows how desirous all who know Sir Roger are of giving him marks of their esteem. When we were arrived upon the verge of his estate, we stopped at a little inn to rest ourselves and our horses. The man of the house had, it seems, been formerly a servant in the knight's family; and to do honour to his old master, had some time since, unknown to Sir Roger, put him up in a sign-post before the door; so that the knight's head hung out upon the road about a week before he himself knew anything of the matter. As soon as Sir Roger was acquainted with it, finding that his servant's indiscretion proceeded wholly from affection and good-will, he only told him that he had made him too high a compliment; and when the fellow seemed to think that could hardly be, added with a more decisive look, that it was too great an honour for any man under a duke; but told him at the same time, that it might be altered with a very few touches, and that he himself would be at the charge of it. Accordingly they got a painter by the knight's directions to add a pair of whiskers to the face, and by a little aggravation to the features to change it to the Saracen's Head.

I should not have known this story, had not the inn-keeper, upon Sir Roger's alighting, told him in my hearing that his honour's head was brought last night with the alterations that he had ordered to be made in it. Upon this, my friend, with his usual cheerfulness, related the particulars above-mentioned, and ordered the head to be brought into the room. I could not forbear discovering greater expressions of mirth than ordinary upon the appearance of this monstrous face, under which, notwithstanding it was made to frown and stare in a most extraordinary manner, I could still discover a distant resemblance of my old friend. Sir Roger, upon seeing me laugh, desired me to tell him truly if I thought it possible for people to know him in that disguise. I at first kept my usual silence; but upon the knight's conjuring me to tell him whether it was not still more like himself than a Saracen, I composed my countenance in the best manner I could, and replied, 'that much might be said on both sides'.

These several adventures, with the knight's behaviour in them, gave me as pleasant a day as ever I met with in any of my travels.

Joseph Addison: from The Spectator, *no. 122,*

1855—From Concord, Massachusetts, Ralph Waldo Emerson 'greeted' Walt Whitman 'at the beginning of a great career'

Dear Sir: – I am not blind to the worth of the wonderful gift of 'Leaves of Grass'. I find it the most extraordinary piece of wit and wisdom that America has yet contributed. I am very happy in reading it, as great power makes us happy. It meets the demand I am always making of what seemed the sterile and stingy nature, as if too much handiwork, or too much lymph in temperament, were making our western wits fat and mean. I give you joy of your free and brave thought. I have great joy in it. I find incomparable things said incomparably well, as they must be. I find the courage of treatment which so delights us, and which large perception only can inspire.

I great you at the beginning of a great career, which yet must have had a long foreground somewhere, for such a start. I rubbed my eyes a little, to see if this sunbeam were no illusion; but the solid sense of the book is a sober certainty.

It has the best merits, namely, of fortifying and encouraging.

I did not know until I last night saw the book advertised in a newspaper that I could trust the name as real and available for a post-office. I wish to see my benefactor, and have felt much like striking my tasks and visiting New York to pay you my respects.

Ralph Waldo Emerson

22 July 📖

1941—Eugene O'Neill, having at length completed Long Day's Journey Into Night, *presented the manuscript to his wife, Carlotta, on their twelfth wedding anniversary*

DEAREST: I give you the original script of this play of old sorrow, written in tears and blood. A sadly inappropriate gift, it would seem, for a day celebrating happiness. But you will understand. I mean it as a tribute to your love and tenderness which gave me the faith in love that enabled me to face my dead at last and write this play – write it with deep pity and understanding and forgiveness for all the four haunted Tyrones.

These twelve years, Beloved One, have been a Journey into Light – into love. You know my gratitude. And my love!   GENE

*   *   *   *   *

She and O'Neill were living at Tao House, a Chinese-styled residence they built on a mountainside thirty-five miles from San Francisco, when O'Neill began to plan the autobiographical *Long Day's Journey Into Night* in 1939.

'He wasn't well even then', Mrs. O'Neill said, 'He didn't sleep well, and when he was very worried and nervous, he would call me to come to his room or he would come to mine and he would talk, frequently all night, about his work or about this terrible thing of whether we were going to have a World War again. He was terribly disturbed that mankind was so stupid; to go through war only meant destruction for everybody. It really did something awful to him. Then he explained to me that he had to write this play about his youth and his family. It was a thing that haunted him. He was bedevilled into writing it, it was something that came from his very guts, he had to get it out of his system, he had to forgive whatever it was that caused this tragedy between himself and his mother and father.

'When he started *Long Day's Journey*, it was a most strange experience to watch that man being tortured every day by his own writing. He would come out of his study at the end of a day gaunt and sometimes weeping. His eyes would be all red and he looked ten years older than when he went in in the morning. I think he felt freer when he got it out of his system. It was his way of making peace with his family – and himself.' . . .

O'Neill expressed the wish that *Long Day's Journey* be given its world premiere by the Royal Dramatic Theatre of Stockholm. . . . Its production [in 1956] has been largely responsible, Mrs. O'Neill feels, for the current revival of interest in her husband's work. 'Sweden did this for O'Neill', she said, 'not America. America was not a damn bit interested, excuse my language. . . . In Europe they think it's the greatest play they've had in years. Count it with the Greeks and God knows what.' She smiled. 'That makes me feel nice and warm for Gene', she said.

Seymour Peck in the New York Times, *Nov. 4, 1956*

A.D. 596—Pope Gregory recalled St Augustine to his mission

'... about the one hundred and fiftieth year after the coming of the English to Britain, Gregory was inspired by God to send his servant Augustine with several other God-fearing monks to preach the word of God to the English nation. Having undertaken this task at the Pope's command and progressed a short distance on their journey, they became afraid, and began to consider returning home. For they were appalled at the idea of going to a barbarous, fierce, and pagan nation, of whose very language they were ignorant. They unanimously agreed that this was the safest course, and sent back Augustine – who was to be consecrated bishop in the event of their being received by the English – so that he might humbly request the holy Gregory to recall them from so dangerous, arduous, and uncertain a journey. In reply, the Pope wrote them a letter of encouragement, urging them to proceed on their mission to preach God's word, and to trust themselves to his aid. This letter ran as follows:

GREGORY, Servant of the servants of God, to the servants of God:

My very dear sons, it is better never to undertake any high enterprise than to abandon it when once begun. So with the help of God you must carry out this holy task. Be constant and zealous . . . and be assured that the greater the labour, the greater will be the glory of your eternal reward. When Augustine your leader returns, whom We have appointed your abbot, obey him humbly in all things, remembering that whatever he directs you to do will always be to the good of your souls. May Almighty God protect you with His Grace, and grant me to see the result of your labours in our heavenly home. And although my office prevents me from working at your side, yet because I long to do so, I hope to share in your joyful reward. God keep you safe, my dearest sons.

Dated the twenty-third of July, in the fourteenth year of the reign of our most devout lord Maurice Tiberius Augustus.

Reassured by the encouragement of the blessed father Gregory, Augustine and his fellow-servants of Christ resumed their work in the word of God, and arrived in Britain.

> *Bede :* History of the English Church and People

24 July

1758—The Welsh poet, John Dyer, died, having left to his own generation of English readers one of their favourite topographical poems, and to their successors one much-quoted quatrain

Below me trees unnumbered rise,
Beautiful in various dyes; . . .
And beyond the purple grove,
Haunt of Phyllis, queen of love!
Gaudy as the opening dawn,
Lies a long and level lawn,
On which a dark hill, steep and high,
Holds and charms the wandering eye!
Deep are his feet in Towy's flood,
His sides are clothed with waving wood,
And ancient towers crown his brow,
That cast an awful look below;
Whose ragged walls the ivy creeps
And with her arms from falling keeps;
So both a safety from the wind
In mutual dependence find.
    'Tis now the raven's bleak abode;
'Tis now the apartment of the toad;
And there the fox securely feeds,
And there the poisonous adder breeds,
Concealed in ruins, moss, and weeds,
While ever and anon, there falls
Huge heaps of hoary moulder'd walls.
Yet Time has seen, that lifts the low,
And level lays the lofty brow,
Has seen this broken pile complete,
Big with the vanity of state;
But transient is the smile of fate!
A little rule, a little sway,
A sunbeam in a winter's day,
Is all the proud and mighty have
Between the cradle and the grave.

John Dyer: from Grongar Hill

1745—The Young Pretender landed in Scotland and proclaimed his father James VIII of Scotland and III of England

'Twas on a Monday morning,
  Right early in the year,
When Charlie came to our toun,
  The young Chevalier.

  Oh, Charlie is my darling,
    My darling, my darling,
  Oh, Charlie is my darling,
    The young Chevalier.

As he came marching up the street,
  The pipes play'd loud and clear,
And a' the folk came running out
  To meet the Chevalier.

  Oh, Charlie is my darling . .

Wi' Hieland bonnets on their heads,
  And claymores bright and clear,
They came to fight for Scotland's right,
  And the young Chevalier.

  Oh, Charlie is my darling . . .

They've left their bonnie Hieland hills,
  Their wives and bairnies dear,
To draw the sword for Scotland's lord,
  The young Chevalier.

  Oh, Charlie is my darling . . .

Oh, there were mony beating hearts,
  And mony a hope and fear,
And mony were the prayers put up
  For the young Chevalier.

  Oh, Charlie is my darling,
    My darling, my darling,
  Oh, Charlie is my darling,
    The young Chevalier.

Carolina Oliphant, Baroness Nairne (1766–1845)

26 July 📖

Sir Walter took us in the Sociable a lovely drive: we crossed the Tweed at Darnick bridge and followed the course to the junction of the Leader, a lovely stream on the banks of which Thomas the Rhymer lived, and commemorated in the song of Leader Haughs, which Sir Walter repeated, as he did many other snatches of old ballads as we passed the spots to which they alluded. . . . He told us much of the Liddesdale country in his early days, which he has described so well in Guy Mannering: the following story he had from an old farmer famous for his strength and courage, and known by the name of 'fighting-Charlie': he was a powerful, clean made, active man, and in advanced life able to cope with most men in attack or defence: he was returning from Stanshie Shaw fair with a sum of nearly £400 in his pocket: he stopped for refreshment at a little inn of bad repute, near Gilsland, called Mumps Hall: when he was about to set out for home in the afternoon the landlady anxiously endeavoured to detain him, and was so importunate as to give him suspicion that all was not right: when out of sight he examined his pistols, and did not find that the charge had been drawn, but as he went on, his mind misgave him more, and just as he entered the dangerous part of the Moss, where a narrow horse path intersected the bog, he once more inspected the pistols for fear the powder should be damp: he then found that the charge had been taken out, and tow substituted: he loaded them carefully and in about half a mile three fellows sprung from the side of the bog, and demanded his money; he was certain that one of them was the Landlord of Mumps Hall: he faced them and presented his pistols: the thieves called out, 'we don't care a damn for your pistols'. Charlie, who was a good natured fellow did not want to commit murder, so he singled out the landlord and cried out, 'Aha! lad, the tow's out noo': on hearing this the rogues made off at speed and Charlie reached home in safety: 'on this', said Sir Walter, 'I founded Dandy's adventures'. . . .

Sir Walter's shepherd is brother to Hogg the Ettrick Shepherd; he is a sensible, steady, unimaginative person, rather ashamed of his brother's poetical fame . . . in the course of the summer, poor Hogg had a fit of sickness which brought him to death's door: during this time all his twenty lambs died: Mr. Laidlaw said to him, 'This is very strange, Hogg: I fear ye've been to blame in something: none of Sir Walter's sheep are dead and yours are all gone': he replied 'It is like it may be for a punishment, and weel deserved, for when I was as it seemed on my death bed, God forgive me I had mair thought and care for the twenty lambs than for the state of my puir soul.'

From Mrs. Hughes's Diary

1793—'I set out with [Robert] Burns on a tour through the wilds and cultivated plains of Galloway' – John Syme, in a letter to Alexander Cunningham

I got Burns a grey highland Shelty to ride on. We dined the first day of our Tour at Glendonwynnes of Parton, a beautiful situation on the banks of the Dee. In the evening we walked up a bonny know and had as grand a view of alpine scenery as can well be found. . . . Immediately opposite and within a mile of us we saw Airds, a charming romantic place where dwelt Low, the author of 'Mary, weep no more for me'. This was classical ground for Burns. He viewed the 'highest hill which rises o'er the source of Dee'. He would have staid till 'the passing spirit' had appeared had we not resolved to reach Kenmore that night. . . .

. . . I must tell you that Burns had got a pair of jimmy boots, which the wetness had rendered it an impossible task to get on. The brawny poet tried force, and tore them in shreds. A whiffling vexation like this is more trying to the temper than a serious calamity. We were going to the Isle – Lord Selkirk's – and the forlorn Burns was quite discomfited – a sick stomach, headache, &c. lent their forces, and the man of verse was quite *accablé*. Mercy on me, how he did fume and rage. Nothing could reinstate him in temper. I tried all I could think of; at length I got a lucky hit. Across the bay of Wigtown I showed him Lord Galloway's house. He expectorated his spleen against the aristocratic elf, and regained a most agreeable temper. I have about half a dozen of capital extempores which I dare not write. . . . I declare they possess as much point and classical terseness, if I may so express myself, as any thing I can imagine. O, he was in an epigrammatic humour indeed. I told him it was rash to crucify Lord G—— in the way he was doing, for tho he might receive any favour at his hands yet he might suffer an injury. He struck up immediately –

> Spare me thy vengeance, Ga——ay,
>   In quiet let me live;
> I ask no kindness at thy hand,
>   For thou hast none to give. . . .

We reached Kirkcudbright about one o'Clock. . . . Burns's obstreperous independence would not dine but where he could, as he said, eat like a Turk, drink like a fish, and swear like the Devil. Since he would not dine with Dalzell in his own house, he had nothing for it but Dalzell to dine with us in the Inn. We had a very agreeable party. . . . We had the song 'Lord Gregory', which I asked for to have occasion to call upon Burns to *speak* his own words to that tune. He did speak them, and such was the effect that a dead silence ensued. . . .

28 July 🕮

1653—Andrew Marvell, having been appointed tutor to Oliver Cromwell's ward, sent his first 'report card' to the boy's eminent guardian

It might perhaps seem fit for me to seek out words to giue your Excellence thanks for myselfe. But indeed the onely Ciuility which it is proper for me to practise with so eminent a Person is to obey you, and to performe honestly the worke that you haue set me about. Therefore I shall use the time that your Lordship is pleas'd to allow me for writing, onely to that purpose for which you haue giuen me it: That is to render you some account of Mr Dutton. I haue taken care to examine him seuerall times in the presence of Mr Oxenbridge, as those who weigh and tell ouer mony before some witnesse ere they take charge of it. For I thought that there might possibly be some lightnesse in the Coyn, or errour in the telling, which hereafter I should be bound to make good. Thereafter Mr Oxenbridge is the best to make your Excellence an impartiall relation thereof. I shall onely say that I shall striue according to my best understanding (that is according to those Rules your Lordship hath giuen me) to increase whatsoeuer Talent he may haue already. Truly he is of a gentle and waxen disposition: and, God be praised, I can not say that he hath brought with him any euill Impression, and I shall hope to set nothing upon his Spirit but what may be of good Sculpture. He hath in him two things which make Youth most easy to be managed, Modesty which is the bridle to Vice, and Emulation which is the Spurr to Virtue. And the Care which your Excellence is pleas'd to take of him is no small incouragement and shall be so represented to him. But aboue all I shall labour to make him sensible of his Duty to God. For then we begin to serue faithfully, when we consider that he is our Master. And in this both he and I ow infinitely to your Lordship, for hauing placed us in so godly a family as that of Mr Oxenbridge whose Doctrine and Example are like a Book and a Map, not onely instructing the Eare but demonstrating to the Ey which way we ought to trauell. And Mrs Oxenbridge hath a great tendernesse ouer him also in all other things. She has lookd so well to him that he hath already much mended his Complexion: And now she is busy in ordering his Chamber, that he may delight to be in it as often as his Studyes require. . . . and truly he is very chearful and I hope thinks us to be good company. I shall upon occasion henceforward informe your Excellence of any particularityes in our little affairs. For so I esteem it to be my Duty. I haue no more at present but to giue thanks to God for your Lordship, and to beg grace of him, that I may approve my selfe

Your Excellencyes most humble and faithfull servant

Andrew Marvell

Mr Dutton presents his most humble Seruice to your Excellence.

1703—Daniel Defoe stood in the Pillory before the Royal Exchange in Cornhill,
'for writing and publishing a seditious libel, intituled The Shortest Way with
the Dissenters'

Hail! Hieroglyphic State Machine,
    Contrived to punish Fancy in!
Men, that are Men, in thee can feel no pain;
    And all thy insignificants disdain!
Contempt, that false new word for Shame,
    Is, without Crime, an empty name!
A Shadow to amuse mankind,
But never frights the wise or well-fixed mind!
    Virtue despises human scorn!
    And scandals, Innocents adorn!

Exalted to thy Stool of State,
What prospect do I see of sovereign Fate! . . .
If a poor Author has embraced thy Wood,
Only because he was not understood;
They punish Mankind but by halves,
    Till they stand here,
Who false to their own principles appear;
    And cannot understand themselves!

Those Nimshites, who with furious zeal drive on
And build up Rome to pull down Babylon,
The real authors of the *Shortest Way*,
Who for destruction, not conversion pray;
They that in vast employments rob the State –
Let them in thy Embraces meet their fate!
Let not the millions they by fraud obtain
Protect them from the scandal, or the pain!
    They who from mean beginnings grow
        To vast estates, but God knows how!
        Who carry untold sums away
    From little Places, but with little pay!
        Who costly palaces erect,
    The thieves that built them to protect: . . .

Tell them, *Mene Tekel's* on the wall!
Tell them, the nation's money paid for all!

Daniel Defoe: from A Hymn to the Pillory

30 July

1771—The start of Benjamin Franklin's two-week visit at Twyford, in Hampshire, during which he wrote the first part of his Autobiography. *['How happy I was in the sweet Retirement of Twyford, where my only Business was a little Scribbling in the Garden Study, and my pleasure your Conversation, with that of your amiable Family!']*

Twyford, at the Bishop of St. Asaph's, 1771

Dear Son,

I have ever had a Pleasure in obtaining any little Anecdotes of my Ancestors. You may remember the Enquiries I made among the Remains of my Relations when you were with me in England: and the Journey I took for that purpose. Now imagining it may be equally agreeable to you to know the Circumstances of *my* Life, many of which you are yet unacquainted with; and expecting a Weeks uninterrupted Leisure in my present Country Retirement, I sit down to write them for you. To which I have besides some other Inducements. Having emerg'd from the Poverty and Obscurity in which I was born and bred, to a State of Affluence and some Degree of Reputation in the World, and having gone so far thro' Life with a considerable Share of Felicity, the conducing Means I made use of, which, with the Blessing of God, so well succeeded, my Posterity may like to know, as they may find some of them suitable to their own Situations, and therefore fit to be imitated. That Felicity, when I reflected on it, has induc'd me sometimes to say, that were it offer'd to my Choice, I should have no Objection to a Repetition of the same Life from its Beginning, only asking the Advantage Authors have in a second Edition to correct some Faults of the first. So would I, if I might, besides correcting the Faults, change some sinister Accidents and Events of it for others more favourable, but tho' this were deny'd, I should still accept the Offer. However, since such a Repitition is not to be expected, the next Thing most like living one's Life over again seems to be a *Recollection* of that Life; and to make that Recollection as durable as possible, the putting it down in Writing. Hereby, too, I shall indulge the Inclination so natural in old Men, to be talking of themselves and their own past Actions, and I shall indulge it, without being troublesome to others who thro' respect to Age might think themselves oblig'd to give me a Hearing, since this may be read or not as any one pleases. And lastly, (I may as well confess it, since my Denial of it will be believ'd by no body) perhaps I shall a good deal gratify my own *Vanity*. Indeed I scarce ever heard or saw the introductory Words, *Without Vanity I may say*, &c. but some vain thing immediately follow'd. Most People dislike Vanity in others whatever share they have of it themselves, but I give it full Quarter wherever I meet with it, being persuaded that it is often productive of Good to the Possessor and to others that are within his Sphere of Action: And therefore in many Cases it would not be quite absurd if a Man were to thank God for his Vanity among the other Comforts of Life.

Then Sir Bedivere departed, and went to the sword, and lightly took it up, and went to the water side; and there he bound the girdle about the hilts, and then he threw the sword as far into the water, as he might; and there came an arm and an hand above the water and met it, and caught it, and so shook it thrice and brandished, and then vanished away the hand with the sword in the water. So Sir Bedivere came again to the king, and told him what he saw. Alas, said the king, help me hence, for I dread me I have tarried over long. Then Sir Bedivere took the king upon his back, and so went with him to the water side. And when they were at the water side, even fast by the bank hoved a little barge with many fair ladies in it, and among them all was a queen, and all they had black hoods, and all they wept and shrieked when they saw King Arthur. Now put me into the barge, said the king. And so he did softly; and there received him three queens with great mourning; and so they set them down, and in one of their laps King Arthur laid his head. . . . Then Sir Bedivere cried: Ah my lord Arthur, what shall become of me, now ye go from me and leave me here alone among mine enemies? Comfort thyself, said the king, and do as well as thou mayest, for in me is no trust for to trust in; for I will into the vale of Avilion to heal me of my grievous wound: and if thou hear never more of me, pray for my soul. But ever the queens and ladies wept and shrieked, that it was pity to hear. . . .

Thus of Arthur I find never more written in books that be authorized, nor more of the very certainty of his death heard I never read . . . Yet some say in many parts of England that King Arthur is not dead, but had by the will of our Lord Jesu into another place; and men say that he shall come again, and he shall win the holy cross. I will not say it shall be so, but rather I will say, here in this world he changed his life. But many men say that there is written upon his tomb this verse: HIC JACET ARTHURUS REX, QUONDAM REX QUE FUTURUS . . .

Thus endeth this noble and joyous book entitled Le Morte Darthur. . . . Which book was reduced into English by Sir Thomas Malory, knight, as afore is said, and by me divided into twenty-one books, chaptered and imprinted, and finished in the abbey Westminster the last day of July the year of our Lord MCCCCLXXXV

Caxton me fieri fecit

August.

1798—When Nelson defeated the French fleet in Aboukir Bay, during the battle of the Nile, young Casabianca went down with his father's ship, thus giving occasion for one of the most-quoted verses in English

The boy stood on the burning deck,
    Whence all but him had fled;
The flame that lit the battle's wreck
    Shone round him o'er the dead.

Yet beautiful and bright he stood,
    As born to rule the storm;
A creature of heroic blood,
    A proud, though child-like form.

The flames rolled on – he would not go,
    Without his father's word;
That father, faint in death below,
    His voice no longer heard. . . .

'Speak, Father!' once again he cried,
    'If I may yet begone'
– And but the booming shots replied,
    And fast the flames rolled on. . . .

They wrapt the ship in splendour wild,
    They caught the flag on high,
And streamed above the gallant child,
    Like banners in the sky.

There came a burst of thunder sound –
    The boy – oh! where was he?
– Ask of the winds that far around
    With fragments strewed the sea!

With mast, and helm, and pennon fair,
    That well had borne their part –
But the noblest thing that perished there
    Was that young faithful heart.

Felicia Hemans: from 'Casabianca'

2 August 📖

1740—James Thomson's ode, 'Rule, Britannia', was first performed in his Alfred: A Masque (music by Thomas Arne), in the gardens of Cliffden House, Buckinghamshire, at a fete given by Frederick, Prince of Wales

When Britain *first, at heaven's command,*
Arose from out the azure main;
This was the charter of the land,
   And guardian Angels sung this strain;
   'Rule Britannia, *rule the waves;*
   Britons *never will be slaves.'*

The nations, not so blest as thee,
   Must, in their turns, to tyrants fall:
While thou shalt flourish great and free,
   The dread and envy of them all.
      'Rule, &c.

Still more majestic shalt thou rise,
   More dreadful, from each foreign stroke:
As the loud blast that tears the skies,
   Serves but to root thy native oak.
      'Rule, &c.

Thee haughty tyrants ne'er shall tame:
   All their attempts to bend thee down,
Will but arouse thy generous flame;
   But work their woe, and thy renown.
      'Rule, &c.

To thee belongs the rural reign;
   Thy cities shall with commerce shine:
All things shall be the subject main,
   And every shore in circles thine.
      'Rule, &c.

The Muses, still with freedom found,
   Shall to thy happy coast repair:
Blest isle! with matchless beauty crown'd,
   And manly hearts to guard the fair.
      'Rule, &c.

James Thomson: from Alfred: A Masque, *Act*
1, scene 5

1798—Thomas Holcroft noted in his diary some reminiscences of the methods of research used by the greatest of English biographers

Asked Weld at Debrett's if he knew Boswell. He had met him at coffee-houses, &c. where *B ----- * used to drink hard and sit late. It was his custom during the session to dine daily with Judges, whether invited or not. He obtruded himself everywhere. Lowe (mentioned by him in his life of Johnson) once gave me a humorous picture of him. Lowe had requested Johnson to write him a letter, which Johnson did, and Boswell came in, while he was writing. His attention was immediately fixed, Lowe took the letter, retired, and was followed by Boswell. 'Nothing', said Lowe, 'could surprise me more. Till that moment he had entirely overlooked me, that I did not imagine he knew there was such a creature in existence; and he now accosted me with the utmost over-strained and insinuating compliments possible. "How do you do, Mr. Lowe? I hope you are well, Mr. Lowe. Pardon my freedom, Mr. Lowe, but I think I saw my dear friend, Dr. Johnson, writing a letter for you." – "Yes, Sir" – "I hope you will not think me very rude, but if it would not be too great a favor, you would infinitely oblige me, if you would just let me have a sight of it. Everything from that hand, you know, is so inestimable." – "Sir, it is on my own private affairs, but" – "I would not pry into a person's affairs, my dear Mr. Lowe; by any means. I am sure you would not accuse me of such a thing, only if it were no particular secret" – "Sir, you are welcome to read the letter." – "I thank you, my dear Mr. Lowe, you are very obliging, I take it extremely kind." (having read) "It is nothing, I believe, Mr. Lowe, that you would be ashamed of." – "Certainly not" – "Why, then, if you would do me another favor, you would make the obligation eternal. If you would but step to Peele's coffee-house with me, and just suffer me to take a copy of it, I would do anything in my power to oblige you." –

'I was overcome', said Lowe, 'by this sudden familiarity and condescension, accompanied with bows and grimaces. I had no power to refuse; we went to the coffee-house, my letter was presently transcribed, and as soon as he had put the document in his pocket, Mr. Boswell walked away, as erect and proud as he was half an hour before, and I was ever after unnoticed. Nay, I am not certain', added he sarcastically, 'whether the Scotchman did not leave me, poor as he knew I was, to pay for my own dish of coffee.'

4 August 📖

1749—Samuel Richardson discussed Henry Fielding's novel Tom Jones *in a letter to Astraea and Minerva Hill*

... I must confess, that I have been prejudiced by the Opinion of Several judicious Friends against the truly coarse-titled Tom Jones; and so have been discouraged from reading it. – I was told, that it was a rambling Collection of Waking Dreams, in which Probability was not observed: And that it had a very bad Tendency. And I had Reason to think that the Author intended for his Second View (His *first* to fill his Pocket, by accomodating it to the reigning Taste) in writing it, to whiten a vicious Character, and to make Morality bend to his Practises. What Reason has he to make his Tom illegitimate, in an Age where Keeping is become a Fashion? Why did he make him a common – What shall I call it? – And a Kept Fellow, the Lowest of all Fellows, yet in Love with a young Creature who was traipsing after him, a Fugitive from her Father's House? – Why did he draw his Heroine so fond, so foolish, and so insipid? – Indeed he has one Excuse – He knows not how to draw a delicate Woman – He has not been accustomed to such Company – And is too prescribing, too impetuous, too immoral, I will venture to say, to take any other Bypass that that a perverse and crooked Nature has given him. Do Men expect Grapes of Thorns, or Figs of Thistles? But, perhaps, I think the worse of the Piece because I know the Writer, and dislike his Principles, both Public and Private, tho' I wish well to the *Man*, and love four worthy Sisters of his, with whom I am well acquainted. And indeed should admire him, did he make the Use of his Talents which I wish him to make; for the Vein of Humour, and Ridicule, which he is Master of, might, if properly turned, do great Service to ye Cause of Virtue ...

1844—Thomas Carlyle answered Ralph Waldo Emerson's request for information about Alfred Tennyson, who was then thirty-four years old

Alfred is one of the few British or Foreign Figures (a not increasing number I think!) who are and remain beautiful to me; – a true human soul, or some approximation thereto, to whom your own soul can say, Brother! – However, I doubt he will not come; he often skips me, in these brief visits to Town; skips everybody indeed; being a man solitary and sad, as certain men are, dwelling in an element of gloom, – carrying a bit of Chaos about him, in short, which he is manufacturing into Cosmos!

Alfred is the son of a Lincolnshire Gentleman Farmer, I think; indeed, you see in his verses that he is a native of 'moated granges', and green, fat pastures, not of mountains and their torrents and storms. He had his breeding at Cambridge, as if for the Law or Church; being master of a small annuity on his Father's decease, he preferred clubbing with his Mother and some Sisters, to live unpromoted and write Poems. In this way he lives still, now here, now there; the family always within reach of London, never in it; he himself making rare and brief visits, lodging in some old comrade's rooms. I think he must be under forty, not much under it. One of the finest-looking men in the world. A great shock of rough dusty-dark hair; bright-laughing hazel eyes; massive aquiline face, most massive yet most delicate; of sallow-brown complexion, almost Indian-looking; clothes cynically loose, free-and-easy; – smokes infinite tobacco. His voice is musical metallic, – fit for loud laughter and piercing wail, and all that may lie between; speech and speculation free and plenteous: I do not meet, in these late decades, such company over a pipe! – We shall see what he will grow to. He is often unwell; very chaotic, – his way is through Chaos and the Bottomless and Pathless; not handy for making many miles upon.

Carlyle to Emerson, 5 August 1844

After the rare arch-poet Johnson died,
The sock grew loathsome, and the buskin's pride,
Together with the stage's glory, stood
Each like a poor and pitied widowhood.
The cirque profaned was, and all postures racked,
For men did strut and stride and stare, not act.
Then temper flew from words, and men did squeak,
Look red, and blow, and bluster, but not speak;
No holy rage or frantic fires did stir
Or flash about the spacious theatre.
No clap of hands, or shout, or praise's proof
Did crack the playhouse sides, or cleave her roof.
Artless the scene was, and that monstrous sin
Of deep and arrant ignorance came in;
Such ignorance as theirs was who once hissed
At thy unequalled play, the *Alchemist*.
Oh, fie upon 'em! Lastly too, all wit
In utter darkness did, and still will sit
Sleeping the luckless age out, till that she
Her resurrection has again with thee.

> Robert Herrick: 'Upon M. Ben Jonson,
> Epigram'

When I a verse shall make,
Know I have prayed thee,
For old religion's sake,
Saint Ben, to aid me.

Make the way smooth for me,
When I, thy Herrick,
Honoring thee, on my knee
Offer my lyric.

Candles I'll give to thee,
And a new altar;
And thou, Saint Ben, shalt be
Writ in my psalter.

> Robert Herrick: 'His prayer to Ben Jonson'

1778—Gilbert White summed up his observations of the flight of birds

A good ornithologist should be able to distinguish birds by their air as well as by their colours and shapes; on the ground as well as on the wing; and in the bush as well as in the hand. For, though it must not be said that every species of birds has a manner peculiar to itself, yet there is somewhat in most genera at least, that at first sight discriminates them, and enables a judicious observer to pronounce upon them with some certainty. Put a bird in motion 'and it is truly betrayed by its walk.'

Thus kites and buzzards sail round in circles with wings expanded and motionless; and it is from their gliding manner that the former are still called in the north of England gleads, from the Saxon verb *glidan*, to glide. The kestrel, or windhover, has a peculiar mode of hanging in the air in one place, his wings all the while being briskly agitated. Hen-harriers fly low over heaths or fields of corn, and beat the ground regularly like a pointer or setting-dog. Owls move in a buoyant manner, as if lighter than the air; they seem to want ballast.

There is a peculiarity belonging to ravens that must draw the attention even of the most incurious – they spend all their leisure time in striking and cuffing each other on the wing in a kind of playful skirmish; and, when they move from one place to another, frequently turn on their backs with a loud croak, and seem to be falling to the ground. When this odd gesture betides them, they are scratching themselves with one foot, and thus lose the centre of gravity. Rooks sometimes dive and tumble in a frolicsome manner; crows and daws swagger in their walk; woodpeckers fly *volatu undoso* (in an undulating manner), opening and closing their wings at every stroke, and so are always rising or falling in curves. . . .

Some birds have movements peculiar to the season of love: though strong and rapid at other times, yet in the spring hang about on the wing in a toying and playful manner; thus the cock-snipe while breeding, forgetting his former flight, fans the air like the windhover; and the green-finch in particular, exhibits such languishing and faltering gestures as to appear like a wounded and dying bird; the kingfisher darts along like an arrow; fern-owls, or goat-suckers, glance in the dusk over the tops of trees like a meteor; starlings as it were swim along, while missel-thrushes use a wild and desultory flight; swallows sweep over the surface of the ground and water, and distinguish themselves by rapid turns and quick evolutions; swifts dash round in circles; and the bank-martin moves with frequent vacillations like a butterfly.

Gilbert White: The Natural History of Selborne, *Letter XLI*

8 August 💷

1588—Queen Elizabeth I reviewed her troops at Tilbury on the approach of the Spanish Armada

My Loving People,

We have been persuaded by some that are careful of our safety, to take heed how we commit ourselves to armed multitudes, for fear of treachery; but I assure you, I do not desire to live to distrust my faithful and loving people.

Let tyrants fear; I have always so behaved myself, that, under God, I have placed my chiefest strength and safeguard in the loyal hearts and good wil of my subjects, and therefore I am come amongst you, as you see, at this time, not for my recreation and disport, but being resolved in the midst and heat of the battle, to live or die amongst you all, to lay down for my God, and for my Kingdoms, and for my people, my honour and my blood, even in the dust.

I know I have the body but of a weak and feeble woman; But I have the heart and stomach of a king, and of a king of England too; and think foul scorn that Parma or Spain, or any prince of Europe should dare to invade the borders of my realm; to which rather than any dishonour shall grow by me, I myself will take up arms, I myself will be your general, judge, and rewarder of every one of your virtues in the field.

I know already, for your forwardness you have deserved rewards and crowns; and we do assure you on the word of a prince, they shall be duly paid you. In the mean time my lieutenant-general shall be in my stead, than whom never prince commanded a more noble or worthy subject; not doubting but by your obedience to my general, by your concord in the camp, and your valour in the field, we shall shortly have a famous victory over those enemies of my God, of my kingdoms, and of my people.

Elizabeth R.

1798—Robert Southey's poem 'The Battle of Blenheim' was published in The Morning Post

It was a summer evening;
   Old Kaspar's work was done,
And he before his cottage door
   Was sitting in the sun;
And by him sported on the green
His little grandchild Wilhelmine.

She saw her brother Peterkin
   Roll something large and round,
Which he beside the rivulet
   In playing there had found.
He came to ask what he had found,
That was so large, and smooth, and round.

Old Kasper took it from the boy,
   Who stood expectant by;
And then the old man shook his head,
   And with a natural sigh,
'Tis some poor fellow's skull,' said he,
'Who fell in the great victory. . . .'

'They say it was a shocking sight
   After the field was won;
For many thousand bodies here
   Lay rotting in the sun;
But things like that, you know, must be
   After a famous victory.'

'Great praise the Duke of Marlboro' won,
   And our good Prince Eugene.'
'Why, 'twas a very wicked thing!'
   Said little Wilhelmine.
'Nay, nay, my little girl,' quoth he;
'It was a famous victory. . . .'

Robert Southey: from 'The Battle of Blenheim'

1757—Thomas Gray anxiously awaited the critical reception of his Two Odes
*('The Bard' and 'The Progress of Poesy') which had been the first book printed
at Horace Walpole's Strawberry Hill Press*

[Gray to Walpole]   Stoke. Aug: 10. 1757

. . . Dodsley sent me some copies last week: they are very pleasant to the eye, &
will do no dishonour to your Press. as you are but young in the trade, you will excuse
me if I tell you, that some little inaccuracies have escaped your eye, as in the 9th
page *Lab'rinth's* & *Echo's*, (wᶜʰ are Nominat:ˢ plural,) with Apostrophes after them,
as tho' they were Genitives singular; & P: 16, sorrow & solitude without capital
letters. besides certain Commas here & there omitted. If you do not commit greater
faults in your next work, I shall grow jealous of Hentzerus. [*A Journey into England*,
by Paul Hentzerus, was the second book printed at Strawberry Hill.]

I am going to add to the trouble I have given you by desiring you would tell me,
what you hear any body say, (I mean, if any body says any thing). I know you will
forgive this vanity of an Author, as the vanity of a Printer is a little interested in the
same cause. . . .

[Gray to Bedingfield]   Stoke. Aug: 10. 1757

Dear Sʳ

I have order'd Dodsley long since to send you piping hot from the Press four
copies of the Bard & his Companion . . . you are desired to give me your *honest*
opinion about the latter part of the Bard, wᶜʰ you had not seen before, for I know it
is weakly in several parts; but it is a mercy, that it ever came to an end at all. there
are also six new lines at the end of the 2ᵈ Antistrophe *Fair laughs the Morn* &c:
wᶜʰ my Friends approve & (to say the truth) so do I. you will do me a favour, if you
will inform me what the North says either in good or in bad. as to the South, it is
too busy & too fastidious to trouble its head about any thing, that has no wit in it.
I know, I shall never be admired but in Scotland. By the way I am greatly struck
with the Tragedy of Douglas, tho' it has infinite faults. the Author seems to me to
have retrieved the true language of the Stage, wᶜʰ had been lost for these hundred
years; & there is one Scene (between Matilda & the old Peasant) so masterly, that it
strikes me blind to all the defects in the world.

I will not make you any excuses for my *sulkyness* of late, for in reality I have been
ill ever since I left Cambridge. . . .

Your Friend & humble Servant

TG:

I am at Mʳˢ Rogers's of Stoke near Windsor Bucks.

991—'In this year came Anlaf with three and ninety ships to Stone and ravaged it without and went thence to Sandwich and thence to Ipswich, which he harried ; and so to Maldon [on August 11, according to Register of monastery of Hyde]. And against him there came Byrhtnoth the alderman with his force and fought with him ; and there they slew the alderman and won the battle'

The Anglo-Saxon Chronicle

>   Mid clash of shields the shipmen came on,
> Maddened by battle. Full many a lance
> Home was thrust to the heart of the doomed.
> Then sallied forth Wistan, Wigelin's son;
> Three of the pirates he pierced in the throng,
> Ere he fell, by his friends, on the field of slaughter.
> Bitter the battle-rush, bravely struggled
> Heroes in armor, while all around them
> The wounded dropped and the dead lay thick.
> Oswold and Eadwold all the while
> Their kinsmen and comrades encouraged bravely,
> Both of the brothers bade their friends
> Never to weaken or weary in battle,
> But keep up their sword-play, keen to the end.
> Up spake Byrhtwold, brandished his ash-spear,
> – He was a tried and true old hero –
> Lifted his shield and loudly called to them:
> 'Heart must be keener, courage the hardier,
> Bolder our mood as our band diminisheth.
> Here lies in his blood our leader and comrade,
> The brave on the beach. Bitter shall rue it
> Who turns his back on the battle-field now.
> Here I stay; I am stricken and old;
> My life is done; I shall lay me down
> Close by my lord and comrade dear.'

from 'The Battle of Maldon', translated by J. Duncan Spaeth in Old English Poetry: Translations into Alliterative Verse

12 August 𝍏

. . . Just as the admiral drew near the door, and the company were about to slip out, William said: 'Admiral, are you *certain* about that circumstance concerning the clergymen you mentioned the other day,' – referring to a piece of the admiral's manufactured history. . . .

'*Certain* of it? Am I *certain* of it? Do you think I've been lying about it? What do you take me for? . . . Read up your history! . . .'

'But Admiral, in saying that this was the first stone thrown, and that this precipitated war, you have overlooked a circumstance which you are perfectly familiar with, but which has escaped your memory. Now I grant you that what you have stated is correct in every detail – to wit: that on the 16th of October, 1860, two Massachusetts clergymen, named Waite and Granger, went in disguise to the house of John Moody, in Rockport, at dead of night, and dragged forth two Southern women and their two little children, and after tarring and feathering them conveyed them to Boston and burnt them alive in the State House square; and I also grant your proposition that this deed is what led to the secession of South Carolina on the 20th of December following. . . . But Admiral, why overlook the Willis and Morgan case in South Carolina? . . . On the 12th of August, 1860, *two months* before the Waite and Granger affair, two South Carolina clergymen, named John H. Morgan and Winthrop L. Willis, one a Methodist and the other an Old School Baptist, disguised themselves, and went at midnight to the house of a planter named Thompson – Archibald F. Thompson, Vice-President under Thomas Jefferson – and took thence, at midnight, his widowed aunt (a Northern woman) and her adopted child, an orphan named Mortimer Highie, afflicted with epilepsy and suffering at the time from white swelling on one of his legs, and compelled to walk on crutches in consequence; and the two ministers, in spite of the pleadings of the victims, dragged them to the bush, tarred and feathered them, and afterward burned them at the stake in the city of Charleston. You remember perfectly well what a stir it made. . . . And you remember also that this thing was the *cause* of the Massachusetts outrage. Who, indeed, were the two Massachusetts ministers? And who were the two Southern women they burned? I do not need to remind *you*, Admiral, with your intimate knowledge of history, that Waite was the nephew of the woman burned in Charleston; that Granger was her cousin in the second degree, and that the woman they burned in Boston was the wife of John H. Morgan, and the still loved but divorced wife of Winthrop L. Willis. . . .'

The admiral was conquered. . . . He stammered some awkward, profane sentences about the —— —— Willis and Morgan business having escaped his memory, but that he 'remembered it now', and then, under pretence of giving Fan some medicine for an imaginary cough, drew out of the battle and went away, a vanquished man.

Mark Twain: from Roughing It, *ch. lxii*

1759 or 1760—Christopher Smart, under confinement as insane, recorded this as a red-letter day in the strange 'journal' now known as Rejoice in the Lamb

. . .

For I pray the Lord Jesus to translate my MAGNIFICAT into verse and represent it.

For I bless the Lord Jesus from the bottom of Royston Cave to the top of King's Chapel.

For I am a little fellow, which is intitled to the great mess by the benevolence of God my father.

For I this day made over my inheritance to my mother in consideration of her infirmities.

For I this day made over my inheritance to my mother in consideration of her age.

For I this day made over my inheritance to my mother in consideration of her poverty.

For I bless the thirteenth of August, in which I had the grace to obey the voice of Christ in my conscience.

For I bless the thirteenth of August, in which I was willing to run all hazards for the sake of the name of the Lord.

For I bless the thirteenth of August, in which I was willing to be called a fool for the sake of Christ.

For I lent my flocks and herds and my lands at once unto the Lord.

. . .

For I pray God to bless POLLY in the blessing of Naomi and assign her to the house of DAVID.

For I am in charity with the French who are my foes and Moabites because of the Moabitish woman.

For my Angel is always ready at a pinch to help me out and to keep me up.

For CHRISTOPHER must slay the Dragon with PAEON's head.

For they have seperated me and my bosom, whereas the right comes by setting us together.

For Silly fellow! Silly fellow! is against me and belongeth neither to me nor my family.

For he that scorneth the scorner hath condescended to my low estate.

. . .

For they pass me by in their tour, and the good Samaritan is not yet come.

. . .

For I am possessed of a cat, surpassing in beauty, from whom I take occasion to bless Almighty God.

. . .

For the Fatherless Children and widows are never deserted of the Lord.

Christopher Smart: from Rejoice in the Lamb

14 August ⨆

1834—The brig 'Pilgrim' sailed from Boston, with young Richard Henry Dana aboard

---

The fourteenth of August was the day fixed upon for the sailing of the brig *Pilgrim*, on her voyage from Boston, round Cape Horn, to the western coast of North America. As she was to get under way early in the afternoon, I made my appearance on board at twelve o'clock, in full sea-rig, and with my chest, containing an outfit for a two or three year's voyage, which I had undertaken from a determination to cure, if possible, by an entire change of life, and by a long abscence from books and study, a weakness of the eyes which had obliged me to give up my pursuits, and which no medical aid seemed likely to cure.

I joined the crew, and we hauled out into the stream, and came to anchor for the night. The next day we were employed in preparations for the sea, reeving studding-sail gear, crossing royal-yards, putting on chafing gear, and taking on board our powder. On the following night I stood my first watch. I remained awake nearly all the first part of the night; and when I went on deck, so great were my ideas of the importance of my trust, that I walked regularly fore and aft the whole length of the vessel, looking out over the bows and taffrail at each turn, and was not a little surprised at the coolness of the old salt whom I called to take my place, in stowing himself snugly away under the longboat for a nap.

The next morning was Saturday, and a breeze having sprung up from the southward, we took a pilot on board, and began beating down the bay. As we drew down into the lower harbour, we found the wind ahead in the bay, and were obliged to come to anchor in the roads. We remained there through the day and part of the night. My watch began at eleven o'clock at night. About midnight the wind became fair, and, having called the captain, I was ordered to call all hands. How I accomplished this I don't know, but I am quite sure that I did not give the true hoarse boatswain call of 'A-a-ll ha.a.a.nds! up anchor, a-ho-oy!' In a short time every one was in motion, the sails loosed, the yards braced, and we began to heave up the anchor. I could take but little part in these preparations. My little knowledge of a vessel was all at fault. Unintelligible orders were so rapidly given, and so immediately executed; there was such a hurrying about, and such an intermingling of strange cries and stranger actions, that I was completely bewildered. At length those peculiar, long-drawn sounds which denote that the crew are heaving at the windlass, began, and in a few minutes we were under way. The noise of the water thrown from the bows began to be heard, the vessel leaned over from the damp night-breeze, and rolled with the heavy ground-swell, and we had actually begun our long, long journey.

R. H. Dana : from Two Years Before the Mast

1057—

> *'Though Birnam Wood be come to Dunsinane,*
> *And thou opposed, being of no woman born,*
> *Yet will I try the last'*
>
> Macbeth, *Act V, sc. viii*

But after that Makbeth perceived his enemy's power to increase, by such aid as came to them forth of England with his adversary Malcolme, he recoiled back into Fife, there purposing to abide in camp fortified, at the castle of Dunsinane, and to fight with his enemies, if they meant to pursue him; howbeit some of his friends advised him, that it should be best for him, either to make some agreement with Malcolme, or else to flee with all speed into the Isles, and to take his treasure with him, to the end he might wage sundry great princes of the realm to take his part, & retain strangers, in whom he might better trust than in his own subjects, which stole daily from him: but he had such confidence in his prophecies, that he believed he should never be vanquished, till Birnane wood were brought to Dunsinane; nor yet to be slain with any man, that should be or was born of any woman.

Malcolme following hastily after Makbeth, came the night before the battle into Birnane wood, and when his army had rested a while there to refresh them, he commanded every man to get a bough of some tree or other of that wood in his hand, as big as he might bear, and to march forth therewith in such wise, that on the next morrow they might come closely and without sight in this manner within view of his enemies. On the morrow when Makbeth beheld them coming in this sort, he first marveled what the matter meant, but in the end remembered himself that the prophecy which he had heard long before that time, of the coming of Birnane wood to Dunsinane castle, was likely to be now fulfilled. Nevertheless, he brought his men in order of battle, and exhorted them to do valiantly, howbeit his enemies had scarcely cast from them their boughs, when Makbeth perceiving their numbers, betook him straight to flight, whom Makduffe pursued with great hatred even till he came unto Lunfannaine, where Makbeth perceiving that Makduffe was hard at his back, leaped beside his horse, saying 'Thou traitor, what meaneth it that thou shouldest thus in vain follow me that am not appointed to be slain by any creature that is born of a woman, come on therefore, and receive thy reward which thou hast deserved for thy pains', and therewithal he lifted up his sword thinking to have slain him.

But Makduffe quickly avoiding from his horse, ere he came at him, answered (with his naked sword at his hand) saying: 'It is true Makbeth, and now shall thine insatiable cruelty have an end, for I am even he that thy wizards have told thee of, who was never born of my mother, but ripped out of her womb': therewithal he stepped unto him, and slew him in the place. Then cutting his head from his shoulders, he set it upon a pole, and brought it unto Malcolme.

Raphael Holinshed: from Chronicles of England, Scotland, and Ireland

16 August

1819—In the 'Peterloo Massacre', six hundred people were killed when troops fired into a mass meeting which had peacefully assembled in support of parliamentary reform

Men of England, heirs of Glory,
Heroes of unwritten story,
Nurslings of one mighty Mother,
Hopes of her, and one another; . . .

From the corners uttermost
Of the bounds of English coast;
From every hut, village, and town
Where those who live and suffer moan
For others' misery or their own,

From the workhouse and the prison
Where pale as corpses newly risen
Women, children, young and old
Groan for pain, and weep for cold –

From the haunts of daily life
Where is waged the daily strife
With common wants and common cares
Which sows the human heart with tares –

Ye who suffer woes untold,
Or to feel, or to behold
Your lost country bought and sold
With a price of blood and gold –

Let a vast assembly be,
And with great solemnity
Declare with measured words that ye
Are, as God has made ye, free – . . .

Rise like Lions after slumber
In unvanquishable number –
Shake your chains to earth, like dew
Which in sleep has fallen on you –
Ye are many – they are few.

Percy Bysshe Shelley: from 'The Mask of Anarchy, written on the occasion of the massacre at Manchester'.

1850—The first instalment of Herman Melville's essay on Nathaniel Hawthorne was published in The Literary World

---

Where Hawthorne is known, he seems to be deemed a pleasant writer, with a pleasant style, – a sequestered, harmless man, from whom any deep and weighty thing would hardly be anticipated – a man who means no meanings. But there is no man in whom humor and love, like mountain peaks, soar to such a rapt height as to receive the irradiations of the upper skies – there is no man in whom humor and love are developed in that high form called genius – no such man can exist without also possessing, as the indispensable complement of these, a great, deep intellect, which drops down into the universe like a plummet. Or, love and humor are only the eyes through which such an intellect views the world. The great beauty in such a mind is but the product of its strength. . . .

For in spite of all the Indian-summer sunlight on the hither side of Hawthorne's soul, the other side – like the dark half of the physical sphere – is shrouded in a blackness, ten times black. But this darkness but gives more effect to the ever-moving dawn, that for ever advances through it, and circumnavigates his world. Whether Hawthorne has simply availed himself of this mystical blackness as a means to the wondrous effects he makes it to produce in his lights and shades; or whether there really lurks in him, perhaps unknown to himself, a touch of Puritanic gloom, – this, I cannot altogether tell. Certain it is, however, that this great power of blackness in him derives its force from its appeals to that Calvinistic sense of Innate Depravity and Original Sin, from whose visitations, in some shape or other, no deeply thinking mind is always and wholly free. . . . At all events, perhaps no writer has ever wielded this terrific thought with greater terror than this same harmless Hawthorne. Still more: this black conceit pervades him through and through. You may be witched by his sunlight, – transported by the bright gildings in the skies he builds over you; but there is the blackness of darkness beyond; and even his bright gildings but fringe and play upon the edges of thunder-clouds. In one word, the world is mistaken in this Nathaniel Hawthorne. . . . For it is not the brain that can test such a man; it is only the heart. You cannot come to know greatness by inspecting it; there is no glimpse to be caught of it, except by intuition; you need not ring it, you but touch it, and you find it is gold.

Herman Melville: from 'Hawthorne and His Mosses'

18 August

1838—George Borrow, in the third year of his robustious attempts to sell the Bible in Spain, was, for the first time, really frightened

I reached Abades at nightfall, and found Lopez, with two peasants whom he had engaged, in the house of the surgeon of the place, where I also took up my residence. He had already disposed of a considerable number of Testaments in the neighbourhood, and had that day commenced selling in Abades itself; he had, however, been interrupted by two of the three curas of the village, who, with horrid curses denounced the work, threatening eternal condemnation to Lopez for selling it, and to any person who should purchase it; whereupon Lopez, terrified, forbore until I should arrive. The third cura, however, exerted himself to the utmost to persuade the people to provide themselves with Testaments, telling them that his brethren were hypocrites and false guides, who, by keeping them in ignorance of the word and will of Christ, were leading them to the abyss. Upon receiving this information, I instantly sallied forth to the market-place, and that same night succeeded in disposing of upwards of thirty Testaments. The next morning the house was entered by the two factious curas, but upon my rising to confront them, they retreated, and I heard no more of them, except that they publicly cursed me in the church more than once, an event which, as no ill resulted from it, gave me little concern.

[In the following week, they sold 'from five to six hundred Testaments'; but] at the expiration of that period I received information that my proceedings were known in Segovia . . . and that an order was about to be sent to the alcalde to seize all books in my possession. Whereupon, notwithstanding that it was late in the evening, I decamped with all my people, and upwards of three hundred Testaments, having a few hours previously received a fresh supply from Madrid. That night we passed in the fields, and next morning proceeded to Labajos, a village on the high road from Madrid to Vallodolid. In this place we offered no books for sale, but contented ourselves with supplying the neighbouring villages with the word of God: we likewise sold it in the highways.

We had not been at Labajos a week, during which time we were remarkably successful, when the Carlist chieftain, Balmaseda, at the head of his cavalry, made his desperate inroad into the southern part of Old Castile, dashing down like an avalanche from the pine-woods of Soria. I was present at all the horrors which ensued, – the sack of Arrevalo, and the forcible entry into Martin Muños. Amidst these terrible scenes we continued our labours. Suddenly I lost Lopez for three days, and suffered dreadful anxiety on his account, imagining that he had been shot by the Carlists; at last [on the 21st. inst. I received information] that he was in prison in Villallos, three leagues distant.

George Borrow: from The Bible in Spain, *ch. xliv*

1843—'The Black Cat', one of Edgar Allen Poe's most horrific tales, was first published in the U.S. Saturday Post

For the most wild, yet most homely narrative which I am about to pen, I neither expect nor solicit belief. Mad indeed would I be to expect it, in a case where my very senses reject their own evidence. Yet – mad am I not – and very surely do I not dream. But tomorrow I die, and today I would unburden my soul. My immediate purpose is to place before the world plainly, succinctly, and without comment, a series of mere household events. In their consequences these events have terrified – have tortured – have destroyed me. Yet will I not attempt to expound them. To me they have presented little but horror – to many they will seem less terrible than *baroques*. Hereafter, perhaps, some intellect may be found which will reduce my phantasm to the common-place – some intellect more calm, more logical, and far less excitable than my own, which will perceive in the circumstances I detail with awe, nothing more than an ordinary succession of very natural causes and effects.

From my infancy I was noted for the docility and humanity of my disposition. . . . I married early, and was happy to find in my wife a disposition not uncongenial to my own. Observing my partiality for domestic pets, she lost no opportunity of procuring those of the most agreeable kind. We had birds, goldfish, a fine dog, rabbits, a small monkey, and *a cat*.

*   *   *   *   *

But may God shield and deliver me from the fangs of the Arch-Fiend! No sooner had the reverberations of my blows sunk into silence than I was answered by a voice from within the tomb! – by a cry, at first muffled and broken, like the sobbing of a child, and then quickly swelling into one long, loud, and continuous scream, utterly anomalous and inhuman – a howl – a wailing shriek, half of horror and half of triumph, such as might have arisen only out of hell, conjointly from the throats of the damned in their agony and of the demons that exult in their damnation.

Of my own thoughts it is folly to speak. Swooning, I staggered to the opposite wall. For one instant the party upon the stairs remained motionless, through extremity of terror and or awe. In the next, a dozen stout arms were toiling at the wall. It fell bodily. The corpse, already greatly decayed and clotted with gore, stood erect before the eyes of the spectators. Upon its head, with red extended mouth and solitary eyes of fire, sat the hideous beast whose craft had seduced me into murder, and whose informing voice had consigned me to the hangman. I had walled the monster up within the tomb!

20 August

1917—Major Sir Ronald Ross, in the midst of the Great War, on the twentieth anniversary of his discovery of the role of the malarial mosquito, for which he had received the Nobel prize, reflected on the fickleness of fame

Now twenty years ago
    This day we found the thing;
With science and with skill
    We found: then came the sting –
What we with endless labour won
    The thick world scorned;
Not worth a word today –
    Not worth remembering.

O Gorgeous Gardens, Lands
    Of beauty where the Sun
His lordly raiment trials
    All day with light enspun,
We found the death that lurk'd beneath
    Your purple leaves,
We found your secret foe,
    The million-murdering one;

And clapp'd our hands and thought
    Your teeming width would ring
With that great victory – more
    Than battling hosts can bring.
Ah, well – men laugh'd. The years have pass'd;
    The world is cold –
Some million lives a year,
    Not worth remembering!

Ascended from below
    Men still remain too small;
With belly-wisdom big
    They fight and bite and bawl,
These larval angels! – but when true
    Achievement comes –
A trifling doctor's matter –
    No consequence at all.

Ronald Ross

1764—'... the work [Reliques of Ancient English Poetry] *is on the very threshold of publication; I only wait for some additional remarks as I shall throw to the end of the last volume by way of appendix ...'*

Thomas Percy to Sir David Dalrymple

The Reader is here presented with select remains of our ancient English bards and minstrels, an order of men who were once greatly respected by our ancestors, and contributed to soften the roughness of a martial and unlettered people by their songs and by their music.

The greater part of them are extracted from an ancient folio manuscript* in the editor's possession, which contains near 200 poems, songs, and metrical romances. . . . This manuscript was shewn to several learned and ingenious friends, who thought the contents too curious to be consigned to oblivion, and importuned the possessor to select some of them, and give them to the press. As most of them are of great simplicity, and seem to have been merely written for the people, he was long in doubt, whether, in the present state of improved literature, they could be deemed worthy the attention of the public. At length the importunity of his friends prevailed, and he could refuse nothing to such judges as the author of the *Rambler* and the late Mr. Shenstone.

from 'The Preface' to Percy's Reliques

* When I first got possession of this MS, I was very young, and being no degree an antiquary, I had not then learnt to reverence it; which must be my excuse for the scribble which I then spread over some parts of its margin, and, in one or two instances, for even taking out the leaves to save the trouble of transcribing. I have since been more careful.   T.P.

note pinned to the MS when Percy left it with his publishers

* This very curious old manuscript, in its present mutilated state, but unbound and sadly torn, &c., I rescued from destruction, and begged at the hands of my worthy friend Humphrey Pitt, Esq., then living at Shiffnal, in Shropshire. . . . I saw it lying dirty on the floor, under a Bureau in ye Parlour: being used by the maids to light the fire. It was afterwards sent, most unfortunately, to an ignorant Bookbinder, who pared the margin, when I put it in boards to lend it to Dr. Johnson. Mr. Pitt has since told me that he believes the transcripts into this volume, &c., were made by that Blount who was author of *Jocular Tenures*, &c., who he thought was of Lancashire or Cheshire, and had a remarkable fondness for these old things. . . .

Thomas Percy, from a further memorandum to his publishers, Nov. 7, 1769

22 August 🕮

1754—George Colman and Bonnell Thornton, having converted their Oxford undergraduate periodical to a fashionable London journal, followed the example of generations of commentators in breaking a lance against the English passion for gambling

> Thumps following thumps, and blows succeeding blows
> Swell the black eye, and crush the bleeding nose;
> Beneath the pond'rous fist the jaw-bone cracks,
> And the cheeks ring with their redoubled thwacks.

The amusement of boxing, I must confess, is more immediately calculated for the vulgar, who can have no relish for the more refined pleasures of whist and the hazard table. Men of fashion have found out a more genteel employment for their hands in shuffling a pack of cards and shaking the dice; and, indeed, it will appear, upon a strict review, that most of our fashionable diversions are nothing else but different branches of gaming. What lady would be able to boast a rout at her house consisting of three or four hundred persons, if they were not drawn together by the charms of playing a rubber? and the prohibition of jubilee masquerades is hardly to be regretted, as they wanted the most essential part of their entertainments – the E. O. table.

To this polite spirit of gaming, which has diffused itself through all the fashionable world, is owing the vast encouragement that is given to the turf; and horse races are esteemed only as they afford occasion for making a bet. The same spirit likewise draws the knowing ones together in a cockpit; and cocks are rescued from the dunghill, and armed with gaffles, to furnish a new species of gaming. For this reason, among others, I cannot but regret the loss of our excellent amusements in Oxford Road and Tottenham Court. A great part of the spectators used to be deeply interested in what was doing on the stage, and were as earnest to make an advantage of the issue of the battle as the champions themselves to draw the largest sum from the box. The amphitheatre was at once a school for boxing and gaming. Many thousands have depended upon a match; the odds have often risen at a black eye; a large bet has been occasioned by a 'cross-buttock'; and while the house has resounded with the lusty bangs of the combatants, it has at the same time echoed with the cries of 'Five to one! six to one! ten to one!'

from The Connoisseur, *no. 30*

1939—Mrs E. M. Pretty, on whose estate at Sutton Hoo in Suffolk had been found a seventh-century ship burial containing the richest treasure ever recovered from any medieval site in Europe, presented the hoard to the British nation, to be housed in the British Museum

Scyld the Sheaf-Child from scourging foemen,
From raiders a-many, their mead-halls wrested.
He lived to be feared, though first as a waif,
Puny and frail, he was found on the shore.
He grew to be great, and was girt with power
Till the border-tribes all obeyed his rule,
And sea-folk hardy that sit by the whale-path
Gave him tribute; a good king was he. . . .
    The aged Scyld, when his hour had come,
Famous and praised, departed to God.
His faithful comrades carried him down
To the brink of the sea, as himself had bidden,
The Scyldings' friend, before he fell silent,
Their lord beloved who long had ruled them.
Out in the bay a boat was waiting
Coated with ice, 'twas the king's own barge.
They lifted aboard their bracelet-bestower,
And down on the deck their dear lord laid,
Hard by the mast. Heaped-up treasure
Gathered from afar they gave him along.
Never was ship more nobly laden
With wondrous weapons and warlike gear.
Swords and corselets covered his breast,
Floating riches to ride afar with him
Out o'er the waves at the will of the sea.
No less they dowered their lord with treasure,
Things of price, than those who at first
Had launched him forth as a little child
Alone on the deep to drift o'er the billows.
They gave him to boot a gilded banner,
High o'er his head they hung it aloft,
Then set him adrift, let the surges bear him.
Sad were their hearts, their spirits mournful;
Man hath not heard, no mortal can say
Who found that barge's floating burden.

from Beowulf, *translated by J. Duncan Speath in* Old English Poetry: Translations into Alliterative Verse.

24 August ⨇

A.D. 79—The violent eruption of Mount Vesuvius that destroyed Pompeii

---

The cloud which had scattered so deep a murkiness over the day, had now settled into a solid and impenetrable mass. It resembled less even the thickest gloom of a night in the open air than the close and blind darkness of some narrow room. But in proportion as the blackness gathered, did the lightnings around Vesuvius increase in their vivid scorching glare. . . . In the pauses of the showers, you heard the rumbling of the earth beneath, and the groaning waves of the tortured sea; or, lower still, and audible but to the watch of intensest fear, the grinding and hissing of the escaping gases through the chasms of the distant mountain. Sometimes the cloud appeared to break from its solid mass, and, by the lightning, to assume quaint and vast mimicries of human or of monster shapes, striding across the gloom, hurtling one upon the other, and vanishing swiftly into the turbulent abyss of shade; so that, to the eyes and fancies of the affrighted wanderers, the unsubstantial vapours were as the bodily forms of gigantic foes, – the agents of terror and of death.

The ashes in many places were already knee-deep; and the boiling showers which came from the streaming breath of the volcano forced their way into the houses, bearing with them a strong and suffocating vapour. In some places, immense fragments of rock, hurled upon the house roofs, bore down along the streets masses of confused ruin. . . .

Sometimes the huger stones striking against each other as they fell, broke into countless fragments, emitting sparks of fire, which caught whatever was combustible within their reach; and along the plains beyond the city the darkness was now terribly relieved; for several houses, and even vineyards, had been set to flames; and on various intervals the fires rose suddenly and fiercely against the solid gloom. . . .

Frequently, by the momentary light of these torches, parties of fugitives encountered each other, some hurrying towards the sea, others flying from the sea back to the land . . . the showers fell now frequently, though not continuously, extinguishing the lights, which showed to each band the deathlike faces of each other, and hurrying all to seek refuge beneath the nearest shelter. The whole elements of civilisation were broken up. Ever and anon, by the flickering lights, you saw the thief hastening by the most solemn authorities of the law, laden with, and fearfully chuckling over, the produce of his sudden gains. If, in the darkness, wife was separated from husband, or parent from child, vain was the hope of reunion. Each hurried blindly and confusedly on. Nothing in all the various and complicated machinery of social life was left save the primal law of self-preservation!

Edward Bulwer-Lytton: from The Last Days of Pompeii

1770—Thomas Chatterton, the seventeen-year-old prodigy, 'was found lying on his bed, stiff and cold', presumably having committed suicide in despair over the world's failure to understand him

ELEGY

Joyless I seek the solitary shade,
    Where dusky Contemplation veils the scene,
The dark retreat (of leafless branches made)
    Where sick'ning sorrow wets the yellow'd green.

The darksome ruins of some sacred cell,
    Where erst the sons of Superstition trod,
Tott'ring upon the mossy meadow, tell
    We better know, but less adore our God.

Now, as I mournful tread the gloomy nave,
    Thro' the wide window (once with mysteries dight)
The distant forest, and the dark'ned wave
    Of the swoln Avon ravishes my sight.

But see the thick'ning veil of evening's drawn,
    The azure changes to a sable blue;
The rapturing prospects fly the less'ning lawn,
    And Nature seems to mourn the dying view.

Self-sprighted Fear creeps silent thro' the gloom,
    Starts at the rust'ling leaf, and rolls his eyes;
Aghast with horror, when he views the tomb,
    With every torment of a hell he flies.

The bubbling brooks in plaintive murmurs roll,
    The bird of omen, with incessant scream,
To melancholy thoughts awakes the soul,
    And lulls the mind to contemplation's dream.

A dreary stillness broods o'er all the vale,
    The clouded moon emits a feeble glare;
Joyless I seek the darkling hill and dale;
    Where'er I wander sorrow is still there.

Thomas Chatterton

26 August 🔲

1721—Sir John Vanbrugh, who had been a successful playwright in earlier days, found 'a vast deal to do' in his new profession of architecture

Cou'd you See how busy I have been, ever Since I writ to you last, you wou'd easily forgive my being so long before I did it again. I return'd but last night from the North (for here you must know we are in the South) where I have been near three weeks finding a vast deal to do, both at Delavals and Lumley Castle. Since it is not easy, to go there often, I resolv'd to do all the Service I cou'd while I was there now.

The Admiral is very Gallant in his operations, not being dispos'd to starve the Design at all. So that he is like to have, a very fine Dwelling for himself, now, and his Nephew &c. hereafter.

Lumley Castle is a Noble thing; and well deserves the Favours Lord Lumley designs to bestow upon it; In order to which, I stay'd there near a Week, to form a General Design for the whole, Which consists, in altering the House both for State, Beauty and Convenience, And making the Courts Gardens and Offices Suitable to it; All which I believe may be done, for a Sum, that can never ly very heavy upon the Family. If I had had good weather in this Expedition, I shou'd have been well enough diverted in it; there being many more Valluable and Agreeable things and Places to be Seen, than in the Tame Sneaking South of England.

I am going for three or four days again to Castle Howard, where I must Spend a Week or ten days, to do what is necessary there. My Lord Carlisle going on with his Works as usual; by which the Seat is wonderfully improv'd this last Year. Two Years more, tho' they won't compleat all the Building, will so Beautify the Outworks, of Gardens, Park &c, That I think no Place I ever Saw, will dispute with it, for a Delightfull Dwelling in generall, let the Criticks fish out what particular faults they please in the Architecture. Here are Several Gentlemen in these Parts of the World, that are possess'd with the Spirit of Building, And Seem dispos'd to do it, in so good a Manner, that were they to establish here a sort of Board of Works to conduct their Affairs, I do verily believe, they wou'd sooner make Hawksmr. a Commissioner of it, than that excellent Architect, Ripley.

Vanbrugh: in a letter to General Watkins

Lie heavy on him, earth, for he
Laid many a heavy load on thee.

anonymous 'epitaph' on Sir John Vanbrugh, written after he had completed his grandest design, Blenheim Palace

*1877—Walt Whitman recorded the success of his self-prescribed 'nature-cure',
recovering from a stroke of paralysis*

Another day quite free from mark'd prostration and pain. It seems indeed as if peace and nutriment from heaven subtly filter into me as I slowly hobble down these country lanes and across fields, in the good air – as I sit here in solitude, with Nature – open, voiceless, mystic, far removed, yet palpable, eloquent Nature. I merge myself in the scene, in the perfect day. Hovering over the clear brook-water, I am sooth'd by its soft gurgle in one place, and the hoarse murmurs of its three-foot fall in another. Come, ye disconsolate, in whom any latent eligibility is left – come get the sure virtues of creek-shore, and wood and field. Two months (July and August, '77) have I absorb'd them, and they begin to make a new man of me. Every day, seclusion – every day at least two or three hours of freedom, bathing, no talk, no bonds, no dress, no books, no *manners*.

Shall I tell you, reader, to what I attribute my already much-restored health? That I have been almost two years, off and on, without drugs and medicines, and daily in the open air. Last summer I found a particularly secluded little dell off one side by my creek, originally a large dug-out marl-pit, now abandon'd, fill'd with bushes, trees, grass, a group of willows, a straggling bank, and a spring of delicious water running right through the middle of it, with two or three little cascades. Here I retreated every hot day, and follow it up to this summer. Here I realize the meaning of that old fellow who said he was seldom less alone than when alone. Never before did I get so close to Nature; never before did she come so close to me. By old habit, I pencill'd down from time to time, almost automatically, moods, sights, hours, tints and outlines, on the spot. . . .

An hour or so after breakfast I wended my way down to the recesses of the aforesaid dell, which I and certain thrushes, cat-birds, &c., had all to ourselves. A light south-west wind was blowing through the tree-tops. It was just the place and time for my Adamitic air-bath and flesh-brushing from head to foot. So hanging clothes on a rail near by, keeping old broadbrim straw on head and easy shoes on feet, haven't I had a good time the last two hours? First with the stiff-elastic bristles rasping arms, breast, sides, till they turn'd scarlet – then partially bathing in the clear waters of the running brook – taking everything very leisurely, with many rests and pauses – stepping about barefooted every few minutes now and then in some neighbouring blacke ooze. . . .

Walt Whitman: from Specimen Days

28 August 📖

1819—John Keats confided to his sister, Fanny, some of his hopes and fears for the tragedy, 'Otho the Great' which he and Charles Armitage Brown had just finished – and something of his irrepressible high spirits

. . . I have still been hard at work, having completed a Tragedy I think I spoke of to you. But there I fear all my labour will be thrown away for the present, as I hear Mr Kean is going to America. . . . The delightful Weather we have had for two Months is the highest gratification I could receive – no chill'd red roses – no shivering – but fair atmosphere to think in – a clean towel mark'd with the mangle and a basin of clear Water to drench one's face with ten times a day: no need of much exercise – a Mile a day being quite sufficient. My greatest regret is that I have not been well enough to bathe though I have been two Months by the seaside and live now close to delicious bathing – Still I enjoy the Weather – I adore fine Weather as the greatest blessing I can have. Give me Books, fruit, French wine and fine weather and a little music out of doors, played by somebody I do not know – not pay the price of one's time for a jig – but a little chance music: and I can pass a summer very quietly without caring much about Fat Louis, fat Regent or the Duke of Wellington. . . . Mr Brown is copying out our Tragedy of Otho the Great in a superb style – better than it deserves – there as I said is labour in vain for the present. I had hoped to give Kean another opportunity to shine. What can we do now? There is not another actor of Tragedy in all London or Europe. The Covent Garden company is execrable. Young is the best among them and he is a ranting coxcombical tasteless Actor – a Disgust, a Nausea – and yet the very best after Kean. What a set of barren asses are actors! I should like now to promenade round your Gardens – apple-tasting – pear-tasting – plum-judging – apricot nibbling – peach-scrunching – nectarine-sucking and Melon-carving. I also have a great feeling for antiquated cherries full of sugar cracks – and a white currant tree kept for company. I admire lolling on a lawn by a water lilied pond to eat white currants and see gold-fish: and go to the Fair in the Evening if I'm good. There is not hope for that – one is sure to get into some mess before evening. Have these hot days I brag of so much been well or ill for your health? Let me hear soon.

Your affectionate Brother John –

Winchester, August 28 [1819]

1838—Lady Charlotte Guest dedicated the Mabinogion *to her two small sons, 'in the hope of inciting you to cultivate the literature of "Gwyllt Walia", in whose beautiful language you are being initiated, and amongst whose free mountains you were born'*

King Arthur was at Caerlleon upon Usk; and one day he sat in his chamber; and with him were Owain the son of Urien, and Kynon the son of Clydno, and Kai the son of Kyner; and Gwenhwyvar and her hand-maidens at needlework by the window. And if it should be said that there was a porter at Arthur's palace, there was none. Glewlwyd Gavaelvawr was there, acting as porter, to welcome guests and strangers, and to receive them with honour, and to inform them of the manners and customs of the Court; and to direct those who came to the Hall or to the presence Chamber, and those who came to take up their lodging.

In the centre of the chamber, king Arthur sat, upon a seat of green rushes, over which was spread a covering of flame coloured satin; and a cushion of red satin was under his elbow.

Then Arthur spoke, 'If I thought you would not disparage me', said he, 'I would sleep while I wait for my repast; and you can entertain one another with relating tales, and can obtain a flagon of mead and some meat from Kai.' And the King went to sleep. And Kynon the son of Clydno asked Kai for that which Arthur had promised them. 'I too will have the good tale which he promised to me', said Kai. 'Nay', answered Kynon, 'fairer will it be for thee to fulfil Arthur's behest in the first place, and then we will tell thee the best tale that we know.' So Kai went to the kitchen and to the mead-cellar, and returned, bearing a flagon of mead, and a golden goblet, and a handful of skewers upon which were broiled collops of meat. Then they ate the collops and began to drink the mead. 'Now', said Kai, 'it is time for you to give me my story.' 'Kynon', said Owain, 'do thou pay Kai the tale that is his due.' 'Truly', said Kynon, 'thou art older, and art a better teller of tales, and has seen more marvellous things than I; do thou therefore pay Kai his tale.' 'Begin thyself', quoth Owain, 'with the best that thou knowest'. 'I will do so', answered Kynon.

'I was the only son of my mother and father, and I was exceedingly aspiring, and my daring was very great. I thought there was no enterprise in the world too mighty for me, and after I had achieved all the adventures that were in my own country, I equipped myself and set forth to journey through deserts and distant regions. And at length it chanced that . . . at the extremity of a plain I came to a large and lustrous Castle, at the foot of which was a Torrent. And I approached the Castle, and there I beheld . . .

from the tale of 'The Lady of the Fountain', in the Mabinogion

30 August

1908—'Finished The Old Wives' Tale *at 11.30 a.m. today. 200,000 words'* (*sole entry in Arnold Bennett's Journal on this date*)

Though Constance was too ill to know how ill she was, though she had no conception of the domestic confusion caused by her illness, her brain was often remarkably clear, and she could reflect in long, sane meditations above the uneasy sea of her pain. In the earlier hours of the night, after the nurses had been changed, and Mary had gone to bed exhausted with stair-climbing, and Lucy Hall was recounting the day to Dick up at the grocer's, and the day-nurse was already asleep, and the night-nurse had arranged the night, then, in the faintly-lit silence of the chamber, Constance would argue with herself for an hour at a time. . . . She did not consider that Fate had treated her very badly. She was not very discontented with herself. The invincible commonsense of a sound nature prevented her, in her best moments, from feebly dissolving into self-pity. She had lived in honesty and kindliness for a fair number of years, and she had tested triumphant hours. She was justly respected, she had a position, she had dignity, she was well-off. She possessed, after all, a certain amount of quiet self-conceit. There existed nobody to whom she would 'knuckle down'. True, she was old! So were thousands of other people in Bursley. She was in pain. So there were thousands of other people. With whom would she be willing to exchange lots? . . . When she surveyed her life, and life in general, she would think, with a sort of tart but not sour cheerfulness: '*Well, that is what life is!*' . . .

It was not acute rheumatism, but a supervening pericarditis that in a few days killed her. She died in the night, alone with the night-nurse. . . . In the evening she had requested that Fossette sould be brought upstairs. . . .

When the short funeral procession started, Mary and the infirm Fossette (sole relic of the connection between the Baines family and Paris) were left alone in the house. The tearful servant prepared the dog's dinner and laid it before her in the customary soup-plate in the customary corner. Fossette sniffed at it, and then walked away and lay down with a dog's sigh in front of the kitchen fire. She had been deranged in her habits that day; she was conscious of neglect, due to events which passed her comprehension. And she did not like it. She was hurt, and her appetite was hurt. However, after a few minutes, she began to reconsider the matter. She glanced at the soup-plate, and, on the chance that it might after all contain something worth inspection, she awkwardly balanced herself on her old legs and went to it again.

Arnold Bennett: from The Old Wives' Tale,
the final chapter

1837—Ralph Waldo Emerson, at Harvard University, delivered the speech which became known as America's 'Declaration of Intellectual Independence'

Perhaps the time is already come when the sluggard intellect of this continent will look from under its iron lids and fill the postponed expectation of the world with something better than the exertions of mechanical skill. Our day of dependence, our long apprenticeship to the learning of other lands, is drawing to a close. The millions that around us are rushing into life, cannot always be fed on the sere remains of foreign harvests. Events, actions arise, that must be sung, that will sing themselves. . .

The duties of the scholar are such as become *Man Thinking*. They may all be comprised in SELF-TRUST. The office of the scholar is to cheer, to raise, and to guide men by showing them facts inside appearances. He is the world's eye. He is the world's heart. He is to resist the vulgar prosperity that retrogrades ever to Barbarism, by preserving and communicating heroic sentiments, noble biographies, melodious verse, and the conclusions of history. . . .

The scholar is that man who must take up into himself all the ability of the time, all the contributions of the past, all the hopes of the future. He must be an university of knowledges. If there be one lesson more than another which should pierce his ear, it is, The world is nothing, the man is all . . . This confidence in the unsearched might of man belongs, by all motives, by all prophecy, by all preparation, to the American scholar.

We have listened too long to the courtly muses of Europe. The spirit of the American freeman is already suspected to be timid, imitative, tame. Public and private avarice make the air we breathe thick and fat. The scholar is decent, indolent, and complaisant. See already the tragic consequences. The mind of this country, taught to aim at low objects, eats upon itself. Young men of the fairest promise, who begin life upon our shores, inflated by the mountain winds, shined upon by all the stars of God, find the earth below not in unison with these, but are hindered from action by the disgust which the principles on which business is managed inspire, and turn drudges, or die of disgust, some of them suicides. What is the remedy? . . .

Henceforth, as befits *Man Thinking*, we will walk on our own feet; we will work with our own hands; we will speak our own minds. The study of letters shall be no longer a name for pity, for doubt, and for sensual indulgence. The dread of man and the love of man shall be a wall of defense and a wreath of joy around all. A nation of men will for the first time exist, because each believes himself inspired by the Divine Soul which also inspires all men.

Emerson: from The American Scholar

September.

1798—With the publication of Lyrical Ballads *on or about this date, William Wordsworth and Samuel Taylor Coleridge established their claim to the leadership of the Romantic movement*

. . . The principal object, then, proposed in these poems, was to choose incidents and situations from common life, and to relate or describe them, throughout, as far as was possible, in a selection of language really used by men, and, at the same time, to throw over them a certain colouring of imagination, whereby ordinary things should be presented to the mind in an unusual aspect; and, further, and above all, to make these incidents and situations interesting by tracing in them, truly though not ostentatiously, the primary laws of our nature. . . . Humble and rustic life was generally chosen, because, in that condition, the essential passions of the heart find a better soil in which they can attain their maturity, are less under restraint, and speak a plainer and more emphatic language. . . .

I cannot, however, be insensible to the present outcry against the triviality and meanness, both of thought and language, which some of my contemporaries have occasionally introduced into their metrical compositions. . . . From such verses the poems in these volumes will be found distinguished at least by one mark of difference, that each of them has a worthy *purpose*. . . . Another circumstance must be mentioned which distinguishes these poems from the popular poetry of the day; it is this, that the feeling therein developed gives importance to the action and situation, and not the action and situation to the feeling. . . .

For the human mind is capable of being excited without the application of gross and violent stimulants. . . . It has therefore appeared to me, that to endeavour to produce or enlarge this capability is one of the best services in which, at any period, a writer can be engaged; but this service, excellent at all times, is especially so at the present day. For a multitude of causes, unknown to former times, are now acting with a combined force to blunt the discriminating powers of the mind, and, unfitting it for all voluntary exertion, to reduce it to a state of almost savage torpor. The most effective of these causes are the great national events which are daily taking place, and the increasing accumulation of men in cities, where the uniformity of their occupations produces a craving for extraordinary incident, which the rapid communication of intelligence hourly gratifies. . . . When I think upon this degrading thirst after outrageous stimulation, I am almost ashamed to have spoken of the feeble endeavour made in these volumes to counteract it; and, reflecting upon the magnitude of the general evil, I should be oppressed with no dishonourable melancholy had I not a deep impression of certain inherent and indestructible qualities of the human mind, and likewise of certain powers in the great and permanent objects that act upon it, which are equally inherent and indestructible; and were there not added to this impression a belief that the time is approaching when the evil will be systematically opposed, by men of greater powers, and with far more distinguished success.

William Wordsworth: from the Preface to the second edition of Lyrical Ballads *(1800)*

2 September 🕮

1483—William Caxton published the first printed edition of John Gower's only long poem in English, the Confessio Amantis

Of those who wrote in days of yore
The books remain, and we therefore
May learn by what was written then.
Thus it is fit that living men
Should also in this latter age
Find some new subject for their page,
(Though copied from the tales of old)
If it be cast in such a mould
That when we die and go elsewhere
It lingers on the wide world's ear
In times to follow after this.
Only, men say – and truth it is –
That works of wholly solemn kind
Will often dull a reader's mind,
Who studies in them every day;
So I will walk the middle way,
If you advise me so to do,
And write a book between the two –
Something to please, something to profit –
So that the most or least part of it
May give some readers some delight.
And furthermore, since few men write
In our English, I think to make
One book at least for England's sake.

. . .

Therefore the style of what I write
From this day forth I mean to change,
And treat of what is not so strange –
Something that every creature learns,
And whereupon the whole world turns,
And so has turned since it began,
And shall while yet there is a man:
And it is Love . . .

from Confessio Amantis (*'The Lover's Shrift'*)
(*as translated by Terrence Tiller*)

Women in tea garden at Bramber – a sweltering hot day: rose trellises; white-washed tables; lower middle classes; motor omnibuses constantly passing; bits of grey stone scattered on a paper-strewn greensward, all that's left of the Castle. . . .

For the rest, Charleston, Tilton, *To the Lighthouse*, Vita, expeditions: the summer dominated by a feeling of washing in boundless warm fresh air – such an August not come my way for years; bicycling; no settled work done, but advantage taken of air for going to the river or over the downs. The novel is now easily within sight of the end, but this, mysteriously, comes no nearer. I am doing Lily on the lawn; but whether it's her last lap, I don't know. Nor am I sure of the quality; the only certainty seems to be that after tapping my antennae in the air vaguely for an hour every morning I generally write with heat and ease till 12.30; and thus do my two pages. So it will be done, written over that is, in 3 weeks, I forecast, from today. What emerges? At this moment I'm casting about for an end. The problem is how to bring Lily and Mr. R. together and make a combination of interest at the end. I am feathering about with various ideas. The last chapter which I begin tomorrow is In the Boat: I had meant to end with R. climbing on to the rock. If so, what becomes of Lily and her picture? Should there be a final page about her and Carmichael looking at the picture and summing up R's character? In that case I lose the intensity of the moment. If this intervenes between R. and the lighthouse, there's too much chop and change, I think. Could I do it in a parenthesis? So that one had the sense of reading the two things at the same time?

I shall solve it somehow, I suppose. Then I must go on to the question of quality. I think it may run too fast and free and so be rather thin. On the other hand, I think it is subtler and more human than *Jacob's Room* and *Mrs. Dalloway*. And I am encouraged by my own abundance as I write. It is proved, I think, that what I have to say is to be said in this manner. As usual, side stories are sprouting in great variety as I wind this up: a book of characters; the whole string being pulled out from some simple sentence, like Clara Pater's 'Don't you find that Barker's pins have no points to them?' I think I can spin out all their entrails this way; but it is hopelessly undramatic. It is all oratorio obliqua. Not quite all; for I have a few direct sentences. The lyric portions of *To the Lighthouse* are collected in the 10-year lapse and don't interfere with the text as much as usual. I feel as if it fetched its circle pretty completely this time; and I don't feel sure what the stock criticism will be. Sentimental? Victorian?

Virginia Woolf: from A Writer's Diary, *entry under 'Friday, September 3rd'*

4 September 🕮

1903—'Mr Bennett' witnessed the strange behaviour of the creeping man, which he reported to Sherlock Holmes at the first opportunity

Mr Bennett spoke in a tone of reproach, for it was very clear that Holmes was not listening. His face was rigid and his eyes gazed abstractedly at the ceiling. With an effort he recovered himself.

'Singular! Most singular!' he murmured, 'These details were new to me, Mr Bennett. I think we have now fairly gone over the old ground, have we not? But you spoke of some fresh developments.'

The pleasant, open face of our visitor clouded over, shadowed by some grim remembrance. 'What I speak of occurred the night before last', said he. 'I was lying awake about two in the morning, when I was aware of a dull muffled sound coming from the passage. I opened my door and peeped out. I should explain that the professor sleeps at the end of the passage – '

'The date being – ?' asked Holmes.

Our visitor was clearly annoyed at so irrelevant an interruption.

'I have said, sir, that it was the night before last – that is, September 4th.'

Holmes nodded and smiled.

'Pray continue', said he.

'He sleeps at the end of the passage and would have to pass my door in order to reach the staircase. It was a really terrifying experience, Mr Holmes. I think that I am as strong-nerved as my neighbours, but I was shaken by what I saw. The passage was dark save that one window halfway along it threw a patch of light. I could see that something was coming along the passage, something dark and crouching. Then suddenly it emerged into the light, and I saw that it was he. He was crawling, Mr Holmes – crawling! He was not quite on his hands and knees. I should rather say on his hands and feet, with his face sunk between his hands. Yet he seemed to move with ease. I was so paralyzed by the sight that it was not until he had reached my door that I was able to step forward and ask if I could assist him. His answer was extraordinary. He sprang up, spat out some atrocious word at me, and hurried on past me, and down the staircase. I waited about for an hour, but he did not come back. It must have been daylight before he regained his room.'

'Well, Watson, what make you of that?' asked Holmes with the air of a pathologist who presents a rare specimen.

Sir Arthur Conan Doyle: from 'The Adventure of the Creeping Man' in The Case Book of Sherlock Holmes

1666—The Great Fire of London was finally put out

And now four days the Sun had seen our woes,
    Four nights the Moon beheld th'incessant fire;
It seem'd as if the Stars more sickly rose,
    And farther from the feav'rish North retire.

In th'Empyrean Heaven, (the bless'd abode)
    The Thrones and the Dominions prostrate lie,
Not daring to behold their angry God:
    And an hush'd silence damps the tuneful sky.

At length th'Almighty cast a pitying eye,
    And mercy softly touch'd his melting breast:
He saw the Town's one half in rubbish lie,
    And eager flames drive on to storm the rest.

The vanquish'd fires withdraw from every place,
    Or full with feeding, sink into a sleep:
Each household Genius shows again his face,
    And, from the hearths, the little Lares creep.

. . .

Methinks already, from this Chymick flame,
    I see a City of more precious mold:
Rich as the Town which gives the Indies name,
    With Silver pav'd, and all divine with Gold.

Already Labouring with a mighty fate,
    She shakes the rubbish from her mountain brow,
And seems to have renew'd her Charters date,
    Which Heav'n will to the death of time allow.

More great then humane, now, and more *August*,
    New deifi'd she from her fires does rise:
Her widening streets on new foundations trust,
    And, opening, into larger parts she flies.

John Dryden: from 'Annus Mirabilis'

6 September 📖

1863—'I want you to write to Lord Palmerston to ask him to ask the Queen to ask the King of Greece to give me a "place" . . . the title to be Lord High Bosh and Nonsense Producer, with permission to wear a fool's cap (or mitre) – 3 pounds of butter yearly and a little pig – and a small donkey to ride on'

Edward Lear to Chichester Fortescue

How pleasant to know Mr Lear!
    Who has written such volumes of stuff!
Some think him ill-tempered and queer,
    But a few think him pleasant enough.

His mind is concrete and fastidious,
    His nose is remarkably big;
His visage is more or less hideous,
    His beard it resembles a wig.

He has ears, and two eyes, and ten fingers,
    Leastways if you reckon two thumbs;
Long ago he was one of the singers,
    But now he is one of the dumbs.

He sits in a beautiful parlour,
    With hundreds of books on the wall,
He drinks a great deal of Marsala,
    But never gets tipsy at all.

He has many friends, laymen and clerical,
    Old Foss is the name of his cat;
His body is perfectly spherical,
    He weareth a runcible hat. . . .

He weeps by the side of the ocean,
    He weeps on the top of the hill;
He purchases pancakes and lotion,
    And chocolate shrimps from the mill.

He reads but he cannot speak Spanish,
    He cannot abide ginger-beer:
Ere the days of his pilgrimage vanish,
    How pleasant to know Mr Lear!

Edward Lear

1847—Henry David Thoreau left Walden, having completed the manuscript of A Week on the Concord and Merrimack Rivers

All the world reposes in beauty to him who preserves equipoise in his life, and moves serenely on his path without secret violence; as he who sails down a stream has only to steer, keeping his bark in the middle, and carry it round the falls. The ripples curled away in our wake, like ringlets from the head of a child, while we steadily held on our course, and under the bows we watched

> The swaying soft
> Made by the delicate wave parted in front,
> As through the gentle element we move
> Like shadows gliding through untroubled dreams.

The forms of beauty fall naturally around the path of him who is in the performance of his proper work, as the curled shavings drop from the plane and borings cluster round the auger. Undulation is the gentlest and most ideal of motions, produced by one fluid falling on another. Rippling is a more graceful flight. From a hill-top you may detect it in the wings of birds endlessly repeated. The two *waving* lines which represent the flight of birds appear to have been copied from the ripple. . . .

Art can never match the luxury and superfluity of Nature. In the former all is seen; it cannot afford concealed wealth, and is niggardly in comparison; but Nature, even when she is scant and thin outwardly, satisfies us still by the assurance of a certain generosity at the roots. In swamps, where there is only here and there an evergreen tree amid the quaking moss and cranberry beds, the bareness does not suggest poverty. . . . As we have said, Nature is a greater and more perfect art, the art of God; though, referred to herself, she is genius; and there is a similarity between her operations and man's art even in the details and trifles. When the overhanging pine drops into the water, and the wind rubbing it against the shore, its boughs are worn in fantastic shapes, and white and smooth, as if turned in a lathe. Man's art has wisely imitated those forms into which all matter is most inclined to run, as foliage and fruit. A hammock swung in a grove assumes the exact form of a canoe, broader or narrower, and higher or lower at the ends, as more or fewer persons are in it, and it rolls in the air with the motion of the body, like a canoe in the water. Our art leaves its shavings and its dust about; her art exhibits itself even in the shavings and the dust which we make. She has perfected herself by an eternity of practise. The world is well kept; no rubbish accumulates; the morning air is clear even on this day, and no dust has settled on the grass.

Henry David Thoreau: from A Week on the Concord . . . etc.

8 September

1560—Amy Robsart died

On the next day, when evening approached, Varney summoned Foster to the execution of their plan. Tider and Foster's old man-servant were sent on a feigned errand down to the village, and Anthony himself, as if anxious that the Countess suffered no want of accomodation, visited her place of confinement. He was so much staggered at the mildness and patience with which she seemed to endure her confinement, that he could not help earnestly recommending to her not to cross the threshold of her room on any account whatever, until Lord Leicester should come, 'Which,' he added, 'I trust in God, will be very soon.' Amy patiently promised that she would resign herself to her fate, and Foster returned to his hardened companion with his conscience half-eased of the perilous load that weighed on it. 'I have warned her,' he said; 'surely in vain is the snare set in the sight of any bird!'

He left, therefore, the Countess's door unsecured on the outside, and, under the eye of Varney, withdrew the supports which sustained the falling trap, which, therefore, kept its level position merely by a slight adhesion. They withdrew to hear the issue on the ground-floor adjoining, but they waited long in vain. At length Varney, after walking long to and fro, with his face muffled in his cloak, threw it suddenly back, and exclaimed, 'Surely never was a woman fool enough to neglect so fair an opportunity of escape!'

'Perhaps she is resolved,' said Foster, 'to await her husband's return.'

'True! – most true,' said Varney, rushing out, 'I had not thought of that before.'

In less than two minutes, Foster, who remained behind, heard the tread of a horse in the court-yard and then a whistle similar to that which was the Earl's usual signal; – the instant after the door of the Countess's chamber opened, and in the same moment the trap-door gave way. There was a rushing sound – a heavy fall – a faint groan – and all was over.

At the same instant, Varney called in at the window, in an accent and tone which was an indescribable mixture betwixt horror and railery, 'Is the bird caught? – is the deed done?'

'O God, forgive us!' replied Anthony Foster.

'Why, thou fool,' said Varney, 'thy toil is ended, and thy reward secure. Look down into the vault – what seest thou?'

'I see only a heap of white clothes, like a snowdrift,' said Foster. 'O God, she moves her arm!'

'Hurl something down on her. – Thy gold chest, Tony – it is an heavy one.'

'Varney, thou art an incarnate fiend!' replied Foster; – 'There needs nothing more – she is gone!'

'So pass our troubles,' said Varney, entering the room: 'I dreamed not I could have mimicked the Earl's call so well.'

Sir Walter Scott: from Kenilworth

1513—The Scots were defeated at the Battle of Flodden Field

A Lament for Flodden

I've heard them lilting at our ewe-milking,
    Lasses a' lilting before dawn o' day;
But now they are moaning on ilka green loaning –
    The Flowers of the Forest are a' wede away.

At bughts, in the morning, nae blythe lads are scorning,
    Lasses are lonely and dowie and wae;
Nae daffing, nae gabbing, but sighing and sabbing,
    Ilk ane lifts her leglin and hies her away.

In hairst, at the shearing, nae youths now are jeering,
    Bandsters are lyart, and runkled, and gray:
At fair or at preaching, nae wooing, nae fleeching –
    The Flowers of the Forest are a' wede away.

At e'en, in the gloaming, nae swankies are roaming
    'Bout stacks wi' the lasses at bogle to play;
But ilk ane sits eerie, lamenting her dearie –
    The Flowers of the Forest are a' wede away.

Dool and wae for the order sent our lads to the Border!
    The English, for ance, by guile wan the day;
The Flowers of the Forest, that fought aye the foremost,
    The prime of our land, lie cauld in the clay.

We'll hear nae mair lilting at our ewe-milking;
    Women and bairns are heartless and wae;
Sighing and moaning on ilka green loaning –
    The Flowers of the Forest are a' wede away.

Jane Elliot

loaning – lane, field-track
bughts – sheep-folds
daffing – joking
leglin – milk-pail
hairst – harvest
bandsters – binders

lyart – grey-headed
runkled – wrinkled
fleeching – coaxing
swankies – lusty lads
bogle – bogy, hide-and-seek
dool – mourning

10 September 📖

1854—George Borrow brought his somewhat roundabout scholarship to bear on a murder case in Llangollen

On the tenth of September our little town was flung into some confusion by one butcher having attempted to cut the throat of another. The delinquent was a Welshman, who it was said had for some time past been somewhat out of his mind; the other party was an Englishman, who escaped without further injury than a deep gash in the cheek. The Welshman might be mad, but it appeared to me that there was some method in his madness. He tried to cut the throat of a butcher: didn't this look like wishing to put a rival out of the way? and that butcher an Englishman: didn't this look like wishing to pay back upon the Saxon what the Welsh call *bradwriaeth y cyllyll hirion*, 'the treachery of the long knives'? . . . Perhaps the reader will ask what is meant? . . . whether he does or not I will tell him.

Hengist wishing to become paramount in Southern Britain thought that the easiest way to accomplish his wish would be by destroying the South British chieftains. . . . Accordingly he invited the chieftains to a banquet to be held near Stonehenge, or the Hanging Stones, on Salisbury Plain. The unsuspecting chieftains accepted the invitation, and on the appointed day . . . Hengist received them with a smiling countenance and every appearance of hospitality, and caused them to sit down to a table, placing by the side of every Briton one of his own people. . . . Now Hengist had commanded his people that when he should get up and cry 'nemet eoure saxes', that is, take your knives, each Saxon should draw his long sax or knife which he wore at his side and should plunge it into the throat of his neighbour. . . . The banquet went on, and in the midst of it . . . uprose Hengist and with a voice of thunder uttered the fatal words 'nemet eoure saxes' . . . Almost every blow took effect; only three British chieftains escaping from the banquet of blood. . . . It will be as well to observe that the Saxons derived their name from the saxes, or long knives . . . at the use of which they were terribly proficient. . . .

It was generally held that the prisoner was disordered in his mind; I held my tongue, but judging from his look and manner I saw no reason to suppose that he was any more out of his senses than I myself, or any person present, and I had no doubt that what induced him to commit the act was rage at being looked down upon by a quondam acquaintance, who was rising a little in the world, exacerbated by the reflection that the disdainful quondam acquaintance was one of the Saxon race, against which every Welshman entertains a grudge more or less virulent, which though of course very unchristianlike, is really, brother Englishman, after the affair of the long knives, and two or three other actions of a somewhat similar character, of our noble Anglo-Saxon progenitors, with which all Welshmen are perfectly well acquainted, not very much to be wondered at.

George Borrow: from Wild Wales, *ch. 52*

1847—Coventry Patmore married Emily Augusta Andrews, the first of his three wives

Why, having won her, do I woo?
    Because her spirit's vestal grace
Provokes me always to pursue,
    But, spirit-like, eludes embrace;
Because her womanhood is such
    That, as on court-days subjects kiss
The Queen's hand, yet so near a touch
    Affirms no mean familiarness,
Nay, rather marks more fair the height
    Which can with safety so neglect
To dread, as lower ladies might,
    That grace could meet with disrespect,
Thus she with happy favour feeds
    Allegiance from a love so high
That thence no false conceit proceeds
    Of difference bridged, or state put by;
Because, although in act and word
    As lowly as a wife can be,
Her manners, when they call me lord,
    Remind me 'tis by courtesy;
Not with her least consent of will,
    Which would my proud affection hurt,
But by the noble style that still
    Imputes an unattain'd desert;
Because her gay and lofty brows,
    When all is won which hope can ask,
Reflect a light of hopeless snows
    That bright in virgin ether basks;
Because, though free of the outer court
    I am, this Temple keeps its shrine
Sacred to Heaven; because, in short,
    She's not and never can be mine.

Coventry Patmore: from Canto XII, The Angel in the House

12 September

1846—Elizabeth Barrett and Robert Browning were secretly married in St Marylebone Church ; her wedding present to him, presented when they 'eloped' a week later, was a sheaf of sonnets she had written during their courtship – sonnets which he pronounced 'the finest in any language since Shakespeare'

Sonnet 14

If thou must love me, let it be for nought
Except for love's sake only. Do not say,
'I love her for her smile – her look – her way
Of speaking gently – for a trick of thought
That falls in well with mine, and certes brought
A sense of pleasant ease on such a day' –
For these things in themselves, Beloved, may
Be changed, or change for thee – and love, so wrought,
May be unwrought so. Neither love me for
Thine own dear pity's wiping my cheeks dry –
A creature might forget to weep, who bore
Thy comfort long, and lose thy love thereby!
But love me for love's sake, that evermore
Thou may'st love on, through love's eternity.

Sonnet 43

How do I love thee? Let me count the ways.
I love thee to the depth and breadth and height
My soul can reach, when feeling out of sight
For the ends of Being and ideal Grace.
I love thee to the level of every day's
Most quiet need, by sun and candlelight.
I love thee freely, as men strive for Right;
I love thee purely, as they turn from Praise.
I love thee with the passion put to use
In my old griefs, and with my childhood's faith.
I love thee with a love I seemed to lose
With my lost saints – I love thee with the breath,
Smiles, tears, of all my life! – and, if God choose,
I shall but love thee better after death.

1814—At 7 a.m. a British squadron under Admiral Cockburn began a 25-hour bombardment of Ft McHenry, Baltimore. Francis Scott Key, who had come to the fleet on a truce mission, was detained on a British ship throughout the attack, during which he wrote the poem that has become the National Anthem of the United States

---

Oh, say, can you see by the dawn's early light
What so proudly we hailed at the twilight's last gleaming?
Whose broad stripes and bright stars, through the perilous fight,
O'er the ramparts we watched were so gallantly streaming?
And the rocket's red glare, the bombs bursting in air,
Gave proof through the night that our flag was still there.
Oh, say, does that star-spangled banner yet wave
O'er the land of the free and the home of the brave?

On the shore, dimly seen through the mists of the deep,
Where the foe's haughty host in dread silence reposes,
What is that which the breeze, o'er the towering steep,
As it fitfully blows, now conceals, now discloses?
Now it catches the gleam of the morning's first beam,
In full glory reflected now shines on the stream:
'Tis the star-spangled banner! O long may it wave
O'er the land of the free and the home of the brave.

And where is that band who so vauntingly swore
That the havoc of war and the battle's confusion
A home and a country should leave us no more!
Their blood has washed out their foul footsteps' pollution.
No refuge could save the hireling and slave
From the terror of flight, or the gloom of the grave:
And the star-spangled banner in triumph doth wave
O'er the land of the free and the home of the brave!

Oh! thus be it ever when freeman shall stand
Between their loved homes and the war's desolation!
Blest with victory and peace, may the heav'n-rescued land
Praise the Power that hath made and preserved us a nation.
Then conquer we must, when our cause it is just,
And this be our motto: 'In God is our trust'.
And the star-spangled banner in triumph shall wave
O'er the land of the free and the home of the brave.

Francis Scott Key

14 September 📖

1767—William Cowper and his friends, the Unwins, moved to the rural village of Olney, where he was to live the remainder of his life. It was there that he wrote The Task *and (with the Rev. Mr Newton) the 'Olney Hymns'*

God made the country, and man made the town.
What wonder then that health and virtue, gifts
That can alone make sweet the bitter draught
That life holds out to all, should most abound
And least be threaten'd in the fields and groves?
Possess ye, therefore, ye, who, borne about
In chariots and sedans, know no fatigue
But that of idleness, and taste no scenes
But such as art contrives, possess ye still
Your element; there only can ye shine,
There only minds like your's can do no harm
Our groves were planted to console at noon
The pensive wand'rer in their shades. At eve
The moon-beam, sliding softly in between
The sleeping leaves, is all the light they wish,
Birds warbling all the music. We can spare
The splendour of your lamps; they but eclipse
Our softer satellite. Your songs confound
Our more harmonious notes; the thrush departs
Scar'd, and th'offended nightingale is mute.
There is a public mischief in your mirth;
It plagues your country. Folly such as your's,
Grac'd with a sword, and worthier of a fan,
Has made, what enemies could ne'er have done,
Our arch of empire, steadfast but for you,
A mutilated structure, soon to fall.

William Cowper : The Task, *Bk. I, lines 749 ff.*

1833—Alfred Tennyson's friend, Arthur Hallam, died

Strong Son of God, immortal Love,
  Whom we, that have not seen thy face,
  By faith, and faith alone, embrace
Believing where we cannot prove;

Thine are these orbs of light and shade;
  Thou madest Life in man and brute;
  Thou madest Death; and lo, thy foot
Is on the skull which thou hast made.

Thou wilt not leave us in the dust:
  Thou madest man, he knows not why,
  He thinks he was not made to die;
And thou hast made him: thou art just.

Thou seemest human and divine,
  The highest, holiest manhood, thou.
  Our wills are ours, we know not how;
Our wills are ours, to make them thine.

Our little systems have their day;
  They have their day and cease to be;
  They are but broken lights of thee,
And thou, O Lord, art more than they . . .

Forgive what seemed my sin in me,
  What seemed my worth since I began;
  For merit lives from man to man,
And not from man, O Lord, to thee.

Forgive my grief for one removed,
  Thy creature, whom I found so fair.
  I trust he lives in thee, and there
I find him worthier to be loved.

*Alfred Lord Tennyson: from 'In Memoriam
A.H.H.'*

16 September

1654—Miss Dorothy Osborne, in her long series of love letters to Sir William Temple, finally got down to the monetary side of the proposed marriage contract, and her insufficient dowry

Knowlton, [Saturday 16 Sept. 1654]

I am but newly waked out of an unquiet sleep and I finde it soe late that if I write at all it must bee now. some company was heer last night kept us up till three a clock and then wee lay three in a bed, wch was all one to mee as if wee had not gon to bed at all. Since dinner they are all gon, and our company with them part of the way, and with much adoe I gott to be Excused that I might recover a litle sleep, but am so moaped yet that sure this letter will bee nonsense; I would faine tell you though that your f: [ather] is mistaken and that you are not, if you beleeve that I have all the Kindenesse and Tendernesse for you my heart is capable of. Let mee assure you (what ere your f: thinks) that had you 10000^ll a year I could love you noe more then I doe, and should bee far from showing it soe much, least it should look like a desire of your fortune, wch as to my self I valew as litle as any body breathing; I have not lived thus long in the world, and in this Age of Changes, but certainly I know what an Estate is. I have seen my fathers reduced [from] better than 4000^ll to not 400^ll a yeare, and I thank god I never felt the change in any thing that I thought necessary; I never wanted, nor am confident I never shall; but yet I would not bee thought soe inconsiderat a person as not to remember that it is Expected from all people that have sence that they should act with reason, that to all persons some proportion of fortune is necessarry according to theire severall qualitys . . . if ever this comes to a treaty I shall declare that in my owne choyse I prefferr you much before any Other person in the world, and all that this inclination in mee (in the Judgments of any persons of honnour and discretion) will beare I shall desyre may bee layed upon it to the uttermost of what they can allow, and if your f: please to make up the rest I know nothing that is like to hinder mee from being Yours. . . . good god what an unhappy person I am; but all the world is soe almost. Just now they are telling mee of a gentleman neer us y^t is the most Wretched Creature made (by ye Losse of a wife that hee passionatly Loved) that can bee. if your f: would but in some measure sattisfie my friends, that I might but doe it in any Justifiable manner, you should dispose mee as you pleased, carry mee whither you would. all places of the world would bee alike to mee where you were, & I should not despaire of carryeng my self soe towards him as might deserve a better opinion from him.

I am   Yours

from The Letters of Dorothy Osborne,
Letter 75.

1796—George Washington's 'Farewell Address' on retiring from the Presidency, which was never delivered as a speech, was published in Claypoole's American Daily Advertiser

Nothing is more essential than that permanent, inveterate antipathies against particular nations, and passionate attachments for others, should be excluded; and that, in place of them, just and amicable feelings towards all should be cultivated. The nation which indulges towards another an habitual hatred, or an habitual fondness, is in some degree a slave. It is a slave to its animosity or to its affection, either of which is sufficient to lead it astray from its duty and its interest. Antipathy in one nation against another disposes each more readily to offer insult and injury, to lay hold of slight causes of umbrage, and to be haughty and intractable, when accidental or trifling occasions of dispute occur. Hence, frequent collisions; obstinate, envenomed, and bloody contests. . . .

So likewise, a passionate attachment of one nation for another produces a variety of evils. Sympathy for the favorite nation, facilitating the illusion of an imaginary common interest in cases where no real common interest exists, and infusing into one the enmities of the other, betrays the former into a participation in the quarrels and wars of the latter, without adequate inducement or justification. It leads also to concessions to the favorite nation of privileges denied to others, which is apt doubly to injure the nation making the concessions, by unnecessarily parting with what ought to have been retained, and by exciting jealousy, ill-will, and a disposition to retaliate, in the parties from whom equal privileges are withheld. And it gives to ambitious, corrupted, or deluded citizens . . . facility to betray or sacrifice the interests of their own country, without odium, sometimes even with popularity. . . .

Against the insidious wiles of foreign influence (I conjure you to believe me, fellow-citizens), the jealousy of a free people ought to be constantly awake . . . But that jealousy, to be useful, must be impartial . . . Excessive partiality for one foreign nation, and excessive dislike of another, cause those whom they actuate to see danger only on one side, and serve to veil and even second the arts of influence on the other. Real patriots, who may resist the intrigues of the favorite, are liable to become suspected and odious; while its tools and dupes usurp the applause and confidence of the people, to surrender their interests.

The great rule of conduct for us, in regard to foreign nations, is, in extending our commercial relations, to have with them as little political connection as possible.

Washington: from the 'Farewell Address'

18 September 📖

1879—Through his friend Theodore Watts, Algernon Charles Swinburne got his rooms in The Pines, Putney Hill, where he stayed for the remaining thirty years of his life

'I keep no chambers in town henceforth, or (probably) for ever – finding after too many years' trial that in the atmosphere of London I can never expect more than a fortnight at best of my usual health and strength. Here I am, like Mr Tennyson at Farringford, 'close to the edge of a noble down,' and I might add 'Far out of sight, sound, smell of the town and yet within an easy hour's run of Hyde Park Corner and a pleasant drive of Chelsea, where I have some friends lingering.'

Swinburne to Lord Houghton

> Here, where the world is quiet,
>   Here, where all trouble seems
> Dead winds' and spent waves' riot
>   In doubtful dreams of dreams;
> I watch the green field growing
> For reaping folk and sowing,
> For harvest-time and mowing,
>   A sleepy world of streams.
>
>   . . .
>
> We are not sure of sorrow,
>   And joy was never sure;
> Today will die tomorrow;
>   Time stoops to no man's lure;
> And love, grown faint and fretful
> With lips but half regretful
> Sighs, and with eyes forgetful
>   Weeps that no loves endure.
>
> From too much love of living,
>   From hope and fear set free,
> We thank with brief thanksgiving
>   Whatever gods may be
> That no life lives for ever;
> That dead men rise up never;
> That even the weariest river
>   Winds somewhere safe to sea.

Algernon Charles Swinburne : from 'The Garden of Proserpine'

1630—George Herbert was ordained a priest, and began his career as a country parson

---

'He that will be respected, must respect.'

> *Herbert:* A Priest to the Temple, or The Country Parson

Who would have thought my shrivell'd heart
Could have recovered greenness? It was gone
    Quite underground; as flowers depart
To see their mother-root, when they have blown;
      Where they together
      All the hard weather
Dead to the world, keep house unknown.

These are thy wonders, Lord of power,
Killing and quick'ning, bringing down to hell
    And up to heaven in an hour;
Making a chiming of a passing-bell.
      We say amiss,
      This or that is:
Thy word is all, if we could spell. . . .

And now in age I bud again,
After so many deaths I live and write;
    I once more smell the dew and rain,
And relish versing; O my only light,
      It cannot be
      That I am he
On whom Thy tempests fell all night.

from 'The Flower'

Love and a cough cannot be hid.
Every path hath a puddle.
He that lieth with the dogs, riseth with fleas.
Better a snotty child than his nose wiped off.

> *from* Outlandish Proverbs, *appended to* A Priest to the Temple.

20 September

1592—License was granted for the posthumous publication of A Groatsworth of Wit, bought with a million of Repentance, *in which the dying Robert Greene had sought to warn his fellow-writers against William Shakespeare and other newcomers in the ranks*

If woeful experience may move you, gentlemen, to beware, or unheard-of wretchedness entreat you to take heed, I doubt not but you will look back with sorrow on your time past, and endeavour with repentance to spend that which is to come. . . . Unto none of you (like me) sought those burs to cleave, those puppets I mean that speak from our mouths, those antics garnished in our colours. Is it not strange that I to whom they all have been beholden – shall (were ye in that case that I am now) be both of them at once forsaken? Yes, trust them not; for there is an upstart crow beautified with our feathers, that with his *tiger's heart wrapped in a player's hide*, supposes he is as well able to bombast out a blank verse as the best of you; and being an absolute *Johannes factotum*, is in his own conceit the only *Shake-scene* in a country. Oh, that I might entreat your rare wits to be employed in more profitable courses, and let these apes imitate your past excellence, and never more acquaint them with your admired inventions! I know the best husband of you all will never prove an usurer, and the kindst of them all will never prove a kind nurse: yet, whilst you may, seek you better masters; for it is pity men of such rare wits should be subject to the pleasures of such rude grooms.

In this I might insert two more, that both have writ against these buckram gentlemen; but let their own work serve to witness against their own wickedness, if they persevere to maintain any more such peasants. For other new-comers, I leave them to the mercy of these painted monsters, who (I doubt not) will drive the best minded to despise them; for the rest, it skills not though they make a jest at them. . . .

Remember, gentlemen, your lives are like so many light tapers, that are with care delivered to all of you to maintain; these with wind-puffed wrath may be extinguished, which drunkenness put out, which negligence let fall; for man's time of itself is not so short, but it is more shortened by sin. The fire of my life is now at the last snuff, and the want of wherewith to sustain it, there is no substance for life to feed on. Trust not them (I beseech ye), to such weak stays; for they are as changeable in mind as in many attires. Well, my hand is tired, and I am forced to leave where I would begin; for a whole book cannot contain their wrongs, which I am forced to knit up in some few lines of words:

Desirous that you should live, though himself be dying,
                                                    Robert Greene

19 B.C.—Virgil died; and for the nineteenth centenary in 1881, Alfred, Lord Tennyson wrote 'To Virgil, Written at the request of the Mantuans'

Roman Virgil, thou that singest
 Ilion's lofty temples robed in fire,
Ilion falling, Rome arising,
 wars, and filial faith, and Dido's pyre;

Landscape-lover, lord of language,
 more than he that sang the 'Works and Days', [Hesiod]
All the chosen coin of fancy
 flashing out from many a golden phrase;

Thous that singest wheat and woodland,
 tilth and vineyard, hive and horse and herd;
All the charm of all the Muses
 often flowering in a lonely word;

Poet of the happy Tityrus
 piping underneath his beechen bowers;
Poet of the poet-satyr
 whom the laughing shepherd bound with flowers;

Chanter of the Pollio, glorying
 in the blissful years again to be,
Summers of the snakeless meadow,
 unlaborious earth and oarless sea;

Thou that seest Universal
 Nature moved by Universal Mind;
Thou majestic in thy sadness
 at the doubtful doom of human kind;

Light among the vanished ages;
 star that gildest yet this phantom shore;
Golden branch amid the shadows,
 kings and realms that pass to rise no more; . . .

I salute thee, Mantovano,
 I that loved thee since my day began,
Wielder of the stateliest measure
 Ever molded by the lips of man.

Alfred, Lord Tennyson

22 September

1819—'*How beautiful the season is now – How fine the air. A temperate sharpness about it.... Somehow, a stubble-field looks warm – in the same way that some pictures look warm. This struck me so much in my Sunday's walk that I composed upon it*'

John Keats to John Hamilton Reynolds, from Winchester

Season of mists and mellow fruitfulness,
　　Close bosom-friend of the maturing sun;
Conspiring with him how to load and bless
　　With fruit the vines that round the thatch-eaves run;
To bend with apples the moss'd cottage-trees,
　　And fill all fruit with ripeness to the core;
　　　　To swell the gourd, and plump the hazel shells
　　With a sweet kernel; to set budding more,
And still more, later flowers for the bees,
Until they think warm days will never cease,
　　For summer has o'er-brimmed their clammy cells.

Who hath not seen thee oft amid thy store?
　　Sometimes whoever seeks abroad may find
Thee sitting careless on a granary floor
　　Thy hair soft-lifted by the winnowing wind;
Or on a half-reap'd furrow sound asleep,
　　Drowsed with the fume of poppies, while thy hook
　　　　Spares the next swath and all its twined flowers:
And sometimes like a gleaner thou dost keep
　　Steady thy laden head across a brook;
　　Or by a cider-press, with patient look,
　　　　Thou watchest the last oozings, hours by hours.

Where are the songs of Spring? Ay, where are they?
　　Think not of them, thou hast thy music too, –
While barred clouds bloom the soft-dying day,
　　And touch the stubble-plains with rosy hue;
Then in a wailful choir the small gnats mourn
　　Among the river sallows, borne aloft
　　　　Or sinking as the light wind lives or dies;
And full-grown lambs bleat loud from hilly bourn;
　　Hedge-crickets sing; and now with treble soft
　　The redbreast whistles from a garden-croft,
　　　　And gathering swallows twitter in the skies.

John Keats: 'Ode to Autumn'

1891—'I expect the book [Poems by the Way] *will be all printed tomorrow, and will go to the binder on Monday. They are printing the colophon-sheet today, which is exciting'*

William Morris to his daughter, Jenny

Come hither, lads, and hearken
    for a tale there is to tell,
Of the wonderful days a-coming,
    when all shall be better than well. . . .

For then, (laugh not, but listen
    to this strange tale of mine)
All folk that are in England
    shall be better lodged than swine. . . .

Men in that time a-coming
    shall work and have no fear
For tomorrow's lack of earning
    and the hunger-wolf a-near. . . .

For that which the worker winneth
    shall then be his indeed,
Nor shall half be reaped for nothing
    by him that sowed the seed.

O why and for what are we waiting?
    while our brothers droop and die,
And on every wind of the heavens
    a wasted life goes by. . . .

Come, join in the only battle
    wherein no man can fail,
Where whoso fadeth and dieth
    yet his deed shall still prevail.

Ah! come, cast off all fooling,
    for this, at least, we know:
That the Dawn and the Day is coming,
    and forth the Banners go.

William Morris: from 'The Day is Coming', in
Poems by the Way

24 September

1761—'As to the Erse fragments . . . it seems to be a very favourable era for the appearance of such irregular poetry. . . . The public has seen all that art can do, and they want the more striking effects of wild, original, enthusiastic genius. • . . Here is indeed . . . the very quintessence of poetry'

William Shenstone to John MacGowan

Cuchullin sat by Tura's well, by the tree of the rustling leaf. – His spear leaned against the mossy rock. His shield lay by him on the grass. As he thought of mighty Carbar, a hero whom he slew in war, the scout of the ocean came, Moran the son of Fithil.

Rise, said the youth, Cuchullin rise; I see the ships of Swaran. Cuchullin, many are the foe: many the heroes of the dark-rolling sea.

Moran! replied the blue-eyed chief, thou ever tremblest, son of Fithil; Thy fears have much increased the foe. Perhaps it is the king of the lonely hills coming to aid me on green Ullin's plains.

I saw their chief, says Moran, tall as a rock of ice. His spear is like that blasted fir. His shield is like the rising moon. He sat on a rock on the shore: his dark host rolled, like clouds, around him. . . . He answered, like a wave on a rock, who in this land appears like me? Heroes stand not in my presence: they fall to earth beneath my hand. None can meet Swaran in the fight but Fingal, king of stormy hills. Once we wrestled on the heath of Malmor, and our heels overturned the wood. Rocks fell from their place; and rivulets, changing their course, fled murmuring from our strife. Three days we renewed our strife, and heroes stood at a distance and trembled. On the fourth, Fingal says, that the king of the ocean fell; but Swaran says, he stood. Let dark Cuchullin yield to him that is strong as the storms of Malmor.

No: replied the blue-eyed chief, I will never yield to man. Dark Cuchullin will be great or dead. Go, Fithil's son, and take my spear: strike the sounding shield of Cabait. It hangs at Tura's rustling gate; the sound of peace is not its voice. My heroes shall hear on the hill.

He went and struck the bossy shield. The hills and the rocks replied. The sound spread along the wood: deer start by the lake of roes. Curach leapt from the sounding rock; and Connal of the bloody spear. Crugal's breast of snow beats high. The son of Favi leaves the dark-brown hind. It is the shield of war, said Ronnar, the spear of Cuchullin, said Lugar. – Son of the sea, put on thy arms! Calmar lift thy sounding steel! Puno! horrid hero, rise: Cairbar from thy red tree of Cromla. Bend thy white knee, O Eth; and descend from the streams of Lena. Ca-olt stretch thy white side as thou movest along the whistling heath of Mora; thy side that is white as the foam of the troubled sea, when the dark winds pour it on the murmuring rocks of Cuthon.

James MacPherson: from 'Fingal, an Ancient Epic Poem' in The Works of Ossian, the Son of Fingal.

1904—Rudyard Kipling began writing the 'Puck of Pook's Hill' stories, inspired by the layers of history discovered at 'Batemans', his recently acquired home in Sussex

---

When we wished to sink a well . . . out of the woods that know everything and tell nothing, came two dark and mysterious Primitives. They had heard. They would sink that well, for they had the 'gift'. . . . When we stopped, at twenty-five feet, we had found a Jacobean tobacco-pipe, a worn Cromwellian latten spoon, and, at the bottom of all, the bronze cheek of a Roman horse-bit.

In cleaning out an old pond which might have been an ancient marl-pit or mine-head, we dredged two intact Elizabethan 'sealed quarts' that Christopher Sly affected, all pearly with the patina of centuries. Its deepest mud yielded us a perfectly polished Neolithic axe-head with but one chip on its still venomous edge.

These things are detailed that you may understand how, when my cousin, Ambrose Poynter, said to me: 'Write a yarn about Roman times here', I was interested. 'Write', said he, 'about an old Centurion of the Occupation telling his experiences to his children.' 'What is his name?' I demanded, for I move easiest from a given point. 'Parnesius', said my cousin; and the name stuck in my head. . . .

Just beyond the west fringe of our land, in a little valley running from Nowhere to Nothing-at-all, stood the long, overgrown slag-heap of a most ancient forge, supposed to have been worked by the Phoenicians and Romans and, since then, uninterruptedly till the middle of the eighteenth century. The bracken and rush-patches still hid stray pigs, of iron, and if one scratched a few inches through the rabbit-shaven turf, one came on the narrow mule-tracks of peacock-hued furnace-slag laid down in Elizabeth's day. The ghost of a road climbed up out of this dead arena, and crossed our fields, where it was known as 'The Gunway', and popularly connected with Armada times. Every foot of that little corner was alive with ghosts and shadows. Then, it pleased our children to act for us, in the open, what they remembered of *A Midsummer Night's Dream*. Then a friend gave them a real birch-bark canoe, drawing at least three inches, in which they went adventuring on the brook. And in a near pasture of the water-meadows lay out an old and unshifting Fairy Ring.

You see how patiently the cards were stacked and and dealt into my hands? The Old Things of the Valley glided into every aspect of our outdoor works. Earth, Air, Water and People of the Valley had been – I saw it at last – in full conspiracy to give me ten times as much as I could compass, even if I wrote a complete history of England, as that might have touched or reached our Valley.

Rudyard Kipling: from the chapter called 'The Very-Own House' in Something of Myself.

26 September 📖

1580—'And the 26 of Sept. . . . we safely with ioyfull minds and thankfull hearts to God, arrived at Plimoth, *the place of our first setting forth, after we had spent 2 yeares 10 moneths and some few odde daies beside . . . in this our encompassing of this neather globe, and passing round about the world . . .'*

From The World Encompassed by Francis Drake

And – while the tense world waited him, as men wait
The sound of cannon, quietly one grey morn,
Grey as a ghost, with none to welcome her,
A tattered ship came gliding into the Sound.
There was no voice to hail her from the quay,
And not an eye to read the faded scroll
Around her battered prow – *The Golden Hind.* . . .
Carelessly lying there, in Plymouth Sound –
A glory wrapped her greyness, and no boat
Dared yet approach, save one with Drake's close friends,
Who came to warn him: 'England stands alone.
The Queen perforce must temporize with Spain,
The Invincible! She hath forfeited thy head
To Spain, against her will. Philip, the king,
Is mustering ships and armies. . . .
To whom Drake answered – 'Gloriana lives;
And, while she lives, England can say "All's well!"
I have brought her a good cargo – a world's wealth,
The golden keys of all the power of Spain;
But lest the Queen be driven to yield them up,
I will warp out behind St. Nicholas' Island,
Until I know her will.'
                              And in his heart
He secretly thought to himself: 'If it be death,
I'll out again to sea, strew its rough floor
With costlier largesses than kings can throw,
And, ere I die, I'll singe the Spaniard's beard
And set the fringe of his imperial robe
Blazing along his coasts. Let him come out
And roll his galleons round my *Golden Hind*,
Bring her to bay, if he can, on the high seas. . . .
No power can make us yield. We can still fasten
Our flag's last shred upon the last stump left us,
And sink with our last shot.'

Alfred Noyes: from Drake, *Bk. vii*

1868—Dante Gabriel Rossetti read to his brother William his own recently completed poem, 'Eden Bower', written after he had painted the commissioned portrait of 'Lilith'

Lilith stood on the skirts of Eden;
    (Alas the hour!)
She was the first that thence was driven;
With her was hell and with Eve was heaven.

In the ear of the snake said Lilith: –
    (Sing Eden Bower!)
'To thee I come when the rest is over;
A snake was I when thou wast my lover.

'Take me thou as I come from Adam:
    (Sing Eden Bower!)
Once again shall my love subdue thee;
The past is past and I come to thee.

'O but Adam was thrall to Lilith!
    (Alas the hour!)
All the threads of my hair are golden,
And there in a net his heart was holden. . . .

'O thou Snake, the King-snake of Eden!
    (Sing Eden Bower!)
God's strong will our necks are under,
But thou and I may cleave it in sunder . . .

'In thy shape I'll go back to Eden;
    (Alas the hour!)
In these coils that Tree I will grapple,
And stretch this crowned head forth by the apple.

'Lo, Eve bends to the words of Lilith! –
    (Sing Eden Bower!)
O how then shall my heart desire
All her blood as food to its fire! . . .

Dante Gabriel Rossetti: from 'Eden Bower'

28 September

1066—William of Normandy undertook the Conquest of England

In this year came king Harold from York to Westminster, the Easter following the Christmas of the king's death . . . At that time, throughout all England, a portent such as men had never seen before was seen in the heavens. Some declared that the star was a comet, which some call 'the long-haired star' . . . Soon thereafter came earl Tostig to this country from across the sea . . . because he was informed that William the Bastard was about to invade this land to conquer it, just as subsequently came to pass. . . . Then Harold our king came unexpectedly upon the Norwegians, and met them beyond York at Stamford Bridge with a great host of Englishmen, and that day a very stubborn battle was fought by both sides. . . .

Then duke William sailed from Normandy into Pevensey, on the eve of Michaelmas [28 September]. As soon as his men were fit for service, they constructed a castle at Hastings. When king Harold was informed of this, he gathered together a great host, and came to oppose him at the grey apple-tree, and William came upon him unexpectedly before his army was set in order. Nevertheless the king fought against him most resolutely with those men who wished to stand by him, and there was great slaughter on both sides. King Harold was slain, and Leofwine, his brother, and earl Gurth, his brother, and many good men. The French had possession of the place of slaughter, as God granted them because of the nation's sins. Archbishop Ealdred and the citizens of London wished to have prince Edgar for king, as was indeed his right by birth, and Edwin and Morcar promised that they would fight for him, but always when some initiative should have been shown, there was delay from day to day until matters went from bad to worse, as everything did in the end. . . .

Duke William returned to Hastings, and waited there to see if there would be any surrender; but when he realized that none were willing to come to him, he marched inland with what was left of his host, together with reinforcements lately come from overseas, and harried that part of the country through which he advanced until he came to Berkhamsted. There he was met by bishop Ealdred, prince Edgar, earl Edwin, earl Morcar, and all the best men from London, who submitted from force of circumstances, but only when the depredation was complete. It was great folly that they had not done so sooner when God would not remedy matters because of our sins. They gave him hostages and oaths of fealty, and he promised to be a gracious lord to them. Nevertheless, in the meantime, they [the Normans] harried everywhere they came. Then on Christmas day archbishop Ealdred consecrated him king in Westminster; but before he would accept the crown he gave a pledge on the Gospels, and swore an oath besides that he would govern this nation according to the best practices of his predecessors if they would be loyal to him. Nevertheless he imposed a very heavy tax on the country. . . .

from The Anglo-Saxon Chronicle (*D-version*)

1634—John Milton's masque, Comus, *with music by Henry Lawes, was presented at Ludlow Castle before the Earl and Countess of Bridgewater, with their sons taking the parts of the Two Brothers, and their daughter playing The Lady*

The Scene changes, presenting Ludlow Town, and the President's Castle: then come in Country Dancers; after them the Attendant Spirit *with the two* Brothers *and the* Lady. . . . *This second Song presents them to their Father and Mother.*

SPIRIT: Noble Lord and Lady bright,
I have brought ye new delight.
Here behold so goodly grown
Three fair branches of your own.
Heaven hath timely tried their youth,
Their faith, their patience, and their truth,
And sent them here through hard assays
With a crown of deathless praise,
  To triumph in victorious dance
O'er sensual folly and intemperance.

The dances ended, the Spirit *epiloguises*
SPIRIT: To the Ocean now I fly,
And those happy climes that lie
Where day never shuts his eye,
Up in the broad fields of the sky. . . .

  But now my task is smoothly done:
I can fly or I can run
Quickly to the earth's green end
Where the bow'd welkin slow doth bend,
And from thence can soar as soon
To the corners of the moon.
  Mortals that would follow me
Love Virtue, she alone is free.
She can teach you how to climb
Higher than the sphery chime;
Or if Virtue feeble were
Heaven itself would stoop to her.

30 September

1654—'I was nigh unto death . . . but the God of the spirits of all flesh . . . when I had expected, and had (by his assistance) prepared for a message of death, then did he answer me with life; I hope to his glory, and my great advantage: that I may flourish not with leaf only, but with some fruit'

> Henry Vaughan: *from The Preface to* Silex Scintillans *written at Newton-by-Usk, near Sketh-rock*

Happy those early dayes, when I
Shin'd in my Angell-Infancy!
Before I understood this place
Appointed for my second race,
Or taught my soul to fancy aught
But a white, Celestiall thought;
When yet I had not walkt above
A mile or two from my first love,
And looking back, at that short space,
Could see a glimpse of his bright face;
When on some *gilded Cloud* or *flowre*
My gazing soul would dwell an houre,
And in those weaker glories spy
Some shadows of eternity;
Before I taught my tongue to wound
My Conscience with a sinfull sound,
Or had the black art to dispence
A sev'rall sinne to ev'ry sence,
But felt through all this fleshly dresse
Bright *shootes* of everlastingnesse.
   O how I long to travell back,
And tread again that ancient track!
That I might once more reach that plaine,
Where first I left my glorious traine;
From whence th'Inlightened spirit sees
That shady City of Palme trees.
But ah! my soul with too much stay
Is drunk, and staggers in the way!
Some men a forward motion love,
But I by backward steps would move;
And when this dust falls to the urn,
In that state I came return.

> Henry Vaughan: 'The Retreate' *from* Silex Scintillans

October.

1918—The Allies entered Damascus, bringing the first World War near to its end

As the Germans left Damascus they fired the dumps and ammunition stores, so that every few minutes we were jangled by explosions, whose first shock set the sky white with flame. At each such roar the earth seemed to shake; we would lift our eyes to the north and see the pale sky prick out suddenly in sheaves of yellow points, as the shells, thrown to terrific heights from each bursting magazine, in their turn burst like clustered rockets. I turned to Stirling and muttered 'Damascus is burning', sick to think of the great town in ashes as the price of freedom.

When dawn came we drove to the head of the ridge, which stood over the oasis of the city, afraid to look north for the ruins we expected: but, instead of ruins, the silent gardens stood blurred green with river mist, in whose setting shimmered the city, beautiful as ever, like a pearl in the morning sun. The uproar of the night had shrunk to a stiff tall column of smoke, which rose in sullen blackness from the store-yard by Kadem, terminus of the Hejaz line.

We drove down the straight banked road through the watered fields, in which the peasants were just beginning their day's work. A galloping horseman checked at our head-cloths in the car, with a merry salutation, holding out a bunch of yellow grapes. 'Good news: Damascus salutes you.' . . .

Quite quietly we drove up the long street to the Government buildings on the bank of the Barada. The way was packed with people lined solid on the side-walks, in the road, at the windows and on the balconies or house-tops. Many were crying, a few cheered faintly, some bolder ones cried our names: but mostly they looked and looked, joy shining in their eyes. A movement like a long sigh from gate to heart of the city, marked our course.

At the Town Hall things were different. Its steps and stairs were packed with a swaying mob: yelling, embracing, dancing, singing. They crushed a way for us to the ante-chamber, where were the gleaming Nasir, and Nuri Shaalan, seated. On either side of them stood Abd el Kader, my old enemy, and Mohammed Said, his brother. I was dumb with amazement. Mohammed Said leaped forward and shouted that they, grandsons of Abd el Kader, the Emir, with Shukri el Ayubi, of Saladin's house, had formed the government and proclaimed Hussein 'King of the Arabs' yesterday, into the ears of the humbled Turks and Germans.

T. E. Lawrence: from Seven Pillars of Wisdom

2 October 🚂

1878—Robert Louis Stevenson found, in the Cevennes in France, a surprising toleration

As I began to go up the valley, a draught of wind came down it out of the seat of the sunrise, although the clouds continued to run overhead in an almost contrary direction. A few steps further, and I saw a whole hillside gilded with the sun; and still a little beyond, between two peaks, a centre of dazzling brilliancy appeared floating in the sky, and I was once more face to face with the big bonfire that occupies the kernel of our system.

I met but one human being that forenoon, a dark military-looking wayfarer, who carried a game-bag on a baldric; but he made a remark that seems worthy of record. For when I asked him if he were Protestant or Catholic –

'Oh', said he, 'I make no shame of my religion. I am a Catholic.'

He made no shame of it! The phrase is a piece of natural statistics; for it is the language of one in a minority. I thought with a smile . . . how you may ride rough-shod over a religion for a century, and leave it only the more lively for the friction. Ireland is still Catholic; the Cevennes are still Protestant. It is not a basketful of law-papers, nor the hoofs and pistol-butts of a regiment of horse, that can change one tittle of a ploughman's thoughts. Outdoor rustic people have not many ideas, but such as they have are hardy plants, and thrive flourishingly in persecution. . . .

The villagers whom I saw seemed intelligent after a countrified fashion, and were all plain and dignified in manner. As a Protestant myself, I was well looked upon, and my acquaintance with history gained me further respect. For we had something not unlike a religious controversy at table, a gendarme and a merchant with whom I dined being both strangers to the place, and Catholics. The young men of the house stood around and supported me; and the whole discussion was tolerably conducted, and surprised a man brought up among the infinitesimal and contentious differences of Scotland. The merchant, indeed, grew a little warm, and was far less pleased than some others with my historical acquirements. But the gendarme was mighty easy over all.

'It's a bad idea for a man to change', said he; and the remark was generally applauded. . . .

That was not the opinion of the priest and soldier at Our Lady of the Snows. But this is a different race, and perhaps the same great-heartedness that upheld them to resist, now enables them to differ in a kind spirit. For courage respects courage; but where the faith has been trodden out, we may look for a mean and narrow population.

Robert Louis Stevenson: from Travels with a Donkey

1610—Ben Jonson's The Alchemist *was entered in the Stationers' Register*

Argument

T he sickness hot, a master quit, for fear,
H is house in town, and left one servant there;
E ase him corrupted, and gave means to know

A Cheater and his punk; who now brought low,
L eaving their narrow practice, were become
C ozeners at large; and only wanting some
H ouse to set up, with him they here contract,
E ach for a share, and all begin to act.
M uch company they draw, and much abuse,
I n casting figures, telling fortunes, news,
S elling of flies, flat bawdry with the stone,
T ill it, and they, and all in fume are gone.

Our scene is London, 'cause we would make known,
No country's mirth is better than our own:
No clime breeds better matter for your whore,
Bawd, squire, imposter, many persons more,
Whose manners, now called humours, feed the stage;
And which have still been subject for the rage
Or spleen of comic writers. Though this pen
Did never aim to grieve, but better men;
Howe'er the age he lives in doth endure
The vices that she breeds, above their cure.
But when the wholesome remedies are sweet,
And in their working gain and profit meet,
He hopes to find no spirit so much diseased,
But will with such fair correctives be pleased:
For here he doth not fear who can apply.
  If there be any that will sit so nigh
Unto the stream, to look what it doth run,
They shall find things, they'd think or wish were done;
They are so natural follies, but so shown,
As even the doers may see, and yet not own.

Ben Jonson: from 'The Prologue' to The Achemist

She was a phantom of delight
When first she gleamed upon my sight;
A lovely apparition, sent
To be a moment's ornament;
Her eyes as stars of twilight fair;
Like twilight's, too, her dusky hair;
But all things else about her drawn
From Maytime and the cheerful dawn;
A dancing shape, an image gay,
To haunt, to startle, and waylay.

I saw her upon nearer view,
A spirit, yet a woman too!
Her household motions light and free,
And steps of virgin liberty;
A countenance in which did meet
Sweet records, promises as sweet;
A creature not too bright or good
For human nature's daily food;
For transient sorrows, simple wiles,
Praise, blame, love, kisses, tears, and smiles.

And now I see with eye serene
The very pulse of the machine:
A being breathing thoughtful breath,
A traveller between life and death;
The reason firm, the temperate will,
Endurance, foresight, strength and skill;
A perfect woman, nobly planned,
To warn, to comfort, and command;
And yet a spirit still, and bright
With something of angelic light.

William Wordsworth

1932—Australian literature suffered one of its greatest losses when the poet, Christopher Brennan, died in Lewisham Hospital, Sydney

When window-lamps had dwindled, then I rose
and left the town behind me; and on my way
passing a certain door I stopt, remembering
how once I stood on its threshold, and my life
was offer'd to me, a road how different
from that of the years since gone! and I had but
to rejoin an olden path, once dear, since left.
All night I have walk'd and my heart was deep awake,
remembering ways I dream'd and that I chose,
remembering lucidly, and was not sad,
being brimm'd with all the liquid and clear dark
of the night that was not stirr'd with any tide;
for leaves were silent and the road gleam'd pale,
following the ridge, and I was alone with night.
But now I am come among the rougher hills
and grow aware of the sea that somewhere near
is restless; and the flood of night is thinn'd
and stars are whitening. O, what horrible dawn
will bare me the way and crude lumps of the hills
and the homeless concave of the day, and bare
the ever-restless, ever-complaining sea?

Christopher Brennan: from The Wanderer
(1913)

6 October

1671—William Wycherley's first comedy, Love in a Wood, *was entered in the Stationers' Register. He dedicated it to the Duchess of Cleveland, who had prompted the publication after seeing the play twice*

TO HER GRACE THE DUTCHESS OF CLEVELAND

Madam,

All authors whatever in their Dedication are Poets; but I am now to write to a Lady, who stands as little in need of Flattery as her Beauty of Art; otherwise, I shou'd prove as ill a Poet to her in my Dedication, as to my Reader in my Play: I can do your Grace no Honour, nor make you more admirers than you have already; yet I can do my self the honour to let the world know, I am the greatest you have; you will pardon me, Madam, for you know, 'tis very hard for a new Author, and Poet too, to govern his Ambition; for Poets, let them pass in the world never so much, for modest, honest men, but begin praise to others, which concludes in themselves; and are like Rooks, who lend people money, but to win it back again, and so leave them in debt to 'em for nothing; and perfume themselves. This is true, Madam, upon the honest word of an Author, who never yet writ Dedication; yet though I cannot lye like them, I am as vain as they, and cannot but publickly give your Grace my humble acknowledgements for the favours I have received from you: This, I say, is the Poets Gratitude, which in plain English, is only Pride and Ambition; and that the world might know your Grace did me the honour to see my Play twice together; yet perhaps my Enviers of your Favour will suggest 'twas in Lent, and therefore for your mortification; then, as a jealous Author, I am concern'd not to have your Graces Favours lessen'd, or rather, my reputation; and to let them know, you were pleas'd, after that, to command a copy from me of this play. . . . But Madam, to be obliging to that excess as you are . . . is a dangerous quality, and may be very incommode to you; for Civility makes Poets as troublesom, as Charity makes Beggers; and your Grace will be hereafter as much pester'd with such scurvy offerings as this . . . as you are now with Petitions: And, Madam, take it from me, no man with Papers in's hand, is more dreadful then a Poet, no, not a lawyer with his Declarations; your Grace sure did not well consider what you did, in sending for my Play. . . .

WILLIAM WYCHERLEY

1531—Henry VIII, pleased to have had Sir Thomas Elyot's The Boke namyd the Governour *dedicated to himself, appointed its author ambassador to the court of Charles V*

I late considering (most excellent prince and mine only redoubted sovereign lord) my duty that I owe to my natural country with my faith also of allegiance and oath, wherewith I am double bounden unto your majesty, moreover the account that I have to render for that one little talent delivered to me to employ (as I suppose) to the increase of virtue, I am (as God judge me) violently stirred to divulgate or set forth some part of my study, trusting thereby to acquit me of my duties to God, your Highness, and this my country. Wherefore taking comfort and boldness, partly of your Grace's most benevolent inclination toward the universal weal of your subjects, partly inflamed with zeal, I have now enterprised to describe in our vulgar tongue the form of a just public weal: which matter I have gathered as well of the sayings of most noble authors (Greeks and Latins) as by mine own experience, I being continually trained in some daily affairs of the public weal of this your most noble realm almost from my childhood. . . . And for as much as this present book treateth of the education of them that hereafter may be deemed worthy to be governors of the public weal under your Highness . . . I therefore have named it *The Governour*, and do now dedicate it unto your Highness as the first fruits of my study, verily trusting that your most excellent wisdom will therein esteem my loyal heart and diligent endeavour. . . .

And if, most virtuous Prince, I may perceive your Highness to be herewith pleased, I shall soon after (God giving me quietness) present your Grace with the residue of my study and labours, wherein your Highness shall well perceive that I nothing esteem so much in this world as your royal estate (my most dear sovereign Lord) and the public weal of my country. Protesting unto your excellent Majesty that where I commend herein any one virtue or dispraise any one vice I mean the general description of the one and the other without any other particular meaning to the reproach of any one person. To the which protestation I am now driven through the malignity of this present time all disposed to malicious detraction. Therefore I most humbly beseech your Highness to deign to be patron and defender of this little work against the assaults of malign interpreters which fail not to rend and deface the renown of writers, they themselves being in nothing to the public weal profitable. Which is by no man sooner perceived than by your Highness, being both in wisdom and very nobility equal to the most excellent princes, whom, I beseech God, ye may surmount in long life and perfect felicity.   Amen.

Sir Thomas Elyot: from 'The Proem' to The Boke namyd The Governour

8 October 🏮

1838—Ralph Waldo Emerson drafted a reply to the Rev. H. Ware, Jr., who, in a sermon on 'The Personality of the Deity' had challenged him to argument, an exercise which Emerson considered prejudicial to truth. ('Jesus simply affirmed, never argued')

I ought sooner to have acknowledged your kind letter of last week & the sermon it accompanied. The Letter was right manly and noble The sermon I have read with attention If it assails any statement of mine When perhaps I am not as quick to see it as most writers certainly I felt no disposition to depart from my habitual content-ment that you should speak your thought whilst I speak mine I believe I must tell you what I think of my new position.

It strikes me very oddly & even a little ludicrously that the good & great men of Cambridge should think of raising me into an object of criticism. I have always been from my very incapacity of methodical writing a chartered libertine free to worship & free to rail lucky when I was understood but never esteemed near enough to the institutions & mind of society to deserve the notice of the masters of literature & religion. I have appreciated fully the advantage of my position for I well knew that there was no scholar less willing or less able to be a polemic. I could not give account of myself if challenged I could not possibly give you one of the 'arguments' on which as you cruelly hint any position of mine stands. For I do not know, I confess, what arguments mean in reference to any expression of a thought. I delight in telling what I think but if you ask me how I dare say so or why it is so I am the most helpless of mortal men; I see not even that either of these questions admit of an answer. So that in the present droll posture of my affairs when I see myself suddenly raised into the importance of a heretic, I am very uneasy if I advert to the supposed duties of such a personage who is expected to make good his thesis against all comers. I therefore tell you plainly I shall do no such thing. I shall read what you & other good men write as I have always done glad when you speak my thought & skipping the page that has nothing for me. I shall go on just as before seeing whatever I can & telling what I see and I suppose with the same fortune as has hitherto attended me the joy of finding that my abler & better brothers who work with the sympathy of society & love it, unexpectedly confirm my perceptions, & find my nonsense is only their own thought in motley.

quoted from The Letters of Ralph Waldo Emerson, *vol. II, pp. 166–167. (edited by Ralph L. Rusk, N.Y., 1939–Columbia University Press)*

1844—Poe's 'Annabel Lee' appeared in the New York Tribune, two days after his death. It is generally assumed to refer to his 'child bride', Virginia Clemm

It was many and many a year ago,
    In a kingdom by the sea,
That a maiden there lived whom you may know
    By the name of Annabel Lee; –
And this maiden she lived with no other thought
    Than to love and be loved by me.

She was a child and *I* was a child
    In this kingdom by the sea,
But we loved with a love that was more than love –
    I and my Annabel Lee –
With a love that the winged seraphs of Heaven
    Coveted her and me.

And this was the reason that, long ago,
    In this kingdom by the sea,
A wind blew out of a cloud by night
    Chilling my Annabel Lee;
So that her highborn kinsmen came
    And bore her away from me,
To shut her up in a sepulchre
    In this kingdom by the sea. . . .

But our love it was stronger by far than the love
    Of those who were older than we –
    Of many far wiser than we –
And neither the angels in Heaven above
    Nor the demons down under the sea
Can ever dissever my soul from the soul
    Of the beautiful Annabel Lee: – . . .

And so all the night-tide, I lie down by the side
Of my darling, my darling, my life and my bride,
    In her sepulchre there by the sea –
    In her tomb by the side of the sea.

Edgar Allen Poe: from 'Annabel Lee'

10 October 📖

1918—Wilfred Owen, in his exchange of letters and poems with Siegfried Sassoon during World War I, compared the latter's 'Counter-Attack' with the real thing

An officer came blundering down the trench:
'Stand-to and man the fire-step!' On he went . . .
Gasping and bawling, 'Fire-step . . . Counter-attack!'
Then the haze lifted. Bombing on the right
Down the old sap: machine-guns on the left;
And stumbling figures looming out in front.
'O Christ, they're coming at us!' Bullets spat,
And he remembered his rifle . . . rapid fire . . .
And started blazing wildly. . . . Then a bang
Crumpled and spun him sideways, knocked him out
To grunt and wriggle: none heeded him; he choked
And fought the flapping veils of smothering gloom,
Lost in a blurred confusion of yells and groans. . . .
Down, and down, and down, he sank and drowned,
Bleeding to death. The counter-attack had failed.

Siegfried Sassoon: from 'Counter-Attack'

Your letter reached me at the exact moment it was most needed. – when we had come far enough out of the line to feel the misery of the billets; and I had been seized with writer's cramp after making out my casualty reports. (I'm O. C. D. Coy) The Battalion had a sheer time last week. I can find no better epithet; because I cannot say I suffered anything, having let my brain grow dull. That is to say, my nerves are in perfect order.

It is a strange truth: that your *Counter-Attack* frightened me much more than the real one: though the boy by my side, shot through the head, lay on top of me, soaking my shoulders, for half an hour.

Catalogue? Photographs? Can you photograph the crimson-hot iron as it cools from the smelting? That is what Jones's blood looked like, and felt like. My senses are charred.

I shall feel again as soon as I dare, but now I must not. I don't take the cigarette out of my mouth when I write Deceased over their letters.

But one day I will write Deceased over many books.

Wilfred Owen to Siegfried Sassoon, 10 Oct. 1918

1906—'I have been tasting your Cometary Tale – every inch and ounce of it : a very curious business. You interest me intensely and that work has done so on every page, having, as it seems to me, extraordinary force and sincerity. You have force as really no one has it . . .'

*Henry James to H. G. Wells on reading
the novel* In the Days of the Comet

CHAPTER THE FIRST

Dust in the Shadows

I have set myself to write the story of the Great Change, so far as it has affected my own life and the lives of one or two people closely connected with me, primarily to please myself.

Long ago, in my crude unhappy youth, I concieved the desire of writing a book. To scribble secretly and dream of authorship was one of my chief alleviations, and I read with a sympathetic envy every scrap I could get about the world of literature and the lives of literary people. It is something, even amidst this present happiness, to find leisure and opportunity to take up and partially realize these old and hopeless dreams. But that alone, in a world where so much of vivid and increasing interest presents itself to be done, even by an old man, would not, I think, suffice to set me at this desk. I find some such recapitulation as this will involve, is becoming necessary to my own secure mental continuity. The passage of years brings a man at last to retrospection; at seventy-two one's youth is far more important than it was at forty. And I am out of touch with my youth. The old life seems so cut off from the new, so alien and so unreasonable, that at times I find it bordering upon the incredible. The data have gone, the buildings and places. I stopped dead the other day in my afternoon's walk across the moor, where once the dismal outskirts of Swathinglea straggled towards Leet, and asked, 'Was it here indeed that I crouched among the weeds and refuse and broken crockery and loaded my revolver ready for murder? Did ever such a thing happen in my life? Was such a mood and thought and intention ever possible to me? Rather, has not some queer nightmare spirit out of dream-land slipped a pseudo-memory into the records of my vanished life?' There must be many alive still who have the same perplexities. And I think too that those who are now growing up to take our places in the great enterprise of mankind, will need many such narratives as mine for even the most partial conception of the old world of shadows that came before our day. It chances too that my case is fairly typical of the Change; I was caught midway in a gust of passion; and a curious accident put me for a time in the very nucleus of the new order . . .

H. G. Wells: from In the Days of the Comet

12 October (Columbus Day) 📖

[193-]—Mr Hyman Kaplan made an appointment with destiny

. . . Mr Parkhill opened the class with these ringing words: 'Tonight, let us set aside our routine tasks for a while to consider the man whose – er – historic achievement the world will commemorate tomorrow.'

Expectancy murmured its sibilant way across the room. 'To this man', Mr Parkhill continued, 'the United States – America – owes its very beginning. I'm sure you all know whom I mean, for he – '

'Jawdge Vashington!' Miss Fanny Gidwitz promptly guessed.

'No, no. Not *George W*ashington – watch that "w", Miss Gidwitz. I refer to – '

'Paul Rewere!' cried Oscar Trabish impetuously. . . .

Mr Parkhill shook his head. 'Not Paul "*Rewere*". It's a "v", Mr Trabish, not a "w". . . . Class, let's not guess. What *date* is tomorrow?'

'Mine boitday!' an excited voice sang out.

Mr Parkhill ignored that. 'Tomorrow', he said firmly, 'is October twelfth. And on October twelfth, 1492 – ' He got no further.

'Dat's mine *boit*day! October tvalf! I should live so! Honist!' It was the proud, enraptured voice of Hyman Kaplan. . . .

Stanislaus Wilkomirski growled, 'Kaplan too old for have birthday.'

'October tvalf I'm born; October tvalf I'm tsalebratink!' Mr. Kaplan retorted. 'All mine *life* I'm hevink boitdays October tvalf. No axceptions!' . . .

'*On October twelfth, 1492* – ' Mr Parkhill's voice rose until it brooked no ignoring – 'Christopher Columbus discovered a new continent!'

The class simmered down at last, and Mr Parkhill launched upon the deathless saga of Christopher Columbus and the brave little armada that sailed into the unknown. He spoke slowly, impressively, almost with fervor. And the thirty-odd novitiates of the beginners' grade, caught up in the drama of that great and fearful voyage, hung upon each word. 'The food ran low. Water was scarce. Rumors of doom – of disaster – raced through the sailors' ranks. . . . '

Goldie Pomeranz leaned forward and sighed moistly into Mr Kaplan's ear. 'You soitinly lucky, Mr. Kaplan. Born same day Columbus did.'

Mr Kaplan was in a world of dreams. He kept whispering to himself, 'Christover Colombiss', the name a talisman. 'My!' He closed his eyes to be alone with his hero. 'October tvalf I'm arrivink in de voild, an' October tvalf Colombiss picks ot for discoverink U. S.! Dastiny!'

Leo Rosten: from The Return of H*Y*M*A*N K*A*P*L*A*N

1786—'Fanatics have almost always cold hearts. Mr. Cowper . . . professes himself . . . a contemner of all praise, which has not Deity for its exclusive object. The plain meaning of what he says on the subject is just this: "You fools, with your jubilee for your Shakespeare, and your commemoration for your Handel!"'

Anna Seward to the Rev. Mr Warner

Man praises man. Desert in arts or arms
Wins public honour; and ten thousand sit
Patiently present at a sacred song,
Commemoration-mad; content to hear
(Oh wonderful effect of music's power!)
Messiah's eulogy for Handel's sake!
But less, methinks, than sacrilege might serve – . . .
Much less might serve, when all that we design
Is but to gratify an itching ear,
And give the day to a musician's praise.
Remember Handel? Who, that was not born
Deaf as the dead to harmony, forgets,
Or can, the more than Homer of his age?
Yes – we remember him; and, while we praise
A talent so divine, remember too
That His most holy book from whom it came
Was never meant, was never us'd before,
To buckram out the mem'ry of a man. . . .
       Man praises man; and Garrick's mem'ry next,
When time has somewhat mellow'd it, and made
The idol of our worship while he liv'd
The god of our idolatry once more,
Shall have its altar; and the world shall go
In pilgimage to bow before his shrine . . .
Why, what has charm'd them? Hath he sav'd the state?
No. Doth he purpose its salvation? No. . . .
       Thus idly do we waste the breath of praise,
And dedicate a tribute, in its use
And just direction sacred, to a thing
Doom'd to be dust, or lodg'd already there!
Encomium in old times was poet's work;
But, poets having lavishly long since
Exhausted all materials of the art,
The task now falls into the public hand. . . .

William Cowper: from The Task

14 October 🕮

1861—A reviewer in The Daily News *undertook to correct Charles Reade's use of 'dialect' in* The Cloister and the Hearth, *and was immediately himself corrected by the author, whose scholarship was a bit more reliable*

The strangest part of the tale is the dialect which our author puts into the mouths of his characters. They are Hollanders, Burgundians, Germans, Italians, and English, but by a singular and surprising concurrence of tastes, they all speak on the Lowland Scottish patois. They say 'gar' instead of make, and 'muckle' instead of much, and call a church a 'kirk', and leave out the 'th' from with; and, in short, speak in a style that would well become Edie Ochiltree or Baillie Nicol Jarvie. Now, we cannot excuse Mr Reade for this. The middle ages are consecrated to the Gods. We cannot recall them to mould their dialects to our own taste, and a tale purporting to be a narrative of fact ought to reproduce the very language which prevailed at the period as a material part of these facts, or if this be impossible, the events should be recounted in the language of the people to whom the story is offered. Were Mr Reade a less eminent writer, we should hesitate before making these remarks, but the public have a right to expect more care and attention to natural congruity in the writings of one of its favourites.

anonymous review in The Daily News

I am about to ask you to modify your opinion of my supposed carelessness in introducing Scotch phrases and words into *The Cloister and the Hearth*. This would, I admit, be incongruous; but I have not done it. It is true that the expressions you object to are now current only in Scotland; but at the date of my story they were English. They are all in Chaucer; and (which is more to the point) they are all in the Paston Letters, written at the very epoch I had to reproduce.

As to the word 'kirk', it is neither Scotch nor English, but Dutch; and I think you will find on re-examination that I have written it Dutch-wise, 'kerk', and that it only occurs in my book when the scene lies at Rotterdam or Gouda, and the interlocutor who uses it is Dutch.

Nevertheless, I shall certainly apply the scissors to these *soi-disant* Scotticisms, but on the simple ground that they give an air of incongruity to my work in the eyes of so just and friendly a critic as yourself. All I ask is to be acquitted of ignorance, or a wont of artistic feeling and care in the matter as it stands at present. I am, etc.,

Garrick Club   14th October   Charles Reade

1764—Edward Gibbon conceived the idea of writing The Decline and Fall of the Roman Empire

---

The pilgrimage of Italy, which I had now accomplished, had long been the object of my curious devotion. The passage of Mount Cenis, the regular streets of Turin, the Gothic cathedral of Milan, the scenery of the Boromean Islands, the marble palaces of Genoa, the beauties of Florence, the wonders of Rome, the curiosities of Naples, the galleries of Bologna, the singular aspect of Venice, the amphitheatre of Verona, and the Palladian architecture of Vicenza, are still present to my imagination. I read the Tuscan writers on the banks of the Arno; but my conversation was with the dead rather than the living, and the whole college of Cardinals was of less value in my eyes than the transfiguration of Raphael, the Apollo of the Vatican, or the massy greatness of the Coliseum.

[My temper is not very susceptible of enthusiasm, and the enthusiasm which I do not feel I have ever scorned to affect. But at the distance of twenty-five years I can neither forget nor express the strong emotions which agitated my mind as I first approached and entered the *eternal City*. After a sleepless night, I trod with a lofty step the ruins of the Forum; each memorable spot where Romulus stood, or Tully spoke, or Caesar fell, was at once present to my eye; and several days of intoxication were lost or enjoyed before I could descend to a cool and minute investigation.]

It was at Rome, on the fifteenth of October, 1764, as I sat musing amidst the ruins of the Capitol, while the barefooted fryers were singing Vespers in the temple of Jupiter, that the idea of writing the decline and fall of the City first started to my mind. After Rome has kindled and satisfied the enthusiasm of the Classic pilgrim, his curiosity for all meaner objects insensibly subsides. My father was impatient, and I returned home by the way of Lyons and Paris, enriched with a new stock of images and ideas, which I could never have acquired in the solitude of the Closet.

From The Autobiographies of Edward Gibbon

16 October 🂠

1847—Charlotte Brontë published Jane Eyre, *in which she 'astonished and delighted' her readers (according to Mrs Gaskell) by the 'accurate and Titanic power' with which she depicted 'the strong, self-reliant, racy, and individual characters'*

The vehemence of emotion, stirred by grief and love within me, was claiming mastery, and struggling for full sway; and asserting a right to predominate; to overcome, to live, rise, and reign at last; yes, – and to speak.

'I grieve to leave Thornfield: I love Thornfield: – I love it, because I have lived in it a full and delightful life, – momentarily at least. I have not been trampled on. I have not been petrified. I have not been buried with inferior minds, and excluded from every glimpse of communion with what is bright and energetic, and high. I have talked, face to face, with what I reverence; with what I delight in, – with an original, a vigorous, an expanded mind. I have known you, Mr. Rochester; and it strikes me with terror and anguish to feel I absolutely must be torn from you for ever. I see the necessity of departure; and it is like looking on the necessity of death.' . . .

'No: you must stay! I swear it – and the oath shall be kept.'

'I tell you I must go!' I retorted, roused to something like passion. 'Do you think I can stay to become nothing to you? Do you think I am an automaton? – a machine without feelings? and can bear to have my morsel of bread snatched from my lips, and my drop of living water dashed from my cup? Do you think, because I am poor, obscure, plain, and little, I am soulless and heartless? You think wrong! – I have as much soul as you, – and full as much heart! And if God had gifted me with some beauty, and much wealth, I should have made it as hard for you to leave me, as it is now for me to leave you. I am not talking to you now through the medium of custom, conventionalities, or even of mortal flesh: – it is my spirit that addresses your spirit; just as if both had passed through the grave, and we stood at God's feet, equal, – as we are!'

'As we are!' repeated Mr. Rochester – 'so,' he added, enclosing me in his arms, gathering me to his breast, pressing his lips on my lips: 'so Jane!'

Charlotte Brontë: from Jane Eyre

1856—Elizabeth Barrett Browning dedicated Aurora Leigh *to her cousin, John Kenyon, the 'Romney' of the poem*

The words 'cousin' and 'friend' are constantly recurring in this poem, the last pages of which have been finished under the hospitality of your roof, my own dearest cousin and friend; – cousin and friend, in a sense of less equality and greater disinteredness then 'Romney's'.

Ending, therefore, and preparing once more to quit England, I venture to leave in your hands this book, the most mature of my works, and the one into which my highest convictions upon Life and Art have entered: that as, through my various efforts in literature and life, you have believed in me, borne with me, and been generous to me, far beyond the common use of mere relationship or sympathy of mind, so you may kindly accept, in sight of the public, this poor sign of esteem, gratitude, and affection   from

your unforgetting   E. B. B.

How dreary 'tis for women to sit still
On winter nights by solitary fires . . .
            to sit alone,
And think, for comfort, how, that very night,
Affianced lovers, leaning face to face
With sweet half-listenings for each other's breath,
Are reading haply from some page of ours . . .
            to have our books
Appraised by love, associated with love,
While *we* sit loveless! is it hard, you think?
At least 'tis mournful. Fame, indeed, 'twas said,
Means simply love. It was a man said that.
And then, there's love and love: the love of all
(To risk, in turn, a woman's paradox)
Is but a small thing to the love of one.
            . . .   And since
We needs must hunger, – better, for man's love,
Than God's truth! better, for companions sweet
Then great convictions! let us bear our weights,
Preferring dreary hearths to desert souls.

Elizabeth Barrett Browning: from Aurora Leigh
Bk. V

18 October

1852—'I have the greatest tenderness for the memory of Hood . . . I shall have a melancholy gratification in privately assisting to place a simple and plain record over the remains of a great writer that should be as modest as he was himself, but I regard any other monument . . . as a mistake'

Charles Dickens to John Watkins

With fingers weary and worn,
    With eyelids heavy and red,
A Woman sat, in unwomanly rags,
    Plying her needle and thread –
        Stitch! stitch! stitch!
In poverty, hunger and dirt,
And still with a voice of dolorous pitch
    She sang the 'Song of the Shirt'! . . .

'Work! – work – work
Till the brain begins to swim;
    Work – work – work
Till the eyes are heavy and dim!
    Seam, and gusset, and band,
    Band, and gusset, and seam,
Till over the buttons I fall asleep,
    And sew them on in a dream!

'O! Men with Sisters dear!
O Men! with Mothers and Wives!
It is not linen you're wearing out,
    But human creatures' lives!
    Stitch – stitch – stitch,
In poverty, hunger, and dirt,
Sewing at once, with a double thread,
    A Shroud as well as a Shirt.

'But why do I talk of Death?
    That phantom of grisly bone,
I hardly fear his terrible shape,
    It seems so like my own –
    It seems so like my own
    Because of the fasts I keep,
Oh! God! that bread should be so dear,
    And flesh and blood so cheap! . . .

Thomas Hood: from The Song of the Shirt

1741—David Garrick made his debut, with unprecedented success

'Last Night was perform'd, gratis, the Tragedy of Richard the Third, at the late Theatre in Goodman's Fields, when the Character of Richard was perform'd by a Gentleman who never appear'd before, whose Reception was the most extraordinary and great that was ever known upon such an occasion; and we hear he obliges the Town this Evening with the same Performance.'

> *from the* London Daily Post and General Advertiser, *October 20, 1741*

Richard Now is the winter of our discontent
    Made glorious summer by this sun of York;
    And all the clouds that loured upon our house
    In the deep bosom of the ocean buried.
    Now are our brows bound with victorious wreaths,
    Our bruised arms hung up for monuments,
    Our stern alarums changed to merry meetings,
    Our dreadful marches to delightful measures.
    Grim-visaged War hath smoothed his wrinkled front,
    And now, instead of mounting barbed steeds
    To fright the souls of fearful adversaries,
    He capers nimbly in a lady's chamber
    To the lascivious pleasing of a lute.
    But I, that am not shaped for sportive tricks
    Nor made to court an amorous looking glass,
    I, that am rudely stamped, and want love's majesty,
    To strut before a wanton ambling nymph;
    I, that am curtailed of this fair proportion,
    Cheated of feature by dissembling Nature,
    Deformed, unfinished, sent before my time
    Into this breathing world scarce half made up,
    And that so lamely and unfashionable
    That dogs bark at me as I halt by them;
    Why, I, in this weak piping time of peace,
    Have no delight to pass away the time,
    Unless to spy my shadow in the sun
    And descant on mine own deformity.

> *William Shakespeare: from* Richard III, *Act I, Scene I*

20 October

1660—Thomas Traherne was ordained a priest

You never Enjoy the world aright, till you see how a Sand Exhibiteth the Wisdom and Power of God: and Prize in evry Thing the Service which they do, by Manifesting His Glory and Goodness to your Soul, far more than the Visible Beauty on their Surface, or the Material Surfaces, they can do your Body. Wine by its Moysture quencheth my Thirst, whether I consider it or no: but to see it flowing from his Lov, who gave it unto Man. Quencheth the Thirst even of the Holy Angels. To consider it, is to Drink it Spritualy. To Rejoice in its Diffusion is to be of a Public Mind. And to take Pleasure in all the Benefits it doth to all is Heavenly. for so they do in Heaven. To do so, is to be Divine and Good. and to imitat our Infinit and Eternal Father.

Your Enjoyment of the World is never right, till evry Morning you awake in Heaven: see your self in your fathers Palace: and look upon the skies and the Earth and the Air, as Celestial Joys having such a Reverend Esteem of all, as if you were among the Angels. The Bride of the Monarch, in her Husbands Chamber, hath no such Causes of Delight as you.

You never Enjoy the World aright, till the Sea it self floweth in your Veins, till you are Clothed with the heavens, and Crowned with the Stars: and Perceiv yourself to be the Sole Heir of the whole World: and more than so, becaus Men are in it who are evry one Sole Heirs, as well as you. Till you can Sing and Rejoyce and Delight in GOD, as Misers do in Gold, and Kings in Scepters, you never Enjoy the World.

> *Thomas Traherne: from* Centuries of Meditations.

1809—Walter Scott acknowledged George Crabbe's gift of The Parish Register, *in a letter recalling his introduction to the poet's work twenty years earlier*

―――

. . . It is, I think, fully that time since I was, for great part of a very snowy winter, the inhabitant of an old house in the country, in a course of poetical study, so very like that of your admirably painted 'Young Lad' that I could hardly help saying, 'That's me!' when I was reading the tale to my family. Among the very few books which fell under my hands was a volume or two of Dodsley's Annual Register, one of which contained copious extracts from 'The Village' and 'The Library' . . . beginning with the description of the old Romancers. I committed them faithfully to my memory, where your verses must have felt themselves very strangely lodged, in company with ghost stories, border riding-ballads, scraps of old plays, and all the miscellaneous stuff which a strong appetite for reading, with neither means nor discrimination for selection, had assembled in the head of a lad of eighteen. . . .

* * * * *

Come, let us then with reverend step advance
And greet – the ancient worthies of ROMANCE! . . .
   Hark! Hollow blasts through empty courts resound,
And shadowy forms with staring eyes stalk round;
See! Moats and bridges, walls and castles rise,
Ghosts, fairies, demons, dance before your eyes;
Lo! magic verse inscribed on golden gate,
And bloody hand that beckons on to fate: –
'And who art thou, thou little page, unfold?
Say, doth thy lord my Claribel withhold?
Go tell him straight, Sir Knight, thou must resign
The captive queen; – for Claribel is mine.'
Away he flies; and now for bloody deeds,
Black suits of armour, masks, and foaming steeds;
The giant falls; his recreant throat I seize,
And from his corslet take the massy keys: –
Dukes, lords, and knights in long procession move,
Released from bondage with my virgin love: –
She comes! she comes! in all the charms of youth,
Unequalled love, and unsuspected truth!
   Ah! happy he who thus, in magic themes,
O'er worlds bewitched, in early rapture dreams,
Where wild Enchantment waves her potent wand,
And Fancy's beauties fill her fairly land. . . .

George Crabbe: from The Library

1968—Robert Browning's first play, Pippa Passes, *written in 1841, was given its world premiere as a stage performance at the Oxford Playhouse*

Two Songs from 'Pippa Passes'

i

The year's at the spring
And day's at the morn;
Morning's at seven;
The hill-side's dew-pearled;
The lark's on the wing;
The snail's on the thorn:
God's in his heaven –
All's right with the world.

ii

You'll love me yet! – and I can tarry
    Your love's protracted growing:
June reared that bunch of flowers you carry,
    From seeds of April's sowing.

I plant a heartful now: some seed
    At least is sure to strike,
And yield – what you'll not pluck indeed,
    Not love, but, may be, like.

You'll look at least on love's remains,
    A grave's one violet:
Your look? – that pays a thousand pains.
    What's death? You'll love me yet!

4004 B.C.—'Man was created by the Trinity on October 23, 4004 B.C. at nine o'clock in the morning'

a 17th-century vice-chancellor of Cambridge University

The drowning of the first world, and the repairing that again; the burning of this world, and establishing another in heaven, do not so much strain a mans Reason, as the Creation, a Creation of all out of nothing. For, for the repairing of the world after the Flood, compared to the Creation, it was eight to nothing; eight persons to begin a world upon, then; but in the Creation, none. And for the glory which we receive in the next world, it is (in some sort) as the stamping of a print upon a Coyn; the metal is there already, a body and a soul to receive glory: but at the Creation, there was no soul to receive glory, no body to receive a soul, no stuff, no matter, to make a body of. The less anything is, the less we know it: how invisible, how unintelligible a thing then, is this *Nothing*! We say in the School, *Deus cognoscibilior Angelis*, We have better means to know the nature of God, than of Angels, because God hath appeared and manifested himself more in actions, than Angels have done: we know what they are, by knowing what they have done; and it is very little that is related to us what Angels have done: what then is there that can bring this Nothing to our understanding? what hath that done? A Leviathan, a Whale, from a grain of Spawn; an Oke from a buried Akehorn, is a great; but a great world from nothing, is a strange improvement. We wonder to see a man rise from nothing to a great Estate; but that Nothing is but nothing in comparison; but absolutely nothing, meerly nothing, is the more incomprehensible than any thing, than all things together. It is a state (if a man may call it a state) that the Devil himself in the midst of his torments, cannot wish.

John Donne: from Sermon XXV, 'The Spital'.

24 October 🛍

1887—Gerard Manley Hopkins took Coventry Patmore (and Cardinal Newman and others) to task for the sloppiness of late Victorian prose

My dear Mr Patmore,

I find I began writing to you a fortnight since. I was then examining: I am still, but am nearly at an end. I enclose the Paper you sent, supposing that you could not wait for it longer. I had meant to write some remarks on it, but I cannot delay the Paper for them. I may send them afterwards.

But I make one now which will amaze you and, except that you are very patient of my criticisms, may incense you. It is that when I read your prose and when I read Newman's and some modern writers' the same impression is borne in on me: no matter how beautiful the thought, nor, taken singly, with what happiness expressed, you do not know what *writing prose* is. At bottom what you do and what Cardinal Newman does is to think aloud, to think with pen and paper. In this process there are certain advantages; they may outweigh those of a perfect technic; but at any rate they exclude that; they exclude the belonging technic, the belonging rhetoric, the own proper eloquence of written prose. Each thought is told off singly and there follows a pause and this breaks the continuity, the *contentio*, the strain of address, which writing should usually have.

The beauty, the eloquence, of good prose cannot come wholly from the thought. With Burke it does and varies with the thought; when therefore the thought is sublime so does the style appear to be. But in fact Burke had no style properly so called: his style was colourlessly to transmit the thought. Still he was an orator in form and followed the common oratorical tradition, so that his writing has the strain of address I speak of above.

But Newman does not follow the common tradition – of writing. His tradition is that of cultured, the most highly educated, conversation; it is the flower of the best Oxford life. Perhaps this gives it a charm of unaffected and personal sincerity that nothing else could. Still he shirks the technic of written prose and shuns the tradition of written English. He seems to be thinking 'Gibbon is the last great master of traditional English prose; he is its perfection; I do not propose to emulate him; I begin all over again from the language of conversation of common life'.

You seem to me to be saying to yourself 'I am writing prose, not poetry; it is bad taste and a confusion of kinds to employ the style of poetry and to express one's thought with point'. But the style of prose is a positive thing and not the absence of verse-forms and pointedly expressed thoughts are single hits and give no continuity of style. . . .

Gerard M. Hopkins

University College
St. Stephen's Green, Dublin

1415—St Crispin's Day, on which the Battle of Agincourt was fought

Fair stood the wind for France
When we our sails advance,
Nor now to prove our chance
    Longer will tarry;
But putting to the main
At Kaux, the mouth of Seine,
With all his martial train
    Landed King Harry. . . .

They now to fight are gone,
Armor on armor shone,
Drum now to drum did groan,
    To hear was wonder,
That with the cries they make
The very earth did shake,
Trumpet to trumpet spake,
    Thunder to thunder. . . .

With Spanish yew so strong,
Arrows a cloth-yard long,
That like the serpents stung,
    Piercing the weather;
None from their fellow starts,
But playing manly parts,
And like true English hearts
    Stuck close together. . . .

Upon Saint Crispin's day
Fought we this noble fray,
Which fame did not delay
    To England to carry;
Oh, when shall English men
With such acts fill a pen,
Or England breed again
    Such a King Harry?

Michael Drayton: from 'To the Cambro-
Britons and their harp, this ballad of Agincourt'

26 October 📖

1740—Tobias Smollett set sail for Jamaica, as second surgeon's mate on H.M.S. Chichester. One of his fellow-officers 'thought his account of the expedition, given in Roderick Random, *very accurate and faithful in every particular'*

We staid not long at the Downes, but took the benefit of the first easterly wind to go round to Spithead, where having received on board provisions for six months, we sailed from St. Helen's in the grand fleet bound for the West Indies, on the ever-memorable expedition of Carthagena.

It was not without great mortification I saw myself on the point of being transported to such a distant and unhealthy climate, destitute of every convenience that could render such a voyage supportable; and under the dominion of an arbitrary tyrant, whose command was almost intolerable: However, as these complaints were common to a great many on board, I resolved to submit patiently to my fate. . . . We got out of the Channel with a prosperous breeze, which died away, leaving us becalmed about fifty leagues to the westward of the Lizard: But this state of inaction did not last long; for next night our main-topsail was spilt by the wind, which in the morning increased to a hurricane. I was wakened by a most horrible din, occasioned by the play of the gun-carriages upon the deck above, the cracking of cabins, the howling of the wind through the shrouds, the confused noise of the ship's crew, the pipes of the boatswain and his mates, the trumpets of the lieutenants, and the clanking of the chain-pumps. Morgan, who had never been at sea before, turned out in a great hurry, crying, 'Got have mercy and compassion upon us! I believe we have got upon the confines of Lucifer and the tamn'd!' – while poor Thomson lay quaking in his hammock, putting up petitions to Heaven for our safety. I rose and joined the Welshman, with whom, after having fortified ourselves with brandy, I went above; but, if my sense of hearing was startled before, how must my sight have been appalled in beholding the effects of the storm! The sea was swelled into billows mountain-high, on the top of which, our ship sometimes hung as if it was to be precipitated to the abyss below! Sometimes we sunk between the waves that rose on each side higher than our topmast-head, and threatened, by dashing together, to overwhelm us in a moment! . . . While I considered this scene with equal terror and astonishment, one of the main braces broke, by the shock whereof two sailors were flung from the yard's arm into the sea, where they perished, and poor Jack Rattlin was thrown down upon the deck, at the expence of a broken leg. Morgan and I ran immediately to his assistance, and found a splinter of the shin-bone thrust by the violence of the fall through the skin: As this was a case of too great consequence to be treated without the authority of the doctor, I went down to his cabin . . . I entered the apartment without any ceremony, and by the glimmering of a lamp, perceived him on his knees, before something that very much resembled a crucifix. . . .

Tobias Smollett: from Roderick Random

1949—Dylan Thomas celebrated his thirty-fifth birthday

In the mustardseed sun,
By full tilt river and switchback sea
    Where the cormorants scud,
In his house on stilts high among beaks
    And palavers of birds
This sandgrain day in the bent bay's grave
    He celebrates and spurns
His driftwood thirty-fifth wind turned age;
    Herons spire and spear.

Under and round him go
Flounders, gulls, on their cold, dying trails,
    Doing what they are told,
Curlews aloud in the congered waves
    Work at their ways to death,
And the rhymer in the long tongued room,
    Who tolls his birthday bell,
Toils towards the ambush of his wounds;
    Herons, steeple stemmed, bless.

In the thistledown fall,
He sings towards anguish: finches fly
    In the claw tracks of hawks
On a seizing sky: small fishes glide
    Through wynds and shells of drowned
Ship towns to pastures of otters. He
    In his slant, racking house
And the hewn coils of his trade perceives
    Herons walk in their shroud,

The livelong river's robe
Of minnows wreathing around their prayer;
    And far at sea he knows,
Who slaves to his crouched, eternal end
    Under a serpent cloud,
Dolphins dive in their turnturtle dust,
    The rippled seals streak down
To kill and their own tide daubing blood
    Slides good in the sleek mouth. . .

Dylan Thomas, from 'Poem on his Birthday'

28 October

1853—Henry David Thoreau received a shipment of books

For a year of two past, my *publisher*, falsely so called, has been writing from time to time to ask what disposition should be made of the copies of 'A Week on the Concord and Merrimack Rivers' still on hand, and at last suggesting that he had use for the room they occupied in his cellar. So I had them all sent to me here, and they have arrived today by express, filling the man's wagon, – 706 copies out of an edition of 1,000 which I bought of Munroe four years ago and have been ever since paying for, and have not quite paid for yet. The wares are sent to me at last, and I have an opportunity to examine my purchase. They are something more substantial than fame, as my back knows, which has borne them up two flights of stairs to a place similar to that to which they trace their origin. Of the remaining two hundred and ninety odd, seventy-five were given away, the rest sold. I have now a library of nearly nine hundred volumes, over seven hundred of which I wrote myself. Is it not well that the author should behold the fruits of his labor? My works are piled up on one side of my chamber half as high as my head, my *opera omnia*. This is authorship; these are the work of my brain. There was just one piece of good luck in the venture. The unbound were tied up by the printer four years ago in stout paper wrappers, and inscribed, –

H. D. Thoreau's
Concord River
50 cops.

So Munroe had only to cross out 'River' and write 'Mass.' and deliver them to the expressman at once. I can see now what I write for, the result of my labors.

Nevertheless, in spite of this result, sitting beside the inert mass of my works, I take up my pen to-night to record what thought or experience I may have had, with as much satisfaction as ever. Indeed, I believe that this result is more inspiring and better for me than if a thousand had bought my wares. It affects my privacy less and leaves me freer.

H. D. Thoreau: from the Journals

1630—Robert Herrick was installed as vicar of Dean Prior in Devon, a living which he held, with mingled emotions, for a total of nearly thirty years

Dean-bourn, farewell; I never look to see
Deane, or thy warty incivility.
Thy rockie bottome, that doth teare thy streams,
And make them frantick, ev'n to all extreames;
To my content, I never sho'd behold,
Were thy streames silver, or thy rocks all gold.
Rockie thou art; and rockie we discover
Thy men; and rockie are thy ways all over.
O men, O manners; Now, and ever knowne
To be *A Rockie Generation*!
A people currish; churlish as the seas;
And rude (almost) as rudest Salvages.
With whom I did, and may re-sojourne when
Rockes turn to Rivers, Rivers turn to Men.

＊　　＊　　＊　　＊　　＊

More discontents I never had
    Since I was born, than here;
Where I have been, and still am, sad,
    In this dull *Devon-shire*:
Yet justly too I must confesse;
    I ne'r invented such
Ennobled numbers for the Presse,
    Then where I loath'd so much.

＊　　＊　　＊　　＊　　＊

How well contented in this private *Grange*
Spend I my life (that's subject unto change:)
Under whose Roofe with *Mosse-worke* wrought, there I
Kisse my *Brown wife*, and *black Posterity*.

30 October 〔W〕

1832—Washington Irving investigated a prairie-dog 'town' in Oklahoma Territory

---

The prairie dog is an animal of the coney kind, and about the size of a rabbit. He is of a sprightly mercurial nature; quick, sensitive, and somewhat petulant. He is very gregarious, living in large communities, sometimes of several acres in extent, where innumerable little heaps of earth show the entrances to the subterranean cells of the inhabitants, and the well beaten tracks, like lanes and streets, show their mobility and restlessness. According to the accounts given of them, they would seem to be continually full of sport, business, and public affairs; whisking about hither and thither, as if on gossiping visits to each other's houses, or congregating in the cool of the evening, or after a shower, and gambolling together in the open air. Sometimes, especially when the moon shines, they pass half the night in revelry, barking or yelping with short, quick, yet weak tones, like those of very young puppies. While in the height of their playfulness and clamor, however, should there be the least alarm, they all vanish into their cells in an instant, and the village remains blank and silent. . . .

It was toward evening that I set out with a companion, to visit the village in question. Unluckily, it had been invaded in the course of the day by some of the rangers, who had shot two or three of its inhabitants, and thrown the whole sensitive community in confusion. As we approached, we could perceive numbers of the inhabitants seated at the entrances of their cells, while sentinels seemed to have been posted on the outskirts, to keep a look-out. At sight of us, the picket guards scampered in and gave the alarm; whereupon every inhabitant gave a short yelp, or bark, and dived into his hole, his heels twinkling in the air as if he had thrown a somerset. We traversed the whole village, or republic, which covered an area of about thirty acres; but not a whisker of an inhabitant was to be seen. . . .

The dusk of the evening put an end to our observations, but the train of whimsical comparisons produced in my brain by the moral attributes which I had heard given to these little politic animals, still continued after my return to camp; and late in the night, as I lay awake after all the camp was asleep, and heard in the stillness of the hour, a faint clamor of shrill voices from the distant village, I could not help picturing to myself the inhabitants gathered together in noisy assemblage and windy debate, to devise plans for the public safety, and to vindicate the invaded rights and insulted dignity of the republic.

Washington Irving: from A Tour on the Prairies, *ed. J. F. McDermott, 1956*

1611—The Maid's Tragedy, *a play by Francis Beaumont and John Fletcher, was licensed*

Beaumont and Fletcher, of whom I am next to speak, had, with the advantage of Shakespeare's wit, which was their precedent, great natural gifts, improved by study: Beaumont especially being so accurate a judge of plays, that Ben Johnson, while he lived, submitted all his writings to his censure, and, 'tis thought, used his judgment in correcting, if not contriving, all his plots. What value he had for him, appears by the verses he writ to him; and therefore I need speak no farther of it.

The first play that brought Fletcher and him esteem was their *Philaster*; for before that, they had written two or three very unsuccessfully, as the like is reported of Ben Johnson, before he writ *Every Man in His Humour*. Their plots were generally more regular than Shakespeare's, especially those which were made before Beaumont's death; and they understood and imitated the conversation of gentlemen much better; whose wild debaucheries, and quickness of wit in reparties, no poet before them could paint as they have done. Humour, which Ben Johnson derived from particular persons, they made it not their business to describe: they represented all the passions very lively, but above all, love. I am apt to believe the English language in them arrived to its highest perfection: what words have since been taken in, are rather superfluous than ornamental. Their plays are now the most pleasant and frequent entertainments of the stage; two of theirs being acted through the year for one of Shakespeare's or Johnson's: the reason is, because there is a certain gaiety in their comedies, and pathos in their more serious plays, which suits generally with all men's humours. Shakespeare's language is likewise a little obsolete, and Ben Johnson's wit comes short of theirs.

John Dryden: from An Essay of Dramatic Poesy

Lay a garland on my hearse of the dismal yew,
Maidens, willow branches bear, say I died true.
My love was false, but I was firm from my hour of birth;
Upon my buried body lay lightly, gently, earth.

Beaumont and Fletcher: from The Maid's Tragedy

Nouember.

1611—'By the Kings players: Hallowmas nyght was presented at Whithall before ye kinges Maiestie a play Called the Tempest'

Revels Account

PROSPERO: Though with their high wrongs I am struck to the quick,
               Yet with my nobler reason 'gainst my fury
               Do I take part: the rarer action is
               In virtue than in vengeance: they being penitent,
               The sole drift of my purpose doth extend
               Not a frown further. Go, release them, Ariel.
               My charms I'll break, their senses I'll restore,
               And they shall be themselves.

ARIEL: I'll fetch them, sir.   *Exit*

PROSPERO: Ye elves of hills, brooks, standing lakes, and groves;
               And ye that on the sands with printless foot
               Do chase the ebbing Neptune and do fly
               When he comes back; you demi-puppets, that
               By moonshine do the green sour ringlets make
               Whereof the ewe not bites; and you, whose pastime
               Is to make midnight mushrooms; that rejoice
               To hear the solemn curfew; by whose aid, –
               Weak masters though ye be – I have bedimm'd
               The noontide sun, call'd forth the mutinous winds,
               And 'twixt the green sea and the azur'd vault
               Set roaring war: to the dread-rattling thunder
               Have I given fire and rifted Jove's stout oak
               With his own bolt: the strong-bas'd promontory
               Have I made shake; and by the spurs pluck'd up
               The pine and cedar: graves at my command
               Have wak'd their sleepers, op'd, and let them forth
               By my so potent art. But this rough magic
               I here abjure; and, when I have requir'd
               Some heavenly music, – which even now I do, –
               To work my end upon their senses that
               This airy charm is for, I'll break my staff,
               Bury it certain fathoms in the earth,
               And, deeper than did ever plummet sound
               I'll drown my book.   *Solemn music*

William Shakespeare, from The Tempest, V. i

2 November

1831—Thomas Carlyle confided to his Notebooks *his personal opinion of Charles Lamb and his coterie*

How few people speak for Truth's sake, even in its humblest modes! I return from Enfield, where I have seen Lamb etc etc. Not one of that class will tell you a straightforward story, or even a credible one, about any matter under the sun. All must be perked up into epigrammatic contrasts, startling exaggerations, claptraps that will get a plaudit from the galleries! I have heard a hundred anecdotes about W. Hazlitt (for example); yet cannot, by never so much cross-questioning even, form to myself the smallest notion of how it really stood with him. – Wearisome, inexpressibly wearisome to me is that sort of clatter: it is not walking (to the end of time you would never advance, for these persons indeed have no WHITHER); it is not bounding and frisking in graceful natural joy; it is dancing – a St. Vitus dance. *Heigho!* – Charles Lamb I sincerely believe to be in some considerable degree *insane*. A more pitiful, ricketty, gasping, staggering, stammering Tom fool I do not know. He is witty by denying truisms, and abjuring good manners. His speech wriggles hither and thither with an incessant painful fluctuation; not an opinion in it or a fact or a phrase even that you can thank him for: more like a convulsion fit than natural systole and diastole – Besides he is now a confirmed shameless drunkard; *asks* vehemently for gin-and-water in strangers' houses; tipples until he is utterly mad, and is only not thrown out of doors because he is too much despised for taking such trouble with him. Poor Lamb! Poor England where such a despicable abortion is named genius! – He said: There are just two things I regret in English History; first that Guy Faux's plot did not take effect (there would have been so glorious an *explosion*); second that the Royalists did not hang Milton (then we might have laughed at them); etc., etc.,

Thomas Carlyle: from Notebooks, *November 2, 1831*

1871—Walt Whitman replied to the two letters in which Mrs Anne Gilchrist had proposed marriage to him

[Earl's Colne, Halstead, Essex]

. . . In May, 1869, came the voice over the Atlantic to me – O, the voice of my Mate; it must be so – my love rises up out of the very depths of the grief & tramples upon despair . . .

Do not say I am forward, or that I lack pride because I tell this love to thee who have never sought or made sign of desiring to seek me. Oh, for all that, this love is my pride my glory. Source of sufferings and joys that cannot put themselves into words. Besides, it is not true thou hast not sought or loved me. For when I read the divine poems I feel all folded round in thy love: I feel often as if thou wast pleading so passionately for the love of the woman that can understand thee – that I know not how to bear the yearning answering tenderness that fills my breast. I know that a woman may without hurt to her pride – without stain or blame – tell her love to thee. I feel for a certainty that she may. Try me for this life, my darling – see if I cannot so live so grow, so learn, so love, that when I die you will say, 'This woman has grown to be a very part of me. My soul must have her loving companionship everywhere in all things. I alone & she alone are not complete identities – it is I and she together in a new, divine, perfect union that form the one complete identity. . . .

Anne Gilchrist to Walt Whitman, 6 Sept. and
23 October

I have been waiting quite a while for time and the right mood, to answer your letter in a spirit as serious as its own, and in the same unmitigated trust and affection. But more daily work than ever has fallen to me to do the present season, and though I am well and contented, my best moods seem to shun me. I wish to give to it a day, a sort of Sabbath, or holy day, apart to itself, under serene and propitious influences, confident that I could then write you a letter which would do you good, and me too. But I must at least show without further delay that I am not insensible to your love. I too send you my love. And do you feel no disappointment because I now write so briefly. My book is my best letter, my response, my truest explanation of all. In it I have put my body and spirit. You understand this better and clearer and fuller than any one else. And I too fully and clearly understand the loving letter it has evoked. Enough that there surely exists so beautiful and delicate a relation, accepted by both of us with joy.

Walt Whitman to Anne Gilchrist, Nov. 3, 1871

4 November 🔲

1743—John Wesley went to see a farce attacking Methodism but found it did not hinder his missionary efforts

Nov. 2, *Wed.* – The following advertisement was published:

FOR THE BENEFIT OF MR. ESTE,
By the Edinburgh Company of Comedians, on Friday,
November 4, will be acted a Comedy called
THE CONSCIOUS LOVERS:
To which will be added a Farce, called,
TRICK UPON TRICK, or METHODISM DISPLAYED.

On Friday a vast multitude of spectators were assembled in the Moot Hall to see this. It was believed there could not be less than fifteen hundred people, some hundred of whom sat on rows of seats built upon the stage. Soon after the comedians had begun the first act of the play, on a sudden all those seats fell down at once, the supports of them breaking like a rotten stick. The people were thrown upon one another, about five foot forward, but none of them hurt. After a short time the rest of the spectators were quiet, and the actors went on. In the middle of the second act all the shilling seats gave a crack and sunk several inches down. A great noise and shrieking followed; and as many as could readily get to the door went out and returned no more. Notwithstanding this, when the noise was over, the actors went on with the play. In the beginning of the third act the entire stage suddenly sank about six inches. The players retired with great precipitation: yet in a while they began again. At the latter end of the third act all the sixpenny seats, without any kind of notice, fell to the ground. There was now a cry on every side, it being supposed that many were crushed in pieces; but, upon inquiry, not a single person (such was the mercy of God!) was either killed or dangerously hurt. Two or three hundred remaining in the hall, Mr. Este (who was to act the Methodist) came upon the stage and told them, for all this, he was resolved the farce should be acted. While he was speaking the stage sunk six inches more; on which he ran back in the utmost confusion, and the people as fast as they could out of the door, none staying to look behind him.

Which is most surprising – that those players acted this farce the next week, or that some hundreds of people came again to see it?

Sun. 6 – We had an useful practical sermon at St. Nicholas's church in the morning, and another at St. Andrew's in the afternoon. At five I preached to a willing multitude, on the Prodigal Son. How many of these were lost, and now are found!

In the following week I endeavoured to speak severally to each member of the society. The numbers I found neither to rise nor fall; but many had increased in the knowledge and love of God.

From An Extract of the Reverend Mr. John Wesley's Journal

1702–1815—Nicholas Rowe's tragedy, Tamerlane, *whose hero is a somewhat glorified portrait of King William III, was performed annually for 113 years on November 5, the anniversary of William's landing in England in the Glorious Revolution of 1688*

Some people (who do me very great honour in it) have fancied, that in the person of Tamerlane, I have alluded to the greatest character of the present age. . . . There are many features, 'tis true, in that great man's life, not unlike his majesty; his courage, his piety, his moderation, his justice, and his fatherly love of his people; but above all, his hate of tyranny and oppression, and his zealous care for the common good of mankind, carry a strong resemblance of him. Several incidents are alike in their stories; and there wants nothing to his majesty, as such a deciding victory, as that by which Tamerlane gave peace to the world. That is yet to come; but I hope we may reasonably expect it . . .

> *Nicholas Rowe: from the Dedication of* Tamerlane *to the Marquess of Hartingdon.*

Of all the muses' various labours, none
Have lasted longer, or have higher flown,
Than those who tell the fame by ancient heroes won.
With pleasure, Rome, and great Augustus, heard
'Arms and the man' sung by the Mantuan bard.
In spite of time, the sacred story lives,
And Caesar and his empire still survives.
Like him (though much unequal to his flame)
Our author makes a pious prince his theme:
High with the foremost names, in arms he stood,
Had fought, and suffer'd, for his country's good,
Yet sought not fame, but peace, in fields of blood.
Safe under him his happy people sat,
And griev'd, at distance, for their neighbour's fate;
Whilst with success a Turkish monarch crown'd,
Like spreading flame, deform'd the nations round;
With sword and fire he forc'd his impious way
To lawless pow'r, and universal sway,
Some abject states, for fear, the tyrant join,
Others, for gold, their liberties resign,
And venal princes sold their right divine:
Till Heav'n, the growing evil to redress,
Sent Tamerlane, to give the world a peace . . .

> *Nicholas Rowe: from the 'Prologue' to* Tamerlane

6 November 📖

1699—Lemuel Gulliver awakened in Lilliput

On the fifth of November, which was the beginning of summer in those parts, the weather being very hazy, the seamen spied a rock, within half a cable's length of the ship; but the wind was so strong, that we were driven directly upon it, and immediately split. Six of the crew, of whom I was one, having let down the boat into the sea, made a shift to get clear of the ship, and the rock. . . . in about half an hour the boat was overset by a sudden flurry from the north. What became of my companions in the boat, as well as of those who escaped on the rock, or were left in the vessel, I cannot tell; but conclude they were all lost. For my own part, I swam as fortune directed me, and was pushed forward by wind and tide. I often let my legs down, and could feel no bottom; but when I was almost gone and able to struggle no longer, I found myself within my depth; and by this time the storm was much abated. The declivity was so small, that I walked near a mile before I got to the shore, which I conjectured was about eight o'clock in the evening. I then advanced forward near half a mile, but could not discover any sign of houses or inhabitants; at least I was in so weak a condition, that I did not observe them. I was extremely tired, and with that, and the heat of the weather, and about half a pint of brandy that I drank as I left the ship, I found myself much inclined to sleep.

I lay down on the grass, which was very short and soft, where I slept sounder than ever I remember to have done in my life, and, as I reckoned, above nine hours; for when I awaked, it was just daylight. I attempted to rise, but was not able to stir: for as I happened to lie on my back, I found my arms and legs were strongly fastened on each side to the ground; and my hair, which was long and thick, tied down in the same manner. I likewise felt several slender ligatures across my body, from my armpits to my thighs. I could only look upwards, the sun began to grow hot, and the light offended my eyes. I heard a confused noise about me, but, in the posture I lay, could see nothing except the sky. In a little time I felt something alive moving on my left leg, which advancing gently forward over my breast, came almost up to my chin; when, bending my eyes downwards as much as I could, I perceived it to be a human creature not six inches high, with a bow and arrow in his hands, and a quiver at his back. In the mean time, I felt at least forty more of the same kind (as I conjectured) following the first. I was in utter astonishment, and roared so loud, that they all ran back in a fright; and some of them, as I was afterwards told, were hurt in the falls they got by leaping from my sides upon the ground.

Jonathan Swift: from Travels into Several Remote Nations of the World, *By Lemuel Gulliver, First a Surgeon, and then a Captain of several Ships.* (London, *1726*)

1724—John Kyrle, 'the Man of Ross', died in his ninetieth year

But all our praises why should lords engross?
Rise, honest Muse! and sing the Man of Ross:
Pleased Vaga echoes through her winding bounds,
And rapid Severn hoarse applause resounds.
Who hung with woods yon mountain's sultry brow?
From the dry rock who bade the waters flow?
Not to the skies in useless columns toss'd,
Or in proud falls magnificently lost,
But clear and artless, pouring through the plain
Health to the sick, and solace to the swain.
Whose causeway parts the vale with shady rows?
Whose seats the weary traveller repose?
Who taught that heaven-directed spire to rise?
'The Man of Ross', each lisping babe replies.
Behold the market-place with poor o'erspread!
The Man of Ross divides the weekly bread:
He feeds yon almshouse, neat, but void of state,
Where Age and Want sit smiling at the gate;
Him portion'd maids, apprenticed orphans bless'd,
The young who labour, and the old who rest.
Is any sick? the Man of Ross relieves,
Prescribes, attends, the medicine makes, and gives. . . .
　　B. Thrice happy man! enabled to pursue
What all so wish, but want the power to do!
Oh say, what sums that generous hand supply?
What mines to swell that boundless charity?
　　P. Of debts and taxes, wife and children clear,
This man possess'd – five hundred pounds a year! . . .
　　B. And what? no monument, inscription, stone?
His race, his form, his name almost unknown?
　　P. Who builds a church to God, and not to fame,
Will never mark the marble with his name:
Go, search it there,* where to be born, and die,
Of rich and poor makes all the history;
Enough that Virtue fill'd the space between;
Proved, by the ends of being, to have been.

　　　　　　Alexander Pope: from Moral Essays, Epistle
　　　　　　III, *'Of the Use of Riches', to Lord Bathurst*

*in the parish register

8 November 🏛

1602—The Bodleian Library at Oxford was opened to the public

I must truly confess of my self, that though I did never yet repent me of those . . . my often refusals of Honourable Offers, in respect of enriching my private Estate; yet somewhat more of late, I have blamed my self and my Nicety that way, for the love that I bear to my Reverend Mother the *University* of *Oxon*, and to the Advancement of her Good, by such kind of means, as I have since undertaken. For thus I fell to discourage, and debate in my mind, That altho' I might find it fittest for me, to keep out of the Throng of Court Contentions, and address my Thoughts and Deeds to such Ends althogether, as I myself could best affect; yet withal I was to think, that my Duty towards God, the Expectation of the World, and my natural Inclination, and very Morality did require, that I should not wholly so hide those little Abilities that I had, but that in some measure, in one kind or other, I should do the true part of a profitable Member of the State; whereupon examining exactly for the rest of my Life, what course I might take, and having sought (as I thought) all the ways to the Wood, to select the most proper, I concluded at the last, to set up my Staff at the Library-Door in *Oxon*; being thoroughly perswaded, that in my Solitude, and Surcease from the Common-Wealth Affairs, I could not busy my self to better purpose, than by reducing that Place (which then in every Part lay ruined and wast) to the publick use of Students. For the effecting whereof, I found my self furnished in a competent Proportion of such four kinds of Aids, as unless I had them all, there was no hope of good Success: For without some kind of Knowledge, as well in the Learned and Modern Tongues, as in sundry other sorts of scholastical Literature, without some Purse-ability to go through with the Charge, without great store of Honourable Friends, to further the Design, and without special good leisure to follow such a Work, it could have proved a vain Attempt and inconsiderate. But how well I have sped in all my Endeavours, and how full Provision I have made for the Benefit and Ease of all frequenters of the *Library*, that which I have already performed in Sight, that which besides I have given for the Maintenance of it, and that which hereafter I prupose to add, by way of Enlargement of that Place, (for the Project is cast, and whether I live or die, it shall be, God Willing, put in full Execution) will testify so truly and abundantly for me, as I need not be the Publisher of the Dignity and Worth of mine own Institution.

Written with mine own Hand, T. B.

from 'The Life of Sir Thomas Bodley, Written by himself' in Reliquiae Bodleianae

1816—Harriet (Westbrook) Shelley committed suicide by drowning herself in the Serpentine, in a fit of despair over Shelley's abandonment of her and their children in order to live with Mary Wollstonecraft Godwin

When the lamp is shattered
The light in the dust lies dead –
When the cloud is scattered
The rainbow's glory is shed.
When the lute is broken,
Sweet tones are remembered not;
When the lips have spoken,
Loved accents are soon forgot.

As music and splendour
Survive not the lamp and the lute,
The heart's echoes render
No song when the spirit is mute –
No song but sad dirges,
Like the wind through a ruined cell,
Or the mournful surges
That ring the dead seaman's knell.

When hearts have once mingled
Love first leaves the well-built nest;
The weak one is singled
To endure what it once possessed.
O Love! who bewailest
The frailty of all things here,
Why choose you the frailest
For your cradle, your home, and your bier?

Its passions will rock thee
As the storms rock the ravens on high;
Bright reason will mock thee,
Like the sun from a wintry sky.
From thy nest every rafter
Will rot, and thine eagle home
Leave the naked to laughter,
When leaves fall and cold winds come.

Percy Bysshe Shelley: 'Lines' (1824)

10 November 🖩

1739—Samuel Richardson began writing his first novel, Pamela

Dear Father and Mother,
I have great trouble, and some comfort, to acquaint you with. The trouble is that my good lady died of the illness I mentioned to you, and left us all much grieved for the loss of her: she was a dear good lady, and kind to all us her servants. Much I feared, that as I was taken by her ladyship to wait upon her person, I should be quite destitute again, and forced to return to you and my poor mother, who have enough to maintain yourselves; and, as my lady's goodness had put me to write and cast such accounts, and made me a little expert at my needle, and otherwise qualified above my degree, it was not every family that could have found a place that your poor Pamela was fit for: but God, whose graciousness to us we have so often experienced, put it into my good lady's heart, just an hour before she expired, to recommend to my young master all her servants, one by one; and when it came to my turn to be recommended, (for I was sobbing and crying at her pillow,) she could only say, – 'My dear son!' and so broke off a little; and then recovering, 'remember my poor Pamela.' – And these were some of her last words. O how my eyes run! Don't wonder to see the paper so blotted.
Well, but God's will must be done. And so comes the comfort, that I shall not be obliged to return back to be a clog upon my dear parents! For my master said, 'I will take care of you all, my good maidens. And for you, Pamela, (and took me by the hand; yes, he took my hand before them all,) 'for my dear Mother's sake, I will be a friend to you, and you shall take care of my linen.' God bless him! and pray with me, my dear father and mother, for a blessing upon him; for he has given mourning and a year's wages to all my lady's servants, and I having no wages as yet, (my lady having said she would do for me as I deserved) he ordered the housekeeper to give me mourning with the rest; and gave me with his own hand four golden guineas, and some silver, which were in my old lady's pocket when she died; and said, if I was a good girl, and faithful and diligent, he would be a friend to me, for his mother's sake. . . .

Samuel Richardson: from Pamela, *ch. 1*

A.D. 887—Asser began to teach Kind Alfred to translate from Latin, and the king immediately started to compile a book of his favourite quotations

In the same year also Alfred, king of the Anglo-Saxons, by divine inspiration began, on one and the same day, to read and to interpret . . . [On the sacred solemnity of St. Martin] we were both of us sitting in the king's chamber, talking on all kinds of subjects, as usual, and it happened that I read to him a quotation out of a certain book. He heard it attentively with both his ears, and addressed me with a thoughtful mind, showing me at the same moment a book which he carried in his bosom, wherein the daily courses and psalms, and prayers which he had read in his youth, were written, and he commanded me to write the same quotation in that book. Hearing this, and perceiving his ingenuous benevolence, and devout desire of studying the words of divine wisdom, I gave, though in secret, boundless thanks to Almighty God, who had implanted such a love of wisdom in the king's heart. But I could not find any empty space in that book wherein to write the quotation, for it was already full of various matters; wherefore I made a little delay, principally that I might stir up the bright intellect of the king to a higher acquaintance with the divine testimonies. Upon his urging me to make haste and write it quickly, I said to him, 'Are you willing that I should write that quotation on some leaf apart? For it is not certain whether we shall not find one or more other such extracts which will please you; and if that should so happen, we shall be glad that we have kept them apart.' 'Your plan is good', said he, and I gladly made haste to get ready a sheet, in the beginning of which I wrote what he bade me; and on that same day, I wrote therein, as I had anticipated, no less than three other quotations which pleased him; and from that time we daily talked together, and found out other quotations which pleased him, so that the sheet became full, and deservedly so; according as it is written, 'The just man builds upon a moderate foundation, and by degrees passes to greater things.' Thus, like a most productive bee, he flew here and there, asking questions as he went, until he had eagerly and unceasingly collected many various flowers of divine Scriptures, with which he thickly stored the cells of his mind.

Now when the first quotation was copied, he was eager at once to read, and to interpret in Saxon, and then to teach others; . . . and he continued to learn the flowers collected by certain masters, and to reduce them into the form of one book, as he was then able, although mixed one with another, until it became almost as large as a psalter. This book he called his ENCHIRIDION or MANUAL, because he carefully kept it at hand day and night and found, as he told me, no small consolation therein.

from Asser's Life of Alfred

12 November 🗓

1660—John Bunyan was arrested at the beginning of his twelve-year imprisonment in Bedford gaol

Upon the 12th of this instant November, 1660, I was desired by some of the friends in the country to come to teach at Samsell, by Harlington, in Bedfordshire. To whom I made a promise, if the Lord permitted, to be with them on the time aforesaid. The justice hearing thereof, (whose name is Mr. *Francis Wingate*) forthwith issued out his warrant to take me and bring me before him, and in the mean time to keep a very strong watch about the house where the meeting should be kept, as if we that was to meet together in that place did intend to do some fearful business, to the destruction of the country; when alas, the constable, when he came in, found us only with our Bibles in our hands, ready to speak and hear the word of God; for we was just about to begin to exercise. Nay, we had begun in prayer for the blessing of God upon our opportunity, intending to have preached the Word of the Lord unto them there present: But the constable coming in prevented us. So that I was taken and forced to depart the room. But had I been minded to have played the coward, I could have escaped, and kept out of his hands. For when I was come to my friend's house, there was whispering that that day I should be taken, for there was a warrant out to take me; which when my friend heard, he being somewhat timourous, questioned whether we had best have our meeting or not: And whether it might not be better for me to depart, lest they should take me and have me before the Justice, and after that send me to prison, (for he knew better than I what spirit they were of, living by them) to whom I said, no: By no means, I will not stir, neither will I have the meeting dismissed for this. Come, be of good cheer, let us not be daunted, our cause is good, we need not be ashamed of it, to preach God's word, it is so good a work, that we shall be well rewarded, if we suffer for that . . . After this I walked into the close, where I somewhat seriously considering the matter, this came into my mind: That I had shown myself hearty and courageous in my preaching, and had, blessed be Grace, made it my business to encourage others; therefore thought I, if I should now run, and make an escape, it will be of a very ill savour in the country. For what will my weak and newly converted brethren think of it? But that I was not so strong in deed, as I was in word. . . . Besides I thought, that seeing God of his mercy should chuse me to go upon the forlorn hope in this country; that is, to be the first, that should be opposed, for the Gospel; that if I should fly, it might be a discouragement to the whole body that might follow after . . . And so, as aforesaid, I begun the meeting: But being prevented by the constable's coming in with his warrant to take me, I could not proceed: But before I went away, I spake some words of counsel and encouragement to the people . . .

John Bunyan: from A Relation of the Imprisonment

1894—The Times *reported word received from the* Samoa Times *about Robert Louis Stevenson's last public speech, in which he thanked Samoan chiefs who had constructed a section of road for him*

Mr Stevenson proceeded:

'I will tell you, chiefs, that when I saw you working on that road, my heart grew warm, not with gratitude only, but with hope. It seemed to me that I read the promise of something good for Samoa; it seemed to me, as I looked at you, that you were a company of warriors in a battle fighting for the defence of our common country against all aggression. For there is a time to fight and a time to dig. You Samoans may fight, you may conquer twenty times and 30 times, and all will be in vain. There is but one way to defend Samoa. Hear it, before it is too late. It is to make roads and gardens, and care for your trees, and sell their produce wisely, and, in one word, to occupy and use your country. If you do not others will . . . It will not continue to be yours or your children's, if you occupy it for nothing. You and your children will in that case be cast out into outer darkness where shall be weeping and gnashing of teeth. For that is the law of God that passeth not away. I who speak to you have seen these things. I have seen them with my eyes, these judgements of God. I have seen them in Ireland, and I have seen them in the mountains of my own country, Scotland, and my heart was sad. . . . I do not speak of this lightly, because I love Samoa and her people. I love the land; I have chosen it to be my home while I live and my grave after I am dead; and I love the people and have chosen them to be my people to live and die with. And I see that the day is come now of the great battle – of the great and the last opportunity by which it shall be decided whether you are to pass away like these other races of which I have been speaking or to stand fast and have your children living and honouring your memory in the land you have received from your fathers. . . . Now is the time for the true champions of Samoa to stand forth. And who is the true champion of Samoa. It is not the man who blackens his face, and cuts down trees, and kills pigs and wounded men. It is the man who makes roads, who plants trees for food, who gathers harvests, and is a profitable servant before the Lord, using and improving that great talent that has been given him in trust. That is the brave soldier; that is the true champion; because all things in a country hang together like the links of the anchor cable, one by another; but the anchor itself is industry. . . .

14 November

[1667]—'To Knipp's lodging, whom I find not ready to go home with me ; and there stayed reading of Waller's verses, while she finished dressing, her husband being by . . .'

Samuel Pepys : Diary

On a girdle

That which her slender waist confined
Shall now my joyful temples bind;
No monarch but would give his crown
His arms might do what this has done.

It was my heaven's extremest sphere,
The pale which held that lovely deer,
My joy, my grief, my hope, my love,
Did all within this circle move!

A narrow compass, and yet there
Dwelt all that's good and all that's fair;
Give me but what this riband bound,
Take all the rest the sun goes round.

Song

Go, lovely rose!
Tell her that wastes her time and me
That now she knows,
When I resemble her to thee,
How sweet and fair she seems to be.

Tell her that's young
And shuns to have her graces spied,
That hadst thou sprung
In deserts where no men abide,
Thou must have uncommended died.

Small is the worth
Of beauty from the light retired;
Bid her come forth,
Suffer herself to be desired,
And not blush so to be admired.

Then die, that she
The common fate of all things rare
May read in thee;
How small a part of time they share
That are so wondrous sweet and fair!

Edmund Waller

1836—At her party for the ladies and gentleman of 'Cranford', Miss Jenkyns, carried the field on behalf of Dr Johnson, against such 'young beginners' as Mr Charles Dickens

When the trays reappeared with biscuits and wine, punctually at a quarter to nine, there was conversation, comparing of cards, and talking over tricks; but by and by Captain Brown sported a bit of literature.

'Have you seen any numbers of *The Pickwick Papers*?' said he. (They were then publishing in parts.) 'Capital things!'

Now Miss Jenkyns was daughter of a deceased rector of Cranford; and, on the strength of a number of manuscript sermons, and a pretty good library of divinity, considered herself literary, and looked upon any conversation about books as a challenge to her. . . .

'I must say, I don't think they are by any means equal to Dr. Johnson. Still, perhaps, the author is young. Let him persevere, and who knows what he may become if he will take the great Doctor for his model.' This was evidently too much for Captain Brown to take placidly . . .

'It is quite a different sort of thing, my dear madam', he began. . . . 'Just allow me to read you a scene out of this month's number. I had it only this morning, and I don't think the company can have read it yet.'

'As you please', said she, settling herself with an air of resignation. He read the account of the "swarry" which Sam Weller gave at Bath. Some of us laughed heartily. *I* did not dare, because I was staying in the house. Miss Jenkyns sat in patient gravity. When it was ended, she turned to me, and said, with mild dignity – 'Fetch me *Rasselas*, my dear, out of the bookroom.' When I had brought it to her she turned to Captain Brown – 'Now allow *me* to read you a scene, and then the present company can judge between your favourite, Mr. Boz, and Dr. Johnson.'

She read one of the conversations between Rasselas and Imlac, in a high-pitched majestic voice; and when she had ended she said, 'I imagine I am now justified in my preference of Dr. Johnson as a writer of fiction.' The Captain screwed his lips up, and drummed on the table, but he did not speak. She thought she would give a finishing blow or two. 'I consider it vulgar, and below the dignity of literature, to publish in numbers.'

'How was *The Rambler* published, ma'am?' asked Captain Brown, in a low voice, which I think Miss Jenkyns could not have heard. . . . She drew herself up with dignity, and only replied to Captain Brown's last remark by saying, with marked emphasis on every syllable, 'I prefer Dr. Johnson to Mr. Boz.'

It is said – I won't vouch for the fact – that Captain Brown was heard to say, *sotto voce*, 'D--n Dr. Johnson!' If he did, he was penitent afterwards, as he showed by going to stand near Miss Jenkyns's arm-chair, and endeavouring to beguile her into conversation on some more pleasing topic. But she was inexorable. . . .

Elizabeth Cleghorn Gaskell: from Cranford

1874—Joel Chandler Harris published the story of 'Brer Rabbit, Brer Fox, and the Tar Baby' in the Atlanta Constitution

===

'Didn't the fox *never* catch the rabbit, Uncle Remus?' asked the little boy the next evening.

'He come mighty nigh it, honey, sho's you bawn . . . Brer Fox went ter wuk en got 'im some tar, en mix it wid some turkentime, en fix up a contrapshun wat he call a Tar-Baby, en he tuck dish yer Tar-Baby en he sot 'er in de big road, en den he lay off in de bushes fer ter see wat de news wuz gwineter be. En he didn't hatter wait long, nudder, kaze bimeby here come Brer Rabbit pacin' down de road – lippity-clippity, clippity-lippity, – dez es sassy ez a jay-bird. Brer Fox, he lay low. Brer Rabbit come prancin' 'long twel he spy de Tar-Baby, en den he fotch up on his behime legs like he was 'stonished. De Tar-Baby, she sot dar, she did, en Brer Fox, he lay low.

'"Mawnin" sez Brer Rabbit, sezee – "nice wedder dis mawnin" sezee. . . . "How duz yo' sym'tums seem ter segashuate?" . . . Brer Fox, he wink his eye slow, en lay low, en de Tar-Baby, she ain't sayin' nuthin'.

"How you come on, den? Is you deaf?" sez Brer Rabbit, sezee. "Kaze if you is, I kin holler louder," sezee. . . . "Youer stuck up, dat's w'at you is . . . en I'm gwineter kyore you, dat's w'at I'm gwineter do," sezee.

'Brer Fox, he sorter chuckle in his stummuck, he did, but Tar-Baby ain't sayin' nuthin'.

'"I'm gwineter larn you howter talk ter 'spectubble fokes ef hit's de las' ack'," sez Brer Rabbit, sezee. "Ef you don't take off dat hat en tell me howdy, I'm gwineter bus' you wide open", sezee.

'Tar-Baby stay still, en Brer Fox, he lay low. Brer Rabbit keep on axin' 'im, en de Tar-Baby, she keep on sayin' nuthin', twel present'y Brer Rabbit draw back wid his fis', he did, en blip he tuck 'er side er de head. Right dar's whar he broke his merlasses jug. His fis' stuck, en he can't pull loose. De tar hilt 'im. But Tar-Baby, she stay still, en Brer Fox, he lay low.

"Ef you don't lemme loose, I'll knock you again," sez Brer Rabbit, sezee, en wid dat he fotch 'er a wipe wid de udder han', en dat stuck. Tar-Baby, she ain't sayin' nuthin', en Brer Fox, he lay low.

"Tu'n me loose, fo' I kick de nat'al stuffin' outen you", sez Brer Rabbit, sezee, but de Tar-Baby . . . she des hilt on, en den Brer Rabbit lose de use er his feet in de same way. . . . Den Brer Rabbit squall out dat ef de Tar-Baby don't tu'n 'im loose he butt 'er cranksided. En den he butted, en his head got stuck. Den Brer Fox, he sa'ntered fort', lookin' dez ez innercent ez wunner yo' mammy's mockin birds.

"Howdy, Brer Rabbit", sez Brer Fox, sezee. "You look sorter stuck up dis mawnin", sezee, en den he rolled on de groun', en laft en laft. . . .'

Joel Chandler Harris: from Uncle Remus and his Legends of the Old Plantations

1590—Sir Henry Lee resigned his office of Champion to Queen Elizabeth at the annual tourney described by George Peele in Polyhymnia

. . . these annuall exercises in armes . . . were first begun and occasioned by the right vertuous and honourable Sir Henry Lee . . . who . . . in the beginning of her happy reigne, voluntarily vowed (unlesse infirmity, age, or other accident did impeach him), during his life, to present himselfe at the tilt armed, the day aforesayd yeerely, there to performe, in honor of her sacred maiestie, the promise he formerly made . . . though true it is, that the author of that custome (being now by age overtaken) in the 33. yeere of her maiesties reigne resigned and recommended that office unto the right noble George Earle of Cumberland . . . On the 17. day of November, anno 1590, this honourable gentleman, together with the Earle . . . having first performed their service in armes, presented themselves unto her highnesse, at the foot of the staires under her gallery-window in the Tilt-yard at Westminster . . . Her maiestie, beholding these armed knights comming toward her, did suddenly heare a musicke so sweet and secret, as every one thereat greatly marveiled. . . . The music aforesayd was accompanied with these verses:

> His golden locks time hath to silver turn'd;
>   O time too swift, O swiftness never ceasing!
> His youth 'gainst time and age hath ever spurn'd,
>   But spurn'd in vain; youth waneth by increasing:
> Beauty, strength, youth, are flowers but fading seen;
> Duty, faith, love, are roots, and ever green.
>
> His helmet now shall make a hive for bees,
>   And, lovers' sonnets turn'd to holy psalms,
> A man-at-arms must now serve on his knees,
>   And feed on prayers, which are age his alms:
> But though from court to cottage he depart,
> His saint is sure of his unspotted heart.
>
> And when he saddest sits in homely cell,
>   He'll teach his swains this carol for a song, –
> 'Bless'd be the hearts that wish my sovereign well,
>   Cursed be the souls that think her any wrong!'
> Goddess, allow this aged man his right,
> To be your beadsman now that was your knight.

. . . After all these ceremonies for divers dayes hee ware upon his cloake a crown embroidered, with a certaine motto or device, but what his intention was, hemselfe best knoweth.

George Peele : from Polyhymnia

18 November 📖

1865—Mark Twain's first famous story, and the one which established his reputation as an outstanding humourist, was published in The Saturday Press *of New York, under its original title of 'Jim Smiley and His Jumping Frog'*

There was a feller here once by the name of *Jim* Smiley, in the winter of '49 – or may be it was the spring of '50 – I don't recollect exactly, somehow, though what makes me think it was one or the other is because I remember the big flume wasn't finished when he first came to the camp; but anyway, he was the curiosest man about always betting on anything that turned up you ever see, if he could get anybody to bet on the other side; and if he couldn't, he'd change sides. Anyway that suited the other man would suit him – anyway so's he's got a bet, *he* was satisfied . . .

Well, thish-yer Smiley had rat-terriers, and chicken cocks, and tom-cats, and all them kind of things, till you couldn't rest, and you couldn't fetch nothing for him to bet on but he'd match you. He ketched a frog one day, and took him home, and said he cal'klated to edercate him; and so he never done nothing for three months but set in his back yard and learn that frog to jump. And you bet you he *did* learn him, too? He'd give him a little punch behind, and the next minute you'd see that frog whirling in the air like a doughnut – see him turn one summerset, or may be a couple, if he got a good start, and come down flat-footed and all right, like a cat. He got him up so in the matter of catching flies, and kept him in practise so constant, that he'd nail a fly every time as far as he could see him. Smiley said all a frog wanted was education, and he could do most anything – and I believe him. Why, I've seen him set Dan'l Webster down here on the floor – Dan'l Webster was the name of the frog – and sing out, 'Flies, Dan'l, flies!' and quicker'n you could wink, he'd spring straight up, and snake a fly off'n the counter there, and flop down on the floor again as solid as a gob of mud, and fall to scratching the side of his head with his hind foot as indifferent as if he hand't no idea he'd been doin' any more'n any frog might do. You never see a frog so modest and straightfor'ard as he was, for all he was so gifted. And when it come to a fair and square jumping on a dead level, he could get over more ground at one straddle than any animal of his breed you ever see. Jumping on a dead level was his strong suit, you understand; and when it come to that, Smiley would ante up money on him as long as he had a red. Smiley was monstrous proud of his frog, and well he might be, for fellers that had travelled and been everywheres, all said he laid over any frog that ever *they* see.

Well, Smiley kept the beast in a little lattice box, and he used to fetch him down town sometimes and lay for a bet . . .

Mark Twain: from 'The Famous Jumping Frog of Calaveras County'

1863—The military cemetery was dedicated at Gettysburg, Pennsylvania. The shortest speech made on the occasion was that of President Lincoln

---

Fourscore and seven years ago our fathers brought forth on this continent a new nation, conceived in liberty and dedicated to the proposition that all men are created equal.

Now we are engaged in a great civil war, testing whether that nation or any nation so conceived and so dedicated can long endure. We are met on a great battlefield of that war. We have come to dedicate a portion of that field, as a final resting-place for those who here gave their lives that that nation might live. It is altogether fitting and proper that we should do this.

But, in a larger sense, we cannot dedicate – we cannot consecrate – we cannot hallow – this ground. The brave men, living and dead, who struggled here, have consecrated it, far above our poor power to add or detract. The world will little note, nor long remember, what we say here, but it can never forget what they did here. It is for us the living, rather, to be dedicated here to the unfinished work which they who fought here have so nobly advanced. It is rather for us to be here dedicated to the great task remaining before us – that from these honored dead we take increased devotion to that cause for which they gave the last full measure of devotion – that we here highly resolve that these dead shall not have died in vain – that this nation, under God, shall have a new birth of freedom – and that government of the people, by the people, for the people, shall not perish from the earth.

Abraham Lincoln: The Gettysburg Address

20 November

1777—William Pitt, Earl of Chatham, informed the House of Lords that in his opinion 'You cannot conquer America'

My Lords, this ruinous and ignominious situation, where we cannot act with success, nor suffer with honour, calls upon us to remonstrate in the strongest and loudest language of truth, to rescue the ear of Majesty from the delusions which surround it. The desperate state of our arms abroad is in part known: no man thinks more highly of them than I do: I love and honour the English troops: I know their virtues and their valour: I know they can achieve anything except impossibilities; and I know that the conquest of English America is an impossibility. You cannot, I venture to say it, you cannot conquer America. . . . What is your present situation there? We do not know the worst; but we know that in three campaigns we have done nothing and suffered much. . . . As to conquest, therefore, my lords, I repeat, it is impossible. – You may swell every expense, and every effort, still more extravagantly; pile and accumulate every assistance you can buy or borrow; traffic and barter with every pitiful little German prince; your efforts are for ever vain and impotent – doubly so from this mercenary aid on which you rely; for it irritates, to an incurable resentment, the minds of your enemies – to overrun them with the mercenary sons of rapine and plunder; devoting them and their possessions to the rapacity of hireling cruelty. If I were an American, as I am an Englishman, while a foreign troop was landed in my country, I would never lay down my arms – never – never – never. . . .

But, my Lords, who is the man, that in addition to these disgraces and mischiefs of our army, has dared to authorise and associate to our arms the tomahawk and scalping-knife of the savage? To call into civilised alliance, the wild and inhuman savage of the woods; to delegate to the merciless Indian the defence of disputed rights, and to wage the horrors of his barbarous war against our brethren? My Lords, these enormities cry aloud for redress and punishment; unless thoroughly done away, it will be a stain on our the national character – it is a violation of the Constitution – I believe it is against law. . . .

1769—The signature 'Junius' first appeared on a letter in the Publick Advertiser, *and started the speculation about their authorship which has not yet ceased*

'Call *Junius*!' From the crowd a shadow stalked,
    And at the name there was a general squeeze,
So that the very ghosts no longer walk'd
    In comfort, at their own aërial ease,
But all were ramm'd, and jamm'd (but to be balk'd,
    As we shall see), and jostled hands and knees,
Like wind compress'd and pent within a bladder,
Or like a human colic, which is sadder.

The shadow came – a tall, thin, grey-hair'd figure,
    That look'd as it had been a shade on earth;
Quick in its motions, with an air of vigour,
    But nought to mark its breeding or its birth;
Now it wax'd little, then again grew bigger,
    With now an air of gloom, or savage mirth;
But as you gazed upon its features, they
Changed every instant – to *what*, none could say.

The more intently the ghosts gazed, the less
    Could they distinguish whose the features were;
The Devil himself seem'd puzzled even to guess;
    They varied like a dream – now here, now there;
And several people swore from out the press,
    They knew him perfectly; and one could swear
He was his father; upon which another
Was sure he was his mother's cousin's brother.

For sometimes he like Cerberus would seem –
    'Three gentlemen at once' (as sagely says
Good Mrs. Malaprop); then you might deem
    That he was not even *one*; now many rays
Were flashing round him; and now a thick steam
    Hid him from sight – like fogs on London days:
Now Burke, now Tooke, he grew to people's fancies,
And certes often like Sir Philip Francis.

Lord Byron: from 'The Vision of Judgment'

22 November 📖

[1697]—St Cecilia's Day, for which John Dryden wrote 'Alexander's Feast, or, The Power of Music', the second of his productions for this occasion

---

Virgil was hardly finished when our author distinguished himself by the immortal Ode to St. Cecilia's Day, commonly called 'Alexander's Feast'. . . . He had been solicited to undertake it by the stewards of the Musical Meeting, which had for several years met to celebrate the feast of St. Cecilia, their patroness, and whom he had formerly gratified by a similar performance. In September 1697, Dryden writes to his son: – 'In the meantime, I am writing a song for St. Cecilia's feast: who, you know, is the patroness of music. This is troublesome, and no way beneficial; but I could not deny the stewards, who came in a body to my house to desire that kindness, one of them being Mr. Bridgeman, whose parents are your mother's friends.' . . . On the other hand, the following anecdote is told upon very respectable authority. 'Mr. St. John, afterwards Lord Bolingbroke, happening to pay a morning visit to Dryden, whom he always respected, found him in an unusual agitation of spirits, even to a trembling. On inquiring the cause, "I have been up all night", replied the old bard: "my musical friends made me promise to write them an Ode for their feast of St. Cecilia. I have been so struck with the subject which occurred to me, that I could not leave it till I had *completed* it; here it is, *finished* at one sitting." And immediately he showed him *this* Ode which places the British lyric poetry above that of any other nation.' . . .

Derrick, in his 'Life of Dryden', tells us . . . that the society paid Dryden £40 for this sublime Ode, which seems to have been more than the bard expected at commencing his labour. The music for this celebrated poem was originally composed by Jeremiah Clarke . . . [but] his composition was not judged worthy of publication. The Ode, after some impertinent alterations, made by Hughes, at the request of Sir Richard Steele, was set to music by Clayton, who, with Steele, managed a public concert in 1711; but neither was this a successful essay to connect the poem with the art it celebrated. At length, in 1736, 'Alexander's Feast' was set by Handel, and performed in the Theatre Royal, Covent Garden, with the full success which the combined talents of the poet and the musician seemed to insure. 'The public expectations and the effects of this representation (says Dr. Burney) seem to have been correspondent, for the next day we are told in the public papers that "there never was, upon the like occasion, so numerous and splendid an audience at any theatre in London, there being at least thirteen hundred persons present. . . ."'

Indeed, although the music was at first less successful, the poetry received, even in the author's time, all the applause which its unrivalled excellence demanded. 'I am glad to hear from all hands', says Dryden in a letter to Tonson, 'that my Ode is esteemed the best of all my poetry, by all the town. I thought so myself when I writ it; but, being old, I mistrusted my own judgment.'

from Sir Walter Scott's 'Life of Dryden', vol. I
of his The Dramatic Works of John Dryden,
ed. by George Sainsbury, Edinburgh, 1882

1850—'Mr. John Oakhurst, gambler' . . . 'struck a streak of bad luck'

As Mr. John Oakhurst, gambler, stepped into the main street of Poker Flat on the morning of the twenty-third of November, 1850, he was conscious of a change in the moral atmosphere since the preceding night. Two or three men, conversing earnestly together, ceased as he approached, and exchanged significant glances. There was a Sabbath lull in the air, which, in a settlement unused to Sabbath influences, looked ominous.

Mr. Oakhurst's calm, handsome face betrayed small concern in these indications. Whether he was conscious of any pre-disposing cause, was another question. 'I reckon they're after somebody', he reflected; 'likely it's me'. . . .

In point of fact, Poker Flat was 'after somebody'. It had lately suffered the loss of several thousand dollars, two valuable horses, and a prominent citizen. It was experiencing a spasm of virtuous reaction, quite as lawless and ungovernable as any of the acts that had provoked it. A secret committee had determined to rid the town of all improper persons. This was done permanently in regard of two men who were then hanging from the boughs of a sycamore in the gulch, and temporarily in the banishment of certain other objectionable characters. I regret to say that some of these were ladies. . . .

Mr. Oakhurst was right in supposing that he was included . . . A few of the committee had urged hanging him as a possible example, and a sure method of reimbursing themselves from his pockets of the sums he had won from them. 'It's agin justice', said Jim Wheeler, 'to let this yer young man from Roaring Camp – an entire stranger – carry away our money.' But a crude sentiment of equity residing in the breasts of those who had been fortunate enough to win from Mr. Oakhurst overruled this narrower local prejudice.

Mr. Oakhurst received his sentence with philosophic calmness, none the less coolly that he was aware of the hesitation of his judges. He was too much of a gambler not to accept Fate. With him life was at best an uncertain game, and he recognized the usual percentage in favour of the dealer.

A party of armed men accompanied the deported wickedness of Poker Flat to the outskirts of the settlement. . . . . As the escort disappeared, their pent-up feelings found vent in a few hysterical tears from the Duchess, some bad language from Mother Shipton, and a Parthian volley of expletives from Uncle Billy. The philosophic Oakhurst alone remained silent. . . .

Bret Harte : from The Outcasts of Poker Flat

24 November

1859—Charles Darwin published The Origin of Species, *of which Thomas Huxley became one of the great defenders and proponents*

Do not allow yourselves to be misled by the common notion that an hypothesis is untrustworthy simply because it is an hypothesis. It is often urged, in respect of some scientific conclusion, that, after all, it is only an hypothesis. But what more have we to guide us in nine-tenths of the most important affairs of daily life than hypotheses, and often very ill-based ones? So that in science, where the evidence of an hypothesis is subjected to the most rigid examination, we may rightly pursue the same course. You may have hypotheses and hypotheses. A man may say, if he likes, that the moon is made of green cheese: that is an hypothesis. But another man, who had devoted a great deal of time and attention to the subject, and availed himself of the most powerful telescopes and the results of the observations of others, declares that in his opinion it is probably composed of materials very similar to those of which our own earth is made up: and that is also an hypothesis. But I need not tell you that there is an enormous difference in the value of the two hypotheses. The one which is based on sound scientific knowledge is sure to have a corresponding value; and that which is a mere hasty random guess is likely to have but little value.

Every great step in our progress in discovering causes has been made in exactly the same way as that which I have detailed to you. A person observing the occurrence of certain facts and phenomena asks, naturally enough, what process, what kind of operation known to occur in Nature applied to the particular case, will unravel and explain the mystery? Hence you have the scientific hypothesis; and its value will be proportionate to the care and completeness with which its basis has been tested and verified. It is in these matters as in the commonest affairs of practical life: the guess of the fool will be folly, while the guess of the wise man will contain wisdom. In all cases, you will see that the value of the result depends on the patience and faithfulness with which the investigator applies to his hypothesis every possible kind of verification.

Thomas Huxley: Darwiniana

📖 25 November (St Catherine's Day)

1925—D. H. Lawrence, having fled to Italy, when unable to get a re-entry permit to the United States, found himself homesick for his ranch in New Mexico

There is a bright moon, so that even the vines make a shadow, and the Mediterranean has a broad white shimmer between its dimness. By the shore, the lights of the old houses twinkle quietly, and out of the wall of the headland advances the glare of a locomotive's lamp. It is a feast day, St. Catherine's Day, and the men are all sitting round the little tables, down below, drinking wine or vermouth.

And what about the little ranch in New Mexico? The time is different there: but I too have drunk my glass to St. Catherine, so I can't be bothered to reckon. I consider that there, too, the moon is in the south-east, standing, as it were, over Santa Fë beyond the bend of those mountains of Picoris.

Sono io! say the Italians. I am I. Which sounds simpler than it is.

Because which I am I, after all, now that I have drunk a glass also to St. Catherine, and the moon shines over the sea, and my thoughts, just because they are fleetingly occupied by the moon on the Mediterranean, and ringing with the last farewell: *Dunque, Signore! di nuove!* – must needs follow the moon-track south-west, to the great South-west, where the ranch is.

They say: *in vino veritas*. Bah! They say so much. But in the wine of St. Catherine, my little ranch, and the three horses down among the timber. Or if it has snowed, the horses are gone away, and it is snow, and the moon shines on the alfalfa slope, between the pines, and the cabins are blind. Only the big pine-tree in front of the house, standing still unconcerned, alive.

Perhaps when I have *Weh* at all, my *Heimweh* is for the tree in front of the house, the overshadowing tree whose green top one never looks at. But on the trunk one hangs the various odds and ends of iron things. It is so near. One goes out of the door, and the tree-trunk is there, like a guardian angel. . . .

And the Mediterranean whispers in the distance, a sound like in a shell. And save that somebody is whistling, the night is very bright and still. The Mediterranean, so eternally, the very symbol of youth! And Italy, so reputedly old, yet forever so childlike and naive! Never, never for a moment able to comprehend the wonderful, hoary age of America, the continent of the afterwards.

I wonder if I am here, or if I am just going to bed at the ranch. Perhaps looking in Montgomery Ward's catalogue for something for Christmas, and drinking moonshine and hot water, since it is cold. Go out and look if the chickens are shut up warm: if the horses are in sight: if Susan, the black cow, has gone to her nest among the trees, for the night . . .

D. H. Lawrence: from the essay ' A Little Moonshine with Lemon', in Mornings in Mexico

26 November 🔖

[1812?]—At the Netherfield Ball, the prejudiced Miss Elizabeth Bennett danced with the proud Mr Darcy

---

The latter part of this address was scarcely heard by Darcy; but Sir William's allusion to his friend seemed to strike him forcibly, and his eyes were directed with a very serious expression towards Bingley and Jane, who were dancing together. Recovering himself, shortly, he turned to his partner and said, 'Sir William's interruption has made me forget what we were talking of.'

'I do not think we were speaking at all. Sir William could not have interrupted any two people in the room who had less to say for themselves. We have tried two or three subjects already without success, and what we are to talk of next I cannot imagine.'

'What think you of books?' said he, smiling.

'Books – Oh! no. I am sure we never read the same, or not with the same feelings.'

'I am sorry you think so; but if that be the case, there can at least be no want of subject. We may compare our different opinions.'

'No – I cannot talk of books in a ball-room; my head is always full of something else.'

'The *present* always occupies you in such scenes – does it?' said he, with a look of doubt.

'Yes, always', she replied, without knowing what she said, for her thoughts had wandered far from the subject, as soon afterwards appeared by her suddenly exclaiming, 'I remember hearing you once say, Mr. Darcy, that you hardly ever forgave, that your resentment once created was unappeasable. You are very cautious, I suppose, as to its *being created*.'

'I am', said he, with a firm voice.

'And never allow yourself to be blinded by prejudice?'

'I hope not.'

'It is particularly incumbent on those who never change their opinion, to be secure of judging properly at first.'

'May I ask to what these questions tend?'

'Merely to the illustration of *your* character', said she, endeavouring to shake off her gravity. 'I am trying to make it out.'

'And what is your success?'

She shook her head. 'I do not get on at all. I hear such different accounts of you as puzzle me exceedingly. . . . But if I do not take your likeness now, I may never have another opportunity.'

'I would by no means suspend any pleasure of yours', he coldly replied. She said no more, and they went down the other dance and parted in silence; on each side dissatisfied, though not to an equal degree, for in Darcy's breast there was a tolerable powerful feeling towards her, which soon procured her pardon, and directed all his anger against another.

Jane Austen: from Pride and Prejudice, *ch. 18*

1797—George Canning's 'Sapphics. The Friend of Humanity and the Knife-grinder', a parody of Robert Southey's poem 'The Widow', was published in The Anti-Jacobin

---

Friend of Humanity: 'Needy Knife-grinder! whither are you going?
Rough is the road, your wheel is out of order –
Bleak blows the blast; your hat has got a hole in't,
So have your breeches! . . .

'Tell me, Knife-grinder, how came you to grind knives?
Did some rich man tyrannically use you?
Was it the squire? or parson of the parish?
Or the attorney? . . .

'Have you not read the Rights of Man, by Tom Paine?
Drops of compassion tremble on my eyelids,
Ready to fall, as soon as you have told your
Pitiful story.'

Knife-grinder: 'Story! God bless you! I have none to tell, sir,
Only last night a-drinking at the Chequers,
This poor old hat and breeches, as you see
Were torn in a scuffle . . .

'I should be glad to drink your Honour's health in
A pot of beer, if you will give me sixpence;
But for my part, I never love to meddle
With politics, sir.'

Friend of Humanity: 'I give thee sixpence! I will see thee damned first –
Wretch! whom no sense of wrong can rouse to vengeance –
Sordid, unfeeling, reprobate, degraded,
Spiritless outcast!'

(Kicks the Knife-grinder, overturns his wheel, and exits in a transport of Republican enthusiasm and universal philanthropy.)

1660—The 'meeting which founded the Royal Society' took place, with a lecture given by Sir Christopher Wren

With Courage and Success you the bold work begin;
    Your cradle has not idle bin:
None e're but Hercules and you could be
At five years Age worthy a History.
    And ne're did Fortune better yet
    Th'Historian to the Story fit.
    As you from all old Errors free
And purge the Body of Philosophy;

Philosophy the great and only Heir
    Of all that Human Knowledge which has bin
Unforfeited by Man's rebellious Sin,
    Though full of years He do appear,
(Philosophy I say, and call it, He,
For whatsoe'er the Painters Fancy be,
    It a Male Virtu seems to me)
Has still bin kept in Nonage till of late,
Nor manag'd or enjoy'd his vaste Estate;
Three or four thousand years one would have thought
To ripeness and perfection might have brought
    A Science so well bred and nurst.

From you great Champions, we expect to get
These spacious Countries but discover'd yet;
Countries where yet instead of Nature, we
Her Images and Idols worship'd see.
These large and wealthy Regions to subdue,
Though Learning has whole Armies at command,
    Quarter'd about in every Land,
A better Troop she ne're together drew.

Abraham Cowley: from 'To the Royal Society,' which was published as a prefatory 'blurb' to Sprat's History of the Royal Society

1698—'Mr. Dennis, his book, called a Vindication of the Stage, in answer to Collier . . . for asserting that the people of England are most prone to rebellion of any in the world . . . the court ordered an indictment against him, and the Attorney general to prosecute him'

Luttrell: Brief historical relation of State Affairs . . .

In short; Nothing can be more disserviable to Probity and Religion, than the management of the *Stage*. It cherishes those Passions, and rewards those Vices, which 'tis the business of Reason to discountenance. It strikes at the Root of Principle, draws off the Inclinations from Virtue, and spoils good Education: 'Tis the most effectual means to baffle the Force of Discipline, to emasculate Peoples Spirits, and Debauch their Manners. How many of the Unwary have these *Syrens* devour'd? And how often has the best Blood been tainted with this Infection? . . . the Mischief spreads dayly, and the Malignity grows more envenom'd. The Feavour works up towards Madness, and will scarely endure to be touch'd. . . .

Jeremy Collier: from A Short View of the Immorality and Profaneness of the English Stage

Now, there is no nation in *Europe*, as has been observ'd a thousand times, that is so generally addicted to the Spleen, as the *English* . . . from the reigning Distemper of the Clime, which is inseparable from the Spleen; from that gloomy and sullen Temper, which is generally spread through the Nation; from that natural Discontentedness, which makes us so uneasy to one another, because we are so uneasy to ourselves; and lastly, from our Jealousies and Suspicions, which . . . have so often made us dangerous to the Government, and, by consequence, to ourselves. . . . it follows, That the *English*, to be happy, have more need, than other people, of something that will raise their Passions in such a manner, as shall be agreeable to their Reasons, and that, by consequence, they have more need of the Drama. . . .

The Drama, and particularly Tragedy, is among other Reasons useful to Government, because it is proper to restrain a People from Rebellion and Disobedience, and to keep them in good Correspondence among themselves; For this Reason, the Drama may be said to be instrumental in a peculiar Manner to the Welfare of the *English* government; because there is no People on the Face of the Earth, so prone to Rebellion as the *English* . . . and the only Civil War which has been amongst us . . . is notoriously known to have been begun, and carried on by those, who had an utter Aversion to the Stage . . .

John Dennis: from The Usefulness of the Stage, to the Happiness of Mankind

30 November (St Andrew's Day) 🚩

1533–41(?)—Nicholas Udall was headmaster of Eton College. Since plays were acted annually under the headmaster's direction 'about the Feast of St. Andrew', his Ralph Roister-Doister, *one of the first English comedies, was probably written and first acted during this period*

Roister Doister is my name,
A lusty brute I am the same,
    I mun be married a Sunday.   *Chorus:* I mun be married a Sunday,
                                         I mun be married a Sunday,
                             Whosoever shall come that way,
                                          I mun be married a Sunday.

Christian Custance have I found,
A widow worth a thousand pound,   I mun . . . &c.

Custance is as sweet as honey,
I her lamb and she my coney,   I mun . . . &c.

When we shall make our wedding feast,
There shall be cheer for man and beast,   I mun be married a Sunday . . . &c.

                   *   *   *   *   *

Whoso to marry a minion wife,
    Hath had good chance and hap,
Must love her and cherish her all his life,
    And dandle her in his lap.

If she will fare well, if she will go gay,
    A good husband ever still,
Whatever she lust to do, or to say,
    Must let her have her own will.

About what affairs soever he go,
    He must show her all his mind.
None of his counsel she may be kept fro,
    Else is he a man unkind.

Nicholas Udall: from 'Certain Songs to be Sung by those which shall use this comedy or interlude',
i.e., Ralph Roister-Doister

December.

1589—The first instalment of Edmund Spenser's The Faerie Queene *was entered at Stationers' Hall*

Lo I the man, whose Muse whilome did maske,
　　As time her taught, in lowly Shepheards weeds,
　　Am now enforst a far unfitter taske,
　　For trumpets sterne to chaunge mine Oaten reeds,
　　And sing of Knights and Ladies gentle deeds;
　　Whose prayers having slept in silence long,
　　Me, all too meane, the sacred Muse areeds
　　To blazon broad emongst her learned throng:
Fierce warres and faithful loves shall moralize my song.

Helpe then, O holy Virgin chiefe of nine,
　　Thy weaker Novice to performe thy will,
　　Lay forth out of thine everlasting scryne
　　The antique rolles, which there lye hidden still,
　　Of Faerie knights and fairest Tanaquill,
　　Whom that most noble Briton Prince so long
　　Sought through the world, and suffered so much ill,
　　That I must rue his undeserved wrong:
O helpe thou my weake wit, and sharpen my dull tong.

And thou most dreaded impe of highest Jove,
　　Faire Venus sonne, that with thy cruell dart
　　At that good knight so cunningly didst rove,
　　That glorious fire it kindled in his hart,
　　Lay now thy deadly Heben bow apart,
　　And with thy mother milde come to mine ayde:
　　Come both, and with you bring triumphant Mart,
　　In loves and gentle jollities arrayd,
After his murdrous spoiles and bloudy rage allayd.

And with them eke, O Goddesse heavenly bright,
　　Mirrour of grace and Majestie divine,
　　Great Lady of the greatest Isle, whose light
　　Like Phoebus lampe throughout the world doth shine,
　　Shed thy faire beames into my feeble eyne,
　　And raise my thoughts too humble and too vile,
　　To thinke of that true glorious type of thine,
　　The argument of mine afflicted stile:
The which to heare, vouchsafe, O dearest dred a-while.

From Book I

2 December 🎭

1603—As You Like It *was reportedly performed by Shakespeare's company at Wilton House, home of the Earl of Pembroke, with Shakespeare appearing in one of the roles*

Under the greenwood tree
Who loves to lie with me,
And tune his merry note
Unto the sweet bird's throat,
Come hither, come hither, come hither:
Here shall he see
No enemy
But winter and rough weather.

Who doth ambition shun
And loves to live i' the sun,
Seeking the food he eats,
And pleased with what he gets,
Come hither, come hither, come hither:
Here shall he see
No enemy
But winter and rough weather.

*   *   *   *   *

Blow, blow, thou winter wind,
Thou art not so unkind
   As man's ingratitude;
Thy tooth is not so keen
Because thou art not seen,
   Although thy breath be rude.
Heigh-ho! sing, heigh-ho! unto the green holly;
Most friendship is feigning, most loving mere folly:
   Then, heigh-ho, the holly!
     This life is most jolly.

Freeze, freeze, thou bitter sky,
Thou dost not bite so nigh
   As benefits forgot:
Though thou the waters warp,
Thy sting is not so sharp
   As friend remembered not.
Heigh-ho! sing, heigh-ho!... etc.

1896—The second edition of Hilaire Belloc's The Bad Child's Book of Beasts
appeared, and sold out in four days as the first edition had done before

I call you bad, my little child,
    Upon the title page,
Because a manner rude and wild
    Is common at your age.

The moral of this priceless work
    (If rightly understood)
Will make you – from a little Turk –
    Unnaturally good.

Do not as evil children do,
    Who on the slightest grounds
Will imitate the Kangaroo,
    With wild unmeaning bounds.

Do not as children badly bred,
    Who eat like little Hogs,
And when they have to go to bed
    Will whine like Puppy Dogs:

Who take their manners from the Ape,
    Their habits from the Bear,
Indulge the loud unseemly jape,
    And never brush their hair.

But so control your actions that
    Your friends may all repeat,
'This child is dainty as the Cat,
    And as the Owl discreet.'

> *Hilaire Belloc: 'The Introduction' to* The Bad
> Child's Book of Beasts

4 December

1877—Samuel Butler's Life and Habit *was published on his forty-second birthday*

. . . we are in the habit of considering that our personality, or soul, no matter where it begins or ends, and no matter what it comprises, is nevertheless a single thing, uncompounded of other souls. Yet there is nothing more certain than that this is not at all the case, but that every individual person is a compound creature, being made up of an infinite number of distinct centres of sensation and will, each one of which is personal, and has a soul and individual existence, a reproductive system, intelligence, and memory of its own, with probably its hopes and fears, its times of scarcity and repletion, and a strong conviction that it is itself the centre of the universe.

True, no one is aware of more than one individuality in his own person at one time. We are, indeed, often greatly influenced by other people, so much so, that we act on many occasions in accordance with their will rather than our own, making our actions answer to their sensations, and register the conclusions of their cerebral action and not our own; for the time being, we become so completely part of them, that we are ready to do things most distasteful and dangerous to us, if they think it for their advantage that we should do so. Thus we sometimes see people become mere processes of their wives or nearest relations. Yet there is a something which blinds us, so that we cannot see how completely we are possessed by the souls which influence us upon these occasions. We still think we are ourselves, and ourselves only, and are as certain as we can be of any fact, that we are single sentient beings, uncompounded of other sentient beings, and that our action is determined by the sole operation of a single will.

But in reality, over and above this possession of our souls by others of our own species, the will of the lower animals often enters into our bodies and possesses them, making us do as they will, and not as we will; as, for example, when people try to drive pigs, or are run away with by a restive horse, or are attacked by a savage animal which masters them. It is absurd to say that a person is a single 'ego' when he is in the clutches of a lion. Even when we are alone, and uninfluenced by other people except in so far as we remember their wishes, we yet generally conform to the usages which the current feeling of our peers has taught us to respect; their will having so mastered our original nature, that, do what we may, we can never again separate ourselves and dwell in the isolation of our own single personality. . . .

Samuel Butler : from Life and Habit

1620—Robert Burton, having prepared The Anatomy of Melancholy *for the press, wrote 'The Conclusion of the Author to the Reader' to be appended to it*

. . . since I have now put my selfe upon the stage, I must undergo and abide the censure of it, *iacta est alea*, and I may not escape it. It is most true . . . our style bewrayes us, and as hunters find their game by the trace, so is a man described by his writings. I have laid my selfe open (I know it) in this Treatise, and shall be censured I doubt not, yet this is some comfort, *ut palata sic iudicia*, our censures are as various as our palates: If I be taxed, exploded by some, I shall happily be as much approved and commended by others. It was *Democritus* fortune . . . and 'tis the common doome of all writers: I seeke not to be commended; . . . I would not be vilified. I feare good mens censures, & *linguas mancipiorum contemno*, as the barking of a dogge, I securely contemne the malitious and scurrile obloquies, flouts, calumnies of those railers and detracters, I scorne the rest. . . . I am none of the best of you, I am none of the meanest; Howsoever, I am now come to retract some part of that which I have writ . . .

> When I peruse this tract which I have writ,
> I am abash'd, and much I hold vnfit.

I could wish it otherwise, expunged, and to this end I have annexed this Apologetical *Appendix*, to crave pardon for that which is amisse. I doe suspect some precedent passages have bin distasteful, as too Satyricall & bitter; some again as too Comicall, homely, broad, or slightly spoken. . . . I should have perused, corrected and amended this Tract, but I had not that happy leasure, no *amanuenses*, assistants, and was enforced as a Beare doth her whelpes, to bring forth this confused lumpe, and had not space to licke in into form, as she doth her young ones; but even to publish it, as it was written at first, once for all, in an extemporanean stile . . . out of a confused company of notes; *effudi quicquid dictavit Genuis meus*, and writ with as small deliberation, as I doe ordinarily speake. So that as a river runs precipitate & swift, & sometimes dull and slow; now direct, now *per ambages* about; now deepe then shallow; now muddy then cleere; now broad, then narrow doth my style flowe, now more serious, then light, now more elaborate or remisse; Comicall, Satyricall, as the present subject required, or as at that time I was affected. And if thou vouchsafe to read this Treatise, it shall seeme no otherwise to thee, then the way to an ordinary traveller; sometimes faire, sometimes foule, here Champion, there inclosed; barren in one place, better soile in another; by woods, groues, hills, dales, plaines, &c. I shal lead thee . . . through variety of objects, that which thou shalt like and dislike.

Robert Burton: from The Anatomy of Melancholy, *'The Conclusion . . . to the Reader'*

6 December

1933—Judge John M. Woolsey of the U.S. District Court (New York) handed down his decision to lift the ban on James Joyce's novel, Ulysses

In writing 'Ulysses', Joyce sought to make a serious experiment in a new, if not wholly novel, literary genre. He takes persons of the lower middle class living in Dublin in 1904 and seeks not only to describe what they did on a certain day early in June of that year as they went about the City bent on their usual occupations, but also to tell what many of them thought about the while.

Joyce has attempted – it seems to me, with astonishing success – to show how the screen of consciousness with its ever-shifting kaleidoscopic impressions carries, as it were on a plastic palimpsest, not only what is in the focus of each man's observation of the actual things about him, but also in a penumbral zone residua of past impressions, some recent and some drawn up by association from the domain of the subconscious. He shows how each of these impressions affects the life and behaviour of the character which he is describing. . . .

To convey by words an effect which obviously lends itself more appropriately to a graphic technique, accounts, it seems to me, for much of the obscurity which meets a reader of 'Ulysses'. And it also explains another aspect of the book, which I have further to consider, namely, Joyce's sincerity and his honest effort to show exactly how the minds of his characters operate.

If Joyce did not attempt to be honest in developing the technique which he has adopted in 'Ulysses' the result would be psychologically misleading and thus unfaithful to his chosen technique. Such an attitude would be artistically inexcusable. It is because Joyce has been loyal to his technique and has not funked its necessary implications, but has honestly attempted to tell fully what his characters think about, that he has been the subject of so many attacks and that his purpose has been so often misunderstood and misrepresented. For his attempt sincerely and honestly to realize his objective has required him incidentally to use certain words which are generally considered dirty words. . . .

The words which are criticized as dirty are old Saxon words known to almost all men and, I venture, to many women, and are such words as would be naturally and habitually used, I believe, by the types of folk whose life, physical and mental, Joyce is seeking to describe. In respect of the recurrent emergence of the theme of sex in the minds of his characters, it must always be remembered that his locale was Celtic and his season Spring. . . . 'Ulysses' is not an easy book to read. It is brilliant and dull, intelligible and obscure by turns. In many places, it seems to me disgusting, but although it contains, as I have mentioned above, many words usually considered dirty, I have not found anything that I consider dirt for dirt's sake. . . .

If one does not wish to associate with such folk as Joyce describes, that is one's own choice. In order to avoid indirect contact with them one may not wish to read 'Ulysses'; that is quite understandable. But when such a real artist in words . . . seeks to draw a true picture of the lower middle class in a European city, ought it to be impossible for the American public legally to see that picture?

1875—'Five Franciscan Nuns, exiles by the Falk Laws, drowned between midnight and morning' in the wreck of the 'Deutschland', and gave the occasion for Gerard Manley Hopkins to begin writing seriously

You ask do I write verse myself. What I had written I burnt before I became a Jesuit and resolved to write no more, as not belonging to my profession, unless it were by the wish of my superiors; so for seven years I wrote nothing but two or three little presentation pieces which occasion called for. But when in the winter of '75 the Deutschland was wrecked in the mouth of the Thames and five Franciscan nuns, exiles from Germany by the Falck Laws, aboard of her were drowned I was affected by the account and happening to say so to my rector he said that he wished someone would write a poem on the subject. On this hint I set to work, and though my hand was out at first, produced one. I had long had haunting my ear the echo of a new rhythm which I now realized on paper. To speak shortly, it consists in scanning by accents or stresses alone, without any account of the number of syllables, so that a foot may be one strong syllable or it may be many light and one strong. I do not say the idea is altogether new; there are hints of it in music, in nursery ryhmes and popular jingles, in the poets themselves, and, since then, I have seen it talked about as a thing possible in critics. Here are instances – 'Díng, dóng, béll Pússy's ín the wéll; *Whó pút* her ín? Líttle Jóhnny Thín. *Whó púlled* her óut? Líttle Jóhnny Stóut.' For if each line has three stresses or three feet it follows that some of the feet are of one syllable only. So too Óne, twó, Búckle my shóe' *passim.* In Campbell you have 'Ánd the fléet alóng the *déep próudly* shóne' – 'It' was tén of Ápril *mórn bý* the chime' etc.; in Shakespeare 'Whý shd. *thís* désert bé? 'corrected wrongly by the editors; in Moore a little melody I cannot quote; etc. But no one has professedly used it and made it the principle throughout, that I know of. Nevertheless to me it appears, I own, to be a better and more natural principle than the ordinary system, much more flexible, and capable of much greater effects. However I had to mark the stresses in blue chalk, and this and my rhymes carried on from one line into another and certain chimes suggested by the Welsh poetry I had been reading (what they call *cynghanedd*) and a great many more oddnesses could not but dismay an editor's eye, so that when I offered it to our magazine the *Month*, though at first they accepted it, after a time they withdrew and dared not print it. After writing this I held myself free to compose, but cannot find it in my conscience to spend time upon it; so I have done little and shall do less. But I wrote a shorter piece on the Eurydice, also in 'sprung rhythm', as I call it, but simpler, shorter, and without marks, and offered the *Month* that too, but they did not like it either. . . .

Gerard Manley Hopkins to R. W. Dixon, 5 October 1878

1709—Mr Isaac Bickerstaff, bachelor, condescended to advise his sister on the way to hold her husband's affection

My Brother *Tranquillus* being gone out of Town for some Days, my sister *Jenny* sent me Word she would come and dine with me, and therefore desired me to have no other Company. I took Care accordingly, and was not a little pleased to see her enter the Room with a decent and Matron-like Behaviour, which I thought very much became her. I saw she had a great deal to say to me, and easily discovered in her Eyes, and the Air of her Countenance, that she had abundance of Satisfaction in her Heart, which she longed to communicate. . . .

I have every Thing, says she, in *Tranquillus* that I can wish for; and enjoy in him (what indeed you have told me were to be met with in a good husband) the Fondness of a Lover, the Tenderness of a Parent, and the Intimacy of a Friend. It transported me to see her Eyes swimming in Tears of Affection when she spoke: And is there not, Dear Sister, said I, more Pleasure in the Possession of such a Man, than in all the little Impertinences of Balls, Assemblies, and Equipage, which it cost me so much pains to make you contemn? She answered, smiling, *Tranquillus* has made me a sincere Convert in a few Weeks, tho' I am afraid you could not have done it in your whole Life. To tell you truly, I have only one Fear hanging upon me, which is apt to give me Trouble in the midst of all my Satisfactions: I am afraid, you must know, that I shall not always make the same amiable Appearance in his Eye that I do at present. You know, Brother *Bickerstaff*, that you have the Reputation of a Conjuror; and if you have any one Secret in your Art to make your Sister always beautiful, I should be happier than if I were Mistress of all the Worlds you have shown me in a Starry Night – *Jenny* (said I) without having Recourse to Magick, I shall give you one plain Rule, that will not fail of making you always amiable to a Man who has so great a Passion for you, and is of so equal and reasonable a Temper as *Tranquillus*. Endeavour to please, and you must please; be always in the same Disposition as you are when you ask for this Secret, and you may take my Word, you will never want it. An inviolable Fidelity, good Humour, and Complacency of Temper, outlive all the Charms of a fine Face, and make the Decays of it invisible.

Sir Richard Steele : from The Tatler

To the Memory of Mr Oldham

Farewell, too little, and too lately known,
Whom I began to think and call my own:
For sure our souls were near allied, and thine
Cast in the same poetic mold with mine.
One common note on either lyre did strike,
And knaves and fools we both abhorred alike.
To the same goal did both our studies drive;
The last set out the soonest did arrive.
Thus Nisus fell upon the slippery place,
While his young friend performed and won the race.
O early ripe! to thy abundant store
What could advancing age have added more?
It might (what nature never gives the young)
Have taught the numbers of thy native tongue.
But satire needs not those, and wit will shine
Through the harsh cadence of a rugged line:
A noble error, and but seldom made,
When poets are by too much force betrayed.
Thy generous fruits, though gathered ere their prime,
Still showed a quickness, and maturing time
But mellows what we write to the dull sweets of rhyme.
Once more, hail and farewell; farewell, thou young,
But ah too short, Marcellus of our tongue;
Thy brows with ivy, and with laurels bound;
But fate and gloomy night encompass thee around.

John Dryden

1948—The General Assembly of the United Nations adopted and proclaimed the Universal Declaration of Human Rights, many of whose clauses have to do with the functions of writers and readers in civilized societies, and constitute new landmarks in the long struggle for unhampered communication

WHEREAS recognition of the inherent dignity and of the equal and inalienable rights of all members of the human family is the foundation of freedom, justice, and peace in the world;

WHEREAS disregard and contempt for human rights have resulted in barbarous acts which have outraged the conscience of mankind, and the advent of a world in which human beings shall enjoy freedom of speech and belief and freedom from fear and want has been proclaimed as the highest aspiration of the common people; . . .

Now, Therefore, THE GENERAL ASSEMBLY *proclaims* THIS UNIVERSAL DECLARATION OF HUMAN RIGHTS as a common standard of achievement for all peoples and all nations, to the end that every individual and every organ of society, keeping this Declaration constantly in mind, shall strive by teaching and education to promote respect for these rights and freedoms and by progressive measures, national and international, to secure their universal and effective recognition and observance, both among the peoples of Member States themselves and among the peoples of territories under their jurisdiction.

Article 1. All human beings are born free and equal in dignity and rights. They are endowed with reason and conscience and should act towards one another in a spirit of brotherhood.

Article 2. Everyone is entitled to all the rights and freedoms set forth in this Declaration, without distinction of any kind, such as race, colour, sex, language, religion, political or other opinion, national or social origin, property, birth, or other status. . . .

Article 18. Everyone has the right to freedom of thought, conscience, and religion; this right includes freedom to . . . manifest his religion or belief in teaching, practice, worship, and observance.

Article 19. Everyone has the right to freedom of opinion and expression; this right includes freedom to hold opinions without interference and to seek, receive, and impart information and ideas through any media and regardless of frontiers. . . .

Article 27. (1) Everyone has the right freely to participate in the cultural life of the community, to enjoy the arts and to share in scientific advancement and its benefits. (2) Everyone has the right to the protection of the moral and material interests resulting from any scientific or artistic production of which he is the author.

1815—Jane Austen answered the request of the Prince Regent's librarian for a copy of her forthcoming novel

---

Dear Sir,

My 'Emma' is now so near publication that I feel it right to assure you of my not having forgotten your kind recommendation of an early copy for Carlton House, and that I have Mr Murray's promise of its being sent to His Royal Highness, under cover to you, three days previous to the work being really out. I must make use of this opportunity to thank you, dear Sir, for the very high praise you bestow on my other novels. I am too vain to wish to convince you that you have praised them beyond their merits. My greatest anxiety at present is that this fourth work should not disgrace what was good in the others. But on this point I will do myself the justice to declare that, whatever may be my wishes for its success, I am strongly haunted with the idea that to those readers who have preferred 'Pride and Prejudice' it will appear inferior in wit, and to those who have preferred 'Mansfield Park' inferior in good sense. Such as it is, however, I hope you will do me the favour of accepting a copy. Mr Murray will have directions for sending one. I am quite honoured by your thinking me capable of drawing such a clergyman as you gave the sketch of in your note of November 16th. But I assure you I am *not*. The comic part of the character I might be equal to, but not the good, the enthusiastic, the literary. Such a man's conversation must at times be on subjects of science and philosophy, of which I know nothing; or at least be occasionally abundant in quotations and allusions which a woman who, like me, knows only her own mother tongue, and has read little in that, would be totally without the power of giving. A classical education, or at any rate a very extensive acquaintance with English literature, ancient, and modern appears to me quite indispensable for the person who would do any justice to your clergyman; and I think I may boast myself to be, with all possible vanity, the most unlearned and uninformed female who ever dared to be an authoress.

Believe me, dear Sir,
Your obliged and faithful humbl Sert.

Jane Austen

Dec. 11 [1815]

12 December 🕮

1786—Three days after Henry Mackenzie had hailed the Kilmarnock edition of Poems, Chiefly in the Scottish Dialect *as the work of 'a genius of no ordinary rank', the following anonymous verses appeared in the Edinburgh* Evening Courant:

EPISTLE to Robert Burns, the Ayrshire Poet

Weel, RAB, I conn'd a' o'er your beuk,
As I sat i' the ingle neuk,
Yestreen, nor coost a sidelin' look,
   I was sae keen,
Nor pried my gill, no bannock breuk,
   Till a' was deen.

And, by my saul, ye are a wag
May FERGUSON or RAMSAY brag,
Ye jog awa' your aiver nag
   At a bra' lilt;
But criesh o' whip, or prickle jag,
   To had her til't.

Whare win ye, man? gin ane may spier,
Our Embrugh fouk say ye're at Ayr,
Lord lad, gif I could meet ye there,
   Tho' few my placks,
Ane o' *Sir Willie's notes* I'd ware
   Upo' your cracks.

Or should you this way cast your louman,
An, show yoursel in likeness human,
Ye'd prove to *College hashes* view, man,
   A sair affliction,
The *Prince of poets an' o' ploughmen*
   Nae lyin' fiction. . . .

And now, my honest cock, fareweel,
Lang may ye ca' your rhiming wheel,
An' whan your bluid begins to jeel
   An' shanks grow fozie,
May *Abram's bosom* be your biel',
   To had you cozie.

                       Anonymus

[Before 1752]—Before the change in the calendar, this date, which is still dedicated to St Lucy, coincided with the winter solstice (now December 20)

A Nocturnall upon S. Lucies Day
Being the Shortest Day

Tis the yeares midnight, and it is the dayes,
Lucies, who scarce seaven houres herself unmaskes,
　　The Sunne is spent, and now his flasks
　　Send forth light quibs, no constant rayes:
　　　The world's whole sap is sunk:
The generall balme th'hydroptique earth hath drunk,
Whither, as to the beds-feet, life is shrunk,
Dead and enterr'd; yet all these seeme to laugh,
Compar'd with mee, who am their Epitaph.

Study me then, you who shall lovers bee
At the next world; that is, at the next Spring:
　　For I am every dead thing,
　　In whom love wrought new Alchimie.
　　　For his art did expresse
A quintessence even from nothingnesse,
From dull privations, and lean emptinesse:
He ruin'd me, and I am re-begot
Of absence, darknesse, death; things which are not. . . .

But I am None; nor will my Sunne renew.
You lovers, for whose sake, the lesser Sunne
　　At this time to the Goat is runne
　　To fetch new lust, and give it you,
　　　Enjoy your summer all.
Since she enjoys her long nights festivall,
Let me prepare towards her, and let mee call
This houre her Vigill, and her Eve, since this
Both the yeares, and the dayes midnight is.

John Donne

1738—The Bank of England, for the first time, issued 'post bills', thus giving further point to Alexander Pope's satire on 'blest paper-credit' already in circulation in 1732

> *B*[athurst]. What Nature wants, commodious gold bestows,
> 'Tis thus we eat the bread another sows.
>   *P*[ope]. But how unequal it bestows, observe,
> 'Tis thus we riot, while who sow it starve:
> What Nature wants (a phrase I much distrust)
> Extends to luxury, extends to lust:
> Useful, I grant, it serves what life requires,
> But dreadful, too, the dark assassin hires.
>   *B*. Trade it may help, society extend:
>   *P*. But lures the pirate, and corrupts the friend.
>   *B*. It raises armies in a nation's aid:
>   *P*. But bribes a senate, and the land's betray'd.
> In vain may heroes fight, and patriots rave;
> If secret gold sap on from knave to knave.
> Once, we confess, beneath the patriot's cloak,
> From the crack'd bag the dropping guinea spoke,
> And jingling down the back-stairs, told the crew,
> 'Old Cato is as great a rogue as you'.
> Blest paper-credit! last and best supply!
> That lends corruption lighter wings to fly!
> Gold imp'd by thee can compass hardest things,
> Can pocket states, can fetch or carry kings;
> A single leaf shall waft an army o'er,
> Or ship off senates to some distant shore;
> A leaf, like Sibyl's, scatter to and fro
> Our fates and fortunes, as the winds shall blow:
> Pregnant with thousands flits the scrap unseen,
> And silent sells a king, or buys a queen!

> *Alexander Pope: from* Moral Essays, Epistle III, to Allen, Lord Bathurst. (*written in 1732*)

1846—The Hakluyt Society was founded for the purpose of encouraging the publication of books of travel, and particularly of re-issuing the works of its namesake

To the Right Honourable Sir Francis Walsingham Knight, Principall Secretarie to her Majestie, Chancellor of the Dutchie of Lancaster, and one of her Majesties most honourable Privie Councell.

Right Honorable, I do remember that being a youth, and one of her Majesties scholars at Westminster that fruitfull nurserie, it was my happe to visit the chamber of M. Richard Hakluyt my cousin, a Gentleman of the Middle Temple, well knowen unto you, at a time when I found lying open upon his boord certaine bookes of Cosmographie, with an universall Mappe: he seeing me somewhat curious in the view thereof, began to instruct my ignorance, by shewing me the division of the earth into three parts after the olde account, and then according to the latter, & better distribution, into more: he pointed with his wand to all the knowen Seas, Gulfs, Bayes, Straights, Capes, Rivers, Empires, Kingdomes, Dukedomes, and Territories of each part, with declaration also of their speciall commodities, & particular wants, which by the benefit of traffike, & entercourse of merchants, are plentifully supplied. From the Mappe he brought me to the Bible, and turning to the 107 Psalme, directed mee to the 23 & 24 verses, where I read, that they which go downe to the sea in ships, and occupy by the great waters, they see the works of the Lord, and his woonders in the deepe, &c. Which words of the Prophet together with my cousins discourse (things of high and rare delight to my yong nature) tooke in mee so deepe an impression, that I constantly resolved, if ever I were preferred to the University, where better time, and more convenient place might be ministred for these studies, I would by Gods assistance prosecute that knowledge and kinde of literature, the doores whereof (after a sort) were so happily opened before me.

According to which my resolution, when, not long after, I was removed to Christ-church in Oxford, my exercises of duety first performed, I fell to my intended course, and by degrees read over whatsoever printed or written discoveries and voyages I found extant either in the Greeke, Latine, Italian, Spanish, Portugall, French, or English languages, and in my publike lectures was the first, that produced and shewed both the olde imperfectly composed, and the new lately reformed Mappes, Globes, Spheares, and other instruments of this Art for demonstration in the common schooles. . . .

From the 'Epistle Dedicatorie' of Richard Hakluyt's The Principal Navigations Voyages Traffiques & Discoveries of the English Nation *Made by Sea or Overland to the Remote and Farthest Distant Quarters of the Earth at any Time within the Compass of these 1600 Years. (First edition 1589)*

Like the vain Curlings of the Watry maze,
Which in smooth streams a sinking Weight does raise;
So Man, declining always, disappears
In the weak Circles of increasing Years;
And his short Tumults of themselves Compose,
While flowing Time above his Head does close.
    Cromwell alone with greater Vigour runs,
(Sun-like) the Stages of succeeding Suns:
And still the Day which he doth next restore,
Is the just Wonder of the Day before.
Cromwell alone doth with new Lustre spring,
And shares the Jewel of the yearly Ring.
    'Tis he the force of scatter'd Time contracts,
And in one Year the work of Ages acts:
While heavy Monarchs make a wide Return,
Longer, and more malignant than *Saturn*:
And though they all *Platonique* years should raign,
In the same posture would be found again.
Their earthy Projects under ground they lay,
More slow and brittle then the *China* clay. . . .
Unhappy Princes, ignorantly bred,
By Malice some, by Errour more misled;
If gracious Heaven to my Life give length,
Leisure to Time, and to my Weakness Strength,
Then shall I once with graver Accents shake
Your Regal sloth, and your long Slumbers wake:
Like the shrill Huntsman that prevents the East,
Winding his Horn to Kings that chase the Beast.
    Till then my Muse shall hollow far behind
Angelique *Cromwell* who outwings the wind . . .
For to be *Cromwell* was a greater thing,
Then ought below, or yet above a King . . .
'Twas Heav'n would not that his Pow'r should cease,
But walk still middle betwixt War and Peace;
Choosing each Stone, and poysing every weight,
Trying the Measures of the Bredth and Height;
Here pulling down, and there erecting New,
Founding a firm State by Proportions true . . .

Andrew Marvell: from The First Anniversary of the Government under Oliver Cromwell, 1654

1679—Forty-eight-year-old John Dryden was waylaid and beaten by thugs hired for the job by thirty-two-year-old John Wilmot, Earl of Rochester, on the mistaken assumption that Dryden had written the following lines :

On Rochester

R—— I despise for his meer want of wit,
Though thought to have a Tail and Cloven Feet;
For while he mischief means to all mankind,
Himself alone the ill effects does find;
And so like Witches justly suffers shame,
Whose harmless malice is so much the same;
False are his words, affected is his wit,
So often he does aim, so seldom hit;
To every face he cringes while he speaks,
But when the Back is turn'd the head he breaks;
Mean in each action, lewd in every Limb,
Manners themselves are mischievous in him:
A proof that chance alone makes every Creature
A very *Killigrew* without good Nature;
For what a *Bessus* has he always liv'd,
And his own *Kickings* notably contriv'd:
(For there's the folly that's still mixt with fear)
Cowards more blows than any Heroe bear;
Of fighting sparks some may her pleasures say,
But 'tis a bolder thing to run away:
The World may well forgive him all his ill,
For ev'ry fault does prove his penance still:
Falsly he falls into some dangerous Noose,
And then as meanly labours to get loose;
A life so infamous is better quitting,
Spent in base injury and low submitting.

from An Essay upon Satyr, *by John Sheffield,
Earl of Mulgrave*

Killigrew – Thomas Killigrew, dramatist, who became Master of the Revels in 1679
Bessus – the Persian who assassinated the defeated Darius

18 December 〔〕

1792—Henry Lord Erskine defended Tom Paine in the Court of the King's Bench from the charge of having written a seditious and slanderous book – The Rights of Man

The proposition which I mean to maintain as the basis of the liberty of the press, and without which it is an empty sound, is this: that every man, not intending to mislead, but seeking to enlighten others with what his own reason and conscience, however erroneously, have directed to him as truth, may address himself to the universal reason of a whole nation, either upon the subject of governments in general, or upon that of our own particular country: that he may analyse the principles of its constitution, point out its errors and defects, examine and publish its corruptions, warn his fellow-citizens against their ruinous consequences, and exert his whole faculties in pointing out the most advantageous changes in establishments which he considers to be radically defective, or sliding from their object by abuse. All this every subject of this country has a right to do, if he contemplates only what he thinks would be for its advantage, and but seeks to change the public mind by the conviction which flows from reasonings dictated by conscience. . . .

I do contend that it is lawful to address the English nation on these momentous subjects; for had it not been for this inalienable right (thanks be to God and our fathers for establishing it!), how should we have had this constitution which we so loudly boast of? If, in the march of the human mind, no man could have gone before the establishments of the time he lived in, how could our establishment, by reiterated changes, have become what it is? If no man could have awakened the public mind to errors and abuses in our Government, how could it have passed on from stage to stage, through reformation and revolution, so as to have arrived from barbarism to such a pitch of happiness and perfection, that the Attorney General considers it as a profanation to touch it further, or to look for any further amendment?

In this manner has reasoned every age; but the Government, in *its own estimation*, has been at all times a system of perfection; but a free press has examined and detected its errors, and the people have from time to time reformed them. This freedom has alone made our Government what it is; this freedom alone can preserve it; and therefore, under the banners of that freedom, today I stand up to defend Thomas Paine. . . .

1785—King George III displayed his abilities as a drama critic to Miss Fanny Burney, who was at that time lady-in-waiting to the Queen

In the evening, while Mrs Delaney, Miss Port, and I were sitting and working together in the drawing-room, the door opened and the king entered. We all started up; Miss Port flew to her modest post by the door, and I to my more comfortable one opposite the fire . . .

Some time afterwards, the king said he found by the newspapers that Mrs Clive was dead. Do you read the newspapers? thought I. O, King! you must then have the most unvexing temper in the world, not to run wild.

This led on to more players. He was sorry, he said, for Henderson, and the more as Mrs Siddons had wished to have him play at the same house with herself. Then Mrs. Siddons took her turn, and with the warmest praise. 'I am an enthusiast for her', cried the king, 'quite an enthusiast. I think there was never any player in my time so excellent – not Garrick himself' . . .

From players he went to plays, and complained of the great want of good modern comedies, and of the extreme immorality of most of the old ones. 'And they pretend', cried he, 'to mend them; but it is not possible. Do you think it is? – what?'

'No, sir, not often, I believe; – the fault, commonly, lies on the very foundation.'

'Yes, or they might mend the mere speeches; – but the characters are all bad from beginning to the end.'

Then he specified several; but I had read none of them, and consequently could say nothing about the matter; – till, at last, he came to Shakespeare. 'Was there ever', cried he, 'such stuff as great part of Shakespeare? Only one must not say so! But what think you? – What? – Is there not sad stuff? What? – what?'

'Yes, indeed, I think so, sir, though mixed with such excellences that – '

'O!' cried he, laughing good-humouredly, 'I know it is not to be said! but it's true. Only it's Shakespeare, and nobody dare abuse him.'

Then he enumerated many of the characters and parts of plays that he objected to; and when he had run over them, finished with again laughing, and exclaiming, 'But one should be stoned for saying so!'

'Madame de Genlis, sir', said I, 'had taken such an impression of the English theatre, that she told me she thought no woman ought to go to any of our comedies.' This, which, indeed, is a very overstrained censure of our dramas, made him draw back. . . . and he vindicated the stage from so hard an aspersion, with a warmth not wholly free from indignation. This led on to a good deal more dramatic criticism . . .

From The Diary and Letters of Madame d'Arblay (*Frances Burney*)

20 December

1786—Anna Seward, the redoubtable 'Swan of Lichfield', stoutly defended her poetic method in a letter to her critic, George Hardinge, by appeal to higher authority

I see you are displeased with me, for the perhaps too ingenious manner in which I have combated the prejudices that govern your criticisms. You say I want temper in argument. It certainly exhausts my patience to see a man of ability, with an air of unappealable decision, perpetually denouncing in *modern* poets *that* to be obscure, which is as clear as day-light; if the language is elevated, calling it stiff and stilted; while, if simplicity be the character of the passage, he terms it heavy, mean and prosaic.

In your observations upon Mason's, Hayley's, the Bard of Derby's, and even upon my much inferior compositions, I cannot guess at the ideas which stimulate your censure, or inspire your praise; because the passages you commend, in our separate writings, appear to me no way superior to those you condemn.

I am still sure of the fact, that where Milton and Shakespeare mean to describe, they use epithets quite as lavishly as our best moderns. The passages you quote to oppose my assertion are merely colloquial and narrative.

It would be a fine opiate truly to read a descriptive poem, in which the author should talk of hills, and vallies, and rocks, and seas, and streams, and youths, and nymphs, without giving us the picturesque noun-adjective, which alone conveys to us any distant idea, what sort of hill, and valley, rock, ocean, stream, youth, or maid, he means to place before us.

I was reading Henry the sixth yesterday, without any design of searching for added instances to prove a truth so self-evident, as that picture and appropriation in general depend upon the epithet. That is not one of Shakespeare's best plays, and though generally natural, and therefore interesting, though it contains much good sense, and strong characteristic strokes, it has certainly less poetry than most of his other dramas; yet in the poetic, or even in his impassioned passages, mark how the epithets pour in!

> —— 'Wizards know their time,
> *Deep* night, *dark* night, the *silent* of the night.'

See how the great poet depends upon the thrice-repeated epithets to produce a growing impression of horror! . . .

Milton, as well as Shakespeare, sometimes produces a beautiful effect, by placing his substantive in the midst of epithets, thus:

> —— 'Now is the *pleasant* time,
> The *cool*, the *silent*.'

And again,

> 'Save what the glimmering of these *livid* flames,
> Casts *pale*, and *dreadful*.'

The breaking waves dashed high
   On a stern and rock-bound coast,
And the woods against a stormy sky
   Their giant branches tossed;

And the heavy night hung dark
   The hills and waters o'er,
When a band of exiles moored their bark
   On the wild New England shore.

Not as the conqueror comes,
   They, the true-hearted, came;
Not with the roll of stirring drums
   And the trumpet that sings of fame:

Not as the flying come,
   In silence and in fear;
They shook the depths of the desert gloom
   With their hymns of lofty cheer.

Amidst the storm they sang,
   And the stars heard, and the sea;
And the sounding aisles of the dim woods rang
   To the anthem of the free. . . .

What sought they thus afar?
   Bright jewels of the mine?
The wealth of seas, the spoils of war? –
   They sought a faith's pure shrine!

Ay, call it holy ground,
   The soil where first they trod;
They have left unstained what there they found, –
   Freedom to worship God.

         Felicia D. Hemans: 'The Landing of the Pilgrim
         Fathers'

22 December 🪺

1854—John Bright informed the House of Commons that in continuing the Crimean War they were backing a dead horse

. . . there is not a Gentleman in this House who is not aware that the Mahometan portion of the population of the Turkish Empire is in a decaying and dying condition, and that the two great Empires which have undertaken to set it on its legs again will find it about the most difficult task in which they ever were engaged. What do your own officers say? Here is an extract from a letter which appeared in the papers the other day . . . and it is said that a third great Empire is about to engage in the task. The Turk wants to borrow money, but he cannot borrow it today in London at less than from eight to nine per cent. Russia, on the other hand, is an Empire against which three great Empires, if Turkey can be counted one still, are now combined . . . But Russian funds at this moment are very little lower than the stock of the London and North-Western Railway. You have engaged to set this Turkish Empire up again – a task in which everybody knows you must fail – and you have persuaded the Turk to enter into a contest, one of the very first proceedings in which has forced him to mortgage to the English capitalist a very large portion – and the securest portion, too, of his revenues – namely, that which he derives from Egypt, amounting, in fact, in a fiscal and financial point of view, to an actual dismemberment of the Turkish Empire by a separation of Egypt from it. . . . whatever may be the result of the war in which Turkey has plunged Europe, this one thing is certain, that at its conclusion there may be no Turkish Empire to talk about. . . . Now Sir, I have only to speak on one more point . . . there are a hundred officers who have been killed in battle, or who have died of their wounds; forty have died of disease; and more than two hundred others have been wounded more or less severely. This has been a terribly destructive war to officers. They have been, as one would have expected them to be, the first in valour as the first in place, they have suffered more in proportion to their numbers than the commonest soldiers in the ranks. This has spread sorrow over the whole country. I was in the House of Lords when the vote of thanks was moved. In the gallery were many ladies, three-fourths of whom were dressed in the deepest mourning. Is this nothing? And in every village cottages are to be found into which sorrow has entered, and, as I believe, through the policy of the Ministry, which might have been avoided. No one supposes that the Government wished to spread the pall of sorrow over the land; but this we had a right to expect – that they would at least show becoming gravity in discussing a subject the appalling consequences of which may come home to individuals and to the nation. . . .

1823—Clement Charles Moore's 'A Visit from St Nicholas' (later entitled 'The Night before Christmas') was first published in the Troy (N.Y.) Sentinel

'Twas the night before Christmas, when all through the house
Not a creature was stirring, not even a mouse;
The stockings were hung by the chimney with care,
In hopes that St. Nicholas soon would be there;
The children were nestled all snug in their beds,
While visions of sugarplums danced in their heads;
And Mamma in her 'kerchief, and I in my cap,
Had just settled our brains for a long winter's nap;
When out on the lawn there arose such a clatter,
I sprang from the bed to see what was the matter. . . .
When what to my wondering eyes should appear
But a miniature sleigh, and eight tiny reindeer,
With a little old driver, so lively and quick
I knew in a moment it must be St. Nick.
More rapid than eagles his coursers they came,
And he whistled, and shouted, and called them by name;
'Now, *Dasher*! Now, *Dancer*! Now, *Prancer* and *Vixen*!
On, *Comet*! On, *Cupid*! On, *Donder* and *Blitzen*!
To the top of the porch! To the top of the wall!
Now, dash away! Dash away! Dash away all!' . . .
And then, in a twinkling, I heard on the roof
The prancing and pawing of each little hoof –
As I drew in my head, and was turning around,
Down the chimney St. Nicholas came with a bound.
He was dressed all in fur, from his head to his foot,
And his clothes were all tarnished with ashes and soot;
A bundle of toys he had flung on his back,
And he looked like a pedlar just opening his pack. . . .
He spoke not a word, but went straight to his work,
And filled all the stockings; then turned with a jerk,
And laying his finger aside of his nose,
And giving a nod, up the chimney he rose;
He sprang to his sleigh, to his team gave a whistle,
And away they all flew like the down of a thistle.
But I heard him exclaim, ere he drove out of sight,
'Happy Christmas to all, and to all a good night.'

24 December 🎭

1896—'The Pilgrim's Progress: *a mystery play, with music, in four acts, by C. G. Collingham; founded on John Bunyan's immortal allegory*' *was presented at the Olympic Theatre*

When I saw a stage version of 'The Pilgrim's Progress' announced for production, I shook my head, knowing that Bunyan is far too great a dramatist for our theatre which has never been enough resolute even in its lewdness and venality to win the respect and interest which positive, powerful wickedness always engages, much less the services of men of heroic conviction. Its greatest catch, Shakespeare, wrote for the theatre because, with extraordinary artistic powers, he understood nothing and believed nothing. Thirty-six big plays in five blank verse acts, and (as Mr. Ruskin, I think, once pointed out) not a single hero! Only one man in them all who believes in life, enjoys life, thinks life worth living, and has a sincere, unrhetorical tear dropped over his deathbed, and that man – Falstaff!

All that you miss in Shakespeare you find in Bunyan, to whom the true heroic came quite obviously and naturally. The world was to him a more terrible place than it was to Shakespeare; but he saw through it a path at the end of which a man might look not only forward to the Celestial City, but back on his life and say: 'Tho' with great difficulty I am got hither, yet now I do not repent me of all the trouble I have been at to arrive where I am. My sword I give to him that shall succeed me in my pilgrimage, and my courage and skill to him that can get it.' The heart vibrates like a bell to such utterances as this: to turn from it to 'Out, out, brief candle', and 'The rest is silence', and 'We are such stuff as dreams are made on', and 'our little life is rounded with a sleep' is to turn from life, strength, resolution, morning air and eternal youth to the terrors of a drunken nightmare.

Let us descend now to the lower ground where Shakespeare is not disabled by this inferiority in energy and elevation of spirit. Take one of his big fighting scenes, and compare its blank verse, in point of mere rhetorical strenuousness, with Bunyan's prose. Macbeth's famous cue for the fight with Macduff runs thus:

> Yet will I try the last: before my body
> I throw my warlike shield. Lay on, Macduff,
> And damned be he that first cries, 'Hold, enough!'

Turn from this jingle, dramatically right in feeling, but silly and resourceless in thought and expression, to Apollyon's cue for the fight in the Valley of Humiliation: 'I am void of fear in this matter. Prepare thyself to die; for I swear by my infernal den that thou shalt go no farther: here will I spill thy soul.' This is the same thing done masterly. Apart from its superior grandeur, force, and appropriateness, it is better clap-trap and infinitely better word-music.

Bernard Shaw, Dramatic Opinions and Essays

1752—'Glastonbury. – A vast concourse of people attended the noted thorn on Christmas-day, new style *; but, to their great disappointment, there was no appearance of its blowing, which made them watch it narrowly on the 5th of January, the Christmas-day,* old style, *when it blowed as usual'*

The Gentleman's Magazine, *January 1753*

Where is this stupendous stranger?
    Swains of Solyma, advise;
Lead me to my Master's manger,
    Show me where my Saviour lies.

O Most Mighty! O Most Holy!
    Far beyond the seraph's thought,
Art thou then so mean and lowly
    As unheeded prophets taught?

O the magnitude of meekness!
    Worth from worth immortal sprung;
O the strength of infant weakness,
    If eternal is so young!

If so young and thus eternal,
    Michael tune the shepherd's reed,
Where the scenes are ever vernal,
    And the loves be love indeed! . . .

Nature's decorations glisten
    Far above their usual trim;
Birds on box and laurel listen,
    As so near the cherubs hymn. . . .

Spinks and ouzles sing sublimely,
    'We too have a Saviour born';
Whiter blossoms burst untimely
    On the blest Mosaic thorn.

God, all-bounteous, all-creative,
    Whom no ills from good dissuade,
Is incarnate, and a native
    Of the very world he made.

Christopher Smart: 'On the Nativity'

26 December 📖

1662—Mr Samuel Pepys lost a shilling, as a result of a bad judgement in matters literary which, after six weeks, he revised

---

'26th. Up, my wife to the making of Christmas pies all day, and I abroad to several places. To the Wardrobe. Hither come Mr Battersby; and we falling into discourse of a new book of drollery in verse, called "Hudibras", I would needs go and find it out, and met with it at the Temple; cost me 2s. 6d. But when I came to read it, it is so silly an abuse of the Presbyter Knight going to the wars, that I am ashamed of it; and by and by meeting at Mr Townsend's at dinner, I sold it to him for 18d. . . .'

Samuel Pepys: from the Diary

For his *Religion*, it was fit
To match his learning and his wit:
'Twas Presbyterian true blue;
For he was of that stubborn crew
Of errant Saints whom all men grant
To be the true Church Militant;
Such as do build their faith upon
The holy text of pike and gun;
Decide all controversies by
Infallible artillery;
And prove their doctrine orthodox
By apostolic blows and knocks:
Call fire, and sword, and desolation
A godly thorough reformation,
Which always must be carried on,
And still be doing, never done:
As if Religion were intended
For nothing else but to be mended
A Sect whose chief devotion lies
In odd perverse antipathies: . . .

Samuel Butler: from Hudibras

. . . And so to a bookseller's in the Strand, and there bought "Hudibras" again, it being certainly some ill humour to be so against that which all the world cries up to be the example of wit; for which I am resolved once again to read him, and see whether I can find it or no.'

Pepys: the Diary, *6 February 1663*

1904—The first performance of James Barrie's Peter Pan, *as described by Daphne du Maurier in the biography of her actor-father Sir Gerald du Maurier, who played the part of Hook in this performance*

In December, James Barrie, who was a great friend of the Llewellyn Davieses, and adored Sylvia and her boys, wrote for them his immortal *Peter Pan*, and Gerald played the parts of Captain Hook and Mr Darling. The play was unlike anything had ever been written before, and nobody expected it to be a success. . . . Befogged journalists gave inaccurate and premature descriptions of the piece, saying that Mr. Barrie had written about an unconventional Fairyland which was inhabited by cuddlesome Eskimos and a quaint little person called Peter, dressed in red leaves, and that Mr. du Maurier would play the fierce Pirate King, a melodramatic and romantic individual.

The result became history, as everyone knows. . . . The Play has grown into a tradition that will never die, an annual joy that time cannot dim, a necessary part of childhood, familiar, lovable, and gloriously shabby. . . .

Can it be that children are less timid nowadays . . . ? When Hook first paced his quarter-deck in the year 1904, children were carried away from their stalls, and even big boys of twelve were known to reach for their mother's hand in the friendly shelter of the boxes. How he was hated, with his flourish, his poses, his dreaded diabolical smile! That ashen face, those blood-red lips, the long, dark, greasy curls; the sardonic laugh, the maniacal scream, the appalling courtesy of his gestures; and that above all most terrible of moments when he descended the stairs and with slow, most merciless cunning poured the poison into Peter's glass. There was no peace in those days until the monster was destroyed, and the fight upon the pirate ship was a fight to the death. Gerald *was* Hook; he was no dummy dressed from Simmons' in a Clarkson wig, ranting and roaring about the stage, a grotesque figure whom the modern child finds a little comic. He was a tragic and rather ghastly creation who knew no place, and whose soul was in torment; a dark shadow; a sinister dream; a bogey of fear who lives perpetually in the grey recesses of every small boy's mind. All boys had their Hooks, as Barrie knew; he was the phantom who came by night and stole his way into their murky dreams. . . .

28 December

1817—'Wordsworth was in town, and as Keats wished to know him I made up a party to dinner of Charles Lamb, Wordsworth, Keats, and Monkhouse, his friend'

Benjamin Haydon

On December 28 the immortal dinner came off in my painting-room, with Jerusalem towering up behind us as a background. Wordsworth was in fine cue, and we had a glorious set-to – on Homer, Shakespeare, Milton, and Virgil. Lamb got exceedingly merry and exquisitely witty; and his fun in the midst of Wordsworth's solemn intonations of oratory was like the sarcasm and wit of the fool in the intervals of Lear's passion. He made a speech and voted me absent, and made them drink my health, 'Now', said Lamb, 'you old lake poet, you rascally poet, why do you call Voltaire dull?' We all defended Wordsworth, and affirmed there was a state of mind when Voltaire would be dull. 'Well', said Lamb, 'here's Voltaire – the Messiah of the French nation, and a very proper one, too.'

He then, in a strain of humour beyond description, abused me for putting Newton's head into my picture; 'a fellow', said he, 'who believed nothing unless it was as clear as the three sides of a triangle'. And then he and Keats agreed he had destroyed all the poetry of the rainbow by reducing it to the prismatic colours. It was impossible to resist him, and we all drank 'Newton's health, and confusion to mathematics'. It was delightful to see the good humour of Wordsworth in giving in to all our frolics without affectation and laughing as heartily as the best of us.

By this time other friends joined, amongst them poor Ritchie, who was going to penetrate Fezzan to Timbuctoo. . . .

It was indeed an immortal evening. Wordsworth's fine intonation as he quoted Milton and Virgil, Keats' eager inspired look, Lamb's quaint sparkle of lambent humour, so speeded the stream of conversation, that in my life I never passed a more delightful time. All our fun was within bounds. Not a word passed that an apostle might not have listened to. It was a night worthy of the Elizabethan age, and my solemn Jerusalem flashing up by the flame of the fire, with Christ hanging over us like a vision, all made up a picture which will long glow upon 'that inward eye/Which is the bliss of solitude'.

Keats made Ritchie promise he would carry his *Endymion* to the great desert of Sahara and fling it in the midst.

Poor Ritchie went to Africa, and died . . . in 1819. Keats died in 1821, at Rome. C. Lamb is gone, joking to the last. Monkhouse is dead, and Wordsworth and I are the only two now living of that glorious party [1841].

from The Autobiography of Benjamin Haydon

I peeled bits of straw and I got switches too
From the grey peeling willow as idlers do,
And I switched at the flies as I sat all alone
Till my flesh, blood and marrow was turned to dry bone.
My illness was love, though I knew not the smart,
But the beauty of love was the blood of my heart.
Crowded places, I shunned them as noises too rude
And fled to the silence of sweet solitude,
Where the flower in green darkness buds, blossoms, and fades,
Unseen of all shepherds and flower-loving maids –
The hermit bees find them but once and away;
There I'll bury alive and in silence decay.
I looked on the eyes of fair woman too long,
Till silence and shame stole the use of my tongue:
When I tried to speak to her I'd nothing to say,
So I turned myself round and she wandered away.
When she got too far off, why, I'd something to tell,
So I sent sighs behind her and walked to my cell.
Willow switches I broke and peeled bits of straws,
Ever lonely in crowds, in nature's own laws –
My ball-room the pasture, my music the bees,
My drink was the fountain, my church the tall trees.
Who ever would love and be tied to a wife
When it makes a man mad all the days of his life?

John Clare

30 December

1816—By way of entertaining his young friend, John Keats, Leigh Hunt proposed as a parlour game that they try which could compose the better sonnet on a set subject, and suggested 'crickets and grasshoppers'. . . . Pleased with the results of their extempore efforts, he later published both productions in The Examiner

Green little vaulter in the sunny grass
   Catching your heart up at the feel of June,
   Sole voice that's heard amidst the lazy noon,
When ev'n the bees lag at the summoning brass;
And you, warm little housekeeper, who class
   With those who think the candles come too soon,
   Loving the fire, and with your tricksome tune
Nick the glad silent moments as they pass;
Oh sweet and tiny cousins, that belong,
   One to the fields, the other to the hearth,
Both have your sunshine; both though small are strong
   At your clear hearts: and both were sent on earth
To sing in thoughtful ears this natural song, –
   In doors and out, summer and winter, Mirth.

Leigh Hunt

The poetry of earth is never dead:
   When all the birds are faint with the hot sun,
   And hide in cooling trees, a voice will run
From hedge to hedge about the new-mown mead;
That is the Grasshopper's – he takes the lead
   In summer luxury, – he has never done
   With his delights; for when tired out with fun,
He rests at ease beneath some pleasant weed.

The poetry of earth is ceasing never:
   On a lone winter evening, when the frost
      Has wrought a silence, from the stove there shrills
The Cricket's song, in warmth increasing ever,
   And seems to one, in drowsiness half lost,
      The Grasshopper's among some grassy hills.

John Keats

Ring out, wild bells, to the wild sky,
    The flying cloud, the frosty light:
    The year is dying in the night;
Ring out, wild bells, and let him die.

Ring out the old, ring in the new,
    Ring, happy bells, across the snow:
    The year is going, let him go;
Ring out the false, ring in the true.

Ring out the grief that saps the mind,
    For those that here we see no more;
    Ring out the feud of rich and poor,
Ring in redress to all mankind.

Ring out a slowly dying cause,
    And ancient forms of party strife;
    Ring in the nobler modes of life,
With sweeter manners, purer laws.

Ring out the want, the care, the sin,
    The faithless coldness of the times;
    Ring out, ring out my mournful rhymes,
But ring the fuller minstrel in.

Ring out old shapes of foul disease;
    Ring out the narrowing lust of gold;
    Ring out the thousand wars of old,
Ring in the thousand years of peace.

Ring in the valiant man and free,
    The larger heart, the kindlier hand;
    Ring out the darkness of the land,
Ring in the Christ that is to be.

Alfred, Lord Tennyson: from In Memoriam

INDEX OF AUTHORS QUOTED AND MENTIONED

(an asterisk indicates authors mentioned,
other dates refer to authors quoted)

A

Addison, Joseph – 12 Mar.; 29 Mar.; 3 July*; 20 July
Alfred, King – 7 May*; 11 Nov.*
anon. (Anglo-Saxon Chronicle) – 11 Aug.; 28 Sept.
  „ ('Battle of Maldon') – 11 Aug.
  „ ('Beowulf') – 23 Aug.
  „ ('Billy the Kid') – 15 July
  „ (Declaration of Human Rights) – 10 Dec.
  „ ('Epistle to Robert Burns') – 12 Dec.
Arnold, Matthew – 21 Mar.; 11 May
Ascham, Roger – 12 Feb.
Asser – 11 Nov.
Aubrey, John – 9 Apr.
Austen, Jane – 26 Nov.; 11 Dec.

B

Bacon, Francis – 27 Jan.; 9 Apr.
Ball, John – 12 June
Barlow, William – 16 Jan.
Barrie, James – 27 Dec.
Beaumont, Francis – 31 Oct.*
Bede, The Venerable – 11 Feb.; 25 May*; 22 June; 23 July
Beerbohm, Max – 21 May*
Belloc, Hilaire – 3 Dec.
Bennett, Arnold – 30 Aug.
Berners, Lord – 12 June; 12 July
Bible, The Holy (A. V.) – 16 Jan.*
Blake, William – 11 Jan.
Bodley, Thomas – 8 Nov.
Borrow, George – 18 Aug.; 10 Sept.
Boswell, James – 27 Mar.; 28 Mar.; 6 Apr.; 16 May; 3 Aug.*
Bradstreet, Anne – 10 July
Brennan, Christopher – 5 Oct.
Brews, Margery (later Mrs John Paston) – 14 Feb.
Bridges, Robert – 22 Apr.*
Bright, John – 22 Dec.
Brontë, Charlotte – 28 Jan.; 21 Mar.*; 29 June; 16 Oct.
Brontë, Emily – 28 Jan.*; 9 May
Browne, Sir Thomas – 26 Apr.*; 6 July
Browning, Elizabeth Barrett – 26 Apr.*; 12 Sept.; 17 Oct.
Browning, Robert – 3 April.; 6 Apr.; 26 Apr.*; 12 Sept.*; 22 Oct.
Bulwer-Lytton, Edward – 24 Aug.
Bunyan, John – Dedication, iv; 18 Feb.; 12 Nov.; 24 Dec*.

Burne-Jones, Edward – 3 June
Burnet, Gilbert – 25 June*
Burney, Frances (Mme d'Arblay) – 19 Dec.
Burns, Robert – 25 Jan.; 1 Apr.; 24 June; 27 July*; 12 Dec.*
Burton, Robert – 5 Dec.
Butler, Samuel ('Hudibras') – 26 Dec.
Butler, Samuel ('Erewhon') – 13 June; 4 Dec.
Byron, George Gordon Noel, Lord – 24 Apr.*; 3 May; 21 Nov.

C

Caedmon – 11 Feb.*
Canning, George – 27 Nov.
Carew, Thomas – 5 Apr.
Carlyle, Thomas – 24 Feb.; 6 Mar.*; 5 Aug.; 2 Nov.
Carroll, Lewis (Charles Dodgson) – 25 Apr.; 4 May
Caxton, William – 1 Mar.; 31 July*; 2 Sept.*
Chapman, George – 8 Apr.
Chatterton, Thomas – 25 Aug.
Chaucer, Geoffrey – 3 June; 17 June
Cheke, Sir John – 16 July
Chesterfield, Earl of (Philip Dormer Stanhope) – 7 Feb.*; 22 Feb.
Chesterton, Gilbert Keith – 7 May
Clare, John – 20 June; 29 Dec.
Coleridge, Samuel Taylor – 7 Jan.; 23 Mar.; 4 Apr.; 10 Apr.*; 24 Apr.*; 1 Sept.*
Collier, Jeremy – 29 Nov.
Colman, George – 22 Aug.
Congreve, William – 11 Mar.
Conrad, Joseph – 10 June
Cowley, Abraham – 28 Nov.
Cowper, William – 14 Sept.; 13 Oct.
Crabbe, George – 21 Oct.
Crane, Hart – 27 Apr.
Cuthbert (monk of Jarrow) – 25 May

D

Dana, Richard Henry – 14 Aug.
Daniel, Samuel – 8 Jan.
Darwin, Charles – 1 July; 24 Nov.*
Davies, Sir John – 1 June
Defoe, Daniel – 17 July; 29 July
Dekker, Thomas – 1 Jan.
Denham, Sir John – 15 June
Dennis, John – 29 Nov.
Dickens, Charles – 7 Apr.; 23 Apr.; 7 June; 18 Oct.; 15 Nov.*

Index

L

Lamb, Charles – 22 Mar.; 2 Nov.*; 28 Dec.*
Langland, William – 14 Apr.
Lanigan, George Thomas – 22 Jan.
Latimer, Hugh – 18 Jan.
Lawrence, D. H. – 25 Nov.
Lawrence, T. E. – 1 Oct.
Lear, Edward – 6 Sept.
Lincoln, Abraham – 19 Nov.
Lindsay, Vachel – 5 Feb.
Locke, John – 6 May
London, Jack – 12 Jan.
Longfellow, Henry Wadsworth – 27 Feb.; 18 Apr.
Lovelace, Richard – 30 Apr.
Lydgate, John – 4 June*

M

MacDiarmid, Hugh (Dr Christopher Grieve) – 13 Feb.
MacPherson, James – 24 Sept.
Malory, Sir Thomas – 31 July
Mandeville, Bernard de – 11 July
Marlowe, Christopher – 18 May; 1 June*; 19 June
Marryat, Capt. Frederick – 18 July*
Marston, John – 1 June
Martineau, Harriet – 21 Mar.*
Marvell, Andrew – 28 July; 16 Dec.
Mason, William – 6 April.
Melville, Herman – 3 Jan.; 14 July; 17 Aug.
Meredith, George – 9 June; 9 July*
Mill, John Stuart – 24 Feb.*; 6 Mar.*
Milton, John – 9 Feb.; 4 Mar.; 30 Mar.; 31 May*; 14 June; 29 Sept.; 2 Nov.*; 20 Dec.*
Minot, Laurence – 19 July
Moore, Clement Charles – 23 Dec.
More, Sir Thomas – 12 May; 5 July
Morris, William – 23 Sept.

N

Nairne, Baroness (Carolina Oliphant) – 25 July
Newman, John Henry – 21 Jan.; 24 Oct.*
North, Sir Thomas – 15 Mar.
Norton, Thomas – 6 Jan.
Noyes, Alfred – 26 Sept.

O

O'Casey, Sean – 2 Mar.*
Oldham, John – 9 Mar.; 9 Dec.*
O'Neill, Eugene – 22 July
Osborne, Dorothy – 16 Sept.
'Ossian' – 24 Sept.
Owen, Wilfred – 19 Mar.; 10 Oct.

P

Paine, Thomas – 10 Jan.; 18 Dec.*
Paston, Mrs John (née Brews) – 14 Feb.
Patmore, Coventry – 11 Sept.; 24 Oct.*
Peacock, Thomas Love – 24 Apr.
Pearson, Hesketh – 14 Mar.
Peele, George – 17 Nov.
Pepys, Samuel – 13 Jan.; 19 Feb.*; 23 Feb.; 22 May; 8 June*; 14 Nov.; 26 Dec.
Percy, Thomas – 21 Aug.
Pitt, William, Earl of Chatham – 20 Nov.
Poe, Edgar Allen – 19 Aug.; 9 Oct.
Pope, Alexander – 25 Mar.; 15 May; 3 July*; 7 Nov.; 14 Dec.
Potter, Beatrix – 4 Feb.
Pound, Ezra – 16 Mar.*

R

Raleigh, Sir Walter – 23 Jan.*; 29 March
Reade, Charles – 14 Oct.
Richardson, Samuel – 20 Feb.; 2 June; 4 Aug.; 10 Nov.
Robinson, Henry Crabb – 31 May
Rochester, John Wilmot, Earl of – 25 June; 17 Dec.*
Ross, Maj. Sir Ronald – 20 Aug.
Rossetti, Dante Gabriel – 6 Apr.; 27 Sept.
Rosten, Leo – 12 Oct.
Rowe, Nicholas – 5 Nov.
Ruskin, John – 26 Apr.*

S

Sackville, Thomas, Earl of Dorset – 6 Jan.; 4 June
Sassoon, Siegfried – 10 Oct.
Scott, Sir Walter – 26 July*; 8 Sept.; 21 Oct.; 22 Nov.
Seward, Anna – 28 Mar.; 13 Oct.; 20 Dec.
Shakespeare, William – 14 Jan.*; 6 Feb.; 23 Apr.*; 20 May; 23 June; 15 Aug.*; 20 Sept.*; 19 Oct.; 31 Oct.*; 1 Nov.; 2 Dec.; 7 Dec.*; 19 Dec.*; 20 Dec.*; 24 Dec.*
Shaw, George Bernard – 21 Apr.; 21 May; 24 Dec.
Sheffield, John, Earl of Mulgrave – 17 Dec.
Shelley, Percy Bysshe – 26 Feb.; 24 Apr.*; 29 May; 16 Aug.; 9 Nov.
Shenstone, William – 21 Aug.*; 24 Sept.
Sheridan, Richard Brinsley – 17 Jan.
Sidney, Sir Philip – 6 Jan.; 30 Jan.
Sitwell, Edith – 24 Jan.
Smart, Christopher – 6 Apr.; 1 May; 13 Aug.; 25 Dec.
Smith, Adam – 29 Apr.
Smith, Sidney – 26 Jan.
Smollett, Tobias – 26 Oct.